THIRD EDITION

PAKISTAN'S FOREIGN POLICY

A Reappraisal

Shahid M. Amin

OXFORD

UNIVERSITY PRESS

OXFORD
UNIVERSITY PRESS

Oxford University Press is a department of the University of Oxford.
It furthers the University's objective of excellence in research, scholarship,
and education by publishing worldwide. Oxford is a registered trade mark of
Oxford University Press in the UK and in certain other countries

Published in Pakistan by
Oxford University Press
No. 38, Sector 15, Korangi Industrial Area,
PO Box 8214, Karachi-74900, Pakistan

ISBN 978-0-19-070393-6

Typeset in Adobe Garamond Pro
Printed on 55gsm Book Paper

Printed by Mas Printers, Karachi

Contents

Introduction to the Third Edition

Twenty years have passed since the first edition of this book was published in 2000. Much has changed in global politics since then, notably, after the terrorist attacks by Al-Qaeda in New York and Washington on 9/11 (11 September 2001). The US launched a 'War on Terror', mainly against Al-Qaeda, and went on to invade Afghanistan and Iraq. Islamist terrorism became the bugbear for many countries. More terrorist groups such as ISIS (more commonly known as Islamic State/Da'esh) emerged to pose new threats in the Middle East. The 'Arab Spring' (early 2010), dethroned long-established dictatorial regimes. It also led to a civil war in Syria which became an international battleground. Differences between Saudi Arabia and Iran assumed the shape of a cold war, further destabilizing the region.

However, the main contours of Pakistan's foreign policy remained unchanged, which proved that foreign policy reflects national interests—more specifically, the search for security and economic welfare—which are permanent in nature and transcend changes of governments. Ideological yearnings are also a component of national interests and do not change with the passage of time.

In the past two decades, Pakistan's foreign and defence policies continued to be based on the perception of a grave threat from its larger neighbour India. Such a perception began right from Pakistan's independence in 1947 and saw two outright wars and some mini-wars between the South Asian neighbours. However, matters have worsened since the coming to power of the stridently Hindu nationalist Bharatiya Janata Party (BJP) regime in India since 2014. Tensions intensified as India's Prime Minister Narendra Modi raised the stakes by launching 'surgical strikes' inside Pakistan, in retaliation for alleged terrorist incidents that took place in India and in India-occupied Kashmir, for which India blamed Pakistan. Islamabad's repeated denials of any complicity and its demands for proof to back up such allegations, made no impact on India, which had convinced itself that Pakistan was involved in a cross-border campaign of terror in India. Toeing the official line, the Indian news media whipped up anti-Pakistan feelings in India through a campaign of systematic vilification/demonization of Pakistan. Having built up such an environment, India refused to hold any talks until Pakistan satisfied India that it had taken effective action against terrorist groups based in Pakistan. Though Pakistan has taken many steps against such groups, which are leftovers from Afghan jihad of 1980s against Soviet occupation, and also launched a major military operation against the terrorists, India is unconvinced about Pakistan's sincerity.

At the bottom of differences between India and Pakistan is the deadlock on Kashmir dispute. Described as an unfinished agenda item from the Partition of India in 1947, Kashmir has long caused a head-on clash of national egos of the two countries. According to the Partition formula, the contiguous Muslim majority areas would become part of Pakistan and contiguous non-Muslim majority areas would constitute India. According to this logic, Kashmir should have become a part of Pakistan because Muslims were in majority there and it was contiguous with Pakistan. However, through intrigue and deception, India manoeuvred and seized half of Kashmir and sought resolution of the Kashmir dispute through the UN Security Council. The UNSC adopted several resolutions that free plebiscite be held and the people of Kashmir be given the opportunity to exercise their right of self-determination to join either India or Pakistan. Such a plebiscite was never held as India went on to declare that Kashmir was its integral part and there could be no third party role to resolve the issue. However, the people of Kashmir never accepted this assertion and have all along continued to protest against Indian occupation. Disregarding the ground reality, India has chosen to interpret their resistance as the handiwork of Pakistan, and any act of militancy in Kashmir is branded by India as a part of 'cross-border terrorism by Pakistan'. Since the Kashmiri opposition to Indian rule has continued, Indian allegations of 'Pakistani involvement in terrorism' also continue, in a deadly stalemate.

In August 2019, India unilaterally declared that it had ended the special status of Kashmir in the Constitution of India (Article 370) and fully integrated it as a part of India. This was a defiant move by India, in direct contradiction of UN resolutions and promises made repeatedly since 1947 by several Indian governments to the Kashmiri people, as well as to Pakistan. Pakistan protested vigorously against this unilateral step, and appealed to the UN and world governments. India sought to muzzle the protests of Kashmiris by imposing draconian measures that, in effect, turned eighty million Kashmiris into prisoners, for many months, confined to their homes with no access to any means of communication with the rest of the world. When the restrictions were partially eased, the Kashmiri protests in some cases took the form of militancy, for which India promptly blamed Pakistan. India refuses to accept that the Kashmiris simply do not want to be ruled by India. They have their own specific reasons for opposing India and do not take any orders from Pakistan. It is India's persistent refusal to accept the reality of the situation in Kashmir—and its attempts to make Pakistan the scapegoat for the unrest and militancy in occupied Kashmir—which is the cause of tension between the two countries and constitutes a grave threat to peace.

If the two countries have avoided a military confrontation since the 1980s, it has been mainly because of the existence of the nuclear deterrent. Both possess an arsenal of nuclear weapons and also have delivery systems. Pakistan has the capability to strike any city in India with nuclear weapons and, vice versa, India has the capability to destroy any city in Pakistan with nuclear weapons. A nuclear war between the two countries would be a case of Mutually Assured Destruction (MAD) and must be avoided at all costs. Despite periodic flare-ups and bellicose threats, it is the nuclear deterrent that has prevented these two countries from going to war, in the same manner as it kept peace between the two rival world blocs—the USA and the USSR—during the Cold War.

Sanity suggests that since war would be a case of mutual suicide, dialogue is the only option left to the two countries. At some point in time, wise leadership on both sides would have to opt for peace and mutual collaboration. Peace would bring all kinds of benefits. The two peoples have so many things in common. They want to live together in peace. They want to visit each other, particularly the numerous holy shrines in the two countries. A reduction in defence expenditure would enhance economic welfare and raise living standards. Regional collaboration under SAARC would benefit everyone and help eliminate poverty and disease, which are the real issues faced by the common man in both the countries. A lasting peace between India and Pakistan must be the hope of all people of goodwill but when and how this will happen, only time will tell. No doubt, Prime Minister Imran Khan has such a vision of peace but progress depends on resolution of the Kashmir dispute.

Pakistan and China drew even closer together in the last two decades. This has become a time-tested friendship not only between the two governments but, more importantly, between the two peoples. Apart from important joint defence production projects, the launching of CPEC (China–Pakistan Economic Corridor) has become the most important joint venture between the two countries. It is transforming Pakistan's infrastructure and significantly boosting its economy. The Chinese interest is to secure a shorter access to the Persian Gulf and an overland transit route through friendly territory, unlike the existing long and relatively insecure sea route via the Indian Ocean and South China Sea. On completion of projects worth over US$60 billion in the near future, CPEC would give long-term stability to this great alliance and fruitful mutual collaboration.

Since the 1950s, Pakistan has maintained close relations with the USA, and has been a recipient of nearly US$75 billion in economic and military aid. However, the relationship has been strained from time to time, mainly due to a lack of trust. Since 9/11 and the US invasion of Afghanistan in 2001, the distrust has grown alarmingly. In spite of incurring enormous financial and physical losses, the US found itself trapped in the longest war in its history, which increasingly looks like a military defeat, since the Afghan Taliban have been gaining ground. Afghanistan defeated earlier foreign invasions and the US failure is true to the Afghan pattern. Instead of accepting its inability to win the war, the US, for a long time, sought to make Pakistan a scapegoat for its military failure in Afghanistan by alleging that sanctuaries provided by Pakistan had enabled the Taliban to make military gains. Relations reached an all-time low when, in January 2018, the new US President Donald Trump accused Pakistan of duplicity and fooling the US governments. He cut off all US aid to Pakistan. Pakistan rejected these allegations and pointed out its key role in support of the War on Terror, including the provision of the invaluable access route across Pakistan to the US/NATO/Kabul forces. It had launched a big military operation against the terrorists. By joining the War on Terror, which many felt was not Pakistan's own war, Pakistan had suffered a huge loss of over 70,000 lives and economic loss of over US$100 billion. Since Trump's outburst, however, matters have eased between the US and Pakistan as Trump had to turn to Pakistan for help in promoting a dialogue between the US and the Taliban to secure a face-saving formula to end the war in Afghanistan. In February 2020, an agreement was signed between the US and the Taliban which will secure withdrawal of US troops from Afghanistan within fourteen months.

Pakistan's relations with Afghanistan were similarly affected by the latter's failure to understand that the Taliban were making gains in Afghanistan due to their ideological and ethnic appeal. Instead, the Kabul regime evidently persuaded itself that the Taliban's military advance in Afghanistan was mainly because Pakistan was providing them with sanctuaries and other help. It tended to blame Pakistan for every new act of militancy by the Taliban. India sought to play up these fears and extended aid to the Kabul regime to win goodwill. As a result, Afghan public opinion clearly turned against Pakistan. This was ironical against the background of the great help given by Pakistan to the Afghan resistance in their jihad against Soviet military occupation, including asylum to three million Afghan refugees. The US military withdrawal from Afghanistan is likely to weaken the Kabul regime but peace in Afghanistan will only be possible if the Taliban show the wisdom to cooperate with non-Pakhtun groups such as Tajiks, Uzbeks, and Hazaras.

For years, a pillar of Pakistan's foreign policy has been the maintenance of a special relationship with Saudi Arabia. Pakistan is seen by Saudi Arabia as a key partner in ensuring its security, whereas Saudi economic assistance to Pakistan is viewed as crucial by Pakistan. In the past two decades, Pakistan's relations with Saudi Arabia remained strong despite change of governments in Pakistan. The Saudis felt more comfortable with the regimes of Pervez Musharraf and Nawaz Sharif and less so with the PPP governments. Prime Minister Imran Khan has strengthened these relations by establishing a personal equation with Crown Prince Mohammed bin Salman, the new Saudi strongman, who paid a triumphal visit to Pakistan in February 2019. At the same time, Pakistan has learned to accept that Saudi Arabia and UAE, another old ally, have been reaching out to India to further their economic interests. This need not affect the special relationship because Saudi Arabia realises that no country other than Pakistan can provide the kind of security, both external and internal, that Pakistan has done in the past fifty years.

Pakistan's international importance will continue in the days ahead because of several reasons. It is the only nuclear power in the Muslim world and one of the foremost military powers in the world. It has a key geostrategic location: a South Asian country which is also a part of Central Asia and the Middle East. It is one of the most important countries in the Muslim world, which consists of over fifty states, constituting one-fourth of the UN. Pakistan is seen as a moderate, progressive and traditionally pro-West Muslim state that serves as a counter-balance to radical Islam. The West and many other states have a stake in keeping Pakistan afloat, since its weakening could destabilise a highly volatile area in the world. Pakistan has good natural resources and a talented people. Given political stability, it could reach an economic 'take-off' in the foreseeable future. At present, its priority must be to improve its economy.

Introduction to the First Edition

The first fifty years of Pakistan's existence have been unusually eventful, marked by many ups and downs for the country. Foreign policy has played a pivotal role, for better or for worse, in several of these developments. The purpose of this study is to analyse, as dispassionately as possible, the successes and failures of the foreign policy pursued so far by Pakistan. The intention here is not to give a comprehensive narrative of Pakistan's foreign policy over the past fifty years, as that exercise has been carried out elsewhere by several other writers. Instead, this study is basically an argument, albeit a long one, about the merits and demerits of the policies followed by Pakistan so far. The author, who spent nearly thirty-nine years in Pakistan's diplomatic service, witnessed from a relatively close range some of the historical developments, which form the subject matter of this book. However, by and large, personal reminiscences have been avoided.

The policymakers in any country, no doubt, often have a hard time choosing between the various options before them. It is difficult, and sometimes impossible, to predict what will be the end result of the policy chosen. Yet, choices have to be made and decisions taken. Obviously, there is a tremendous responsibility on the shoulders of policymakers who have to handle national matters anywhere. In particular, those entrusted with taking difficult foreign policy decisions, affecting not only the present but also the future generations, have a truly onerous task. The benefit of hindsight is a luxury available to historians because they know the final outcome of a given policy decision. Moreover, with the passage of time, it is much easier to conduct an impassive scrutiny of the merits and demerits of policies followed. However, those in authority who take the original decisions, can only guess the consequences of their actions and decisions. Nevertheless, this cannot be used as a general excuse for governments and policymakers to defend the failures of their foreign policy. Most governments usually have a mass of information available to them. They have trained professionals and experts at their service. Above all, great leaders are blessed with an historic vision, the sagacity, and even the instinctive ability, to take the right decisions.

Foreign policy is often considered the first line of defence of any country. This is probably even more pronounced in the case of Pakistan, which has been beset by a difficult security situation from the very beginning. Indeed, the country can be said to have had a baptism of fire. It was more or less thrown into the vortex of international crosscurrents before it could even stand on its feet. Pakistan inherited a complex antagonistic relationship with India, a neighbour who was several times its size. Moreover, Pakistan's odd and almost indefensible frontiers consisting, initially, of two separated wings across a thousand miles of hostile territory, added to the intricacies of its security problems.

It is generally agreed that foreign policy is influenced by a country's history and geography. This has certainly been the case in Pakistan. The Islamic identity and consciousness of its people have been dominant influences on their history throughout. Indeed, without that particular background, there could have been no Pakistan. It was the distinctive Islamic identity and peculiar historical experiences of the Muslims living in the South Asian subcontinent which provided the motivation for seeking a separate and independent Muslim homeland that finally came into being on 14 August 1947. Moreover, this historical legacy has profoundly affected the security concerns and foreign policy pursued by Pakistan.

While most states in the world have existed for a long time within defined geo-political limits, Pakistan's borders were carved out for the first time in 1947. In this case, ideology had clearly preceded the delineation of borders. Pakistan emerged as a state because of the Islamic consciousness of its people which had evolved over several centuries, nourished by the ideas of a number of rulers, religious leaders, scholars, thinkers and poets. In this long list, the poet-philosopher Muhammad Iqbal (1877–1938) was a more recent but, perhaps, the most influential exponent. Moreover, he is regarded the first top-ranking figure to set forth the concept of an independent Muslim state comprising the Muslim-majority areas in the north-west of what was then British India. Thus, he is also known as the 'thinker' of Pakistan. Pakistan is probably the first state in the world carved out in the name of Islam. It is not surprising, therefore, that the Pakistani people have always shown a deep commitment to Islam, not only in the religious sense but also in their political and global outlook. Moreover, it is this peculiar background which has profoundly influenced the formulation of the country's foreign policy after independence. Any attempt to understand the various policies followed by Pakistan would be incomplete, if not impossible, without keeping this Islamic dimension in mind.

Apart from history and ideology, Pakistan's geographical location has also profoundly affected its fortunes as an independent state. Had Pakistan been located in some other part of the world, its course of action and policies after gaining independence might have been entirely different. However, as the saying goes, one can choose one's friends but not one's neighbours. It so happened that Pakistan, a relatively big country itself, is located right next door to India, which is much larger, and with whom Pakistan has always had a relationship of distrust and antagonism. Thus, Pakistan has been preoccupied, for the greater part of its existence, in a difficult and unequal contest with India. This has produced the most decisive impact on the formulation of Pakistan's foreign policy.

However, in addition to the Indian dimension, the geostrategic location of Pakistan has had important repercussions on its foreign policy. To begin with, Pakistan consisted of two wings and was both a neighbour of Central Asia as well as Southeast Asia. The post-1971 Pakistan has borders with India, Iran, Afghanistan, and China. Moreover, until 1991, only a narrow 40-km stretch of land separated it from a superpower, the former Soviet Union. Pakistan has thus been surrounded by three big neighbours: India, China, and the Soviet Union, the latter two being communist powers. Out of these, China has been a friend whereas India has been the adversary. The Soviet Union, for the greater part, had been close to India. It is also notable that though Pakistan is situated in South Asia, it is adjacent to Central Asia and Middle East and is located at the mouth of the strategic Persian Gulf region. While it is a South Asian country, on the basis of its physical location, Pakistan is in some ways also an extension of the Middle East and Central Asia from where it draws most of its spiritual roots and some of its ethnic and cultural origins. The best natural access to the sea for several land-locked countries in Central Asia is via Afghanistan and Pakistan. Western China, which has common borders with Pakistan, also has an outlet to the sea via Pakistan.

In terms of size, Pakistan is among the ten most populous countries in the world. In the Islamic world, which consists of over fifty independent states, Pakistan is second only to Indonesia in population. Moreover, among the Third World countries as also in the Islamic world, Pakistan ranks high in military capability, industrial and agricultural progress, scientific and intellectual development, as also in culture and, in some respects, in education. Pakistan has served as a think-tank and laboratory of the Islamic world in political and economic matters. Its thinkers like Iqbal and Maudoodi have influenced Muslims in many parts of the world. All of these factors, which account for Pakistan's importance and notable geo-strategic significance, have also influenced its foreign policy in one way or the other.

The fiftieth year of Pakistan's independence is perhaps a fitting milestone for taking stock of the successes and failures of its foreign policy so far. However, in a country where emotions run deep and strong partisanship often clouds judgement, any effort to make an objective evaluation can be a hazardous exercise. This seems unfortunate, since the formulation of foreign policy of any country should really be an exercise conducted with cool precision and clear thinking. A country's self-preservation and well-being over-rides all other factors. National self-interest has to be given priority in the making of a country's foreign policy. Governments come and go but a country's interests have permanence. Moreover, historical records show that there are few permanent friends or permanent enemies in global politics. The foreign policy of most states has been mainly motivated by self-interest and not by personal factors. The record also shows that ideology has, in general, played a minor role in the formulation of foreign policy.

A successful foreign policymaker seeks to promote a country's strategic interests by devising policies based on brutal realism, bereft of all kinds of illusions, romanticism, and emotions. In diplomatic parlance, this approach has been described as '*realpolitik*.' On the other hand, foreign policy failures have been generally attributable to a lack of realism or, what is even worse, self-delusion. A study of the first fifty years of Pakistan's foreign policy, unfortunately, bears out this truth in a number of important instances. On several crucial occasions, Pakistan's policymakers and, indeed, even the nation as a whole, have allowed illusions to get the better of their judgement, resulting in disastrous consequences for the country. This has been a major flaw in the formulation of Pakistan's foreign policy and, unless the policymakers draw the right lessons from historical experience, such unrealistic evaluations are capable of causing further harm to the country.

The other main weakness in the formulation of Pakistan's foreign policy has been '*ad hocism*' or the tendency to take decisions to tide over an immediate exigency without any long-term planning. There have been several instances where there was a lack of foresight in the country's considered response to given developments. Pakistan has thus more often reacted than acted according to a definite plan.

Such *ad hocism* has been, in part, due to the absence of an effective and relatively autonomous policy planning and research division in the Pakistan Foreign Office and the lack of involvement of think tanks, top scholars, and academic experts in policy planning. While a research wing has long been in existence in the Foreign Office, it has rarely been manned by the best brains in the Foreign Service. Usually, it has been a dumping ground for officers for whom no other posting could be found. They, in turn, have tended to consider their posting in the research wing of little importance and have thus generally worked without any commitment. Not surprisingly, they have, in a kind of vicious cycle, received little encouragement or appreciation. Also, in the actual functioning of the Foreign Office, the research wing has been rarely consulted by the political desks while formulating policies. The research wing has, moreover, been unable to have systematic access to important current information with the result that it has often been starved of vital input needed for any kind of meaningful contribution.

In general, the political desks in the Pakistan Foreign Office have played a more decisive role in the formulation of foreign policy. However, here too, matters have not been helped, in many instances, by the posting of officers who have had little previous experience or specialization regarding the given geographical area. Many of them indeed get to learn the more precise nature of the issues affecting their area of responsibility on the job. Hence, they have lacked real insight into political under-currents in the countries under their charge. Moreover, there never seems to be time for anyone in the Foreign Office or in Pakistan embassies abroad to go through old records to get the full historical perspective of relations with a given country. All of this has accounted for *ad hocism* in the formulation of Pakistan's foreign policy.

Finally, *ad hoc* policies have resulted from the continuous practice of the head of government to give directives on a given issue without any kind of advance consultation with the Foreign Office. As the culture of opportunism has grown in Pakistan over the years, the Foreign Office has, for its part, rarely shown the backbone to suggest any kind of reconsideration of such political directives. More often than not, the Foreign Office merely accompanies the many sycophants surrounding the top leadership in applauding every brainchild of the chief executive. The result, of course, has been that policy decisions have been made first and the duty of the Foreign Office has merely been to produce the rationale for such decisions subsequently. This has distorted and even negated the very concept of policymaking. Not surprisingly, Pakistan's foreign policy has suffered as a consequence.

However, in all fairness it needs to be said that over the past fifty years, the majority of Pakistani diplomats, despite the many constraints imposed upon them and their own occasional failures, have performed well in the pursuit of Pakistan's national interests. This is shown, among other factors, by the high reputation that many of them have enjoyed in the international arena. That Pakistan has been able to hold back a much larger adversary over the years, by itself, speaks well of its diplomatic efforts.

One oft-repeated line of criticism of Pakistan's foreign policy should also perhaps be rejected at the outset. There are some cynical observers, both inside and outside Pakistan, who argue that Pakistan has never had a foreign policy of its own or that its foreign policy has generally been made in the USA. Any careful scrutiny of the record would show that this is a flawed argument. If this accusation had been true, then, for instance, it would not have been possible for Pakistan to have maintained a solidly pro-Arab and anti-Israel stance throughout its history, in total contrast to the US attitude. How could one explain Pakistan's befriending China, prior to 1971, when that country was regarded as an enemy by the US; or how could Pakistan have remained very friendly with Iran, after the Islamic Revolution in 1979, despite Iran's strained relations with Washington. For that matter, how could one explain Pakistan's solidly pro-Islamic stance in general; its persistently anti-India policies including two wars which were fought in disregard of American advice; the development of its nuclear and missile programmes in total rejection of US wishes that Pakistan sign the Nuclear Non-Proliferation Treaty (NPT) and the Comprehensive Nuclear Test Ban Treaty (CTBT)? Surely, Pakistan could not have pursued these policies if it were taking dictation from Washington. In fact, the record shows that, in the last fifty years Pakistan–America relations have seen several highs and lows. Such vicissitudes could not have arisen if Pakistan's foreign policy had been tailored in the US.

Actually, this kind of criticism can be traced back to the era of the Cold War when Pakistan's membership of the US-sponsored military pacts in the mid-1950s brought a howl of disapproval from the pro-Moscow leftists and supporters of nonalignment, as also from India. These circles would taunt that Pakistan's membership of the pacts meant that it had become an American stooge and was left with no option but to take orders from Washington. Later on, the more hard line Islamic parties in Pakistan also joined in this criticism. They tended to see the hand of the US in all that was wrong with the Islamic world, citing in particular its support for Israel against the Arabs. In the context of Pakistan, the Islamists along with the leftists have been critical of the US for its perceived failure to come to Pakistan's assistance in the wars against India even though, at that time, Pakistan was a military ally of the US. In more recent years, the US has been criticised for the pressures on Pakistan's economy—bordering on dictates—from the World Bank and the International Monetary Fund (IMF), which are considered to be US-dominated bodies. Based on this logic, Islamabad's often close relations with the US have been viewed as a case of subservience to Washington.

In addition, over the years, a cynical view has grown in Pakistan which holds, without being able to advance much by way of credible evidence, that the all-powerful USA must be behind not only all changes of regimes and policies in Pakistan but also behind all that is wrong with it since, in their view, nothing could happen here without US blessings. America-bashing, rather than a realistic understanding of the situation in Pakistan, is clearly responsible for this kind of criticism of Pakistan's foreign policies.

In reality, an objective study would show that Pakistan's foreign policy, even during the phase when the military pacts were relatively vibrant (1954–61), had always reflected Pakistan's preoccupations with India, and could not be described as subservient to the US. In the years that followed, Pakistan's relations with the US lost much of their earlier warmth. The military pacts were, in fact, more or less dead even before they were dissolved in the 1970s. Thus, there remained little possibility of American dictation. However, around 1980, it was a convergence of interests between the US and Pakistan in the wake of the Soviet military intervention in Afghanistan, which induced the two countries to work together to dislodge the Soviets from Pakistan's neighbouring Muslim country. Incidentally, in this bid a similar anti-Soviet position was taken by Iran as well, despite its known hostile attitude towards the US. Moreover, China, Saudi Arabia, Japan, and most other countries in the world were also opposed to the Soviet military occupation of Afghanistan. It was, without doubt, a case of mutuality of interests that had brought Pakistan and these diverse countries together on the Afghan issue and not any kind of dictation from Washington.

Nonetheless, it can be said that over the years, a degree of American influence on Pakistan can be traced in certain instances. But there have been similar influences on Pakistan by certain other countries that have had close relations with Pakistan like Saudi Arabia, Turkey, China, etc. For instance, Pakistan's policy towards Taiwan and Tibet has been influenced by the desire to keep China happy. Pakistan's stance on Northern Cyprus has been influenced by Turkey. Pakistan's policy towards Israel has been influenced by the sensitivities of the Arab countries. Pakistan's stance towards Iraq in the Gulf War of 1991 was influenced by its close friendship with Saudi Arabia and Kuwait. Similarly, Pakistan had eschewed all contacts with South Africa before 1993 to show solidarity with black Africa.

Moreover, it should not be forgotten that Pakistan too has in certain situations influenced the foreign policies of friendly countries, including that of the US (e.g. during the 1971 War, President Richard Nixon 'tilted' in favour of Pakistan). Similarly, many of Pakistan's friends have remained cool towards India, mainly so as not to ruffle Pakistan's feelings. For instance, Turkey and Iran would have drawn much closer to India but for the considerations of friendship with Pakistan. The same applies to some of Pakistan's closest friends in the Arab world, including Saudi Arabia. In fact, bilateral influences are not uncommon in international relations and do not necessarily prove the subservience of one country to another country. There have been historical instances of subservience, such as those of the East European countries after 1945 who became vassals of the Soviet Union. But probably few leftists, while accusing Pakistan of toeing the American line, have ever been willing to admit that reality.

The fact of the matter is that Pakistan, like most other states, has had to chart out its own course in international relations based on the evaluation of its national interests by the various governments which have ruled the country. Their decisions might or might not have been sound in all cases, but it is misleading to say that Pakistan has had no foreign policy and that its policies were made in Washington or elsewhere.

Reviewing the past fifty years of Pakistan's foreign policy as objectively as possible, it can be said that the over-riding motivation in determining Pakistan's foreign policy has been the desire to safeguard the country's independence and territorial integrity. For Pakistan, the main danger has come from India. Thus, the quest for security *vis-à-vis* India has been an unvarying, and almost obsessive, dimension of Pakistan's foreign policy from the very beginning. Much that Pakistan has done in its foreign relations has been influenced greatly by its perception of a mortal threat from India. At the same time, there has also been a kind of sibling rivalry with India resulting in an abiding competition even in areas unrelated to a security threat. Apart from India, until 1991, the former Soviet Union and, in a lesser way, Afghanistan as well, posed a potential threat.

In addition to considerations of security, the other motivations of Pakistan's foreign policy have revolved around its ideological yearnings, as also its economic interests. Being a new state on the world map, having liberated itself from British colonialism and owing its origin to its Islamic identity, Pakistan's foreign policies have reflected a certain ideological orientation. In the first place, the Pakistani people have always shown a genuine commitment to the concept of Islamic solidarity and have been keen, from the very beginning, to foster unity among Islamic countries. Pakistan has, therefore, always taken a deep interest in Islamic issues around the globe, foremost of which has been the Palestinian problem. However, apart from ideological reasons, Pakistan's rivalry with India has been a contributing factor, in establishing friendly relations with Islamic countries—an important plank of Pakistan's foreign policy.

Similarly, Pakistan's colonial past also influenced it to sympathize with other Third World countries on issues relating to the struggle against colonialism, neo-colonialism, imperialism, and racial discrimination. Moreover, being a developing country, Pakistan has common interests with the countries of the South in their negotiations with the North. Pakistan has sought to promote an equitable international economic system, which does not discriminate against countries producing raw materials. Arising out of its preoccupation with security as well as ideology, an important dimension of Pakistan's foreign policy has been the maintenance of special relationships with certain countries in the region like Saudi Arabia, the Gulf states, Iran and Turkey as also with China. With Saudi Arabia, Pakistan developed a very close relationship motivated by common strategic interests, ideological affinity as well as the pull of its enormous oil wealth. The same applies to the other Gulf countries.

On the other hand, China, though not an Islamic country, emerged around 1960 as one of Pakistan's best friends. A mutuality of interests, particularly with respect to India, originally brought these two very diverse countries together. In the 1960s, China was also a very isolated country in the international arena and it welcomed an opening to the rest of the world via Pakistan. On the other hand, China's position as one of the great powers of the world, apart from being an immediate neighbour, enhanced its importance in Pakistan's eyes. Friendship with China has remained a pillar of Pakistan's foreign policy and has withstood the test of time. It has, moreover, enjoyed enormous public support in Pakistan.

In addition, economic interests have strongly influenced the formulation of Pakistan's foreign policy. The Gulf countries, including Saudi Arabia and Iran, have had a strong economic pull for Pakistan. During the period of the oil boom (1974–84), Pakistan received substantial financial assistance from these countries. With the emigration of hundreds of thousands of Pakistanis in search of jobs, this region has become pivotal for Pakistan's economic wellbeing.

However, the main trading links have always been with the US, UK, Western Europe, and Japan. The Western way of life has also been a powerful influence on many Pakistanis, especially the ruling elite. Their ideas on politics and commerce have been influenced by the West. Even after the departure of the British, a kind of colonial hangover has persisted, which is not unlike the attitude found in many former colonies in other parts of the world. A kind of love–hate relationship has prevailed for the greater part between Pakistan and Britain, and—in a wider context—with the USA and Western Europe. The latter have, however, shown a preference for India over Pakistan, mainly because India is a bigger power and has greater economic attraction. For its part, Pakistan has always remained eager to win over the sympathies of the West and has perhaps paid preponderant attention to these countries, though the results have not been commensurate with the efforts made. Nonetheless, the bulk of the economic aid to Pakistan over the years has come from Western countries. Japan too has been a principal aid-giver. Special attention has, therefore, always been paid to bilateral relations with these countries.

Multilateral diplomacy has also been an important preoccupation of Pakistan's foreign policy. Pakistan has always been quite active at the United Nations (UN) and its various subsidiary bodies as well as in the Organisation of Islamic Cooperation (OIC), the Non-Aligned Movement (NAM), South Asian Association for Regional Cooperation (SAARC), and the Economic Cooperation Organization (ECO). Motivated largely by the desire to find an equalizer against India, Pakistan's foreign policy has focused a great deal on the UN and the OIC, the latter being the main political body of Muslim countries since it was set up in 1969. Moreover, Pakistan has sought to promote the regional grouping, formerly known as the Regional Cooperation for Development (RCD), consisting of Iran, Pakistan, and Turkey. It has since been renamed as the ECO and expanded to include seven other Central Asian countries.

Pakistan has also been active in seeking friendship with its immediate neighbours in South Asia viz. Nepal, Sri Lanka, Maldives and, since 1975, with Bangladesh. While SAARC, the grouping of South Asian countries, has made slow progress mainly due to the political tensions between two of its larger members, Pakistan has been able to achieve a good understanding with all of its other South Asian neighbours. Relations with these countries have always been given considerable attention by Pakistan.

1

The Rationale for Partition and Peaceful Co-existence

The founder of Pakistan, Quaid-i-Azam Mohammad Ali Jinnah, the great leader who is credited as having almost single-handedly created Pakistan had declared, shortly before the country's independence, that Pakistan wanted 'to live peacefully and maintain cordial and friendly relations with our immediate neighbours.' Indeed, the main argument of the Muslims in pressing for the partition of British India was that durable peace in this region could only be achieved when the Muslims have a sovereign state of their own, which would exist side by side with Hindu-majority India.

In voicing hope for a friendly relationship with India after independence, Jinnah was certainly conscious of the bitterness between the Hindus and Muslims, which had preceded the creation of Pakistan in 1947. Yet, he was optimistic that having achieved independence, the two newly independent countries and neighbours—Muslim-majority Pakistan and Hindu-majority India—would be able to live as friends. His evident logic was that time had shown beyond doubt that a united India was no longer feasible because of the unbridgeable and conflicting interests, as also the disparate national yearnings, of the two principal groups and hence partition was the only practical means of achieving peace and tranquillity.

When Pakistan finally emerged, Jinnah said in his famous speech of 11 August 1947:

> I know there are people who do not quite agree with the division of India...
> But the question is, whether it was possible or practicable to act otherwise
> than what has been done. A division had to take place...I am sure future
> history will record its verdict in favour of it. And what is more, it will be
> proved by actual experience as we go on, that it was the *only solution* of
> India's constitutional problem. *Any idea of a United India could never have
> worked* and in my judgement it would have led us to terrific disaster.
> (My italics)

1

Jinnah was convinced that separation alone was the solution which would enable the two peoples to live peacefully, side by side according to their own aspirations and beliefs, in separate sovereign states. Having secured their national objectives and being able to go their different ways, the two peoples would have every reason to bury the hatchet and live together in the region in peaceful co-existence.

The rationale for the Partition perhaps needs to be elaborated here, particularly because of the persistent distortion of historical facts by many circles in India and beyond. In the words of S.M. Burke, a non-Muslim historian, 'it is difficult to think of any two religions more antithetical to each other than Islam and Hinduism.' Despite living in the same region for over a thousand years, they were '...like two streams, which continue to run parallel to each other indefinitely, never becoming one body of water.'[1]

To understand the extent of the insurmountable differences between the Hindus and the Muslims, which led to the creation of Pakistan, a few instances need to be mentioned. The historical recollections of the two communities were mutually contradictory: the Muslim heroes in Indian history were villains for the Hindus, and vice versa. Thus, the golden age for the Muslims of a thousand years of rule over India was the period of shame and national humiliation for the Hindus. The Hindus worshipped idols whereas the Muslims, being fiercely monotheistic, were appalled by idol-worship. The Hindus treated the Muslims like untouchables. Inter-marriages were severely frowned upon by both groups. Their attitude towards language was mutually exclusive. Urdu was the lingua franca as also the main language used in the government and the media at the end of the nineteenth century. Growing Hindu nationalism resulted in a sustained campaign in the twentieth century to promote Hindi and to suppress Urdu which was branded as the language of the Muslims. The latter obviously resented this step-motherly treatment of a widely spoken language, which moreover, was the repository of the best in their literature and culture. The culinary habits of the two communities were conflicting: the Muslims eat beef whereas the Hindus regard this as abominable since they worship the cow. The Hindus dressed differently from the Muslims. Their festivals, their manner of salutations and their system of burial of the dead were all strikingly different from those of the Muslims.

Moreover, as prospects of independence from British colonial rule increased in the early twentieth century, the religious tensions grew alarmingly. A fierce jockeying for power began at all levels between the two communities and the general conditions deteriorated rapidly, so much so that a civil war seemed imminent. Hindus and Muslims felt unsafe *vis-à-vis* each other and, in fact, small and big communal riots were endemic in British India. Thus, it seemed to the Muslims, who were in a minority and nearly always suffered more in these riots, that their life and honour was at stake in a Hindu-dominated India. The Muslims feared that in a united India, after independence, the chauvinism of the Hindu majority would deny them their due rights in political, economic, and other matters. Indeed, there were deep fears about the very survival of the Muslims as a religious and cultural group in a post-independence, Hindu-dominated India.

Such fears were not imaginary. The Hindu intolerance of the Muslims had become increasingly apparent as the time of independence from British colonialism drew nearer, more particularly, when Hindu-dominated governments were formed in several provinces of British India in 1937 and proceeded to impose Hindu ideas over others. Thus, the contrary argument by the secularists—indeed those masquerading as secularists—that Muslims and Hindus were one and the same people made little sense to the overwhelming majority of Muslims. They found that even under British colonial rule, the Hindu majority was denying the Muslims their due share in the political, cultural, and economic fields. The Muslims felt that they did not even have the basic security of life and honour. Attempts were being made to forcibly convert them and to suppress their culture. For these reasons they were deeply apprehensive that, after the departure of the British, in a Hindu-dominated independent India, a worse fate awaited the Muslims.

The repeated attempts of Muslim leaders from around 1880, to secure constitutional safeguards for Muslims in a united India were roundly spurned by the Hindu majority which was intoxicated by the confidence that they would always have a 75 per cent vote in a democratic set-up. Thus, for the most part, they were insensitive to, and even scornful of, the genuine concerns of the Muslims and rejected with disdain all formulas which could have given the Muslims a sense of security and fair play in a united India. In fact, the demand for a separate Muslim homeland was made as late as 1940 only after the Muslim masses had lost all hopes of justice in a united, but Hindu-dominated, independent India.

There is an oft-repeated argument in India that the British colonialists had planted the demand for Pakistan as a part of their policy of 'divide and rule.' However, there is little historical evidence to support this argument which is both simplistic and self-serving. In fact, the British always took great pride in having secured the unity of India, which was the 'Jewel in the Crown' for them. Even as late as 1947, when Louis Mountbatten took over as the last viceroy, the 'unity of the subcontinent' was still 'the top priority'[2] for the British who opposed the creation of Pakistan till the very end. In fact, the British rulers of the period (Linlithgow, Zetland, Wavell, Amery, Attlee, and Mountbatten) were generally hostile to the concept of Pakistan as well as to Jinnah personally. Mountbatten's dislike for Jinnah is well documented. Clement Attlee, the prime minister of the Labour Party government in Britain when the subcontinent gained independence, confirmed in an interview given later in 1959 that he had 'never liked Jinnah' whom he had known since 1927.[3] Another British historian observed that the Labour Party's 'political bias, its belief in centralization and planning, its concept of a socialist state, all predisposed its leaders in favour of the aspirations of the left wing of the Congress, and made them if not antipathetic, at least allergic to Muslim League demands for partition and a separate Muslim state.'[4]

Even more importantly, if the demand for Pakistan was merely a British concoction, then how could one explain why the Muslim masses supported it so overwhelmingly? The truth of the matter was that it was the Hindu majority's intolerance and narrow-mindedness, bordering on arrogance, which eventually pushed the Muslims—who in any case always had a sense of being a distinct national group—to make the demand for a separate homeland of their own.

The demand for Pakistan has been misrepresented from the beginning by most Indian Hindus, as also by those of a secular mind set in the West and elsewhere, as a retrograde and narrow-minded demand. Some of them argue that if the Catholics and Protestants in Europe could live together as one nation, why could not this be done by Hindus and Muslims in India? However, what is forgotten in this line of thinking is that the Catholics and Protestants, for instance, in England as well as France did go through torrid times, including civil wars, till one or the other of the two groups came to a position of total dominance. Secondly, in the last century religion has lost its hold in many of the Western societies and thus differences on a religious basis no longer have much meaning for them. This was not the situation in British India in the early part of the twentieth century. Hence, the parallel with the Western experience was simply not there. Also, the degree of differences dividing the Hindus and Muslims is far greater than the differences which existed between Catholics and Protestants. Hindus and Muslims in the South Asian subcontinent have two different ways of life and belong to two different civilizations, which was not the case in Europe.

In addition to the Hindu majority's chauvinistic intolerance, the Muslims were also propelled by another powerful impulse leading towards the demand for a separate country. The Indian Muslims had a proud history of a thousand years of having ruled the major portions of India until they were displaced by the British colonialists in 1857. Thus, it was particularly difficult for them to accept the permanent status of second-class citizens in an independent India, ruled by a chauvinistic majority who had been their subjects for centuries. Besides, though a minority in overall numbers, the Muslims had a huge population of almost one hundred million—more than the population of Britain and Germany put together. They were unwilling to accept the permanent status of a minority. Rather fortuitously for the Muslims, the division of the country was demographically possible because the Muslim population was concentrated in two large regions in the north-west and the north-east of the subcontinent, even though in the whole of India, they were outnumbered three to one by the Hindus. Moreover, these two Muslim-majority regions were relatively fertile and economically viable. Statehood was, therefore, quite feasible.

The creation of Pakistan left a large number of Muslims and great centres of Muslim heritage (like Delhi, Lucknow, and Hyderabad) in India. Nonetheless, the agonizing logic prevailed that in a united India all Muslims faced the threat of ruthless subjugation. Hence, it was deemed worthwhile to save at least some Muslim areas from such a dismal fate. It is notable that the Muslims from the minority provinces, who had tasted at first hand the oppression of the Hindus, were in the forefront of the demand for Pakistan. It was in this context and not due to any inherent Muslim fanaticism or obscurantism, that the slogan 'Islam is in danger' did become a kind of rallying cry. In fact, the demand for Pakistan was in essence defensive in nature, motivated by the instinct for self-preservation. It is manifestly wrong to portray it as indicative of any kind of Muslim militancy or irrationality.

Those who accuse the Muslims of religious fanaticism should also not forget that the division of India had never been the first priority of the Muslims and was demanded by them only when all other remedies had failed. Even as late as 1946, when the campaign for Pakistan was already in full momentum, the Muslim League had accepted the Cabinet Mission Plan, which meant foregoing the demand for Pakistan, on the stipulation that satisfactory constitutional safeguards could be given to the Muslims of an undivided India. It is also notable that the Cabinet Mission Plan was rejected, after having been first accepted, by the Hindu-dominated, and seemingly power-drunk, Indian National Congress.

From the early part of the twentieth century, the Muslims had made all possible efforts to preserve the unity of India, firstly, by supporting the Congress in large numbers, and secondly, by working shoulder-to-shoulder with all parties for the common objective of securing liberation from colonial rule. However, the Hindu majority showed little understanding for the Muslim pleas for constitutional safeguards such as separate electorates, reservation of seats for the Muslims, or greater autonomy for the provinces. After the rise of Mahatma Gandhi in Indian politics around 1920, there was a gradual change in the character of the Congress as it began to reflect the Hindu viewpoint more rather than maintaining a truly national, non-communal stance. Thus, the Congress summarily rejected even a modest list of Muslim demands in 1929, incorporated in Jinnah's Fourteen Points. In fact, the attitude of the Congress had been unaccommodating even when the Muslims were supporting a united India and there was no demand for a separate state.

It was against this backdrop of growing Muslim alienation that the great poet-philosopher Muhammad Iqbal, addressing the annual session of the Muslim League at Allahabad in 1930, made the prophetic observation:

> I would like to see the Punjab, North-West Frontier Province, Sind and Baluchistan amalgamated into a single state. Self-government within the British Empire or without the British Empire, the formation of a consolidated North-West Indian Muslim State appears to me to be the final destiny of the Muslims, at least of North-West India.[5]

The above dimensions of the situation have to be kept in mind in order to understand why the call for a separate homeland, when it was eventually made by a major party, the Muslim League, in the famous Lahore Resolution on 23 March 1940, brought such an overwhelming response from the Muslim masses in general. They readily flocked under its banner to launch a vigorous campaign for the creation of Pakistan and succeeded in achieving it on 14 August 1947.

The demand for a separate Muslim state was immediately opposed by many Hindus who saw it as a vivisection of 'mother' India. However, in reality, there was nothing outlandish or shocking in the demand, nor was there anything sacrosanct about India's unity. In its recorded history of about 2500 years, India had nearly always consisted of small and big states, mostly in conflict with each other, and it was hardly ever ruled as one unified country. Hence, division rather than unity had been the tradition.

The Hindu leadership fought tooth and nail against this demand. They argued, in a clear distortion of facts, that Hindus and Muslims belonged to a common Indian nation and shared the same culture and language. (They were blithely disregarding the fact that at that very time they themselves were seeking to crush the Urdu language.) The argument that Muslims and Hindus were the same people or were brothers, therefore, seemed almost ludicrous, since the prevalent conditions bordered on a civil war in many parts of India.

For the foregoing reasons, the Muslim League was convinced that practical wisdom clearly dictated that it was better to separate and live side by side as independent nations rather than go on fighting each other interminably in a forced union. The point was that, even within one household, if two brothers were constantly at loggerheads, and their differences seemed irreconcilable, it made better sense for them to live separately in two different houses in order to establish a smoother relationship.

Motivated by this spirit, Jinnah said in a statement issued only a week before Pakistan gained independence: 'Our object should be peace within and peace without. We want to live peacefully and have cordial and friendly relations with *our immediate neighbours* and with the world at large. We have no aggressive designs against anyone. We stand by the United Nations' Charter.'[6] (My italics)

In fact, the founder of Pakistan had initially visualized active collaboration after independence between Pakistan and India, even in security matters. For instance, he said soon after independence, 'It is of vital importance to Pakistan and India as independent sovereign states to collaborate in a friendly way jointly to defend their frontiers both on land and sea against aggression.'[7] Even earlier, on 14 October 1944 and 15 November 1946, Jinnah had said that India and Pakistan would proclaim a 'Monroe Doctrine' of their own for the defence of the subcontinent against all outsiders.[8] In a more personal context, Jinnah had been hopeful that sometime after the creation of Pakistan, he might even go back to Bombay in India to spend his last years in the city where he had spent most of his life.[9]

This kind of friendly cooperation after independence was Jinnah's sincere hope. In the years that followed, had the leaders of Pakistan and India shown even a small degree of goodwill and accommodation, as well as the necessary statesmanship, it would not have been difficult for the two countries to adopt the mutually beneficial course of compromise and cooperation. This could have, for one thing, saved the backbreaking expenditure on armaments, warfare, and defence, which has kept hundreds of millions of their peoples so deeply impoverished. In fact, South Asia has remained one of the lowest per capita income groups in the world, along with the ills that accompany poverty, viz. disease, illiteracy, and malnourishment. Perennial tensions between India and Pakistan have, in addition, caused so many other avoidable sufferings at a human level, apart from thwarting the two countries' national growth and leaving them behind in the economic field.

NOTES

1. S.M. Burke and Lawrence Ziring, *Pakistan's Foreign Policy: An Historical Analysis*, 2nd ed. (Karachi: Oxford University Press, 1990), pp. 5–6.
2. Cited by Dr Sikandar Hayat, article in *Dawn*, 14 August 1997. Similarly, Lord Birdwood observed that the accusation of 'divide and rule' against the British was a complete misapprehension. Burke and Ziring, op. cit., p. 6.
3. Burke and Ziring, op. cit., p. 111, quoting a BBC-TV interview printed in *Listener*, 22 January 1959.
4. Nicholas Mansergh, cited in Chaudhri Muhammad Ali, *The Emergence of Pakistan* (New York: Columbia University Press, 1967), p. 117.
5. Chaudhri Muhammad Ali, *The Emergence of Pakistan*, p. 25.
6. M. Rafique Afzal (ed.), *Selected Speeches and Statements of the Quaid-i-Azam Mohammad Ali Jinnah (1911–34 and 1947–48)*, 4th ed. (Lahore: Research Society of Pakistan, 1980), p. 418. Similar views were expressed by Jinnah in his interview to Reuters on 21 May 1947 and his press conference on 13 July 1947, reported at p. 75 and p. 85 respectively by Mohammad Hanif Shahid, *The Quaid-i-Azam on Important Issues* (Lahore: Sang-e-Meel Publications, 1989).
7. Ibid., p. 459, cited in Burke and Ziring, p. 55.
8. Jamil-ud-Din Ahmad (ed.), *Some Recent Speeches and Writings of Mr Jinnah*, vol. 2, (Lahore: Shaikh Muhammad Ashraf, 1964), pp. 225, 274, cited in Burke and Ziring, p. 55.
9. Chris Mitchell, Director of BBC documentary on Jinnah, cited in Mohsin S. Jafri, *The News*, 25 December 1997.

2

India–Pakistan Relations: The First Phase

Any impartial observer would have to hold that the ruling classes of both Pakistan and India must share the blame for the unending tensions and, indeed, confrontation between the two countries since independence. However, behind the actions of the two governments, there has been a certain narrow-mindedness of official and non-official circles. In particular, from the very beginning the atmosphere has been vitiated by the extremist 'hate lobbies' in both countries, mostly consisting of right-wing religious parties, demagogues, the 'super patriots', and rabid nationalists who could only thrive when relations were strained between the two neighbours.

The religious parties, incidentally, played a minor role in the creation of Pakistan. Some of them had even actively opposed the division of India for one reason or the other. But after independence, they have assumed the mantle of champions of Pakistan's integrity and have emerged as the most relentless foes of any softening of stance towards India. Similarly, the Hindu fundamentalist parties in India which, unlike the case of Pakistan, have even succeeded in gaining political power, have all along thrived on a 'hate Pakistan' motto. Driven by such lobbies, the masses in the two countries have shown both a propensity for emotional frenzies as well as a susceptibility to manipulation by demagogy. It seems that the intellectuals and scholars have also not been immune to such poison. Then there are powerful vested interests, including some in the military establishment and in the business world, who stand to lose in case there is any lessening of tensions. In building the general atmosphere of distrust, sections of the print media in both countries have, more often than not, played a key part by fanning suspicions and hatred through systematic distortion and misrepresentation of facts. The few voices for sanity and compromise, raised periodically in either country, have been drowned in a sea of hatred and misrepresentation.

Nonetheless, it can still be argued, in retrospect, that there could have been much better chances of peace and stability, and even friendship and cooperation, if the bigger country, India, had shown forbearance, particularly in the early years after independence. It would have been so much more sensible if a policy of 'let bygones be bygones' had been adopted by both sides, right from the time of independence. But, in reality, such an attitude was rarely forthcoming, in particular, from India in the formative years. Big power chauvinism seems to have been a permanent part of the Indian psyche. Thus, the record shows that India–Pakistan relations in the past fifty years have been, with very few exceptions, almost persistently characterized by suspicion, acrimony, crises, and wars.

Indian Efforts to Undo Pakistan

It appears that the Indian leadership, certainly in the early years after independence, held on to the belief that the Partition would shortly be undone. The top leaders of the Indian National Congress, including M.K. Gandhi, Jawaharlal Nehru, and Vallabhbhai Patel, had only unwillingly accepted the creation of Pakistan in 1947, evidently more as a tactical move, to expedite the departure of the British colonialists. But in ideological terms they had remained unreconciled to the Partition and treated it as an unfortunate and temporary aberration. For instance, Prime Minister Nehru, in his speech on 3 June 1947, while conceding the demand for Pakistan, added that 'it may be that in this way we shall reach united India sooner than otherwise.'[1] According to Maulana Abul Kalam Azad, a close associate and chronicler of the Congress leaders, Patel 'was convinced that the new State of Pakistan was not viable and could not last. He thought the acceptance of Pakistan would teach the Muslim League a bitter lesson. Pakistan would collapse in a short time.'[2]

The Indian leaders evidently expected that due to its inherent weaknesses, including its separation in two wings located a thousand miles apart, Pakistan would soon burst like a bubble and rejoin the 'mother' country. Grossly misreading the reasons for the alienation of the Muslims and their national aspirations, the Indian leaders saw the Partition as an unfortunate transient misunderstanding which needed to be rectified. With this in view, they clearly did what they could to make things as difficult as possible for Pakistan at the very outset.

In this antagonistic environment, the departing British colonial admin-istration headed by the last Viceroy, Lord Mountbatten, could at least have played a helpful neutral role so as to ensure that Partition took place much more peacefully. Had this been done, millions need not have been killed, injured, or displaced, and the invidious Kashmir dispute, in particular, would not have arisen.

Unfortunately, the British attitude towards the freedom struggle in India was a mixture of cynicism and unprincipled self-interest. As long as the British thought that they could continue to rule India as a colony, they sought to suppress the Congress Party, which was the biggest political force in India and, in particular, enjoyed the support of most of the Hindus, the majority group in Indian population. In this phase, the British also favoured a 'divide and rule' policy and sought to encourage the various smaller parties, including the Muslim League, as a counterpoise to the Congress.

However, Britain was severely weakened by the Second World War during which the US emerged as the senior partner in the war alliance. The war was being fought in the name of democracy and President Franklin D. Roosevelt, a liberal thinker, pressed London to let India, the world's largest colony, become independent. Meanwhile, the freedom movement in India had also acquired an increasing momentum. Once the British came to the conclusion that they could no longer keep India as a colony and would have to grant it independence, they made a switch in their policy and now tilted in favour of the Congress, on the apparent logic that Britain's future interests lay with India, the larger country in the subcontinent.

Moreover, in ideological terms also, the Labour government ruling Britain found a greater affinity with the Congress Party of Gandhi and Nehru rather than with Jinnah's Muslim League. Nehru's attachment to socialism obviously struck the right chord with Labour. Moreover, the call of the Congress for a secular, multi-ethnic, and multi-religious state (though, in reality, it was little more than double talk for Hindu domination of India) made more sense to the party of Clement Attlee and Stafford Cripps than the Muslim League's demand for the division of India, and that too on the basis of religion. The reluctance of the British to partition the 'Jewel in the Crown' was another reason for favouring the Congress. In this particular scenario, the last British Viceroy, Lord Mountbatten—a vain man with strong prejudices and personal ambitions of his own—was, if anything, two steps ahead of London in the bid to woo and even appease the Congress. The personal equation, which Mountbatten established with Nehru, and his dislike for Jinnah, also became a factor.

Mountbatten at first discouraged Jinnah from pressing ahead with the demand for Pakistan. When he found that the latter was absolutely firm, Mountbatten reversed his tactics. He then insisted on advancing the date of independence from June 1948 to August 1947, in spite of the complaint of the Muslim League that it would be impossible to set up a new country within the space of two months after the announcement to partition India.[3] This change had evidently been done by Mountbatten at the bidding of the Congress as a *quid pro quo* for India remaining in the Commonwealth after independence, which was his main interest. The logic of the Congress clearly was that if the newly created and truncated state of Pakistan were set up in great haste, bordering on confusion and panic, without a proper government in the saddle, it would not survive its fiery birth.[4] There is also some evidence that Mountbatten conspired with the Indian Hindu leaders to draw a highly contorted border to produce what Jinnah could only describe as a 'moth-eaten and truncated Pakistan.' This thinking of Hindu leaders was, later in 1949, personally confirmed by Patel, the strongman of the Congress, who was also Nehru's chief lieutenant. He said, 'I agreed to partition as a last resort…Mr Jinnah did not want a truncated Pakistan but he had to swallow it. *I made a further condition that in two months' time, power should be transferred.*[5] (My italics).

As a part of the same strategy, at the dawn of independence, the key province of Punjab, and some other regions, were thrown into a state of turmoil and more than a million were killed in communal massacres in the midst of an unparalleled exodus. The system of communications and the very fabric of society almost entirely broke down in this bloodshed and anarchy. Millions of Hindus and Sikhs living in Pakistan left the fledgling state *en masse* and many more Muslim refugees from India sought refuge in or were pushed into Pakistan. Many of the Hindus and Sikhs who left Pakistan were prominent in trade and various professions; their abrupt departure could have and was probably designed to cripple the newly born state. In the same manner, the Partition assets of British India, which were inherited by Pakistan as its share, were largely denied to it by India creating a severe handicap for the former at the very outset. Also, soon after independence, there were serious attempts by India, disregarding existing agreements, to block the supply of water in the canals flowing into Pakistan from India, which were so vital for Pakistan's agriculture and could have resulted in famine on a large scale.

All of this was clearly done to create the maximum confusion and hardship in the expectation that Pakistan, at its very birth, would collapse under such burdens. *Akhand Bharat*, or united India, remained the conviction of many top Indian Hindu leaders in the early years after independence. The then president of the Congress Party, J.B. Kripalani (popularly known as Acharya Kripalani), declared: 'Neither the Congress nor the nation has given up its claim of a united India.'[6] This mentality, obviously, could not but create bitterness and deep suspicions in Pakistan. Jinnah's own expectations about peaceful co-existence had been shattered just two months after independence when he had to say that:

...it is very unfortunate that vigorous propaganda has been going on.... that Pakistan is...merely a temporary madness and that Pakistan will have to come into the Indian Union as a penitent, repentant, erring son...It is now clear beyond doubt that it was well-planned, well-organised, and well-directed and the object of it all...was to paralyse the new-born Dominion of Pakistan.[7]

Not surprisingly, having been born in such circumstances, Pakistan quickly developed a siege mentality. India's hostile posture was, justifiably, perceived by Pakistani policymakers as a mortal threat to their newly born country's very existence. Some successive events further aggravated their misgivings and deepened their perception of threat. Firstly, in the formative years after the independence, bloody riots were regularly taking place in India, in which the Muslim minority always suffered the most, pushing ever more refugees into Pakistan. As a reaction, in some instances, there were anti-Hindu riots in East Pakistan, which had a large Hindu minority. In this manner, the flames of mutual distrust and bitterness were given fresh fuel. Thus, the two countries almost came to war, both in 1950 and 1951, because of the passions raised by communal riots. Moreover, Pakistan's awkward division into two wings separated by a 1000 miles of Indian territory, added to the complexities of the situation, allowing India to fish in troubled waters. In fact, in the years that followed, India's perceived insidious role in fanning separatist feelings in East Pakistan was destined to arouse even deeper misgivings and resentment in West Pakistan, eventually leading to war.

The Kashmir Dispute

More than anything else, in the aftermath of independence, it was the Kashmir dispute which was to create special bitterness in the bilateral relations between Pakistan and India. In fact, this has remained the crux of the difficulties between the two countries. It seems that both sides view it not merely as a territorial dispute or an issue of the right of the Kashmiri people to self-determination but there have been deep underlying ideological antagonisms and centuries-old prejudices and misgivings. Pakistan describes the Kashmir dispute as an 'unfinished item on the agenda of the Partition' of the subcontinent in 1947, viz. that the contiguous Muslim-majority areas, which obviously must include Kashmir, would constitute Pakistan. In fact, Kashmir was always viewed as an integral part of the Pakistan scheme: its initial letter 'K' forming part of the name chosen for the new country.

On the other hand, India has been adamant in hanging on to Kashmir as symbolizing its rejection of the philosophy of Partition, namely, separation on the basis of religion. Asserting its belief in a secular polity, India has argued that religion should not have been the basis for the 'vivisection' of the country in 1947. In the legal context, India has contended that the princely ruler of the state of Jammu & Kashmir had duly opted for India by signing the Instrument of Accession. A more personal reason, initially responsible for India's hanging on to Kashmir, was the Kashmiri origin of Prime Minister Nehru.[8]

However, in addition to the ideological dimension, the Kashmir issue has been complicated by considerations of strategic interest. Perhaps, more than anything else, the factor of national prestige or face has hardened the respective stances of both countries. Last but not the least, the issue has been aggravated by demagogues and unscrupulous politicians on both sides who have always fanned the flames of the Kashmir dispute to secure their own political ambitions.

In Pakistan's eyes, Kashmir became a test case for resisting what it perceived as India's hegemonic ambitions. In Pakistan's view, from the very beginning India's actual conduct, as against what it professed, was far from reassuring. India showed a propensity to use force to settle various territorial disputes. In the first instance, when the princely states of Junagarh and Manavadar decided to accede to Pakistan in September 1947, India quickly moved in and occupied them. Next, Hyderabad, the largest amongst the princely states, which had indicated that it wanted to join neither India nor Pakistan and would prefer to become independent, was occupied by India in September 1948. India launched a full military invasion, cynically calling it a 'police action,' and conquered the territory. The matter went to the UN Security Council which turned a blind eye to the Indian action as *fait accompli*.

Some years later, in 1961, it was the turn of Goa, the small Portuguese colony, which too was forcibly occupied. This time, the Security Council did protest, but the Indian ambassador to the UN stated flatly that irrespective of what the Security Council had to say or what the UN Charter laid out, India would not be stopped from annexing Goa. A few years later, Sikkim, a small state in the Himalayas, was also taken over by India. In all of these instances, India had clearly used force as an instrument of foreign policy. For its part, India justified its conduct by arguing that these relatively small territories which were more like enclaves, had no viable option but to join India. It claimed this was also the wish of the people inhabiting these territories. However, the fact remained that instead of waiting for negotiations to produce a peaceful solution, India had, every time, ruthlessly imposed its will by force. In fact, in the case of Goa, Nehru had categorically ruled out the use of force, as early as 1954.[9] But he was later to renege on his solemn word. A similar disregard of solemn commitments had earlier taken place in the case of Kashmir.

Such behaviour seemed paradoxical and even ironic for a country which swore by its leader Mahatma Gandhi, the great exponent of the philosophy of non-violence. In its actual conduct as a state India has, in several instances, shown an open ruthlessness and utter disregard of principles. Indeed, even during Gandhi's own lifetime, India had followed policies of *realpolitik*, more reminiscent of Otto von Bismarck; Nehru himself confirmed that Gandhi had approved the Indian government's decision to send troops to Kashmir.[10] He had earlier also approved the annexation of Junagarh and Manavadar. And yet, Gandhi was assassinated early in 1948 by a Hindu hardliner for being 'soft' towards the Muslims. Such a mentality could hardly be reassuring for Pakistan where the chilling perception was that if a bitter opponent of the creation of Pakistan—which Gandhi certainly had been—could be killed, allegedly for being 'soft' towards the Muslims, then Pakistan could expect little accommodation from such a people. Incidentally, just a few months after Gandhi's death, India invaded and conquered Hyderabad.

It could be argued that Pakistan was not a parallel case with these smaller entities, nor could it be annexed by similar 'police action.' In each of the above-mentioned instances, the territories conquered by India could hardly put up any serious resistance, whereas Pakistan was a much larger power and a far harder nut to crack. Nevertheless, each such Indian military adventure only reinforced the apprehension in Pakistan that India had hegemonic designs and could not be trusted; and that whenever the opportunity arose, it would strike against Pakistan. Thus, Pakistan's peculiar 'siege mentality' was not a mere case of paranoia, as has been contended by some observers but had behind it a specific background.

To return in greater detail to the dispute over the princely state of Jammu and Kashmir, which began almost immediately after independence, the position here was that the ruler was Hindu while the majority of the population was Muslim. Furthermore, the territory had many more links with Pakistan than with India. Three rivers flow from Kashmir into Pakistan making the whole a single geographical unit. There have been strong ethnic, cultural, and economic linkages between the Kashmiris and the Pakistani people from times immemorial. Thus, by the logic that India had itself applied, while forcibly annexing Junagarh and Hyderabad, as also in keeping with the Partition formula, to which India was a party, Kashmir should have gone to Pakistan. To wit, the principle on which the Partition of the subcontinent had taken place was that the contiguous Muslim majority areas should be separated from the contiguous non-Muslim majority areas in order to form the two Dominions. It was beyond doubt that Kashmir had a large Muslim majority and was contiguous to Pakistan.

Indeed, India would not even have had access to Kashmir but for the collusion of Mountbatten, who manoeuvred with Cyril Radcliffe, the British adjudicator, to secure the adjoining Gurdaspur district for India, thus opening a gateway for it into Kashmir.[11] The Hindu ruler vacillated in deciding which country he should opt for. When this triggered a pro-Pakistan rebellion, he decided to join India, in defiance of the Partition formula. Next, by prior arrangement with the ruler, Indian troops were flown to Kashmir in a rush. For more than a year, there was fierce, though inconclusive, fighting between the Indian troops and the local Kashmiris, who were initially supported by tribesmen from Pakistan's Frontier province who crossed over into Kashmir to support their Muslim compatriots. They were later joined by regular Pakistani troops. On 1 January 1948, the matter had been taken to the UN by India who accused Pakistan of having committed aggression in Kashmir. Incidentally, this accusation was never accepted by the Security Council. On 1 January 1949, a ceasefire was arranged under the UN's supervision, with India holding on to more than half of the territory, including the main Kashmir valley.

The UN took the principled position that the issue should be resolved by allowing the people of Kashmir to vote in an impartial plebiscite whether they wanted to join India or Pakistan. The Cold War had not as yet fully polarized the world and India and Pakistan were also new on the world scene. Hence the UN was able to adopt a relatively neutral position in the matter. Indian Prime Minister Jawaharlal Nehru, who was at that time confident that under his old Kashmiri friend Sheikh Abdullah's leadership the Kashmiris would opt for India, solemnly promised to uphold the Kashmiris' right of self-determination which, he said, was 'not merely a pledge to (the Pakistan) Government but also to the people of Kashmir and to the world.'[12] In the Security Council, India pledged that, after the tribal raiders had been expelled, the people of Kashmir 'would be free to decide their future by the recognized democratic method of a plebiscite or referendum under international auspices.'[13]

As Nehru's confidence in Sheikh Abdullah faded, he reneged on his oft-repeated promises on a plebiscite, eventually using the lame excuse that Pakistan's joining of the US-sponsored military pacts around 1954 had altered the situation and a plebiscite was no longer possible.[14] Sheikh

Abdullah was arrested by Nehru and was to stay behind bars for the next ten years. The pliant Kashmir Assembly, elected through rigged polling, was in the meanwhile made to declare that the decision to join India had the people's support. It is also noteworthy that this assembly did not have any representation from the portion of Kashmir under the control of Pakistan. Hence, it could not possibly speak for the whole of Jammu and Kashmir. Moreover, the UN Security Council, by its resolution dated 24 January 1957, expressly rejected the Indian contention that the Kashmir Assembly's support for accession to India was tantamount to a popular verdict. The UN reaffirmed that the wishes of the Kashmiri people could only be ascertained through an impartial plebiscite.

Nonetheless, since then India has unilaterally insisted that the Kashmir issue was a settled matter and that Kashmir was an integral part of India. It has also persistently contended that the only issue for discussion is Pakistan's 'vacation' of the Kashmiri territory held by it since 1948. Of course, neither the UN nor Pakistan nor the overwhelming majority of states has ever accepted the Indian contention. Moreover, Pakistan has time and again reaffirmed that a decision of this kind could only be made in an impartial plebiscite held under UN auspices, as per India's original commitments.

Pakistan has also consistently maintained that Kashmir is the 'core' problem between the two countries and without its resolution, on the basis of the UN resolutions, there could be no durable peace in the subcontinent. India and Pakistan have remained largely inflexible in their positions. Bilateral talks at various levels have been held repeatedly but to no avail. Mediatory efforts by friendly countries have fared no better. In fact, since the 1970s, India has even refused to let any third country use its good offices in the matter. Pakistan's repeated offers to refer the dispute to international mediation or adjudication have also been rejected by India.

Thus, the Kashmir dispute has remained unresolved. It has been the single most important cause for the deadlock and adversarial relations, which have continued between India and Pakistan ever since their independence. In fact, two wars have been fought over the Kashmir dispute and the energies of the two countries have been greatly consumed over the unending polemics and tension generated by this issue.

Here, some historical footnotes in the context of Kashmir need to be recalled even though, with the passing of time, they may now seem to have only some academic interest.

There is one historical version[15] according to which, soon after independence, India had shown interest in 'exchanging' Hyderabad for Kashmir. The powerful Indian Home Minister Sardar Patel is believed to have conveyed such an offer to Jinnah who is said to have summarily rejected it. His reported argument was that he had no right to reach a deal behind Hyderabad's back. Hyderabad, an important Muslim princely state, was at the time seeking to become independent. As Jinnah saw it, Hyderabad was entitled to opt for independence if it so chose. Jinnah held that the legal position was that 'with the lapse of Paramountcy on the transfer of power by the British, all Indian States would automatically regain their full sovereign and independent status. They are, therefore, free to join either of the two Dominions or to remain independent.'[16] The Nizam of Hyderabad had, of course, been an important supporter of Muslim causes, including the struggle for the creation of Pakistan. Hence, both Jinnah's penchant for constitutionalism as well as sympathy for Hyderabad's aspirations for becoming independent evidently influenced his response to the reported suggestion from Patel.

As it turned out, two days after Jinnah's death, India invaded and occupied Hyderabad. There was little that Pakistan could do to save Hyderabad, which was like an enclave, surrounded by India from all sides. Moreover, Hyderabad had a majority Hindu population. No doubt, the ruler was a Muslim and, over the centuries, Hyderabad had even become an important centre of Muslim civilization. But, according to the Partition formula, which incidentally was Pakistan's moral and legal case in Kashmir, Hyderabad should have gone to India. Furthermore, *realpolitik* dictated that Pakistan should have, in effect, 'traded' Kashmir for Hyderabad, which was practically defenceless against India; Pakistan could not, and in fact did not, save Hyderabad when India launched its remorseless 'police action' against it.

However, it needs to be noted that the above version has not been, so far, supported by solid historical evidence, even though it has been reported by some important individuals. As far as is known, the offer by Patel was evidently not made in writing and India has never confirmed that such an offer was ever made.[17] Secondly, Patel was the deputy of Nehru who was the real leader of India and the actual head of government. If Patel had made such an offer behind Nehru's back, it could have had little practical or legal meaning. Nehru himself was of Kashmiri origin and the Indian stance on Kashmir was at least in part influenced by Nehru's personal emotional commitment to Kashmir.[18] It seems implausible that he would have subscribed to such an offer. Moreover, the dice was heavily loaded against Hyderabad and India knew that it was only a matter of time before Hyderabad would have fallen in its lap, which it did a few months later. Hence, there was no real need or urgency for India to offer such a deal in earnest. It, therefore, seems more likely that Patel's offer, if it was actually made, was conveyed with a view to demoralise the ruler of Hyderabad in his bid to secure independence.

At the same time, however, Pakistan's sympathy for the cause of Hyderabad did weaken its moral and legal case in Kashmir. Practically, all the arguments which Pakistan had advanced in the context of Kashmir's accession to Pakistan were also applicable to the Indian case for securing Hyderabad. In the reverse, of course, it is also true that the Indian arguments *vis-à-vis* Hyderabad worked *mutatis mutandis* in favour of Pakistan's case on Kashmir.

The same reasoning applied even more in the cases of the small princely state of Junagarh and its even smaller neighbour Manavadar where again the rulers were Muslim but the majority of the population consisted of Hindus. Moreover, Junagarh and Manavadar were surrounded by India and were not contiguous to Pakistan. And yet, when the two rulers signed the instruments of accession in favour of Pakistan, the latter showed poor judgement by accepting the accession. India strongly protested saying that this action was *'in utter violation of principles on which partition was agreed upon and effected.'*[19] (My italics) Incidentally, the same principle had been invoked by India when the state of Jodhpur had shown interest in joining Pakistan. Mountbatten had then warned the Maharaja that, his subjects being predominantly Hindu, his accession to Pakistan *'would surely be in conflict with the principle underlying the partition of India on the basis of Muslim and non-Muslim majority areas.'*[20] (My italics)

Incidentally, the case of Junagarh's accession to Pakistan arose before India made its move in Kashmir. Pakistan's stance on Junagarh, apart from eroding Pakistan's case on Kashmir, was untenable for another reason. The reality was that Pakistan was in no position to save Junagarh in the event of an Indian military intervention. However, by endorsing the Junagarh ruler's emotional decision to join Pakistan, the latter merely diluted the strength of its much more valid case on Kashmir. In essence, of course, the situation in Hyderabad was the same. In the reverse, there can be no doubt that the Indian position on the issue of Junagarh and Manavadar, as also Jodhpur, was in utter violation of its own subsequent stance on Kashmir. Neither country had been consistent on the issue of accession. However, Pakistan stood to gain much more by adopting a principled and consistent position since as between Hyderabad, Junagarh, and Kashmir, the last-mentioned was much more important for Pakistan. Kashmir had always figured as an integral part in the concept of Pakistan and it clearly had far greater importance for economic, ethnic, and strategic reasons. As it turned out, at the end of the exercise, Pakistan came out the loser in all of these cases.

NOTES

1. S.M. Burke and Lawrence Ziring, *Pakistan's Foreign Policy: An Historical Analysis*, 2nd ed., p. 8.
2. M.A.K. Azad, *India Wins Freedom*, p. 242, cited in Burke and Ziring, p. 9.
3. M. Rafique Afzal, *Speeches and Statements of Quaid-i-Millat Liaquat Ali Khan* (1941–51) (Lahore: Research Society of Pakistan. University of Punjab, 1967), p. 209, cited in Burke and Ziring, p. 113.
4. Chaudhri Muhammad Ali, *The Emergence of Pakistan*, pp. 135–8.
5. Kewal L. Panjabi, *The Indomitable Sardar* (Bombay: Bharatiya Vidya Bhavan, 1990), p. 124, cited in Chaudhri Muhammad Ali, *The Emergence of Pakistan*, p. 123. See also M.A.H. Ispahani, *Quaid-e-Azam Jinnah: As I Knew Him*, 3rd ed. (Karachi: Royal Book Co., 1976), p. 263.
6. Burke and Ziring, *Pakistan's Foreign Policy: An Historical Analysis*, p. 9.
7. *Statesman*, 25 October 1947, cited in Burke and Ziring, p. 10.
8. Jawaharlal Nehru, *Speeches*, I, p. 195, cited in Burke and Ziring, pp. 20–21, 284.
9. *Rajya Sabha Debates*, 27 August 1954, col. 578, cited in Burke and Ziring, p. 235.
10. *Hindu Weekly Review*, 1 January 1962, cited in Burke and Ziring, p. 235.
11. Chaudhri Muhammad Ali, *The Emergence of Pakistan*, pp. 287, 213, has provided the authentic details
12. Telegram from Nehru to Liaquat Ali Khan, 30 October 1947, cited in Burke and Ziring, p. 27.
13. Security Council Records, India's complaint against Pakistan, 1 January 1948, cited in Burke and Ziring, p. 28.
14. Burke and Ziring, p. 226.
15. Chaudhri Muhammad Ali, *The Emergence of Pakistan*, pp. 299–300.
16. Ibid., p. 230.
17. See also an article by A.A. Musalman, 'The Myth Surrounding Patel's offer on Kashmir,' *Dawn*, 27 February 1999.
18. Chaudhri Muhammad Ali, *The Emergence of Pakistan*, p. 276.
19. Burke and Ziring, pp. 21, 284.
20. V.P. Menon, *The Story of the Integration of the Indian States* (New Delhi: Orient Blackswan Pvt. Ltd., 1956, 1999), pp. 112–3, cited in Burke and Ziring, p. 18.

3

Pakistan's Quest for Security

India's efforts immediately after independence to undo Pakistan, particularly its attempt to seize Kashmir, were the main causes for the bitterness and sense of insecurity which gripped the Pakistani policymakers from the very outset. This perception was to have a profound influence on the formulation of their defence and foreign policies. In the years that followed, the Pakistani policymakers remained convinced that India, which is several times bigger than Pakistan in size and resources, was conspiring against Pakistan's very independence and territorial integrity. In their perception, India's hostile designs not only consisted of the conventional methods of warfare (to begin with in Kashmir) but also included diverse political and other pressures, including a psychological war of relentless propaganda questioning the very *raison d'être* of Pakistan's creation.

In addition to applying direct pressures, India also sought to isolate and encircle Pakistan with the help of other countries. On Pakistan's western border, Afghanistan, its Muslim neighbour, entertained irredentist claims against Pakistan, and was willing to collude with India, and later on with the USSR, against Pakistan's security. Thus, the possibility of a pincer movement always worried Pakistani strategists.

More ominously for Pakistan, from around 1954, the Soviet Union adopted a hostile posture towards Pakistan and extended vital military and other aid to India. In addition, Moscow posed a more distant but nevertheless a real threat to Pakistan's security due to the perceived expansionist nature of Soviet communism and the old Russian ambitions of reaching the warm waters of the Arabian Sea.

To overcome these grave challenges to Pakistan's security, the first task of Pakistani diplomacy was, therefore, to somehow find an equalizer against India. This has, ever since, remained the most important preoccupation of Pakistan's foreign and defence policies. However, through the years, Pakistan's quest for security went through various phases. In the early years after independence, Pakistan had banked its hopes on the UN to protect it against any Indian aggression and, at least, to help to resolve the dispute with India on Kashmir. The UN began positively enough but as time passed India managed to frustrate the implementation of the various UN resolutions on Kashmir. Since then the UN has seemed impotent in the face of Indian intransigence.

Similarly, Pakistan also placed its hopes in the British Commonwealth and Britain, in particular, for assistance in resolving the Kashmir dispute and Pakistan's other problems with India. However, Pakistan found the British unhelpful and even leaning towards India. For instance, at the UN the British tried to water down the resolutions on Kashmir in favour of India.[1] Furthermore, the British decision in 1949 to make a special allowance for India to remain in the Commonwealth, even after it became a republic, convinced Pakistani policymakers that India would always get its way with the British. In fact, Pakistan found out soon enough that the Commonwealth, under British patronage, was not willing to discuss any bilateral disputes between member states.

Soon after independence, Pakistan also explored Pan-Islamism to see if it could bring the weightage of the numerous Islamic states behind it with respect to India. However, it drew a blank and its call for an Islamic bloc even aroused uneasiness in countries like Egypt which were seemingly worried that Pakistan would become a rival for leadership in the Islamic world. Pakistan's efforts thus brought the sneering comment from Egypt's King Farouk[2] that the Pakistanis held that 'Islam was born on 14 August 1947,' the date of Pakistan's independence. Egypt's opposition to the formation of an Islamic bloc was reiterated as late as April 1960 by President Gamal Abdel Nasser, who, on a visit to Pakistan said: 'I do not wish to use Islam in international politics.'[3] In the meanwhile, a Pakistani Prime Minister himself was to deride the leverage of the Islamic world by arguing that 'zero plus zero is after all equal to zero.'[4]

This left Pakistan with the option of turning to either of the two global power blocs. It needs to be remembered that in the gathering Cold War of the late 1940s, Pakistan had started with an open mind. Three days after Pakistan's independence, Prime Minister Liaquat Ali Khan had declared that Pakistan would take no sides in the conflict of ideologies between the nations.[5]

As it turned out, under Joseph Stalin, the Soviet policy towards both India and Pakistan showed certain ideological reservations. The Soviet Union saw the hand of imperialism behind the developments in the subcontinent and treated both India and Pakistan as bourgeois pro-West states. Moscow thus showed little interest in getting close to either India or Pakistan. However, two developments took place in 1949, which brought new thinking in

Moscow as well as in Karachi. The US extended an invitation to Indian Prime Minister Jawaharlal Nehru to visit the United States and this was readily accepted. Also, India decided to stay on in the Commonwealth even after becoming a republic. Both of these moves drew criticism from the Soviets who now looked more supportively towards Pakistan.

Reacting to these developments, Prime Minister Liaquat Ali Khan declared that 'Pakistan can not afford to wait. She must take her friends where she finds them.'[6] Contacts were initiated with Moscow and Liaquat Ali Khan promptly received an invitation to visit the Soviet Union. However, for reasons which have remained obscure, the Soviets could not mutually settle convenient dates for the visit. Sometime later, an American invitation was received and Liaquat Ali Khan went on to visit the US in May 1950. While on US soil he declared his intention to visit the Soviet Union after the dates had been finalized. However, there was no further progress on the matter and Liaquat Ali Khan was tragically assassinated in 1951.

Later, a myth developed in some Pakistani circles, particularly amongst those with left leanings that Moscow had turned against Pakistan in the years that followed because of Liaquat Ali Khan's failure to visit the Soviet Union whereas he did go to the US. (Incidentally, Moscow itself has hardly ever put forward such reasoning.) This lobby further argued that the alleged rebuff to the Soviet Union inevitably led to profound adverse consequences, as subsequently seen. A careful appraisal, however, shows that there were no noteworthy strains in Pakistan's bilateral relations with the USSR between 1949 and 1953.[7] Most importantly, the Soviet Union did not veto any Security Council resolution on Kashmir. Moreover, Pakistan and the Soviet Union exchanged ambassadors. In fact, relations with the Soviet Union turned sour only around 1954 when Pakistan decided to join the US-sponsored military pacts. That was the cause of Moscow's displeasure with Pakistan and not the inability of Liaquat Ali Khan to visit the Soviet Union for which he could not, in any case, be held personally responsible. It should also be noted that in international diplomacy, invitations are often extended but not always availed. Failure to visit a country in response to its invitation has hardly ever become the cause of long-term estrangement.

India–Pakistan relations kept on deteriorating, with serious war scares during 1950 as also 1951 when India amassed its troops on the Pakistani borders while putting forward No War proposals.[8] This was to become a trademark of Indian diplomacy with Pakistan for many years to come. Pakistan's response from the beginning was that it welcomed such a proposal in principle but it must, at the same time, contain a provision for a fair settlement of the disputes between the two countries. This was never accepted by India thereby making the whole proposal, in Pakistani eyes, no more than a propaganda ploy.

Thus, the Pakistani policymakers found themselves in a dilemma. Tensions with India showed no signs of abatement. The Pakistani efforts to mobilize the UN as well as the Commonwealth against India's intransigence in Kashmir were making no real headway. The Islamic countries were quite weak and, in any event, were not responding to Pakistan's suggestions for an Islamic bloc. The Soviet Union was not forthcoming and was not really in a position to extend large-scale assistance to anyone. Pakistan was in desperate need to somehow find an equalizer against a belligerent India.

It was under these circumstances that Pakistan decided to join the US-sponsored military pacts—the Baghdad Pact (later renamed CENTO) and SEATO. This was not an unnatural alliance. In ideological terms, Pakistan felt closer to the West rather than to communism. Moreover, the Russians had been on an expansionist course southwards since the previous two centuries and had annexed vast Muslim territories in Central Asia with which the Pakistani people had age-old links. This had aroused a negative perception in Pakistan about Russian intentions. Moreover, communist involvement in an abortive *coup d'état* bid in 1951, known as the Rawalpindi Conspiracy Case, had added to these concerns. Pakistan's closest friends in the Islamic world, Iran and Turkey, were keen to join these pacts as both of them felt directly threatened by the Soviet Union; and their attitude clearly influenced Pakistan. In fact, Pakistan was quite eager to secure a military alliance with these two Muslim countries that gave it a sense of security against India and was in harmony with its Pan-Islamic approach.

Thus, the reality was that the decisive factor for Pakistan in joining the military pacts was the need to find an equalizer against India. The Pakistani army chief, General Ayub Khan, was particularly keen to secure the latest American military equipment for the Pakistani armed forces with the conviction that whereas Pakistan had the manpower to take on India, it was only deficient in military equipment. By January 1957, Ayub Khan could declare, 'We are no more short of men and material.'[9] Only a year later, he made the confident claim that 'the Pakistan Army today is the sharpest instrument of peace or war and the greatest deterrent against aggression.'[10]

When Ayub Khan seized power in Pakistan in 1958, he was at first inclined to accept the Western argument that communism was a direct threat to the subcontinent as well. The early rifts in Sino–Indian relations on the border issue had also become known. Thus in early 1959, Ayub Khan came forward with the proposal for 'Joint Defence' of the subcontinent against any encroachment from the north. He evidently meant both the

Soviet Union as well as China. However, Ayub Khan did put a pre-condition with this proposal that the Kashmir dispute should be resolved in a just manner. This might well have been Pakistan's main objective in making this proposal. However, India immediately rejected the idea and Nehru even asked ingenuously as to 'against whom'[11] was there need for a joint defence. Ironically, the emphatic reply came three years later when China dealt a big blow against India during a brief border war. In the meantime, Pakistan had moved away from any possibility of a joint defence with India, as it embarked upon a major effort to improve relations with the two communist giants in its neighbourhood.

On the whole, it was the quest for arms and aid to be used against India, rather than any real fear of communist aggression, which was Pakistan's main motive in joining the Western-sponsored military pacts. It is also a fact, though now largely forgotten in Pakistan, that these pacts did undoubtedly secure very substantial US military and economic assistance for Pakistan in its nascent years and significantly strengthened it in facing India, as seen in the 1965 War. During that war, Pakistan made full use of US-supplied military arms and equipment. In fact the use of US military aid for Pakistan's 'legitimate self-defence' was permitted under Article I(2) of the US–Pakistan Mutual Defence Assistance Agreement of 19 May 1954. According to the then US Ambassador to Pakistan, Horace Hildreth, 'the only limitation' on the use of US military aid was that it would not be used for the purpose of aggression.[12]

Nevertheless, from the very beginning, there was a basic disagreement between Pakistan and the US about the *raison d'être* of these defence pacts. The latter held that the pacts were meant to defend the member states against communist aggression only. For instance, after joining the military committee of the Baghdad Pact, the US had stated that its participation was 'related solely to the Communist menace and carries no connotations with respect to intra-area matters.'[13] The British Minister of Defence had added that both Britain and the US had promised to defend the Baghdad Pact region against communist aggression only.[14] In the case of SEATO, the US had actually entered a reservation in the Treaty that her obligation under Article IV would extend only to cases of communist aggression.[15]

On the other hand, Pakistan continued to insist that these pacts should also be applicable in the case of aggression against Pakistan by India. It held that India was almost a camp follower of the Soviet Union in most matters and in turn enjoyed wholehearted Soviet military and diplomatic support. This was particularly the sentiment in Pakistan because its membership of the pacts had alienated Moscow to the extent that it had made a common cause with both India and Afghanistan in their respective disputes with Pakistan. In particular, Pakistan was hurt that the Soviet veto was being applied at the UN Security Council on any resolution on Kashmir which displeased India. This in effect marginalized the UN's role in the context of the Kashmir dispute. Indeed, in 1960, Pakistan's relations with the USSR reached an all-time low when Soviet leader Nikita Khrushchev threatened to wipe out a Pakistani city, Peshawar, from where a US spy U-2 plane had taken off and was shot down over Soviet territory. In the words of *The New York Times*, the Pakistanis realized with a shock that 'such incidents as the U-2 flight could touch off a war, that Pakistan could be a prime target and that the Soviet Union nearly touches Pakistan's northern border while the United States, her ally, is 9000 miles away.'[16]

Pakistan's standing in the Third World had also suffered because of its military alignment with the US. Pakistan was thus unable to join the Non-Aligned Movement where India became a leading player, despite its close military links with the Soviet Union. Many Pakistanis resented becoming camp followers of the US, which was viewed as the main supporter of Israel. Thus there was a perception that Pakistan had paid a heavy price for joining the Western-sponsored military pacts. There was an understandable expectation that the US should come to Pakistan's help in case of aggression from India, a country enjoying strong diplomatic and military support of the Soviet Union. In this context, it needs to be recalled that the US–Pakistan Agreement of March 1959 had stated that the US 'regards as vital to its national interest and to world peace the preservation of the independence and integrity of Pakistan.'[17] This pledge was to be repeated by the US government on several subsequent occasions. There were also some assurances given to Pakistan by US officials, though not in the form of written agreements, that the US would assist Pakistan in the event of Indian aggression.[18]

In fact, the US was always reluctant to take sides between India and Pakistan. Some top US policymakers evidently believed that the total alignment of India to the Soviet bloc, after China had become communist in 1949, would be a major blow to Western interests in Asia and the world at large. It was only after Washington became increasingly disenchanted with India in the early 1950s due to its attitude towards the Japanese Peace Treaty and the Korean War that the US turned towards Pakistan. US Secretary of State, John Dulles, was now engaged in building a chain of military pacts around the world to 'contain' Soviet expansionism. It was in this context that Pakistan was viewed by the US as a strategically important country and was encouraged to become member of the two military pacts.

India's size and importance continued to attract many American strategists. Despite its own military alliance with Pakistan, and in spite of India's special ties with the USSR, the US was unwilling to let go of India because of its immense size as well as for its democratic, non-communist political system. The liberal school of thought in the US including top Democrats was also of the view that the US should support democratic India and not the military dictatorship in Pakistan as a counter-weight against China. Hence, when President John F. Kennedy came to power, Washington was eager to woo India. Ayub Khan's visit to the US in 1961 helped in restoring some balance in Kennedy's attitude. But in the wake of the India–China border war in 1962, substantial Western military assistance was rushed to strengthen India, in contravention to the understanding given to Pakistan by Kennedy that it would be consulted before any arms aid was given to India.

This fateful decision to send Western aid to India, in disregard of the feelings and security concerns of Pakistan, which was then the West's 'most committed' military ally in Asia, ended the special relationship between Pakistan and the USA. Pakistan could have taken advantage of India's border war with China by stirring up trouble in Kashmir. But the US and the UK appealed to Pakistan to show restraint. To mollify Pakistan they persuaded India to open talks on Kashmir. Several rounds of such talks were actually held between India and Pakistan but there was no real progress. As the fear of war with China subsided, India felt no compulsion to make any kind of concessions to Pakistan, particularly because the West, apart from initiating the talks, showed no real interest in taking these negotiations towards a meaningful conclusion.

Disappointed with these events, Pakistan now looked increasingly towards China to bolster up its security. Pakistan's relations with China had remained quite warm in the 1950s even though Pakistan was a member of SEATO, a military pact aiming to contain China. Unlike the Russians, the Chinese had little difficulty in understanding that Pakistan's membership of this pact was basically meant to strengthen itself against India rather than being motivated by any crusading instincts against communism. As China's relations with India soured in the late 1950s, followed by actual border clashes in 1959 and a serious border war in 1962, the stage was set for Pakistan to forge a closer relationship with China. India argued bitterly that the logic that 'my enemy's enemy is my friend' had brought Pakistan and China closer and that Pakistan had been guilty of 'collusion' with China in its bid to oppose India. However, India itself had shown no hesitation in joining hands with the Soviet Union against Pakistan in the 1950s and, in the 1960s, to turn to the US and the West for military aid against China.

Pakistan was deeply frustrated when the West rushed to help India disregarding the latter's strong links with the communist Soviet Union. Under these circumstances, Pakistan felt it had no option but to get closer to communist China. Unfortunately, Pakistan's overtures to China were not judged by the Western countries by their own yardstick. It was all right for them to support India in spite of its close links with the Soviet communists but wrong for Pakistan to get closer to the Chinese communists, even though this was clearly being done for strategic reasons rather than due to any ideological affinity. In fact, there was deep resentment in the US towards Pakistan when it embarked on a policy of closer ties with China. Pakistan felt bitter that its security concerns were not appreciated by Washington. This estrangement increased when US military aid to Pakistan started to dry up and was altogether stopped in 1965. Indeed the 'special relationship' between the two countries was never restored.

This disenchantment with the US in the 1960s should not obscure the fact that US military aid did improve Pakistan's military capability. As Zulfikar Ali Bhutto himself conceded: 'While it is true that military assistance was not made available for use against India, nevertheless its possession did act as a deterrent against India.'[19] Moreover, though US military equipment had been received to fight against communist aggression, this did not prevent Pakistan from fully using it in the 1965 War against India. The equipment received by India from the West to fight China was also used by it against Pakistan. It was thus quite ironic that the US military hardware supplied as aid to both Pakistan and India, to fight against communist aggression, was actually used by both against each other. This was clearly a major failure of US diplomacy and made the US look ridiculous for having been taken for a ride by the two South Asian rivals.

Pakistan felt bitter that the US, its military ally, had declined to come to Pakistan's help when it was attacked by India, insisting that the military pacts could be activated only in case of communist aggression. In fact, the US adopted a neutral position in the 1965 War and put an embargo on the supply of arms to both Pakistan and India. In effect, this hurt only Pakistan since India was not getting its arms from the US around 1965. There was deep anger in Pakistan on this account, particularly at the popular level, and many Pakistanis accused the US of betrayal.

It was primarily due to this growing estrangement with the US that Pakistan made a bid in the early 1960s not only to strengthen its relations with China but also to befriend the Soviet Union, which had been antagonized against Pakistan since 1954 due to its membership of the military pacts. Characteristically, it was the search for an equalizer which influenced Pakistan's bid to grow closer to the two communist giants in response to India's turning to the West for military assistance against China. This illustrated well the old maxim that in diplomacy, there are no permanent friends or enemies, but only permanent interests.

Pakistan's relations with the Soviet Union had started to mend with the signing of an agreement in 1961 for cooperation in the exploration of gas and oil reserves in Pakistan. Moscow was beginning to get worried by India turning to the West for arms and sustenance after the border war with China in 1962. The Soviet Union now took greater interest in mending fences with Pakistan, which seemed simultaneously to be slipping out of the Western-sponsored military pacts. Trade and air services agreements were signed with Pakistan during 1963 and President Ayub Khan was invited to visit the Soviet Union. The new Soviet leaders, Leonid Brezhnev and Alexei Kosygin, were more willing to revise the pro-India tilt of their predecessor. Moscow decided to promote relations with Pakistan without placing any pre-conditions that Pakistan must first renounce the military pacts.

The 1960s were, therefore, the decade of what was termed 'bilateralism' in Pakistan's foreign policy when it sought to establish, with some success, equally good relations with the leading powers in the world—the USA, the USSR, and China—even though these three were deeply antagonistic to each other. This balancing act was a high point in Pakistani diplomacy. Indeed, during the decade of the 1960s, Pakistan appeared to be more genuinely non-aligned than India.

It was no mean achievement of Pakistan's foreign policy that despite its hitherto special relationship with India, the Soviet Union adopted a relatively neutral position, firstly, when there were India–Pakistan clashes in the Rann of Kutch in April 1965 and, a few months later, during the 1965 War. In fact, the Soviets made serious efforts to halt the 1965 War.[20] Their offer of mediation was readily accepted by Pakistan and, a little reluctantly, by India. The Tashkent Agreement of January 1966, brokered by the Soviet Union, marked a high point of Moscow's diplomacy in the subcontinent.

NOTES

1. Burke and Ziring, *Pakistan's Foreign Policy*, pp. 30–1.
2. *Dawn*, 27 September 1956, cited in Burke and Ziring, *Pakistan's Foreign Policy*, p. 67.
3. *Dawn*, 15 April 1960, cited in Burke and Ziring, p. 304.
4. Prime Minister Huseyn Shaheed Suhrawardy's speech on 9 December 1956, cited in Burke and Ziring, op. cit., p. 252.
5. *The New York Times*, 18 August 1947, cited in Burke and Ziring, p. 147.

6. *Pakistan News*, 11 June 1949, cited in Burke and Ziring, p. 99.
7. Burke and Ziring, p. 210 cites Soviet leader Georgy Malenkov as saying in August 1953 that the USSR placed great value on good relations with both India and Pakistan.
8. Ibid., p. 48. India first proposed a No War Declaration in November 1949.
9. *Dawn*, 31 January 1957, cited in Burke and Ziring, p. 264.
10. *Dawn*, 19 September 1958, ibid., p. 265.
11. *Rajya Sabha Debates*, 4 May 1959, cited in Burke and Ziring, p. 233.
12. *Dawn*, 13 March 1957, ibid., p. 165.
13. *Asia Recorder*, 1957, p. 1395, ibid., p. 171.
14. *Dawn*, 13 February 1959, ibid., p. 171.
15. Burke and Ziring, p. 167.
16. *The New York Times*, 4 July 1960, cited by Burke and Ziring, p. 267.
17. Burke and Ziring, op. cit., p. 344.
18. Cf. Assurance by US Asst. Secy. of State George Ball in September 1963, cited in Iqbal Akhund, *Memoirs of a Bystander: A Life in Diplomacy* (Karachi: Oxford University Press, 1997), p. 81.
19. Zulfikar Ali Bhutto, *The Myth of Independence* (New York: Oxford University Press, 1969), p. 111.
20. American Embassy Rawalpindi telegram dated 7 February 1966, in *The American Papers: Secret and Confidential India-Pakistan-Bangladesh Documents 1965–1973*, compiled and edited by Roedad Khan (Karachi: Oxford University Press, 1999), p. 147.

4

The First India–Pakistan War, 1965

Neither India nor Pakistan had planned the 1965 War; in fact, the two countries got drawn into this war through a series of miscalculations. The pride of the Indian army had been greatly hurt by its ignominious performance in the border war with China in 1962 in the high Himalayan region.[1] In April 1965, an old border dispute with Pakistan in the Rann of Kutch region suddenly erupted into a sharp clash with the Pakistani troops during which the latter fared far better than the Indians. The Rann was a marshy area and the Indian troops felt handicapped in the military operation. This setback added to India's sense of humiliation. While accepting a ceasefire in the Rann, brokered by the British, Indian Prime Minister Lal Bahadur Shastri vowed that the next time India would fight 'at a time and place of India's choice'.

In Pakistan the army's demonstration of strength in the Rann of Kutch fighting created 'a state of euphoria'.[2] It encouraged a certain smugness in Pakistan that an uprising could be spurred on in Indian-occupied Kashmir and that India, as in the case of the Rann of Kutch, would dare not risk an all-out war. Pakistan's upbeat mood was also because its armed forces were well equipped as a result of US military aid received over the previous ten years. Just four months after the fighting in the Rann of Kutch, Pakistan commenced Operation Gibraltar, a clandestine campaign of sending infiltrators across into Indian-held Kashmir to stir a popular rising. Contrary to Pakistani expectations, this venture snowballed into becoming the first full-scale war between India and Pakistan.

The 1965 War was a brief and inconclusive war though fought intensely by the two countries on land, air, and the sea. In some respects, the Pakistani forces performed well thus increasing even more the public euphoria. However, in retrospect, it is clear that the miscalculations and illusions on the part of Pakistani military strategists and policymakers—apart from the actual conduct of the war—were quite appalling. It is thus ironic that many Pakistanis, at the time and even now, have idealized it as a 'victory' over India. This misconception also led to some disastrous consequences.

The policymakers in Pakistan had expected that by sending some infiltrators across into the Indian-held Kashmir, a popular uprising against India would be initiated, but a full-scale war with India was not anticipated by them. The infiltrators were not able to generate a popular uprising or even guerrilla war against India. The Indian troops had little real difficulty in isolating the infiltrators. However, in a move to escalate, the Indians went on the offensive across the ceasefire line and, among other places, occupied the main infiltration route in Haji Pir area inside Pakistani-held Kashmir. Indian Minister of Information and Broadcasting, Indira Gandhi, declared that India would not give up the new territory which it had secured in these border clashes. These developments triggered a direct response from the Pakistani army, which also crossed the ceasefire line and launched a successful attack in the Chhamb area to the south. In further escalation, the Pakistanis next started a push to capture Akhnur, a strategically important town, which would have cut off India's main land access to its troops in Kashmir. It was not realized by Pakistani military strategists that such an encirclement of Indian troops in Kashmir, leading to their likely surrender, would be altogether unacceptable to any Indian government, even one headed by the supposedly weak Prime Minister Shastri. In such a situation, it should have been obvious that India would not let the fighting remain confined to Kashmir where it was at a relative military disadvantage.[3]

Faced with the imminent prospect of an ignominious rout in Kashmir, India apparently felt that it had no choice but to strike in 'the place of its own choosing,' as had been forewarned by Shastri. On 6 September 1965, the Indian army attacked Pakistan near Lahore. This had been clearly done to relieve the growing pressure on Indian troops in Kashmir. The astonishing thing was that Pakistani strategists had remained complacent till then assuming that India would keep matters confined to Kashmir and would 'dare not cross the international border.' As a result of such unrealistic thinking, a vitally important city like Lahore was left almost undefended. All the evidence pointed to the fact that the Indian attack on this front had caught the Pakistani troops by surprise. Though gallantly defended by a handful of soldiers, it seems that Lahore escaped capture only fortuitously due to some erroneous suppositions by the Indian army.

In any event, it now became open war on land, air, and sea. The stage was also set for the Pakistan army's crucial counter-attack against India, led by its sophisticated US-supplied armour. Pakistan had highly motivated troops, fortified by the memory of victories of Muslim armies in the past centuries against a succession of Indian Hindu rulers, and the more recent military success in the Rann of Kutch. The moment had come when the massive modern military equipment received during the previous ten years through membership of military pacts could be put to effective use. However, unluckily for Pakistan, through bad planning and even poorer execution, the Pakistani counter-offensive against India quickly fizzled out near Khem Karan and ended in an 'ignominious fiasco.'[4] It is arguable that probably this was Pakistan's best-ever opportunity to cut deep into Indian territory and even resolve the Kashmir issue. Indeed, a breakthrough seemed to be in Pakistan's grasp, which would possibly have changed the power equation in the subcontinent. But Pakistan fumbled and missed the opportunity.

Making no real headway in the fighting, facing a shortage of arms and supplies, as also under international pressure to stop the war, Pakistan was left with no option but to agree to a ceasefire.

There was later the inevitable post-mortem of the war in which the Pakistan military command blamed the Foreign Office for not 'forewarning' them that India would attack across the international border. Actually, the military strategists, or for that matter any alert observer of the situation, should have been able to foresee this possibility. Leaving Lahore virtually undefended made no sense at all, even if an all-out Indian attack had not been expected. Moreover, fighting a war with just two weeks' supply of equipment and fuel showed exceedingly poor planning.

The Pakistanis took satisfaction from the performance of their air force as also from many individual acts of gallantry, particularly by the heroic defenders at Chawinda who were able to stop a major Indian thrust. Indeed, judged by a realistic yardstick rather than by romantic expectations of a victory over India, the very fact that Pakistan had been able to hold back a much bigger foe was in itself creditable. Pakistan's relatively good performance was, no doubt, due also to the military aid received from the US in the previous decade, ostensibly to fight communist aggression. Thus, the strategy and long-term planning under which Pakistan had joined the military pacts also stood vindicated.

At the international level, Pakistan received support from its traditional friends in the Islamic world, particularly Iran, Turkey, and Saudi Arabia as also, surprisingly, from Indonesia which, under its mercurial President Sukarno, who was very pro-China, had drawn close to Pakistan in the early 1960s. However, the most significant help to Pakistan had come from China, which at one point even threatened to attack India. It was this support that has permanently endeared China to the Pakistani people. But what is less well understood in Pakistan is that, more than out of considerations of friendship with Pakistan, China had probably been motivated by its own animosity towards India following its border war with that country as also by a fierce rivalry for the top position in Asia.

Pakistan's main military ally, the USA, shocked the Pakistanis, at the outset of the war, by declaring its neutrality[5] and urging them to agree to an immediate ceasefire. Misreading the existing military situation and the overall mood in Pakistan, the American ambassador reportedly even warned President Ayub Khan that 'the Indians have got you by the throat like a chicken.'[6] Furthermore, the US imposed an arms embargo on both sides with a view to stop the fighting. In actual effect, this worked only to Pakistan's disadvantage since India was hardly getting any arms from the US whereas Pakistan had been largely dependent on American arms supplies. The Pakistanis also felt betrayed because on several past occasions, the US had declared that it regarded 'as vital to its national interest and to world peace the preservation of the independence and territorial integrity of Pakistan.'[7]

The British Prime Minister Harold Wilson was more forthright and did criticize India when it crossed the international border to attack Lahore but, on the whole, the West was neutral and insisted on an immediate ceasefire. The Soviet Union, with which Pakistan's relations were on the mend, adopted a relatively neutral posture and its offer to mediate between India and Pakistan was accepted.

Despite individual gallantry and a good performance by its air force, Pakistan had little to show as its real gains in the 1965 War. Operation Gibraltar was faulty both in conception as well as in implementation. Even worse, Pakistan found itself drawn into a full-scale war with India that it had not anticipated and for which it was caught unprepared. In the actual fighting, the Indians managed to cut deep into the strategic Sialkot sector whereas, at the end of the war, Pakistan was in possession of some desert land. Pakistan's counter-offensive led by its armour failed to make any headway. However, in spite of this, the hype was such that the Pakistani people, by and large, thought that the war was actually being won when perfidious, or at least weak-hearted, elements in the leadership had halted it prematurely in obedience to US commands. This was a gross misreading of the ground situation and as usual was more a product of popular illusions than anything else.

When peace was negotiated at Tashkent, in January 1966, with Soviet mediation which basically restored the *status quo ante bellum* (the state existing before the war) there was widespread disappointment in Pakistan that a favourable settlement of the Kashmir dispute had not been secured, commensurate with Pakistan's perceived success in the war. Of course, it was hardly likely that Pakistan could have secured at the negotiating table what it was unable to achieve in the actual fighting. Nevertheless, the prevalent mood of frustration was skilfully exploited by the ambitious Foreign Minister, Zulfikar Ali Bhutto, who was able to build up a personal political following, in the hawkish circles in West Pakistan, by his tough anti-India posture. His bravado during the war that 'we will fight India for a thousand years' had won him a good deal of public applause. In reality, Pakistan had managed to fight for only two weeks. Bhutto also spread stories about a 'betrayal' by Ayub Khan at Tashkent and, for many years thereafter, he kept the nation in suspense with the promise that he would 'reveal' the true secrets of the Tashkent negotiations. Bhutto never did as there were no secrets to tell.[8] He later confided to his close associate Rafi Raza, in July 1972, that 'there was nothing to convey to the public about Tashkent that was not already known.'[9] The Tashkent Agreement called for fresh negotiations between the two countries to resolve the Kashmir dispute. Several rounds of ministerial-level India–Pakistan talks were in fact held but ended in a stalemate.

The popular disappointment in Pakistan in the context of the 1965 War and the aftermath of the Tashkent Agreement, in addition to some other factors, set in motion the discontent, which eventually led to the downfall of President Ayub Khan in 1969. Under his ten-year rule, Pakistan had made good progress in the economic field and acquired considerable international prestige. It was even cited as a model country for economic development in the Third World. For instance, a leading US newspaper had said in 1965 that 'Pakistan may be on its way toward an economic milestone that so far has been achieved by only one other populous country, the United States.'[10]

By the mid-1960s, Ayub Khan had also been able to establish a good rapport with the Soviet Union. As a result, the Soviets had not been as forthcoming as before in their support of India. It is notable that shortly after Ayub Khan's fall, the Soviet Union was to throw its full weight behind India.

It is also perhaps not a coincidence that internally a process of destabilization set in Pakistan following the 1965 War. Since the days of Ayub Khan, not only the Pakistani people's sense of national solidarity but also the standards of public morality, financial discipline, law and order as well as bureaucratic efficiency—all seem to have gone downhill. In the more immediate context, the 1965 War intensified the sense of estrangement in East Pakistan, which felt that it had been left undefended during the war. This, among other factors, hastened the breakup of Pakistan six years later in the 1971 War.

Another war with India was looming in the air because of the virulent anti-India feelings in Pakistan generated by the 1965 War. It was revealing that in this period the popular slogan in Pakistan was 'Crush India,' reflecting the mood of over-confidence *vis-à-vis* India. Of course, this slogan turned out to be quite ironic in the light of the actual outcome of the next war. In this sense also, the 1965 War has to be blamed for creating the psychological climate, which contributed to expediting the next war with India.[11]

For the foregoing reasons, it can be said that the adverse consequences for Pakistan of the 1965 War—both short-term as well as long-term—were far more damaging than what most people in Pakistan were led to believe. In particular, the internal cohesion of Pakistan was greatly damaged, thus hastening the separation of East Pakistan, whose repercussions continue to be felt in what remains of Pakistan.

The 1965 War also ended Pakistan's special relationship with the US. This not only stopped US military aid to Pakistan but also greatly reduced the extent of American economic assistance. These were tangible losses for a relatively small country like Pakistan. No doubt, Pakistan's estrangement with the US had started from around 1962, but it had intensified due to the bitterness generated by the latter's neutral stand during the 1965 War. Thereafter Pakistan's interest in the two military pacts greatly declined and it continued to remain in CENTO more as a gesture of solidarity with Iran and Turkey, its two main friends in the Islamic world, rather than any enthusiasm for the West.[12]

In the same period, Pakistan's ties with both China and the Soviet Union gained momentum. For the first time, the Soviets agreed to supply weapons to Pakistan. They also agreed to set up Pakistan's first steel mill. However, with the fall of Ayub Khan in March 1969 and the growing signs of a secessionist movement in East Pakistan, Moscow evidently decided that Pakistan was a bad bet and moved decisively closer towards India. A Treaty of Friendship was signed by India and the Soviet Union in the thick of the Bangladesh crisis under which the Soviets extended all-out support to India. That turned out to be one of the decisive factors in the defeat of Pakistan in the 1971 War.

A parallel has sometimes been drawn in Pakistan between the Soviet solidarity with India and Pakistan's experience with the US. It is argued that while remaining a 'non-aligned' country India still enjoyed, from 1954 onwards, a correspondingly greater Soviet commitment and support, whereas Pakistan, though a military ally, was abandoned by the US when India attacked Pakistan in 1965, as well as in the 1971 War. In discussions with their Pakistani counterparts, the Soviets indeed took pride in claiming that they stood four squares behind their friends, unlike the 'fickle' Americans who had wavered in supporting Pakistan. The record no doubt bears out that the Soviets were much more solid in their support for India than the US was in supporting Pakistan. There remains a school of thought in Pakistan, which believes that, had Pakistan befriended the Soviet Union from the beginning, or at least not joined the US-sponsored military pacts, the history of Pakistan and the course of India–Pakistan relations would have been very different. They argue that the Soviets would have proved themselves to be more reliable friends of Pakistan than the Americans and that Moscow would not have extended so much support to India.

What is forgotten in this reasoning is that in the early 1950s, it was essentially the quest for arms and aid which had induced Pakistan to turn to the Americans.[13] At that time the Soviet Union simply could not match the US in generosity. As for reliability, the Soviet record in East Europe after the Second World War was anything but reassuring. It was known to be a power, which used its influence in any country to promote the cause of communism, and once entrenched in that country, it would never let go. Moreover, the abortive *coup* attempt in Pakistan in 1951, known as the Rawalpindi Conspiracy Case, had some degree of communist involvement. It could hardly have been a reassuring prelude for the Pakistan Government to develop a close relationship with Moscow. In ideological terms also, though this need not have been a decisive factor (as shown by Pakistan's friendship with China), Pakistan did feel closer to the West rather than to the atheistic Soviet communists.

The real reason behind the abiding Soviet interest in India was the latter's enormous size and resources. In view of their global rivalry with the West, the Soviets were determined, for strategic reasons, not to lose India's friendship or let it fall into the Americans' lap. Moreover, Nehru's socialist ideas and latent anti-Americanism were music to the Soviet ears. His belief in non-alignment suited the Soviet Union's strategic interests at a time when US Secretary of State, Dulles, was busy building anti-Soviet military alliances all over the world. Motivated by these particular considerations the Soviets could not displease India by getting too close to Pakistan. Had India been a smaller country, the Soviets would have taken much less interest in it. Indeed, time and again, India's huge size has been able to secure for it the attention and respect of other countries, whether it was the Soviet Union or the USA. Pakistan's smaller size made it a comparatively less attractive partner for the Soviets. Whenever they have had to make a choice between India and Pakistan, the Soviets have always chosen India.

The bottom line, of course, is that it is not friendship but interests that influence foreign policy. The Soviets calculated that between India and Pakistan, the former was a more attractive proposition and, therefore, they paid far more attention to India than to Pakistan. The only exception to this pattern were the last five years of President Ayub Khan's rule when the Soviet Union tried to adopt a more even-handed attitude towards Pakistan. This was because, since 1962, the Soviets had seen a special warmth in India's relations with the West, following its border war with China. This had resulted in a massive flow of Western aid to India. These developments had caused anxiety in Moscow and it was, therefore, willing to pay more attention to Pakistan. Pakistan was getting disenchanted with the military pacts for roughly the same reasons, viz. the growing friendship between the US and India. Under these circumstances the Soviets wanted to encourage Ayub Khan to move away from the Americans. This brought unusual warmth in relations between Moscow and Islamabad. But with Ayub Khan's fall in 1969, and the growing secessionist movement in East Pakistan, heralding the partial disintegration of Pakistan, the Soviets decided to throw all their weight behind India, the stronger of the two countries. Moreover, India's ties with the US had not gotten any closer, as the Soviets had at first apprehended. Hence, after 1970, friendship with India, bordering on a special relationship, was to remain the hallmark of Soviet foreign policy till the collapse of the Soviet Union itself in 1991. (Though a much weakened successor of the old Soviet Union, the Russian Federation also remains close to India.)

NOTES

1. *Sunday Times*, 12 September 1965, cited in Burke and Ziring, op. cit., p. 333.
2. Lt. Gen. Gul Hassan Khan, *Memoirs* (Karachi: Oxford University Press, 1993), p. 179.
3. American Embassy, New Delhi, telegram dated 6 September 1965, contained in *The American Papers: Secret and Confidential India-Pakistan-Bangladesh Documents 1965–1973*, compiled and edited by Roedad Khan (Karachi: Oxford University Press, 1999), p. 15.
4. Lt. Gen. Gul Hassan Khan, ibid., p. 205. He was serving as Director Military Operations during the 1965 War.
5. Burke and Ziring, op. cit., p. 341.
6. Based on the writer's personal recollection of record of the meeting.
7. *Dawn*, 6 March 1959, cited in Burke and Ziring, p. 344.
8. Iqbal Akhund, op. cit., p. 115. He was a member of the Pakistan delegation at the Tashkent Conference. See also Sultan M. Khan, *Memories & Reflections of a Pakistani Diplomat* (London: London Centre for Pakistan Studies, 1997), p. 148.
9. Rafi Raza, *Zulfikar Ali Bhutto and Pakistan 1967–1977* (Karachi: Oxford University Press, 1997), pp. 209–10.
10. *The New York Times*, 18 January 1965, cited in Burke and Ziring, p. 317.
11. US Embassy Rawalpindi reported this Pakistani frame of mind in its telegram dated 23 September 1966, in *The American Papers*, p. 187.

12. Foreign Minister Arshad Husain's speech to the National Assembly, 28 June 1968, cited in Burke and Ziring, p. 358. See also ibid., p. 417.
13. By 1965, Pakistan had received $3 billion in US economic aid and $1.5 billion in military assistance. Norman D. Palmer, *India and Pakistan: The Major Recipients*, cited in Burke and Ziring, p. 278. Dean Rusk, US Secretary of State, noted in a secret Memo dated 9 September 1965 that the US had an investment of nearly $12 billion in India and Pakistan. *The American Papers*, op. cit., p. 53.

5

The Second India–Pakistan War, 1971

In retrospect, it seems clear that the main reason for Pakistan's defeat in the 1971 War was the alienation of the East wing's Bengali population, which had taken place in the background of West Pakistan's domination and perceived injustice to East Pakistan. A point of no return was, however, reached in March 1971 when Islamabad decided to attempt the bloody suppression of the Bengali secessionists.

India had played an active role in these developments through years of sustained propaganda and sabotage to spread disaffection in East Pakistan against West Pakistan. By 1967, India was involved in planning the separation of East Pakistan and was willing to provide covert military aid to the secessionists. The project was unearthed and the Awami League leader, Sheikh Mujibur Rahman, and some others were arrested and tried in the Agartala Conspiracy Case. The publicity given to this trial turned conspirators into heroes and spurred the secessionist movement in East Pakistan. Moreover, the political movement against President Ayub Khan, resulting in his ouster in 1969, brought an increase in the separatist activities in East Pakistan, with Indian involvement. India began openly to incite the secessionists as the demand for an independent Bangladesh grew in momentum. After the Pakistan military's crackdown in March 1971, India's assistance included the military training of Bengali secessionists and, later on, the setting up of the Bangladesh government-in-exile on Indian soil.

The military regime of General Yahya Khan proved itself totally inept in handling the growing crisis in East Pakistan. Once Sheikh Mujibur Rahman's Awami League had swept the polls in East Pakistan in the elections held in 1970, and secured a clear majority in the National Assembly, the wiser course would have been to allow him to become the Prime Minister of Pakistan. This might well have diffused his secessionist tendencies and, at any rate, would have avoided the traumatic developments that actually followed. However, a mood of unreality and self-delusion had taken hold of not only the rulers in Islamabad but also the public in West Pakistan in their anti-Mujib feelings. There was a rigid refusal to understand as to how far

the people of East Pakistan had been alienated, and the reasons behind their grievances. Instead, in an ostrich-like fashion, all the blame for the crisis in East Pakistan was conveniently put on India and its 'lackeys' in East Pakistan. In part, this was due to the belligerent feelings, accentuated by Pakistan's perceived success in the 1965 War, which had also produced the belief that, when the time comes, Pakistan would be able to handle India militarily. It was against this background that the military operation was launched on 26 March 1971 to crush Mujibur Rahman's party.

Moreover, Zulfikar Ali Bhutto, the leader of the PPP, the dominant party in West Pakistan, was mainly interested in coming to power himself by one means or the other, even if this meant having two power centres in Pakistan.[1] Hence, neither the military rulers nor the West Pakistani politicians and public made any genuine efforts to come to terms with Mujibur Rahman. As a result, a kind of irreversible momentum developed in East Pakistan under which the demand for provincial autonomy turned into secessionist feelings in a rapidly changing environment. President Yahya Khan's refusal to convene the National Assembly, which would have led to the election of Mujibur Rahman as the new prime minister, eventually turned East Pakistan into a rebel province. It was under these circumstances that the Pakistan army felt compelled to use brutal force to bring East Pakistan to heel. Public opinion in West Pakistan strongly supported this iron-fisted policy. On day the military operation was launched in East Pakistan, Bhutto us fateful words: 'Thank God, Pakistan has been saved.'[2] Actually, this action set in motion the gory process which finally ended with the of East Pakistan just nine months later.

In the very beginning, Pakistan lost the propaganda war b decision to expel all foreign journalists from East Pakistan the world news media against Pakistan. Wildly exaggera 'millions' of Bengalis having been killed and 'hundred Bengali women raped, gained currency in the intern Manipulated mainly by India which spread canard Bengalis by West Pakistani troops—while the grueso by the secessionists against pro-Pakistan elemer ignored—the world opinion largely turned a unwise decision to expel foreign journalists fro into India's hands. But, worst of all, the po was largely ignored by the Pakistani rulers the 'miscreants'.

By and large, the Arab and the Isl others, still remained supportive of Pa

about the heavy-handed policy adopted by Islamabad in suppressing the dissidents in East Pakistan, some of them were opposed to the very idea of the breakup of a country or any change of borders, for reasons of their own.[3] Moreover, President Richard Nixon, who had been an old friend of Pakistan and was, more recently, grateful to Yahya Khan for Pakistan's role in bringing about the US–China *rapprochement*, remained sympathetic to Pakistan and 'tilted' towards it. On the other hand, the US public opinion, in general, veered towards the secessionists.

The battle for East Pakistan was lost because the Bengali majority had turned against West Pakistan's domination; also the logistic difficulties faced by Pakistani troops in reaching East Pakistan which was located at a distance of a thousand miles from West Pakistan; the massive Soviet military support for India; the pressure of international public opinion; and, finally, the shockingly inept Pakistani military planning and the performance by the Eastern Command of the Pakistan army headed by General A.A.K. 'Tiger' Niazi.

There were enough arms stored in East Pakistan for the Pakistani troops to fight a long protracted defensive war to hold on to the 'Dacca Bowl'. Instead, the strategy was adopted to hold back the Indians and the Bengali secessionists along the entire border. This dangerously scattered the resources of the relatively smaller Pakistani forces. The directive given to the army was that 'not one inch of territory be abandoned to the rebels.' This strategy was described by the then Chief of General Staff, Lt. Gen. Gul Hassan Khan, later in his *Memoirs*, thus: 'A more hopelessly disadvantageous position for opposing a superior attacking force I could not visualize.'[4] The Eastern Command was 'deployed along nearly two thousand miles of border with India…and intended to fall back, under pressure, to their strong points …eventually concentrate on Dhaka. This appeared sound on paper and verbal briefing, but the paramount question was: would the rebels and Indians, when operations began in earnest, permit Eastern Command to freely follow their plan of concentrating on Dhaka?'[5] This strategy lay in ruins just three days after the war began.

Niazi, however, kept up his bravado right till the end. He had boasted that Indian troops could enter Dhaka only over his 'dead body'. Far from dead, Niazi was there to sign the surrender document just a few days later, even cracked jokes with his captors. Subsequently, Niazi would put all the blame on his superiors in Islamabad for the debacle in East Pakistan. In fact, due to this unrealistic strategy, based largely on Niazi's own over-optimistic assessments, the Pakistani armed forces were able to put up only a feeble resistance before the much better organized Indians. The number of dead

among the Pakistani troops was a small percentage of their total strength. A total of 1,337 armed forces personnel died in the actual fighting: 115 officers, 40 JCOs and 1,182 soldiers.[6] Despite all the tall talk about 'shedding the last drop of blood' to defend the motherland, this was the hard reality.

The morale of the Pakistani forces in East Pakistan was so low that, in the end, they were keener to surrender to the Indian army so as to prevent themselves from being humiliated, tortured, and massacred by the Bengali insurgents, even though the latter were their own co-religionists and hitherto compatriots. This was a devastating commentary on the state of national feeling, in which the Indian enemy was found preferable to the erstwhile fellow countrymen.

Last-ditch efforts were made by some countries in the UN to provide a face-saving formula under which West Pakistani troops could be withdrawn peacefully from East Pakistan and the latter be given the choice to decide its future links with Pakistan. However, ignoring the desperate military situation in East Pakistan after just one week of the fighting, the head of the Pakistani delegation, Z.A. Bhutto, reportedly tore away the Polish draft resolution and walked out of the Security Council in a melodramatic gesture of defiance.[7] Bhutto won much applause back home for his heroics, but the unpleasant reality caught up with the nation when Pakistani troops surrendered in Dhaka two days later. Thus, the bankruptcy of Pakistani diplomacy stood fully exposed.

Whether it was the battlefield or the diplomatic arena, self-delusion had clearly blurred the judgement of the Pakistani policymakers throughout the 1971 crisis. The Pakistani people, in general, remained in a jingoistic mood, oblivious of the ground realities. It should have been obvious from the beginning that the dice was heavily loaded against Pakistan, but few people in West Pakistan correctly understood what was happening. Thus, defeat came to them as a bolt from the blue.[8]

As stated previously, even in the 1965 War, when Pakistan was in a relatively stronger position, the Pakistani military performance had been patchy. Lahore was left virtually defenceless and Pakistan's superiority in armour was poorly used at Khem Karan where the latest US-supplied tanks were left stranded in waterlogged fields. In 1971, as in 1965, Pakistan faced a serious shortage of weapons and oil supplies within ten days after fighting began. It was nonsensical to enter into a war with a much larger foe while having military supplies of about one week. Finally, the expected major counter-offensive on the West Pakistan front never materialized. Lt. Gen. Gul Hassan Khan has given an insider's account of how this too was mishandled right from the start, and never came about,[9] making a mockery of the military wisdom that the defence of East Pakistan lay in West Pakistan.

While in 1965, the military pacts—CENTO and SEATO—still had some life, this was hardly the case in 1971. Yet Islamabad clung to the hope that the US 7th Fleet would come to its rescue in East Pakistan. Similar hopes were pinned on China although it too had never promised to make a military intervention. Unfortunately, policies based on illusions come to a sorry end, as was proved by the speedy surrender in Dhaka.

East Pakistan had fallen through a combination of factors, both internal and external. In the final phase of the crisis, the Pakistani policymakers showed a total lack of realism in assessing the political and military situation. Self-delusion and irrational behaviour distorted their crucial decisions. Similarly, the Pakistani public was also highly incensed and rational thinking seemed impossible. As usual, the super patriots and demagogues had led the way, creating a charged atmosphere in which any concession would have been seen as a betrayal. This, too, forced the hand of the government against any kind of reconciliation with the Bengali separatists, even at the eleventh hour. Living in a world of make-believe, there was no willingness on the part of Islamabad to understand that almost any compromise would have been better than the abject surrender of 93,000 Pakistani troops and civilians to Indian forces on 16 December 1971.

Even after the 1971 debacle, the illusions continued. The popular slogan in Pakistani streets was 'Bangladesh not accepted.' The unreality of this slogan, instigated by the Bhutto government itself, could not have been more manifest. Pakistan was in no position to undo Bangladesh but the illusions and bravado persisted, as Pakistani opposition parties vied with the government in breathing fire and defiance. It was only later in 1974 that the recognition of Bangladesh took place.

The separation of the eastern wing was a devastating blow to Pakistan and should have been fully recognized as such, followed by a lot of critical introspection. However, no honest self-appraisal has ever been undertaken. Indeed, the report of the official enquiry conducted by the Hamoodur Rahman Commission was belatedly published. No one seems to have been punished for the grievous, indeed criminal, mishandling of the crisis in East Pakistan. The nation by and large opted to look away, as if the tragedy happened in some other part of the world. Thus, it seems odd, and indeed incomprehensible, that even a quarter of a century later, the lessons of the debacle in East Pakistan have not really been learnt either by the ruling elite or perhaps by the majority of the Pakistani people. Under the circumstances, it can be apprehended that an East Pakistan-like situation can arise again in what is left of Pakistan.

In any event, in this disastrous fashion, the country was cut down into two parts by the 1971 War, and even West Pakistan probably remained intact because of the reported US and Chinese warnings to India not to continue the war against West Pakistan, after East Pakistan had fallen.[10] The Pakistani army was again unable to mount any serious counter-offensive against India on the western border and India never came under any pressure in this sector either. Thus, when the war ended, Pakistan possessed little Indian territory that could have been used as a bargaining counter in the peace negotiations. On the other hand, some 93,000 Pakistani prisoners of war, who had surrendered in East Pakistan, were left in India's control which used them as bargaining chips at the peace negotiations at Simla in July 1972 between Indian Prime Minister Indira Gandhi and the new Pakistani President Z.A. Bhutto.

The Simla Agreement was regarded by India as a pledge for peace by Pakistan with the tacit understanding that the Kashmir issue would be kept on the backburner, only to be discussed bilaterally, if at all. Indeed, the Indian officials spoke of a 'secret' understanding between Bhutto and Indira Gandhi at Simla to this effect that while Pakistan could continue to maintain its public position on Kashmir, it would not push the issue in international forums nor allow the Kashmir dispute to vitiate the peace between the two countries. However, Pakistani officials were to deny any such secret understanding and argued that the text of the Simla Agreement had stated that its provisions were 'without prejudice to the recognized position of either side' on Kashmir. Still, it is noteworthy that, apart from any fleeting reference, the Kashmir issue was not pressed by Pakistan in international forums during the remaining five years of the Bhutto government; nor did it figure much in bilateral exchanges between India and Pakistan.

According to Rafi Raza, who was Special Assistant of Bhutto, and a close confidant, there was a deadlock at Simla until Raza was able to secure Indira Gandhi's approval of the phrase 'without prejudice to the recognized position of either side' in the text of the agreement.[11] In the main, the Simla Agreement secured withdrawals from territories acquired by either side during the war, except in Kashmir where the Line of Control replaced the ceasefire line of 1949. The two sides also agreed to the return of the Prisoners of War (POWs). Bhutto was later to claim credit for having secured an honourable peace at Simla including the return of the POWs, even though he had no bargaining chips in his hands. Actually, it took two more years of protracted negotiations before all the POWs returned home. Such a return could not, in any event, have been withheld indefinitely by India which had to incur a good deal of expenditure in keeping this huge number of prisoners in custody, apart from facing world-wide criticism on this score. The delay in the return of the POWs and Bangladesh's insistence on holding trial of 195 among the POWs on 'war crimes' were mainly bargaining tactics to secure Pakistan's recognition of Bangladesh. However, China's veto of Bangladesh's application for membership of the UN in 1972 and 1973, strengthened Pakistan's bargaining position and evidently dissuaded Bangladesh from insisting on trying the 195 POWs for war crimes.

The 1971 War was perhaps a watershed in another way. Until then, there was at least a latent fear in India that, despite its smaller size, Pakistan could inflict a military defeat on India, repeating the centuries-old pattern of such victories gained by smaller Muslim armies on a succession of Indian Hindu rulers. It was, therefore, not surprising that following India's victory in the 1971 War, Prime Minister Indira Gandhi said that the defeats of the past centuries had been 'avenged.' In the words of an Indian writer, because of India's victory, 'the ghost of the Mughal Empire had been finally set at rest.' This gave the Indian people a newfound confidence with respect to Pakistan. The Indian nuclear explosion in 1974 added to this euphoria. In fact, the next Indian Prime Minister Morarji Desai (1977–9) used this self-confidence as the rationale for seeking better relations with Pakistan, arguing that India should have nothing to fear from a small country like Pakistan.

There was a very different reaction in Pakistan. So far, the Pakistan psyche had been that in spite of being smaller than India in size, it could defeat or at least hold its own grounds against India in the battlefield, just as the Muslims in the past centuries had been able to defeat much larger Indian Hindu armies. Indeed, in the first twenty-five years after independence the military wisdom in Pakistan was that the defence of the seemingly vulnerable East Pakistan lay in West Pakistan, namely, that the Pakistani army would cut through, say, up to the Sutlej River or even reach Delhi, before India could penetrate deep into East Pakistan. With the help of modern equipment received in US military aid, Pakistan had been able to hold its own against India in the 1965 War. But the illusions were to be wrecked in 1971 when the battle was lost within ten days in East Pakistan, whereas on the Western front also, no military offensive against India materialized. Shortage of supplies had clearly hampered Pakistan. India had, as always, the advantage of larger size and resources, and this time also had access to an unlimited supply of Soviet arms.

Following the loss of East Pakistan, another manifestation of irrationalism could be seen in Pakistan's abrupt decision to quit the Commonwealth early in 1972. After the surrender in Dhaka, the recognition of Bangladesh by most countries was inevitable. A reunion with Pakistan seemed out of the question. But, Pakistan's new ruler, President Bhutto, chose to react by breaking diplomatic relations with a few countries and by quitting the Commonwealth. It was, however, notable that relations were not broken with the Soviet Union, which had done the greatest harm to Pakistan by its massive military aid to India or with the UK whose powerful news media was most vocal in denunciation of Islamabad's policies in East Pakistan. Oddly, it was the Commonwealth, an assembly of about fifty former British colonies in Asia, Africa and elsewhere—which could not be held guilty of doing anything hostile to Pakistan during the Bangladesh crisis—with which Pakistan broke ties.

Incidentally, even in the case of those few countries with which relations were broken following their recognition of Bangladesh, Pakistan shortly thereafter re-established ties. In fact, Pakistan itself recognized Bangladesh in 1974. But Bhutto never did reverse the decision to quit the Commonwealth, describing it as anachronistic and serving no useful purpose. He took pride for having kicked away 'colonial remnants.' As a result of this decision, Pakistanis residing in the UK suffered many inconveniences and Pakistan deprived itself of the benefits of a fairly useful international forum. Later on when Bhutto's successor, President Ziaul Haq decided to reverse the decision, Indira Gandhi, who had again become the Indian Prime Minister, blocked Pakistan's re-entry into the Commonwealth. She had been embittered by what she considered to be Pakistan's disregard of the undertaking given to her at Simla by Bhutto of not letting the Kashmir issue mar peaceful relations between the two countries. It was thus not until 1989 that Pakistan was able to return to the Commonwealth when, ironically, Pakistan's Prime Minister was Bhutto's daughter—Benazir. Pakistan had needlessly harmed itself for seventeen years by remaining out of the Commonwealth, more out of capriciousness rather than any reasoned judgement of foreign policy.

After the war, the issue of the return of the POWs from Bangladesh became one of the main preoccupations of Pakistan's diplomacy. Bangladesh claimed that some of the POWs had been guilty of 'war crimes' including genocide during the course of the crackdown of the Pakistani army against the Bengali separatists, beginning from March 1971. The Bangladesh government prepared a list of 'war criminals' whom it insisted on trying in a court. This demand was endorsed by India where the POWs were being kept. On the other hand, Pakistan insisted on the immediate return of the POWs in keeping with international law and strongly opposed the holding of any trials for the alleged war crimes. In this context, Pakistan sought the moral and diplomatic help of foreign countries. Wives of the POWs went around the world appealing to the world conscience. This was humiliating for a country which had prior to the 1971 War, enjoyed a reputation as one of the stronger military powers in the Third World.

In the post-1971 War scenario, the hard reality was that Pakistan's prestige had suffered greatly in the rest of the world. The repression of Bengali separatists had aroused severe criticism of Pakistan. The exodus of millions of Bengali refugees to India and their pathetic plight had added to the moral indignation. The quick surrender of the Pakistani army in Dhaka shattered its reputation and led to a reappraisal of Pakistan's military prowess. East Pakistan's separation raised questions about the very viability of Pakistan. There were critical circles worldwide who had never been able to accept the creation of a new state in the name of religion. Pakistan's breakup gave them a *raison d'être* for the negation of its creation.

Having been so comprehensively defeated in the war, Pakistan lost considerable ground in terms of power politics. Pakistan's future as a state was being openly questioned. Pakistan's closest neighbour Iran, in the latter years of Mohammad Reza Pahlavi, the Shah of Iran, adopted an almost patronizing attitude towards Pakistan. The Shah hinted at the possibility of annexing Balochistan province in case of a 'further dismemberment' of Pakistan.[12] Even with the traditionally friendly Gulf countries, which had so far looked up to Pakistan as a big brother, the relationship underwent a subtle change. It was now Pakistan, which needed their support.

In retrospect, it seems that Pakistan had reached its zenith in the 1960s under Ayub Khan when it was being cited as a model among developing countries. In this period, in the military field, Pakistan could hold its own against India. The decline of Pakistan started with the self-inflicted 1965 War and the nadir was reached with its ignominious defeat in the 1971 War. Moreover, with the loss of its eastern part in 1971 Pakistan was, in geo-strategic terms, a different country. Its linkage with Southeast Asia was gone. It now seemed to be more a part of the Middle East and Central Asia.

In August 1975, President Sheikh Mujibur Rahman was assassinated in a military *coup d'état*. It seemed at first that the new rulers had an anti-India bias and might declare the country an Islamic Republic. There was a sense of jubilation in Pakistan and Prime Minister Bhutto prematurely launched a publicity campaign in the expectation that there would be some kind of confederal arrangement with Bangladesh.[13] This was once again a typical case of Pakistani illusions, disregarding the degree of estrangement existing in Bangladesh. The euphoria in Pakistan was, however, short-lived as

Bangladesh basically maintained its course, even though the pro-Indian feelings had long since run out of steam.

Since then, Bangladesh and Pakistan have been able to establish a generally cordial relationship although the issues of the repatriation to Pakistan of 'Biharis' (non-Bengali speaking migrants from India settled in ex-East Pakistan after 1947) and the division of assets have never been resolved.

NOTES

1. Rafi Raza, op. cit., p. 71.
2. Ibid., p. 92.
3. NAM Communiqué of 10 October 1964 pledged to respect existing borders. Burke and Ziring, op. cit., pp. 88–9.
4. Lt. Gen. Gul Hassan Khan, *Memoirs*, p. 315.
5. Ibid., p. 316.
6. Hasan Zaheer, *The Separation of East Pakistan: The Rise and Realization of Bengali Muslim Nationalism* (Karachi: Oxford University Press, 1994), pp. 418–19.
7. Lt. Gen. J.F.R. Jacob, *Surrender at Dacca: Birth of a Nation*, pp. 131–2, cited by Sherbaz Khan Mazari, *A Journey to Disillusionment* (Karachi: Oxford University Press, 1994), pp. 216–17.
8. Sultan M. Khan, op. cit., who was Yahya Khan's Foreign Secretary, p. 336 notes that 'the generals lived in a make-believe world of their own, convinced that the army could take care of the situation.' At p. 386, he says that 'the fantasy of the prevailing mood was unbelievable.'
9. Lt. Gen. Gul Hassan Khan, *Memoirs*, pp. 329–36.
10. Burke and Ziring, op. cit., p. 406, from an interview with President Nixon, published in *Time*, 3 January 1972.
11. Rafi Raza, op. cit., pp. 209–10.
12. C.L. Sulzberger, *The New York Times*, 22 April 1973, cited by Sherbaz Khan Mazari, op. cit., p. 360.
13. Rafi Raza, op. cit., p. 226.

6

The Resurgence of Pakistan after 1971

The 1971 War had been an unmitigated disaster for Pakistan. In the words of British historian Hugh Trevor-Roper, 'In December 1971, Pakistan was divided, defeated, demoralized, and in the eyes of the world, disgraced.' However, in spite of these setbacks, Pakistan's geo-strategic importance remained and indeed came to the country's rescue. A number of developments helped Pakistan to not only recover much lost ground but, in some ways, to emerge even stronger in the international arena.

Pakistan's geo-strategic importance on the world scene had been demonstrated by its ability, even in the midst of the Bangladesh crisis, to play a key role in the normalization of relations between the US and China in 1971. It was from Islamabad that US Secretary of State, Henry Kissinger, flew secretly to Beijing to open a new chapter in Sino–American relations. Pakistan's abiding friendship with China was thus eventually appreciated and put to good use by the US. It was Pakistan, which played the role of the trusted intermediary in bringing China and the US closer. This was not only a belated endorsement by the US of Pakistan's steadfast policy of befriending China but also reaffirmed Pakistan's standing in its region and beyond. Besides, it secured crucial help in meeting Pakistan's strategic concerns with respect to India. It is widely believed that after the fall of Dhaka, India was deterred from invading West Pakistan and imposing its terms on Islamabad because of the strong warnings given by the US and China. The US, moreover, secured the cooperation of the Soviet Union in the efforts to restrain India.[1]

Shortly after the debacle in East Pakistan, Pakistan's new ruler, President Bhutto undertook a tour of several Islamic countries in January 1972, followed by a second trip in May that year. The main purpose was to reassure the Muslim world that Pakistan still remained a viable and important country. Bhutto also sought their moral and material support in the difficult negotiations with India for a peace treaty. The Muslim countries were also persuaded to withhold their recognition of Bangladesh. Bhutto was warmly welcomed and received strong assurances of support. These visits conveyed the message to India that Pakistan still enjoyed the sympathy and support of the Islamic world and was not an isolated country.

Lahore Islamic Summit

The successful holding of the Islamic Summit at Lahore in 1974 by Prime Minister Bhutto reaffirmed Pakistan's continued importance in the Islamic world and served as a morale-booster for the Pakistani people. The summit was called basically to discuss the Middle East situation in the wake of the Arab–Israeli War of October 1973 and the oil embargo imposed by the Arabs. The proposal for holding an extraordinary summit had come from the OIC Secretary General Tunku Abdul Rahman, the former Malaysian Prime Minister, but Bhutto was quick to seize the initiative and offered to host it in Pakistan. The Arab countries obviously welcomed the holding of such a summit to discuss the Middle East situation, with a view to securing the support of the Islamic world for the Arab cause. The response of most of the other Islamic countries was also very enthusiastic since this was only the second time that an Islamic Summit had been arranged since 1969. The oil boom had, in the meantime, greatly enhanced the attraction of the oil-rich Islamic countries. The poorer Islamic countries welcomed participation in any forum where they could be together with their affluent cousins.

Being the host of the Lahore Summit, Pakistan was clearly the main beneficiary of this historic meeting and succeeded in regaining considerable prestige and goodwill. This was in no small way due also to the enthusiastic, even ecstatic, welcome given by the people of Lahore to the visiting delegations. The 'spirit of Lahore' was recalled by leaders and officials of the Islamic countries for some years after this Summit. Bhutto's own stature in the Islamic world also rose due to the successful holding of the Lahore Summit.

In strategic terms, by gathering so many important heads of states in Lahore, Pakistan was able to send a message to India that it did not stand alone but had a large number of friends including some of the world's richest countries. The oil boom had begun about that time and the financial standing of many of the participating countries could not be ignored.

The Lahore Summit also provided a face-saving forum for Pakistan to back down on its hitherto defiant attitude of non-recognition of Bangladesh. In the ambience of Islamic fraternity generated by the Islamic Summit, it seemed easier for Pakistani public opinion to forget the bitterness of the past, embrace Mujibur Rahman, and recognize Bangladesh. Many Arab and

Islamic countries had until then also not recognized Bangladesh, as a gesture of solidarity with Pakistan. The reality was that over two years had passed since Bangladesh came into being and the *fait accompli* could no longer be ignored. The Arab and Islamic countries used the Lahore Summit to induce Pakistan to recognize Bangladesh. Six heads of states flew from Lahore to Dhaka to bring President Mujibur Rahman to the Summit. Pakistan was clearly on a weak wicket in its continued refusal to recognize Bangladesh, which was an irreversible reality. But the Pakistan government had tied its own hands by fomenting public emotions on this issue. Hence, the Lahore Summit provided a way out of this self-inflicted dilemma.

Another important outcome of the Lahore Summit was the acceptance by the Islamic world of the status of the Palestine Liberation Organization (PLO), under its leader Yasser Arafat, as the sole legitimate representative of the Palestinian people. Until then, there had been many reservations in some conservative Arab countries and in Pakistan itself about the PLO for its involvement in terrorism and hijackings. The recognition of the PLO also gave the Palestinian cause an important boost in the international arena. Its hands were also strengthened in securing acceptance at the UN and in other international bodies. Arafat was moved to make the remark that the state of Palestine was 'born in Lahore.'

The Lahore Summit also strengthened the hands of the Arab countries, particularly Egypt, in the negotiations that followed the 1973 Arab–Israel War. Jerusalem was singled out for special mention and it was made clear that its status was of profound interest to the entire Islamic world.

Nuclear Capability

Pakistan's international stature and geo-strategic importance received a yet more decisive boost by two key developments in the late 1970s, namely, Pakistan's known progress towards the acquisition of nuclear capability and the Soviet incursion into Afghanistan.

Pakistan's evident progress in the nuclear field and the impression that Pakistan had actually developed a nuclear weapons capability—the so-called 'Islamic Bomb'—forced the international power brokers to upgrade Pakistan's military importance. The Pakistani nuclear programme had started under President Ayub Khan. However, the decision to develop a nuclear weapons capability was made in January 1972 in a meeting with top scientists held by President Bhutto, a month after the fall of Dhaka. Bhutto reportedly said that Pakistanis would 'eat grass' if necessary in order to develop the nuclear bomb. He had been convinced for several years that Pakistan should develop a nuclear deterrent. He knew that India had embarked upon a programme for the development of nuclear weapons despite its denials.

When India suddenly carried out a nuclear explosion in 1974, Pakistan stepped up its efforts to develop nuclear capability. Under the circumstances, any government in Pakistan would probably have taken the same decision, as already taken by Bhutto, to go nuclear. Also, at about this time, Islamabad was fortunate to secure the services of a Pakistani scientist Dr A.Q. (Abdul Qadeer) Khan who had returned home from Holland with information about a different kind of nuclear technology than the (French-supplied) reprocessing technology which had so far been pursued by Pakistan. Dr A.Q. Khan thus played a key role in the development of Pakistan's nuclear programme.

The Indian explosion gave a strong impetus to the US to work against nuclear proliferation. Until then, the West had been relatively open about sharing nuclear technology for peaceful purposes. However, India had proved how this knowledge could be used towards building of nuclear weapons capability. Ironically, the anxieties generated by India's progress in the nuclear field had more of a fall-out on Pakistan. The West in general and the US in particular from then on strongly opposed Pakistan's acquisition of nuclear technology. No doubt, there were strong reasons for the global concern about nuclear non-proliferation. But it seemed that for the West, the possession of nuclear weapons by an Islamic country like Pakistan was a matter of particular worry.

India had not faced any significant Western disapproval even after carrying out its nuclear test in 1974 at Pokhran. Pakistan, however, came under vigorous scrutiny and strong pressures, as soon as it proceeded to develop its nuclear capability. The West clearly feared that the 'Islamic Bomb' in Pakistan's possession might eventually pass, for ideological as well as financial reasons, into the hands of some of its 'volatile and unstable' Muslim Arab brethren in the Middle East, thereby posing a grave threat to the security of Israel. America's blind partisanship with Israel, which has distorted its Middle East policy in the past fifty years, has survived under successive American presidents.

Against this background the US Congress passed a rider to its Foreign Aid Appropriations Bill in 1976, called the Symington Amendment, barring all economic and military aid to any country involved in importing and exporting reprocessed or un-safeguarded enrichment plants. The US also applied a good deal of pressure on France to rescind its contract for building of a nuclear reprocessing plant in Pakistan. According to a popular version in Pakistan, during a visit to Pakistan in August 1976, US Secretary of State Henry Kissinger, who was Jewish, sought to pressurize Bhutto by threatening that the US would make a 'horrible example' of him if Pakistan went ahead with its nuclear programme.

It is not clear as to what role, if any, was played by the US in the overthrow of Bhutto in July 1977 in a military *coup d'état*. Many of Bhutto's followers have believed that there was US complicity in this as also in his eventual hanging in April 1979 primarily because of his refusal to compromise on the nuclear issue.[2] However, Rafi Raza, a close associate of Bhutto, has produced evidence,[3] which contradicts the belief that Kissinger had ever threatened Bhutto, as he remained in power for nearly a year after the alleged threat by Kissinger. It is more plausible that Bhutto's fall was related primarily to his mishandling of the internal political situation, including massive rigging in the elections held in March 1977, rather than any American intrigue.

If the US had conspired with the Pakistani army chief, General Ziaul Haq, to overthrow Bhutto in order to prevent Pakistan from going ahead with its nuclear programme, then the logic would have been that Ziaul Haq should have, after seizing power, put a halt to this programme. However, Ziaul Haq stood firm against US pressure and Pakistan's nuclear programme went ahead on its secret course. All kinds of means were adopted by Pakistan to secure the required machinery and components for the nuclear programme. These efforts could not remain undetected and a number of articles and books were written in the world media about Pakistan's efforts to develop the 'Islamic Bomb.'[4] These reports were always duly denied by Pakistani spokespersons. Pakistan kept assuring the world that its nuclear programme was entirely peaceful and that it had no intention to develop nuclear weapons.

To ward off international pressure, Pakistan manoeuvred to secure the moral high ground against India by repeatedly proposing a variety of nuclear non-proliferation proposals in various international forums. The international community gave overwhelming support to such proposals. The voting at the UN was usually around 100 for and 2 or 3 against such Pakistan-sponsored resolutions in support of non-proliferation in South Asia. India was compelled in each case to reject such resolutions. This suited Pakistan's interests very conveniently as the onus for the rejection of eminently sensible non-proliferation proposals lay squarely on Indian shoulders, while Pakistan went ahead quietly with its nuclear programme. This was a considerable success for Pakistan's diplomacy.

The critical breakthrough in Pakistan's nuclear programme had been achieved in 1979 and three years later, Pakistan had produced enough fuel for use in a nuclear weapon. According to Pakistan's top nuclear scientist, Dr Abdul Qadeer Khan, the cold tests had been conducted by 1984.[5]

It was thus under President Ziaul Haq's stewardship that Pakistan acquired nuclear capability. His many critics in Pakistan have, however, ensured that he receives little credit for this outstanding achievement which has given an abiding sense of security to Pakistan and has, indeed, served as a deterrent against war in the subcontinent.

While Pakistan's acquisition of the nuclear bomb was not officially confirmed (until May 1998 when it carried out several nuclear explosions in retaliation to the Indian nuclear explosions), what is relevant is that India, among others, has evidently believed for the past two decades that Pakistan did have such a capability. The nuclear deterrent has kept India at bay and established an uneasy but seemingly durable peace in the sub-continent. Despite strong Western pressure, neither Pakistan nor India has so far signed the NPT. India has argued that it would not accept a discriminatory ban on its nuclear capacity while China and other nuclear weapon states remained exempted. Pakistan had, in principle, indicated its willingness to sign the NPT, but made this contingent to India also doing so. This has been basically a tactical manoeuvre to divert international pressure towards India. A similar stance was initially adopted by Pakistan for the signing of the Comprehensive Nuclear Test Ban Treaty (CTBT).

In geo-strategic terms, there can be no doubt that since the early 1980s, Pakistan's importance has increased significantly because of its perceived acquisition of nuclear weapons capability. After carrying out the nuclear explosions, Pakistan has undoubtedly become a nuclear power. Its joining of the 'nuclear club' has thus put it in a league apart from most other states in the world.

NOTES

1. Burke and Ziring, op. cit., p. 406.
2. Zulfikar Ali Bhutto, *If I am Assassinated* (New Delhi: Vikas Publishing House, 1979), pp. 168–71, cited in Burke and Ziring, op. cit., p. 434.
3. Rafi Raza, op. cit., pp. 243–8.
4. For example, Steve Weissman and Herbert Krosney, *The Islamic Bomb: The Nuclear Threat to Israel and the Middle East* (New York: Times Books, 1981).
5. Interview to the daily *Jang*, dated 30 May 1998.

7

The Afghanistan Problem

Soviet Occupation of Afghanistan

Apart from the importance that Pakistan gained from the development of its nuclear capability, Pakistan's geo-strategic importance came to the fore during the same period due to two important developments in the region. In Iran, the pro-West regime of the Shah was overthrown by Islamic radicals, led by Ayatollah Khomeini, who adopted a fiery anti-US posture and seemed ready to destabilize the other conservative regimes as well. A deadly war broke out between Iran and Iraq, which added to the uncertain security situation in the region. But the West was disconcerted more by the Soviet armed intervention in Afghanistan, which sent alarm bells ringing all over the world. Against this background, the importance of Pakistan acquired a new significance in the eyes of the West as well as the oil-rich Gulf states and indeed for most of the non-communist world.

The global concern regarding the Soviet entry in Afghanistan had in its background Imperial Russia's southward expansion in Central Asia which had been taking place for more than a century. The 1917 Communist Revolution did not change that trend. The Soviet Union's ambitions in the region were recorded in November 1940 in the secret agreement with Nazi Germany wherein Soviet Foreign Minister Vyacheslav Molotov had proposed that 'the area south of Batum and Baku in the general direction of the Persian Gulf should be recognized as the *centre of the aspirations* of the Soviet Union.'[1] (My italics). At the end of the Second World War, the Soviet Union had even tried to perpetuate its control over northern Iran. The geo-strategic importance of the region further increased with the discovery of huge oil deposits in the Persian Gulf region in the last fifty years. In fact, by 1970, the dependence of the industrialized West and Japan on oil imports from the Gulf had become crucial for their economic welfare.

The communist coup in Afghanistan in April 1978, followed by the induction of the Red Army in Afghanistan in December 1979, revived fears of the long-dreaded Soviet (Russian) expansion towards the warm waters. The hard reality was that the uninterrupted flow of oil from the Gulf to the rest of the world was of vital strategic interest to the West. President Jimmy Carter warned in January 1980 that the US would even use military force to keep the oil lanes open. The Carter Doctrine declared that 'an attempt by any outside force to gain control of the Persian Gulf region will be regarded as an assault on the vital interests of the United States, and such an assault will be repelled by any means necessary, including military force.'[2] President Carter was clearly referring to the Soviet military presence in Afghanistan and the threat it posed to the Persian Gulf.

The global ambitions and the expansionist nature of Soviet Communism had for long caused deep apprehensions in the capitalist West as well as in Islamic countries and elsewhere. By the end of the Second World War, most of East Europe was firmly under Soviet control. In the case of each country occupied by them, the Soviets proceeded to install communist regimes, which basically acted as Moscow's puppets. In the east, Mongolia had become a Soviet satellite shortly after the communist revolution in Russia. North Korea came under communist control after the Second World War, more or less on the East European pattern. In 1949, communism had a notable success in Asia with the establishment of the People's Republic of China. However, China was too big to become another Soviet satellite although, for the first few years, it was firmly in the Soviet camp.

Alarmed by this pattern of communist expansion, the US adopted the policy of 'containment' in the early 1950s, which involved building military alliances including countries on the periphery of the communist bloc. The 'containment' policy succeeded partially in holding back the tide of communism. However, North Vietnam fought successfully against French colonialism to establish a communist regime by 1955. It subsequently assisted the Vietcong militarily to establish communist rule in South Vietnam. Fearing a domino effect, the US decided now to directly intervene militarily in Vietnam to hold back the communists. After bitter warfare lasting nearly fifteen years, the US eventually had to withdraw in disarray from South Vietnam, as public opinion in the US itself turned against continued involvement there. Shortly thereafter, North Vietnam overran South Vietnam.

But the communist success in Vietnam was not an isolated affair. Cuba had turned communist in 1959 and South Yemen had a Marxist regime a few years later. The 1970s witnessed a gushing rise of communist regimes around the globe. Soon after the fall of South Vietnam, neighbouring Laos and Cambodia came under communist rule and the latter saw unprecedented cruelty under the Pol Pot regime. Next to join the communist camp were Angola, Mozambique, Ethiopia, and Nicaragua.

The communist takeover in Afghanistan in 1978, followed by actual Soviet military intervention, was not an isolated development, but part of the chain wherein Soviet-inspired communism was seizing control in one country after another. Moreover, there were certain exceptional features in the case of Afghanistan. Although there were very few communists in this strongly conservative Islamic country, yet they had manoeuvred to seize power with the help of the Soviet military advisers. Faced with internal resistance to the communist rule, Soviet troops had become directly involved in Afghanistan, unlike the communist take-overs in other countries. Afghanistan had a common border with the Soviet Union. Because of this geographical proximity, it seemed that Afghanistan could even be annexed outright by the Soviet Union. It looked like a potential sixteenth Soviet republic, similar to Uzbekistan and others. More ominously, Afghanistan was only about 500 km away from the strategic Gulf region from where the Soviet Union could impede the flow of oil.

In the immediate context, it seemed that Pakistan, a strategically-located country, with a 2,200 km-long porous border with Afghanistan had become vulnerable to communist expansion. The communist takeover in Afghanistan was, therefore, viewed as an ominous development with strategic global implications and not merely a change of government in a remote country in Central Asia.

Some observers like Selig S. Harrison have argued that 'Moscow did not launch its invasion as the first step in a master plan to dominate the Persian Gulf, as *most observers believed* at the time. Rather, after stumbling into a morass of Afghan political factionalism, the Soviet Union resorted to military force in a last desperate effort to forestall what it perceived as the threat of an American-supported Afghan Tito on its borders.'[3] (My italics). But Harrison himself has noted that Soviet military advisers in Afghanistan played a key role in the success of the coup on 27 April 1978 which brought the communists to power.[4] Later on, when the rift grew between the two main factions of Afghan communists, and the anti-communist resistance gained momentum, the Soviet Politburo considered the possibility of a military intervention. The then KGB chief Yuri Andropov said in the meeting held on 17 March 1979, that '*we cannot afford to lose Afghanistan under any circumstances.*'[5] (My italics). Similarly, Harrison has reported that Mikhail Suslov, the Politburo's ideologue, had argued in favour of Soviet military intervention saying that 'the collapse of the Afghan revolution would imperil Communist regimes everywhere.'[6]

It is difficult to sustain the argument that the Soviet Union 'stumbled' into Afghanistan. In fact, it had built up secret communist cells in the Afghan armed forces over a long period of time. Some of them had participated in the *coup d'état* of Mohammed Daoud in 1973 and served as coalition partners in his regime. Five years later, alarmed by certain moves by Daoud to change his erstwhile pro-Moscow policies, the Afghan communists with Soviet blessings seized power in April 1978. Moscow was the first to recognize the regime. Thus, there can be little doubt that Moscow had long entertained expansionist designs in Afghanistan. Since Afghanistan itself had hardly any resources, its importance lay in being the stepping stone to more attractive objectives lying beyond it. At any rate, whatever might have been Moscow's real motives for entering Afghanistan, there was a general perception in most countries around the world that this action showed that the Soviet Union was on an expansionist course.

To hold back the perceived Soviet expansion via Afghanistan towards the warm waters, the US and Saudi Arabia, supported by Japan and many other countries, decided to extend all-out support to Pakistan which alone seemed physically capable, across a mountainous terrain, to assist the growing popular resistance in Afghanistan against the Soviet occupation. Iran could not fill this role even though it too was strongly opposed to the Soviet presence in Afghanistan and was located next door to it. The reason, of course, was that since its Islamic Revolution in February 1979, there had been a serious deterioration in Iran's relations with the US. Pakistan thus became the main conduit for the flow of arms to the Afghan resistance and a 'front-line' state against the perceived Soviet expansionism. As a *quid pro quo*, Pakistan received strong financial and diplomatic support from the West and several Islamic countries.

In this process, Pakistan also took some fearsome risks, primarily by confronting the Soviet Union, a superpower located in its immediate backyard. Moscow repeatedly warned Pakistan that it was playing with fire and threatened it with dire consequences. There were many strategists who advised caution and retreat. However, President Ziaul Haq saw the communist take-over in Kabul, and the later entry of the Red Army into Afghanistan, as a mortal threat to Pakistan itself and decided, as he put it, 'to fight the battle for Pakistan' inside Afghanistan. He held the view that for more than a century, Russia had been following a policy of relentless expansion in Central Asia as a result of which one Muslim state after another had been conquered and annexed. Imperial Russia's successor, the Soviet Union, had shown itself to be even more expansionist. From this historical perspective, the Soviet entry in Afghanistan could not be considered an isolated event. Afghanistan was to be the gateway to Pakistan and to the warm waters and control of the oil-rich Gulf states which were perceived to be the real Soviet agenda.

President Ziaul Haq clearly also had personal motives in following a policy of activism in Afghanistan, and that was to entrench himself more deeply in power in Pakistan by securing respectability and international aid for his military regime which had become relatively sequestered, in particular, after the execution of former Prime Minister Z.A. Bhutto in April 1979.

In any event, Pakistan was taking great risks by confronting the Soviet Union. It seemed almost like a desperate gamble at the time. Even amongst Ziaul Haq's closest advisers, both in the armed forces as well as in the Foreign Office, there was a sharp division of opinion. The majority view probably was that it would not be wise to further alienate the Soviets who had already done so much harm to Pakistan especially in the 1971 War, and generally, ever since the mid-1950s. There were senior Pakistani diplomats who were convinced that nothing could dislodge the Soviets from Afghanistan, and Pakistan had no option but to accept the *fait accompli* and come to terms with the Soviet Union. It was even argued that Pakistan should opt to become a neutral state on the model of Finland or Austria so as to escape eventual occupation by the Soviet Union. There were some who warned that the Soviet Union was the superpower located in Pakistan's backyard, with the capacity to do grievous harm to Pakistan; and that it made little sense to depend on the other superpower, the US, which was located 10,000 miles away, who, despite being a military ally, had not come to Pakistan's rescue in the previous two wars with India.

President Ziaul Haq stood firm in the view that it made more sense to try to hold back the Soviets in Afghanistan, since Pakistan's turn would inexorably come next, whether or not it acquiesced in the Soviet presence in Afghanistan. Moreover, he calculated that the Afghans had a proud history of resisting foreign occupiers and the country's terrain was well suited for guerrilla resistance. Ziaul Haq and his military associates—particularly DG ISI General Akhtar Abdur Rahman Khan, who was to play a key role in the military planning—were probably also encouraged by the recent example of Vietnam where guerrilla resistance had successfully thwarted the colonial power, France, and then a superpower, the USA.

The fighting in Afghanistan continued for nearly a decade. In spite of the strong support worldwide for the Afghan cause, there was little optimism anywhere that the Soviets would eventually withdraw. The Soviets were known for their ruthlessness and tenacity. Besides, the Soviet Union was a superpower with seemingly unlimited resources. As things turned out,

Ziaul Haq's gamble did pay off and, in his words, 'the miracle of the twentieth century' did take place. Afghanistan's rugged terrain, fanatical resistance by the Afghan Mujahideen, the strong support extended to them by the West and China, as also by key Islamic countries—above all by Pakistan—forced a reassessment in Moscow. Most importantly, though it was not generally known at the time, it was the precarious nature of the Soviet economy, making it imperative to improve relations with the West by cutting down on the Soviet Union's military expenditure, which made the Soviet stay in Afghanistan untenable.

The Soviet Union looked from the outside like a monolith and it was difficult for outsiders to know that there were rifts inside. By 1980, a reformist group had emerged in the Communist Party, which included Andropov and his protégé, Mikhail Gorbachev. Yuri Andropov, then head of the KGB, had some reservations about the wisdom of Soviet intervention in Afghanistan, but had gone along with the decision. When he became general secretary in 1982, Andropov broadly hinted in a meeting with President Ziaul Haq that the original decision to intervene 'might or might not have been right.' However, Andropov was generally ill during his brief tenure, and the material fact on the ground was that he did not change the Soviet policy towards Afghanistan. His successor Konstantin Chernenko, a Leonid Brezhnev loyalist, followed the hard line in Afghanistan.

It was not until Gorbachev came to power in Moscow in March 1985 that there was a material change in the situation. He was willing to take a fresh look on all Soviet policies—internal and external—in the spirit of *glasnost* and *perestroika*. To begin with, Gorbachev had persisted with Moscow's hard line posture *vis-à-vis* Pakistan due to its 'interference' in Afghanistan. Gorbachev was tough and even menacing in a meeting with Ziaul Haq which took place immediately after he took over in Moscow. TASS reported that Gorbachev had told Ziaul Haq that the 'aggressive actions' of the Pakistan government 'cannot but affect in the most negative way Soviet–Pakistani relations.'[7] Indeed, there was a stepping up of Soviet military activities in Afghanistan during the summer of 1985.[8] There were also open threats of punitive strikes against Pakistan itself in the exercise of the right of 'hot pursuit.' Islamabad was warned that it was playing with fire; officially, the Soviets at times described Pakistan as an 'enemy country.' In fact, in this period Pakistan was receiving far more abuse in the Soviet media than the US and the West, which were the principal enemies.

While talking to the Pakistani Ambassador in Moscow in November 1985, Gorbachev sent a conciliatory message for the first time expressing his keenness to improve ties with Pakistan. From 1986 onwards, signs began to appear that a reappraisal of the Afghan policy was taking place in the Kremlin. In a major speech on 25 February 1986, Gorbachev described Afghanistan as having become a 'bleeding wound' for the Soviet Union. It thus began to appear that, in some respects, Afghanistan had become as much of a problem for the Soviets as Vietnam had for the Americans.

The reasons for this change in thinking were multi-dimensional. As the war in Afghanistan went on interminably, it became highly unpopular in the Soviet Union. The average Soviet family simply could not understand as to why its son, brother, or husband should fight, die, or be wounded in fighting a fierce guerrilla resistance movement to make a remote and impoverished country safe for communism. Moscow could not generate any patriotic feelings in favour of a war being fought in a small country, which hardly posed any threat to the security of the Soviet Union itself. The prevalent system of rotating Soviet soldiers in Afghanistan for short spells of duty meant that a very large number of young men had to endure military service in Afghanistan. Millions of Soviet families suffered the trauma over a period of ten years of having their dear ones face the hazards of fighting the fanatical Afghans, whom many in the Soviet Union regarded as little better than savages. At the international level, the Soviet Union was facing strong criticism, even ostracism, because of its military occupation of Afghanistan. It seemed that due to this problem, the tensions with the US would continue unabated, imposing severe financial burdens on Moscow. Probably the last straw which broke the camel's back was the 'Star Wars' project launched by President Ronald Reagan in the mid-1980s which forced the Soviet Union to divert ever more funds to the armament programme.

Nonetheless, in the tradition of totalitarian rule in the Soviet Union, in which decisions were imposed by the supreme leader, these factors might not have made a difference. But Gorbachev was not a traditional Soviet leader and he was acutely conscious that the Afghan war was imposing a severe financial burden on an economy already at the verge of collapse because of the arms race. Moreover, as the then Foreign Minister Eduard Shevardnadze was to recall, the policies of *perestroika* 'would have lost heavily' if the Afghan conflict were not resolved.[9]

The logic finally prevailed in the Kremlin that the losses involved in continuing the war in Afghanistan were more than the gains. In the intensified discussions on Afghanistan, the main interlocutor with the Soviet Union was Pakistan, which had so far also bore the brunt of Soviet displeasure. The status of Pakistan thus changed in Moscow's eyes from that of a despised enemy into one of an earnestly sought dialogue partner. Foreign Minister Eduard Shevardnadze and his deputy Yuli Vorontsov brought a new look to the negotiations on the Afghan issue. Georgi Arbatov, a key adviser of Gorbachev, who maintained a channel of communications with the Pakistan Ambassador in Moscow between 1985 to 1988, played a significant role in establishing an earnest dialogue with Pakistan. Discussions were also taking place with Professor Yuri Gankovsky of the Institute of Oriental Studies, a key Soviet expert on Afghanistan, whose superior during 1985–7 was Yevgeny Primakov, later Prime Minister, who was also involved in the deliberations on Afghanistan.

So far, the Soviets had proceeded on the logic that through a combination of brutal suppression and shrewd local compromises they would be able to succeed in stamping out the pockets of resistance in Afghanistan. They drew a parallel between the Afghan situation and that of the 'Basmachi' revolt in Bukhara in the 1920s where the Uzbek Muslims, despite putting up a fierce resistance for nearly a decade, had been eventually subdued. The Pakistani ambassador countered this reasoning by pointing out that there was a vast difference between Afghanistan of 1985 and Bukhara of 1925. The terrain in Afghanistan, unlike Bukhara, was mountainous and suitable for guerrilla warfare. The Afghans had a long tradition of fighting, with considerable success, all foreign invaders in their country. The Afghans were also known for their fierce devotion to Islam and had a strong motivation to fight against what they considered the un-Islamic ideas of the communist regime in Kabul and, in particular, the occupation of their country by a non-Muslim power. Afghanistan had a long porous border that made it accessible to help from outside which was not the case with the Basmachi. Also, the international opinion was solidly against the Soviet presence in Afghanistan and external assistance was forthcoming for the Afghan guerrillas on a scale which the Uzbeks, in the 1920s, had never received.

Pakistan argued persuasively that the Soviet policy in Afghanistan was based on a false analogy and could not succeed. As a superpower, the Soviet Union certainly had the physical capability to prolong the bloodshed for a very long time but, at the end of the exercise, the situation would remain unchanged. Thus, it made better sense for Moscow to cut its losses by ending this futile campaign in Afghanistan. In so doing, the Soviet Union stood to gain important diplomatic and material dividends. The allegation that Pakistan was hostile to the Soviet Union or was playing the American game had no basis. It was clearly in Pakistan's national interest to have a friendly relationship with the Soviet Union, its neighbour and a superpower as well. So far as Afghanistan was concerned, even after the Soviet withdrawal, it should be beyond doubt that any successive Afghan regime would wish to have friendly relations with Moscow, as had been the case for more than a century.

Eventually, the Soviet policymakers came around to accepting this logic. (Declassified Soviet records show that at a meeting of the Politburo held on 13 November 1986, Gorbachev declared that 'we have been fighting for six years. If we don't change our approach we will fight for another twenty to thirty years! Are we going to fight forever, knowing that our military can't handle the situation?')[10]

The decisive factor behind Moscow's decision to withdraw might well have been the precarious nature of the Soviet economy, though this factor was not really known to the outside world at that time. At any rate, whatever might have been the persuasive consideration for Moscow, the fact was that the Soviet Union did finally agree to leave Afghanistan. This was the first time that, as a result of military pressure the Soviet Union had agreed to quit a country occupied by it. The Soviets had in the past withdrawn from some other places (northern Iran, Manchuria, Finland, and Austria), but for non-military reasons.

The formal negotiations to secure peace in Afghanistan had started as early as 1981 under UN auspices, but were making little headway till Gorbachev came to power. No doubt, the UN mediator (since February 1982) Diego Cordovez as also some Pakistani officials had, at times, sounded optimistic about the progress being made in the 'proximity talks' in Geneva when actually only ancillary details had been settled. For instance, in May 1983, Cordovez had reportedly said that '95 per cent of the settlement was ready.' This was far from the truth since the actual issue all along was when, if ever, the Soviet forces would withdraw from Afghanistan. On this, there had been no real change in Moscow's thinking until a year after Gorbachev took over. For instance, 'the widespread assessment in Washington (in December 1985) was that there was no prospect of a Soviet withdrawal.'[11] Prior to that, it seemed that the Soviets were using these talks to merely ward off international pressure by pretending to hold serious talks to resolve the problem 'around' Afghanistan, as Moscow and Kabul used to describe it. They claimed that the real issue to be addressed was 'foreign interference,' notably by Pakistan, supported by the US and others. Indeed, it was more plausible that the Soviets were using the UN-sponsored talks to buy time to crush the Afghan resistance and convert the country into another Uzbekistan. Thus Babrak Karmal, the head of the communist regime in Kabul, said in a talk with Selig Harrison on 13 March 1984 that the UN negotiations would continue to be a 'charade' until Pakistan agreed to deal with him as a legitimate government.[12]

In the end, Afghanistan turned out to be a different story. The times were different and the terrain was different. This time it was the mighty Soviet Union itself, which had to yield. Thus, the Geneva Accords signed in April 1988 were, above all, a great victory for the heroic Afghan people. At the same time, the Soviet withdrawal from Afghanistan was also a high watermark of Pakistani diplomacy and military strategy.

In the penultimate negotiations before the signing of the Geneva Accords—which secured what had been Pakistan's main demand from the outset, viz. the Soviet military withdrawal from Afghanistan—President Ziaul Haq made a bid to obtain an agreement with Moscow to set up an interim government in Afghanistan, dominated by non-communists, to replace the existing regime of Mohammad Najibullah. To achieve this Ziaul Haq was prepared even for a delay in the Soviet withdrawal.

The question about the composition of the future government in Kabul at the time of Soviet withdrawal was actually first raised by Moscow during 1987. It wanted to install a broad-based government led by the People's Democratic Party of Afghanistan (PDPA—Afghan Communist Party) at the time of Soviet withdrawal. With this in view, the Soviets echoed the arguments of the Kabul regime in favour of 'national reconciliation.' The main motive, as Shevardnadze put it in the internal debate in the Kremlin, was 'to avoid a bloodbath in which our friends would be slaughtered.'[13] His deputy, Vorontsov, was later to reveal that 'our real concern was to make sure that everything did not fall apart the minute we left, which would have humiliated us.'[14]

Pakistan and the US were, at first, opposed to the linkage of a future government to the issue of Soviet withdrawal. Pakistan later enthusiastically joined in the discussion on this issue. However, under the pressure of the Mujahideen leaders, it insisted on a minimal or no role for the PDPA in such a government. During the course of hard bargaining on this issue, Pakistan even indicated that it could accept a delay in the Soviet withdrawal. In early 1988, Ziaul Haq took the position that 'Pakistan would not sign the Geneva Accords unless Moscow removed Najibullah and agreed to an interim government to be chosen through processes dominated by the Pakistan-based resistance groups.'[15] This was an astonishing reversal of Pakistan's position. As Cordovez put it:

> I was dumbfounded. Pakistan had pressed me for a whole year to persuade the Soviets to drop the link between the withdrawal of the troops and the formation of a new government. Soviet arguments in support of such a linkage had been dismissed and laughed at as meaningless and unjustified.

Zia and Yaqub had assured me a hundred times that Pakistan would be ready to sign with anybody but Karmal—even with his brother or with a clone. Islamabad, like Washington, had consistently maintained that once a withdrawal was agreed upon all other matters would 'fall into place.' In Moscow the Soviets had promised to consider a withdrawal time frame of less than a year. What should I tell them? That the withdrawal was no longer needed?[16]

The Soviets refused to accept the sidelining of the PDPA in any interim government, and now dropped their insistence on linkage of withdrawal with the formation of such a government. They further pointed out that the main demand of Pakistan, the US and its supporters from the beginning of the Afghan crisis was that the Soviet Union should withdraw its forces from Afghanistan. Moscow was now willing to do so but to expect it also to install a regime of Pakistan's choice in Kabul was out of the question. The Soviet contention was that there had been no surrender of their forces in Afghanistan and it was absurd to expect Moscow to sign the terms of capitulation by installing a Mujahideen-dominated regime in Kabul. They further reminded Pakistan that it had been saying all along that without Soviet military support, the communist regime in Kabul would not last more than a few days. Now that the Soviet forces were withdrawing Pakistan could, by its own previous logic, expect Najibullah to fall. Thus, it made no sense to ask Moscow to install a non-communist regime in Kabul.

President Ziaul Haq's last minute insistence that an interim government should replace Najibullah before Pakistan would sign the Geneva Accords imperilled the entire agreement. His stance also split the Pakistan government between those who supported the President's ambitious reasoning and those, led by Prime Minister Mohammad Khan Junejo, who argued that securing Soviet military withdrawal from Afghanistan had always been the great objective and now that its realization was within Pakistan's grasp nothing ought to be done to upset it. The latter also pointed out that, in any event, there was nothing to stop the Soviets from unilaterally withdrawing from Afghanistan, with or without the Geneva Accords. They noted further that the Soviet Union had not been militarily defeated in Afghanistan and was withdrawing more for political reasons. Therefore, it was a case of being over-ambitious, as also being altogether unrealistic, to expect the Soviet Union not only to quit Afghanistan but also to hand it over to Pakistan on a silver platter by installing a pro-Pakistan regime there. Moreover, when the general view in Pakistan had been that the communist regime in Kabul would not last more than a few days after the Soviet withdrawal, it made no sense to imperil the Geneva Accords by insisting on Najibullah's eviction as a precondition. The US held the same view and urged that the historic opportunity to sign a mutually advantageous treaty should not be missed. Finally, Ziaul Haq had to accept this reasoning and thus the final hitch in the negotiations was overcome.

Yet another last-minute hitch occurred in the negotiations when the Soviets made it known that even after signing the Geneva Accords and withdrawing their forces from Afghanistan, they would yet continue to extend whatever military assistance might be needed by the Najibullah regime. This would have created an asymmetrical situation as the Kabul regime would have continued to receive Soviet arms and supplies whereas the Afghan Mujahideen would have been denied such help under the provisions of the Geneva Accords regarding 'non-interference' from outside, the coded euphemism for arms supplies via Pakistan reaching the Mujahideen. This dispute was resolved with an exchange of letters between the US secretary of state and the Soviet foreign minister confirming 'positive symmetry' namely, that if the Soviet Union should, after the signing of the Geneva Accords, continue its military assistance to the pro-Moscow regime in Afghanistan, the US would also retain the right to provide military assistance (to the other factions). The Soviets eventually gave their approval in writing of this understanding.[17]

The Geneva Accords were signed on 14 April 1988 in a historic ceremony. The withdrawal of Soviet forces commenced accordingly and was completed on schedule early in 1989. The Soviet Union was thus compelled, against its previous record, to withdraw from a country, which had been under its occupation for nearly a decade. According to Moscow 13,310 Soviet soldiers had lost their lives and 35,478 were wounded in Afghanistan. The actual figure was probably higher. Even more significantly—although it was not foreseen at the time—the Afghan misadventure evidently hastened the collapse of the Soviet Union itself just three years later. That epoch-making unexpected development, of course, entirely changed the geo-strategic realities of global politics by ending the Cold War between the two superpowers which had kept the whole world under the threat of a nuclear holocaust for half a century, apart from causing international tensions all over the globe due to the hostility between the two. The key role played by Pakistan in the Afghan jihad against the Soviet Union, thus, seems to have produced more far-reaching consequences than was realized at the time. For these reasons, it is arguable that Islamabad's support of the Afghan resistance (between 1978 and 1989) perhaps represents the only occasion in Pakistan's fifty-year existence when it has been able to directly influence global history.

This historic achievement could not have been possible without the determination and clairvoyance of President Ziaul Haq. He had on several occasions said frankly that he did not expect to see Soviet withdrawal from Afghanistan during his lifetime and that if this happened, it would constitute 'the miracle of the twentieth century.' Nonetheless, he had held on to Pakistan's risky role in Afghanistan in the belief that any other option would be still worse. In the end, Pakistan managed to come out successfully through this critical test lasting over a decade. However, Ziaul Haq himself was killed four months after signing the Geneva Accords in a mysterious air crash on 17 August 1988. The Soviets had always been highly critical of him: but his supply of covert arms assistance to the Mujahideen, even after the signing of the Geneva Accords and the commencement of the Soviet withdrawal from Afghanistan, angered Moscow to a point that warnings of dire consequences were being issued to Pakistan right up to the time of the air crash.

The circumstantial evidence seemed to point to a Soviet hand in the air disaster, which also killed Arnold Raphel, the American ambassador to Pakistan. Ordinarily, this should have brought a very sharp reaction from Washington which always made a big outcry even in the case of the death of an ordinary American citizen, more so where Moscow's hand was suspected. However, Secretary of State George Shultz was quick to rule out any Soviet complicity even before the American enquiry team had arrived in Pakistan. Evidently, the US was quite content to have the Soviets retreat from Afghanistan in disgrace and did not wish to imperil the implementation of the Geneva Accords. Nor did it want to aggravate relations with Moscow when Gorbachev was cooperating in major arms reduction deals. Even more importantly, he had set in motion reformist policies in the Soviet Union, which could only lead to the loosening of the Soviet totalitarian system. This was highly welcomed by the US.

President Ziaul Haq had probably outlived his utility to the Americans once the Soviet withdrawal from Afghanistan was agreed upon. His Islamic fundamentalist views as also his efforts to develop Pakistan's nuclear capability, apart from his non-democratic credentials, had not endeared him to the Americans. His exit at this particular time suited US global interests. This reasoning has led to the increasing belief in some quarters that the US itself might have engineered the air crash that killed Ziaul Haq. This seems much too Machiavellian and something which, in the American system, could not for long have been kept a secret. At any rate, the fact of the matter is that the US hardly showed any keenness to unearth the causes for the mysterious air crash.[18]

Not long after Ziaul Haq's death, the US went ahead to apply sanctions against Pakistan under the Pressler Amendment on the grounds that Pakistan was developing nuclear capability. Interestingly, while the Afghan crisis lasted, the US presidents had been annually certifying to the Congress that Pakistan was not doing so. Had Ziaul Haq lived, it would have been more embarrassing for the US administration to stage a volte-face of this nature with a leader to whom the US was indebted for his role in confronting the Soviet Union. On the other hand, it was simpler to apply sanctions against the succeeding regime in Pakistan. This cynical behaviour is characteristic of the policies of *realpolitik* pursued by the US and indeed by most other countries. In international diplomacy, it is mostly a country's self-interest which matters. Sentiments of friendship and gratitude usually mean little, if anything, in global politics.

There have always been many observers in Pakistan, including bitter critics of Ziaul Haq, who have questioned the very wisdom of Pakistan's involvement in the Afghan fighting against the Soviet occupation forces. They argue that, in disregard of its national interests, Pakistan had allowed itself to be used merely as a pawn of the Americans in their global confrontation with the Soviets. Pakistan had thus become a tool in a proxy war in which the US was using the Afghans as gun fodder against the Soviets; whereas Pakistan exposed its security to grave risks by antagonizing Moscow. Moreover, by allowing itself to be used as a conduit for supply of arms to the Afghan Mujahideen, Pakistan had jeopardized its internal security. There is a proliferation of arms all over Pakistan; a Kalashnikov culture has since developed in the country resulting in the incessant terrorism in Karachi and elsewhere. These critics conclude that Pakistan got nothing from the Afghan problem except gun-running, religious fanaticism, terrorism, and narcotics.

This line of reasoning has acquired a certain plausibility, with the benefit of hindsight, now that the Soviet Union is no more there and the threat of communist expansion is no longer a real concern. The problem, of course, is that policymakers are not soothsayers and they have got to act in the context of actual and known realities. In 1978, probably no one expected the Soviet Union to collapse in such a short period of time. The reality at that time was that communist expansionism was accelerating and the 1970s had seen several countries going under communist rule. The perception, therefore, was that the communist takeover in Afghanistan and the subsequent arrival of the Soviet army in that country had brought the red tide to Pakistan's very doorsteps. Hence, the threat to Pakistan's security was a real one and simply could not be wished away. It was against this specific background that

Pakistan decided to extend covert armed support to the Afghan resistance against the Soviet-backed communist regime in Kabul.

For more than a year after the communist takeover in Kabul, Pakistan was nearly alone in its support for the Mujahideen. The Western countries were still debating whether the Nur Mohammad Taraki regime in Kabul was a communist one, or they were merely leftist reformers interested in modernizing Afghanistan. For instance, Adolph 'Spike' Dubs, the US ambassador in Kabul, described the regime's strongman Hafizullah Amin as 'a tough cookie who thinks of himself as a "national Communist" and doesn't want to be any more dependent on (the Soviets) than he has to be.'[19] Moreover, President Carter had shown little enthusiasm for Ziaul Haq and had imposed sanctions against Pakistan for continuing its nuclear programme. It was not until Soviet troops landed in Kabul in December 1979 that the Western world was shaken out of its complacency. Even then, the US offered limited assistance to Pakistan, which Ziaul Haq initially rejected as 'peanuts'. It was only after Ronald Reagan was elected as the new US president that the Americans took any real interest in the Afghan resistance. The record thus shows that Pakistan had been ahead of the US in its policy of support for the Afghan Mujahideen, and not the other way around. Pakistan was pursuing a policy based on its own clear national objectives and was neither acting at the bidding of the US nor was being used as its pawn.

In the short term, Pakistan's basic objective was to secure Soviet withdrawal from Afghanistan and an end to the communist rule in that country. The long-term interest of Pakistan was to have a friendly Afghanistan. In this bid, Pakistan received very substantial economic and military assistance from the US, Saudi Arabia, Japan, and others because they were all opposed to communist expansionism in this strategic region. Even Iran, despite its bitter differences with the US, held the view that the Soviets must be made to withdraw from Afghanistan. Pakistan's Afghan policy, therefore, won broad-based international sympathy and support. It could not then be said that the US alone was concerned by the Soviet incursion into Afghanistan and that Pakistan was made to do the dirty work for the Americans. In fact, Pakistan's role won it considerable goodwill as shown by the massive votes at the UN in favour of the Pakistani-sponsored resolutions on Afghanistan. Pakistan's stance also helped it to break out of the isolation in which it had found itself at the time. Pakistan was thus able to receive massive US military and economic assistance and, moreover, Washington was obliged to turn a blind eye to Pakistan's nuclear programme which, according to Dr A.Q. Khan, reached weapon capability by 1983. These were the strategic considerations behind Pakistan's Afghan policy, which produced tangible benefits for the country. No doubt, Pakistan was at the same time taking considerable risks by antagonizing Moscow, but Islamabad correctly calculated that the Soviet Union would not go so far as to attack Pakistan for fear that this would lead to a global war.

There has been the argument that as a consequence of the Afghan policy, there is gun-running all over Pakistan, ensuing terrorism and violent religious fanaticism. However, this again does not stand the test of a careful scrutiny. The greatest accumulation of guns and ammunition had been in Pakistan's bordering provinces of NWFP and Balochistan from where they used to be sent across to the Mujahideen. But in the 1990s there was relatively little terrorism in these two provinces. Clearly, the reasons for the terrorism in Karachi, which is located far from Afghanistan, have to be looked for elsewhere and cannot be mainly attributed to Pakistan's role in the Afghan jihad. Moreover, the fighting against the Soviets had ended by 1988 with the signing of the Geneva Accords. The fact is that during Ziaul Haq's eleven-year tenure (1977–88), terrorism in Karachi was much less than the scale reached after his death. In fact, terrorism increased after the end of the fighting against the Soviets when the arms flow to Afghanistan had already stopped. Hence, there was little linkage between the two events. Also, factional violence inspired by religious fanaticism was in that period more pronounced in the Punjab rather than in the two provinces bordering Afghanistan.

As for the spread of narcotics in Pakistan, this is probably a part of a worldwide phenomenon, in which the pervasive Western way of life, as carried by films, television, and literature, has been a key factor.

The Afghan Problem in the Post-Soviet Era

The Geneva Accords secured the withdrawal of the Soviet troops from Afghanistan on schedule in 1989. Soon thereafter, Moscow witnessed dramatic events when the communist hardliners made a last-ditch effort to seize power from Gorbachev. They failed in this bid, but Gorbachev too had to go. It was his former protégé and subsequent rival Boris Yeltsin who managed to seize power with popular support. As a reaction to the revolt of the communist hardliners, Yeltsin decided to put an end to the entire Soviet State structure under communism. One of the world's two superpowers along with its East European empire thus disintegrated without a shot being fired. The Soviet misadventure in Afghanistan had been a contributory factor in this momentous development which has altogether changed the global equations.

With the demise of the Soviet Union, the old-time fear of Soviet expansionism has disappeared and thus one of Pakistan's security threats has been eliminated. With the emergence of six independent Muslim states in Central Asia, an unfriendly superpower is no longer breathing down Pakistan's neck. The Central Asian Muslims have old linkages with Pakistan. The last great Muslim Empire in India—the Mughal dynasty, which ruled from 1526 to 1857—was established by Babur, the ruler of Ferghana in today's Uzbekistan. Many Uzbeks came over to India during the Mughal period to become part of the ruling elite. Many Pakistanis trace their roots to Central Asia. For these reasons, there is inherent goodwill and fraternal sentiments between Pakistan and the six Muslim countries of Central Asia.

Moreover, all of these countries are land-locked and can secure a natural transit route to the sea via Pakistan. Although Iran is also vying to serve as the land transit route, Pakistan seems to be a better choice for these countries for logistic reasons. Peace in Afghanistan is, however, a prerequisite for such a transit route. Indeed, the concept of a Central Asia enjoying friendly relations with, and giving a strategic depth to Pakistan *vis-à-vis* India is apparently inseparable from the situation in Afghanistan.

Unfortunately, after the Soviet withdrawal and the ouster of the communist regime in Kabul three years later, the seven Mujahideen parties, who had fought the Soviet-backed regime, got involved in an internecine struggle for power. Pakistan tried to play the role of the honest broker between the warring factions (1992–6) with short-term success. On the whole, it seems to have only burnt its fingers. The situation was aggravated by outside involvement in the power struggle, this time from Iran, Tajikistan, and Uzbekistan, as well as by Russia—each of which has its own ethnic or other interests in Afghanistan.

While Pakistan came under suspicion for supporting Gulbuddin Hekmatyar in the initial phase of the civil war, it later found itself in a more awkward position. The sudden rise of the Taliban, a radical Islamic fundamentalist movement, and their ascendancy over most of Afghanistan aroused apprehensions in the neighbouring Central Asian countries, with the possible exception of Turkmenistan. Even after becoming independent in 1991, these Muslim countries continue to be ruled by their old-time communist bosses who were raised on a staple of secularism, atheism, and modernism. During the Soviet era, one of the main security concerns for Moscow in the Muslim-majority areas was any adherence to Islamic orthodoxy. Thus, despite pretensions of religious freedom, everything was done to crush Islam. After the Central Asian states became independent, Islam re-emerged as the dominant religion in these countries and even the former communists now pay lip service to Islam. However, since these rulers are leftovers from the communist era, they have run into serious opposition from Islamic orthodox circles. In their threat perception Islamic 'fundamentalists' top the list and a militant Islamic regime in Afghanistan is seen as a threat.

The influence of Turkey in Central Asia is also a factor in this scenario. Ethnically, the Central Asians are Turkish and see Turkey as a kind of a big brother. For its part, Turkey seems to regard these Central Asian countries as a special preserve of its own. In the beginning of the twentieth century, Pan-Turkism had been an important political movement in Central Asia, until it was crushed by both the Russians and the Chinese. But ever since the Central Asian countries regained independence in 1991, Turkey has been seeking to advance its influence in this region.

The Turkish ruling circles, who are wedded to secularism and are facing opposition from orthodox Islamic circles in their own country, are enthusiastic promoters of secularism in Central Asia as well. A serious tussle is thus taking place in Central Asia between the secular rulers and the orthodox Islamic majority.

Russia continues to hold sway in the Central Asian states, even after their separation. The whole region was colonized by the Russians in the last 200 years and Russian political and cultural influence persists, despite the break-up of the Soviet Union. Moreover, Russian troops are stationed in some Central Asian states in accordance with the provisions of treaties under the aegis of the Commonwealth of Independent States (CIS). It seems that the hangover of the colonial past has not disappeared altogether from the mind-set of Moscow. Pervasive Russian influence in Central Asia is pitted against the spread of Islamic orthodoxy and is working in tandem with the instinct for self-preservation of the Central Asian rulers in their own struggle against the Islamic opposition. These rulers are fearful that the militant Taliban ideology in neighbouring Afghanistan could spread to their own countries, or the Taliban could even extend material support across the Oxus River to the Islamic opponents of the present regimes, thus posing a grave threat to their internal security.

In addition to ideology and security, ethnic considerations are also a factor. Northern Afghanistan is mostly populated by Uzbeks and Tajiks in whose welfare Uzbekistan and Tajikistan clearly have some interest. In the more recent fighting in the Afghan civil war, the Uzbek and Tajik population of northern Afghanistan was undoubtedly the recipient of considerable material aid from their cousins across the borders. The success in the civil war of the mainly Pukhtun Taliban had also raised the fear that Uzbek and Tajik refugees might be pushed across the Oxus River into Central Asia. This adds to the concerns of the Central Asian countries.

On the western side, Iran was bitterly hostile to the Taliban government for reasons of its own. It has come down heavily against the extremist Islamic policies of the Taliban. Ironically, prior to the rise of the Taliban, Iran had been regarded as the Islamic fundamentalist country. However, the Taliban are Sunni Muslims and, hence, Shi'ite Iran has shown little enthusiasm for the former. Moreover, ever since the fall of the communist regime in Afghanistan in 1992, Iran has evidently sought to acquire for itself a position of special influence in Afghanistan, by promoting the power and influence of the Afghan Shia minority as also the Persian-speaking and non-Pukhtun ethnic groups. Iran was extending all out material and moral aid to the Burhanuddin Rabbani regime even after it had been ousted in 1996 from the capital Kabul and, two years later, from its provisional capital Mazar-e-Sharif.

It is thus tragic that for the past three decades, peace has eluded Afghanistan. First there was the long, and ultimately successful, jihad against the Soviet occupation. This was followed by a prolonged civil war in which the Taliban emerged as the victors. The supremacy of the Taliban did, at long last, bring peace and stability to Afghanistan in the areas under their control. However, the threat to peace was coming more from outside because of the apprehensions and hostility towards the Taliban of some of the neighbouring countries, particularly Iran.

Unfortunately, there is an impression among these neighbouring countries that Pakistan has been actively supporting the Taliban in their military successes. Very little evidence has been advanced to support this contention which minimizes the real reason for the rise of the Taliban, namely, their popularity amongst large sections of the Afghan people. It is true, however, that the ascendancy of the Taliban could produce two main advantages for Pakistan. A stable and peaceful Afghanistan would enable Pakistan to promote beneficial cooperation in the region and obtain a natural transit route via Afghanistan. Also the Taliban have much more in common with Pakistan and are more well disposed towards it than the other Afghan groups. Thus, it was natural that Pakistan was the first country to recognize the Taliban regime.

On the other hand, the success of the mainly Pukhtun Taliban, who were controlling nearly 90 per cent area of Afghanistan, seemed to have brought about a congruence in the thinking of some neighbouring countries, though for diverse reasons. Unfortunately, for Pakistan, it found itself the target of criticism from some of its traditional friends and neighbours for a 'sin' which it had not even committed.

Pakistan was thus facing a serious dilemma. Most of the Taliban are ethnic Pukhtuns, like many Pakistanis in the two provinces bordering Afghanistan. Many Taliban leaders had studied in Pakistan's religious schools. (Incidentally, Afghan religious students from all ethnic backgrounds have long been coming to Pakistan.) Thus, the Taliban had strong linkages with Pakistan and were basically well-disposed towards it. At the same time, the Taliban succeeded in holding their sway over most of Afghanistan due to their own policies and the support of Afghanistan's majority Pukhtun population. Pakistan had neither the resources nor the political will to secure the success of the Taliban. However, if Pakistan tried either to distance itself from the Taliban or to adopt a negative attitude towards them, then it ran the risk of annoying the major Afghan ethnic group—indeed the only group—which was well-disposed towards Pakistan. In fact, the Taliban can pose problems across Pakistan's porous border.

The Taliban have been accused of ill-treatment of the Shias and ethnic minorities. They have strongly denied these charges, which have hardly been substantiated. The restrictions imposed by them on women's education and holding of jobs, use of the veil, as well as Islamic punishments have brought charges of human rights violations from international bodies, including the UN. For this reason also, the Taliban remain highly isolated internationally. Pakistan, followed by Saudi Arabia and UAE, were the only countries to extend recognition to the Taliban government. Further, Iran stepped up a war of nerves against the Taliban and even threatened to launch a military invasion against them.

Under these circumstances, Pakistan risked being dragged into a situation where its objectives of securing regional cooperation and the perceived strategic advantages, accruing from the emergence of six Islamic states in Central Asia, might prove illusory. If on the other hand, the Taliban government was able to establish a better equation with its neighbours and peace at home, Pakistan could look forward to a close and highly beneficial political and economic relationship with several countries in its backyard with which Pakistan has had centuries-old links.

Pakistan has always been in favour of establishing a broad-based government in Afghanistan including the main ethnic groups and various factions. The overwhelming success of the Taliban all over Afghanistan, except the north-eastern part and the Panjshir Valley, however, made them less inclined towards having a coalition with the other factions.

In the event that the Taliban regime had been able to maintain its hold over Afghanistan, it is likely that the rest of the world would have, sooner or later, accepted the reality of its existence and come to terms with it. The Taliban would, however, have to show some malleability in their own interest by broadening their ethnic base and by improving their human rights record. On the other hand, Pakistan's interests would be best served by coaxing the Taliban to move towards conciliation and more flexibility. The establishment of a durable peace in Afghanistan and a friendly regime in Kabul, which is at peace at home and with its neighbours, should remain Pakistan's objective. If this can be achieved, Pakistan's strategic interests in the region would receive a big boost.

Pakistan–Iran Differences on the Afghan Issue

The Afghan issue arose almost at the same time as the Islamic Revolution in Iran. The Afghan people's resistance against the communist regime and Soviet occupation forces was steeped in their strong adherence to Islam. This naturally evoked all-out sympathy and support from the Islamic revolutionaries in Iran. At the same time their xenophobia and hatred towards the USA resulted in the adoption of a strange attitude towards Pakistan's role in the Afghan crisis. In the first place, Tehran chose to be suspicious of Pakistan's sincerity in opposing the Soviet occupation of Afghanistan. The fact that American arms were reaching the Afghan Mujahideen via Pakistan aroused Iranian suspicions, since the US was considered to be the 'Big Satan' by the Islamic revolutionaries. It was clearly not understood by Tehran that a common interest to oppose the Soviet designs in Afghanistan had brought the US, Pakistan, China, Saudi Arabia, and the Afghan Mujahideen together. In fact, nearly all countries in the world were opposed to the Soviet occupation of Afghanistan. Furthermore, Iran seemed to be unmindful that it was Pakistan which was making the greatest sacrifices by opposing the Soviets—in terms of security hazards and the burden of refugees—certainly as compared to the losses incurred by Iran in supporting the Afghan resistance.

Even though Pakistan faithfully kept Iran fully informed of all developments, from 1982 onwards, in the context of the UN-sponsored Geneva negotiations to bring about the Soviet withdrawal, still Iran persisted in maintaining a negative attitude. It refused to participate in the talks but only agreed to be kept informed. The Iranians told Diego Cordovez that 'they were much more honest and determined friends of the mujahideen than the Pakistanis.'[20] Iran, however, refused to be 'pinned down' to any agreement.

Thus, Deputy Foreign Minister Ali Larijani told Cordovez that Iran preferred 'to remain a wild card. We will see what we can do when a settlement is nearer.'[21] In fact, Iran kept on apprehending that these negotiations were nothing more than a trick or façade for 'betraying' the Afghan Mujahideen! While Iran did not take even a fraction of the risks incurred by Pakistan in opposing the Soviet military presence in Afghanistan, it was inexplicably suspicious of Pakistan's commitment to the cause of the Mujahideen fighting against the Soviet occupiers. In fact, the Iranian prognosis of the situation was so widely off the mark that, till the actual signing of the Geneva Accords in April 1988 and even for sometime thereafter, the Iranians kept on saying that the Soviets would never withdraw from Afghanistan.

The Soviet withdrawal from Afghanistan in 1989 and the overthrow of the communist regime in Kabul in 1992, were great victories—above all, for Islamic ideology and solidarity. This should have indeed ushered in an era of fraternal cooperation and greater understanding with Pakistan, in the context of Afghanistan, consistent with the Islamic spirit behind Iran's Revolution. In reality, since 1992, Iran has played, from the point of view of Pakistan, an increasingly unhelpful and unfriendly role in Afghanistan.

It seems that since the rise in oil income in the early 1970s, there has been a transformation in Iran's attitude when the Shah began dreaming of a revival of the Persian Empire. Pakistan's defeat in the 1971 War had diminished its earlier importance in his eyes. The Islamic Revolution in Iran has not basically changed this attitude despite all protestations of fraternal feelings for Pakistan. A close analysis of events suggests that, behind the friendly façade, the real problem has been Iran's hegemonic ambitions in Afghanistan. According to Selig S. Harrison, with oil prices rising, the Shah of Iran had 'embarked on his ambitious effort to roll back Soviet influence in neighbouring countries and create a modern version of the ancient Persian empire. Until the eighteenth century, Iran had ruled western Afghanistan, and the fall of Zahir Shah (in 1973) revived Iranian ambitions.'[22] It is ironic, however, that the Islamic radicals, who toppled the hated Shah, have evidently persisted with his hegemonic ambitions, particularly in respect of western Afghanistan. Since the fall of the communist regime in Kabul in 1992, their effort has been to acquire for Iran a position of special influence in Afghanistan. To achieve this objective, Iran has sought to secure a key position for the small Shia minority in Afghanistan's power structure.

In the pursuit of these ambitions, since the ouster of the communist regime, Iran has in effect opposed the control of Afghanistan by the Pukhtun/ Sunni majority, which has ruled Afghanistan for the past 200 years, including the period of the communist rule (1978–92). Iran is, of course, aware that the

Pukhtuns have much more in common with Pakistan; the leaders of the main Pukhtun political groups had lived in Pakistan during the Soviet occupation, and had in fact operated from bases in Pakistan against the Soviets. They are obviously well disposed towards Pakistan. Evidently, conscious of this reality, Iran has thrown its support behind the non-Pukhtun groups in Afghanistan, some of whom also speak the Persian language.

Following the successful outcome of the ten-year long jihad against the Soviet forces and the subsequent ouster of the communist regime, the Afghan people naturally expected that there would at long last be peace and tranquillity in their country, and reconstruction under a Mujahideen-led government. Unfortunately, the loose coalition of the Mujahideen leaders, which had operated successfully against the Soviet forces and the Afghan communist regime, fell apart in the individual lust for power. The Mujahideen leaders soon enough turned into regional warlords each with his own personal agenda. This led to civil war and large-scale bloodshed in the battle for succession. Several attempts at reconciliation, brokered by Pakistan and Saudi Arabia, came to nought. The Mujahideen leaders even broke the pledges they had made in the sanctity of the Holy Ka'aba in Makkah. This caused deep frustration in Saudi Arabia, which had solidly stood by the Mujahideen during the long struggle against the Soviet occupation. As a consequence the Saudis have, subsequently, taken only a marginal interest in developments in Afghanistan. This in turn has weakened Pakistan's ability to manoeuvre in the Afghan imbroglio.

The post-communist civil war in Afghanistan was initially spurred by personal ambitions of the various Mujahideen leaders. Later on ethnic and linguistic considerations have become an increasingly important factor in the power struggle. Significantly, it was disgust with this internecine fighting for power, which gave birth to the Taliban movement. It first emerged in the Pukhtun areas, around 1994, as a third force and speedily gained popularity. The Taliban denounced the existing political factions as un-Islamic, corrupt, and self-centred. They also promised to bring peace and Islamic justice to areas under their control. This message was evidently well-received. The business community also welcomed the prospect of stability and good law and order. Thus, one region after another in the Pukhtun belt came under the control of the Taliban, usually without any fighting. The capital Kabul fell to the Taliban in September 1996 and thus the new regime came to control nearly two-thirds of Afghanistan, including some non-Pukhtun areas.

The sudden ascendancy of the Taliban confounded most observers. Looking for explanations, some analysts concluded, by inference rather than on the basis of concrete evidence, that Pakistan was behind their success, since the movement of the *Taliban* (meaning students) had originally started among Afghan students who had studied in religious schools in Pakistan. The fact that most of the Taliban were Pukhtuns like many Pakistanis and were also well-disposed towards Pakistan was considered as further proof that Pakistan must have had a hand in their successes. In fact, their rapid growth has been due largely to indigenous factors. Pakistan had neither the military capability, financial resources, nor even the political will (under the then ruling Benazir government) to launch such a religiously oriented movement. If Pakistan had possessed such a capability, why could it not secure the success of its former alleged favourite, Hekmatyar, in the power struggle before the Taliban emerged on the scene? It is also noteworthy that, in most instances, the Taliban have succeeded in the Pukhtun belt through political persuasion and appeal to Islamic solidarity, rather than by using military means.

The Taliban are very puritanical and extremely rigid in their version of Islam, which is basically the way in which Islam has been traditionally practiced for centuries in the Pukhtun villages. However, the Taliban's rigid enforcement of these beliefs such as keeping of women behind the veil, confined to their homes, and the shutting down of girls' schools, public flogging for sex offences, etc. quickly aroused deep concern in the West and even more so among the international human rights groups. The fact is that the moral and religious attitudes followed by the Taliban are widely prevalent in even the non-Pukhtun parts of Afghanistan. Some similar practices are to be found in Saudi Arabia, which, however, has generally escaped Western criticism due to its oil wealth and pro-West foreign policy. Afghanistan is poor and of little material interest for the West. Thus, the Taliban have been singled out for strong criticism by the Western countries and human rights organizations. Ironically, Iran has been even more outspoken in criticizing the fundamentalist views of the Taliban, even though Iran has itself been branded by the West as an oppressively fundamentalist regime. The secularists elsewhere (including Pakistan) have also been highly critical of the Taliban.

Hence, an odd combination of liberals and conservatives have joined in condemning the Taliban regime. At the same time, the Taliban themselves have not helped their cause by their handling of the UN offices in Afghanistan, their violation of human rights, and by their poor public relations in general.

The successes of the Taliban regime in winning over most of Afghanistan also aroused deep anxieties amongst its northern neighbours, particularly in Uzbekistan and Tajikistan. Though independent since the break-up of the Soviet Union in 1991, these countries continue to be ruled by their former communist bosses who now profess to be Muslim liberals. Moreover, the Russian presence remains strong in these countries and their southern borders with Afghanistan are in fact guarded by Russian troops. These regimes are facing local opposition in their own countries from the orthodox Islamic circles. Hence, these governments were deeply disturbed at the growing power of the Taliban in Afghanistan. They apprehended that the Taliban would, sooner or later, openly or covertly, give support to the local Islamic movements across the Oxus River.

Thus, for varying reasons, the Western countries, Iran, and Afghanistan's northern neighbours manoeuvred to prevent the Taliban from occupying the seat of Afghanistan at the UN. This seat continued to be held by the ousted Rabbani regime, which, in August 1998, even lost its temporary capital Mazar-e-Sharif. The Taliban controlled nearly 90 per cent of Afghanistan and the Rabbani regime simply did not exist. According to international practice, the Taliban regime had every right to represent Afghanistan in international bodies since it was in effective control of most of the country for over four years. It is notable that the communist regime had immediately secured recognition in 1978 even though it was clearly opposed by the overwhelming majority of the Afghan people. Similarly, Rabbani was given recognition even though he was bitterly opposed by Hekmatyar in a bloody civil war. The Taliban regime had been singled out for stringent criteria for securing recognition. Under International Law, it is for the Afghans alone to decide as to what system of government they want. Whether the Taliban were right or wrong in their interpretation of Islam was their own business and was entirely an internal matter for the Afghans themselves to resolve.

In the region itself, as the Taliban's bid to secure power gained strength in Afghanistan, the strongest opposition to their ascendancy came from Iran. There was also overwhelming evidence that Iran has been supporting the opponents of the Taliban, both materially as well as morally. In fact, even before the emergence of the Taliban, Iran had taken a partisan attitude in the Afghan civil war by backing the regime led by President Rabbani, one of the original Mujahideen leaders, belonging to the Tajik ethnic minority. In the peace agreements brokered by Pakistan and Saudi Arabia in 1992, Rabbani had become interim president for a limited period of time. But even after the expiry of his term, he doggedly refused to relinquish power. This first pitted him against Hekmatyar, another Mujahideen leader and an ethnic Pukhtun, who was next in line for the Presidency. In clear disregard of the principle of non-interference in the internal affairs of other countries, Iran openly supported Rabbani in the conflict against Hekmatyar.

Eventually, neither Rabbani nor Hekmatyar could prevent the Taliban from capturing Kabul and most of Afghanistan. Rabbani thereafter retreated north to Mazar-e-Sharif in the Uzbek–Tajik ethnic majority areas where he enjoyed the support respectively of the Uzbek warlord General Abdul Rashid Dostum and the Tajik warlord Ahmad Shah Massoud, apart from the support of some neighbouring countries. However, the onward march of the Taliban could still not be stopped. In August 1998, they conquered Mazar-e-Sharif and thereafter reached the Oxus River, dividing Afghanistan from the Central Asian countries. Excepting for a few pockets of resistance, most of Afghanistan was controlled by the Taliban.

To stop the Taliban's northwards march, Iran did everything possible to fortify the Rabbani regime by forging understanding with neighbouring Uzbekistan and Tajikistan, as well as with Russia. While the first two have a natural sympathy for their respective ethnic brethren in northern Afghanistan, Russia's interest stems from its lingering ambitions in Central Asia, even after the collapse of the Soviet Union.

Paradoxically, Iran itself has a general reputation as a 'fundamentalist' country. But it has had no hesitation in forging an alliance against the 'fundamentalists' in Afghanistan by joining hands, among others, with Russia, the successor of the Soviet Union, which was responsible for the devastation of Afghanistan following its military intervention in 1979. Moreover, there were reports that Iran had also colluded with India in the efforts to sustain the Rabbani regime. One would have thought that such an unholy alliance with countries which have done so much harm to Muslims would have been totally against Iran's Islamic ideology. But, here again, it would seem that realpolitik and hegemonic ambitions, rather than ideology, have determined Iran's policies towards Afghanistan.

Evidence suggests that Iran has been keen to make Afghanistan its zone of influence and to this end, there has been a shadowy contest with Pakistan, despite all the claims of working hand in hand with Pakistan to restore peace in Afghanistan. Nominally, Iran and Pakistan keep consulting each other to promote reconciliation in Afghanistan but it is clear that they have been working at cross-purposes.

There also seems to be rivalry between Iran and Pakistan on the question of providing the transit route to the sea for the various land-locked countries of Central Asia. On the face of it, the better and shorter transit route from Central Asia would appear to be via Afghanistan and Pakistan. The Iranian route is longer and might take greater efforts to develop. Iran's policies have also kept it isolated in the world and a transit route through Iran might be a riskier proposition. However, the Pakistani transit route becomes feasible only when there is peace in Afghanistan. Hence, it would suit Iran's chances for becoming the preferred transit route if Afghanistan remains in a state of turmoil.

This situation calls for a realistic evaluation by Pakistan of the relationship with Iran. A high-ranking Saudi leader once confided, 'Saudi Arabia understands Pakistan's reasons for seeking friendly relations with Iran. But Pakistan will find out sooner or later that Iran is not sincere in its professions of friendship with Pakistan.'[23] The record would suggest that there is considerable weight in this observation. Pakistan would, therefore, have to take a hard and realistic look at all aspects of its relations with Iran. A new relationship based on a mutually beneficial give-and-take basis would have to be worked out, although obviously Pakistan's motive should remain to seek close cooperation with Iran.

NOTES

1. Burke and Ziring, op. cit., p. 169.
2. Diego Cordovez and Selig S. Harrison, *Out of Afghanistan: The Inside Story of the Soviet Withdrawal* (New York: Oxford University Press, 1995), p. 55.
3. Cordovez and Harrison, 'Afghanistan and the End of the Cold War', in *Out of Afghanistan: The Inside Story of the Soviet Withdrawal* (New York: Oxford University Press, 1995), p. 4.
4. Harrison, 'How the Soviet Union Stumbled into Afghanistan', ibid., p. 27.
5. Ibid., p. 36.
6. Ibid., p. 49.
7. Cordovez, 'The Long Winter', in *Out of Afghanistan*, p. 182.
8. Harrison, '"Bleeders," "Dealers," and *Perestroika*', ibid., p. 187.
9. Cordovez, 'Climax and Anticlimax: The Geneva Accords', ibid., p. 317.
10. Harrison, '"Bleeders," "Dealers," and *Perestroika*', ibid., p. 207.
11. Ibid., p. 194.
12. Harrison, 'The War Escalates', in *Out of Afghanistan,* p. 153.
13. Harrison, 'Realpolitik Vindicated', ibid., p. 248.
14. Ibid., p. 251.
15. Ibid., p. 258.
16. Cordovez, 'The Final Hurdles: "Linkage" and the Time Frame', in *Out of Afghanistan*, p. 326.
17. Harrison, 'Realpolitik Vindicated', ibid., p. 266.
18. Edward Jay Epstein, 'How General Zia Went Down,' *Vanity Fair*, July 1989, cited in Sherbaz Khan Mazari, *Journey to Disillusionment*, (Karachi: Oxford University Press, 1999), pp. 589–95.
19. Harrison, 'How the Soviet Union Stumbled into Afghanistan', in *Out of Afghanistan*, p. 33.
20. Cordovez, 'The Long Winter', in *Out of Afghanistan*, p. 168.
21. Cordovez, 'The Slow Thaw', ibid., p. 232.
22. Ibid., p. 232.
23. Based on the author's personal knowledge while serving as Ambassador to Saudi Arabia.

8

Pakistan's Multilateral Diplomacy

An important factor in Pakistan's foreign policy formulation has been its unflinching support for international law and the principles and purposes of the UN as spelled out in its charter. Pakistan has also been an enthusiastic supporter of the UN system and the main international organizations. Pakistan has always held that disputes should be resolved through recourse to the internationally accepted mediatory procedures including good offices, arbitration, and adjudication.

The founder of Pakistan, Quaid-i-Azam Mohammad Ali Jinnah had stated in February 1948:

> Our foreign policy is one of friendliness and goodwill towards all the nations of the world. We do not cherish aggressive designs against any country or nation. We believe in the principle of honesty and fair play in national and international dealings and are prepared to make our utmost contribution to the promotion of peace and prosperity among the nations of the world. Pakistan will never be found lacking in extending its material and moral support to the oppressed and the suppressed peoples of the world and in upholding the principles of the United Nations' Charter.[1]

In addition to ideological considerations, Pakistan's attitude towards multilateral diplomacy has stemmed from its security anxieties, particularly with India, and the expectation that the UN and the world bodies in general would insist on the implementation of the principle of self-determination for the people of Jammu and Kashmir. In fact, Pakistan's endeavour has been to bring the weight of international opinion behind it in its disputes with India.

In the international arena Pakistan has, in general, played a high-profile role in the last fifty years of its independence. Indeed, a certain amount of over-ambitiousness—the quest for grandeur—has characterized Pakistan's diplomacy over the years. It has always been one of the more active countries on the world stage. In part, this has merely been an extension of the old rivalry with India into the international arena. Pakistan has always been keen to mobilize international support against India on the Kashmir dispute as well as on several other issues including those related to the 1965 and 1971 wars. In part, this high-profile role has been reflective of the Pakistani character.

The support secured by Pakistan in most international forums, apart from the OIC and ECO, has been rather unsatisfactory. The NAM and the Commonwealth have rarely adopted any position or resolution favouring the Pakistani point of view against India. In fact, bilateral problems are not supposed to be raised in some of these forums.

As for the UN, Pakistan's efforts to secure support on Kashmir have followed the pattern of the law of diminishing returns. The resolutions on Kashmir passed by the UN in the early phase (1948–57) calling for an impartial plebiscite, have never been reaffirmed in any subsequent resolution. It is highly unlikely that Pakistan can secure today any resolution at the UN on Kashmir similar to the earlier UN resolutions. In legal terms, the old UN resolutions remain valid but with the passing of time, these resolutions seem rather antiquated and are in effect ignored. It is notable that Pakistan failed in its efforts in 1994 and 1995 to get any kind of fresh endorsement by a UN body of the Kashmiris' right of self-determination or even the mere condemnation of human rights' violations in Kashmir by Indian forces. Such is the apathy—or reluctance to take sides—of the majority of UN members on the Kashmir issue.

It is not surprising that at the UN as well as in other forums, the India–Pakistan disputes have often produced bitter debates between Pakistani and Indian delegates. Sometimes the work of conferences has been held up while Indian and Pakistan delegations have gone hammer and tongs against each other.

Consequently, it is becoming evident that a certain amount of fatigue has developed in many countries with respect to the dispute between India and Pakistan. In fact, the majority of countries have, with the passing of time, tended to adopt a neutral position on India–Pakistan issues.

This kind of international fatigue has worked to Pakistan's disadvantage since it suits India that the Kashmir issue is not debated in international forums. In the case of many countries India's larger size, its greater attraction for trade and investment purposes, as also its military prowess have tilted the balance in its favour, even though, in principle, these countries might, at least, disapprove of India's suppression of the Kashmiri people and its disregard for the UN resolutions on Kashmir.

These are the harsh realities of international diplomacy where a country's self-interest comes above everything else. Pakistani public opinion has found it difficult to understand this reality and there is always a tendency to look for scapegoats and, in particular, Pakistani diplomats have often been accused of failing in their jobs. In recent years, parliamentarians and politicians have been sent on foreign junkets to lobby 'more effectively' for the Kashmir cause. They have singularly failed in these endeavours and have even drawn ridicule for being novices in the field of diplomacy. The failure of the parliamentarians and non-diplomats to change the international realities became manifest when the ill-considered bid of the Benazir government in 1994 and 1995 to revive the Kashmir issue in UN forums produced discouraging and even counter-productive results.

The Organization of Islamic Conference (OIC) has all along extended strong support to Pakistan on Kashmir and other India–Pakistan issues. This has been a source of strength for Pakistan. The OIC meets annually at the level of foreign ministers and, since 1981, it has held Summits every three years. It has a large membership, constituting over one-fourth of the UN member states, and includes several oil-rich countries in its ranks. This is the OIC's major strength. However, the OIC has shown a propensity to adopt resolutions much too liberally. Time has shown that a member country can get practically any resolution adopted by the OIC, provided it is not against another OIC member state. This has tended to deflate the importance of OIC resolutions since member countries have often adopted different stances at the UN or other forums which are diametrically opposed to the position contained in the resolution adopted by them at the OIC meeting. This has reflected a certain non-serious attitude towards the OIC by its members, treating it more as a kind of a debating society of Muslim brothers.

The resolutions on Kashmir adopted by the OIC have had less significance than what has been claimed by the various ruling governments in Pakistan, some of whom have tended to use the OIC as a propaganda platform, mainly to score points at home against their domestic political opponents. They have tried to convince Pakistani public opinion that all is well with Pakistan's policies in terms of international support, by citing the given resolution passed by the OIC. But this too has, in many cases, become more of an illusion of widespread support coming from Islamic countries rather than solid reality.

From the outset, Pakistan has been a leading exponent of the Palestinian and Arab cause at the UN and elsewhere. Its first Foreign Minister Sir Zafrulla Khan played a notable role in the advocacy of the cause of liberation of Muslim countries in North Africa. His eloquent articulation of the Palestinian case won for Pakistan, and for him personally, the abiding gratitude of the Arab world. After the Arab defeat in the 1967 War, Pakistan was one of the authors of Resolution 242 which later became the basis for peace talks in the Middle East. Pakistan was also mainly responsible for the Security Council resolutions on the status of Jerusalem or Al-Quds, which have pitted the international community against Israel's expansionist designs over the third holiest city for the Muslims.

Pakistan's membership of the US-sponsored military pacts prevented it from becoming a member of the Non-Aligned Movement (NAM) till 1979. The seeds of non-alignment were actually laid in the Bandung Conference in 1954 in which Pakistan played an active role. At about this time, the rise of military pacts around the world overtook events. Pakistan decided to join the Baghdad Pact (later CENTO) as well as SEATO, not so much out of concern against any imminent communist aggression but rather to strengthen itself militarily in case of Indian aggression. Consequently, countries like Egypt and Syria, which had opposed the military pacts, gravitated towards India and the Soviet bloc.

NAM, in an institutional form, was set up in 1961 by India, Egypt, and Yugoslavia. In the period of the Cold War between the West and the Soviet communist bloc, many countries in the Third World sought to join NAM as a third option. However, under the influence of Jawaharlal Nehru, Gamal Abdel Nasser, Kwame Nkrumah, and Sukarno, NAM did at times adopt positions which were overly critical of the West. The main reason was that many of the Third World countries were struggling against colonialism and racialism where the West was more often the culprit. This attitude was obviously to the liking of Moscow and worked to its strategic advantage. The fact that the East European countries were like satellites of the Soviet Union hardly drew any comment from the NAM. The concept of neutrality or non-alignment was initially opposed by the US, which saw the Soviet bloc as an evil force seeking to bring the whole world under its subjugation. With the passage of time, however, the US moved away from the policies associated with John Foster Dulles and his 'pactomania' during the 1950s. In fact, NAM had a membership of over one hundred states including big countries like India, and the US could not afford to ignore it or oppose it. With the election of President John F. Kennedy, non-alignment became 'respectable' in the US, which decided to adopt a more even-handed attitude towards NAM.

Meanwhile, Pakistan's membership of the military pacts kept it out of NAM and thus its case in this large international body went unrepresented. It seemed rather unfair that while Pakistan was excluded because of its membership of two nearly moribund military pacts, countries like North Korea, Cuba, Ethiopia, and South Yemen were members of NAM despite having active military alliances with the Soviet Union. India itself signed a

Treaty of Friendship and Cooperation with the Soviet Union in 1971, under which massive Soviet military aid was flown to India which helped it to win the 1971 War against Pakistan.

Pakistan–American relations had been under considerable strain from 1962 onwards, unlike the special relationship existing between New Delhi and Moscow. In the mid-1960s, Pakistan had achieved a kind of parity in its relations with the US, the Soviet Union, and China which made it a more genuine non-aligned country than India. In fact, the record shows that on various issues, Pakistan had supported the US on fewer occasions than India did. Yet, Pakistan was dubbed an aligned country and kept out of NAM until 1979, whereas India has all along been a leading spirit in this body.

In the early 1970s, Pakistan quit SEATO and in 1979 CENTO was dismantled. It was only after this that Pakistan was able to join NAM at the Havana Summit. President Fidel Castro, the host of the NAM Summit, adopted a helpful attitude and the Indian government headed by Prime Minister Morarji Desai decided not to create any hurdles in the way of Pakistan's entry into NAM. (The contrasting attitude of Prime Minister Indira Gandhi, who succeeded Desai, was apparent from her vigorous opposition to Pakistan's re-entry in the Commonwealth soon thereafter.) At any rate, circumstances led to President Ziaul Haq taking Pakistan in the NAM, thereby filling the gap in Pakistan's international profile. Pakistan's exclusion from NAM, which seemed a stigma on Pakistan's foreign policy, had long bothered many Pakistanis, particularly the leftist circles. Moreover, Pakistan's absence from NAM had also left the field open for Indian manipulations in a large international body.

In terms of tangible results, Pakistan's membership of NAM has hardly produced anything worthwhile. Indeed, NAM has all along been rather tall on rhetoric and short on substance. Nevertheless, it has been outspoken on political issues of the Third World like anti-colonialism and racial discrimination. This did contribute in the eventual elimination of both colonialism and apartheid, at least in a visible form. However, with the collapse of the Soviet bloc in 1991, in some ways the *raison d'être* of NAM has ended. The old logic that NAM countries were neither aligned with the East nor with the West is no longer applicable. Nonetheless, even in a unipolar world, the issues of the Third World remain. NAM has a role to play in the context of such issues as development, favourable trade terms, and debt relief. Furthermore, in a unipolar world where the US is the only remaining superpower, NAM does articulate the concerns of the bulk of humanity living in the developing countries. In given instances, NAM can also play a role in defusing regional tensions, particularly among its own members. Pakistan can benefit from its membership of NAM. Above all, NAM is an important forum and provides an opportunity for Pakistan to project its point of view and make useful contacts. It is even arguable that the opportunity such a large forum provides for bilateral contacts between its members is more productive than any deliberations in the meetings of NAM itself. Of course, the same considerations apply in varying degrees to Pakistan's membership of the Commonwealth and other multilateral bodies.

Another dimension of international diplomacy needs to be taken into consideration. In international conferences, the Pakistani delegates are generally among the more articulate and knowledgeable participants and pursue their objectives very actively. While this can be viewed as a tribute to our diplomats, the tendency to try and outshine others is somewhat reflective of the Pakistani national character as also the country's latent quest for grandeur and the yearning to be centre stage. This gives credibility to the criticism that Pakistan is a relatively small country pretending to act like a big power. It is necessary to remember that a nation's real importance can be gauged from the harsh realities being faced at home and not through scoring personal points in multilateral forums.

Over the years, Pakistan has shown a keenness to secure prestigious posts in international bodies, not only in the quest for prestige and influence, but also to satisfy the career ambitions of individuals. To achieve this, Pakistan has spent a lot of money as well as diplomatic energy. Special envoys have been sent regularly to all corners of the globe to woo for votes. By and large, this has been a sheer wastage of the country's meagre resources, especially because Pakistan's efforts to secure such international posts have been generally futile. The opposition to Pakistan's repeated bids for international posts has generally come from India and Israel, supported by their many friends.

In the past fifty years, international diplomacy has spawned numerous conferences where, literally, thousands of resolutions have been passed. Most of these resolutions have been ineffective and even inconsequential with little or no attention being paid to them by the real policymakers in most countries. This has not prevented the participants of such conferences from spending days and weeks arguing over every word and phrase in these resolutions, in an almost surrealistic exercise. They have rarely been discouraged by the scant attention paid to the resolutions passed by them or the sheer repetitiveness of the exercise. It is arguable that personal vested interests of the individual participants in such conferences have been the main reason for the continuation of such barren exercises. The delegates get to travel abroad to exotic places to attend such conferences and make some money by pocketing travelling allowances etc. There is a certain glamour and prestige involved in being participants of these conferences, often in a blaze of publicity. The participants of such conferences have little desire to downplay the importance of these meetings or to make any realistic appraisal of their intrinsic usefulness or otherwise. So this ritual of international conferences and the resolutions passed by them continues unabated.

Pakistani diplomats have always been amongst the busiest in this exercise of make-believe. Many phantom victories have thus been won (and lost) in the passing of such resolutions by international conferences which have at times become the over-riding pivots of Pakistani diplomacy. In fact, over the years, a UN 'Mafia' has emerged among diplomats in most Foreign Offices, including that of Pakistan, who thrive in these ritualistic games. By and large, this has been nothing more than a case of chasing shadows and feeding illusions. The only problem is that while the affluent countries can probably afford such wasteful activities, a cash-starved Third World country like Pakistan is severely financially burdened.

It can be said that Pakistan's high-profile role in international conferences has not been of much tangible benefit to the country. In fact, on the yardstick of cost-effectiveness, Pakistan's international diplomacy has brought meagre advantages weighed against the diplomatic energy spent and the heavy expenditure incurred in the process of chasing shadows rather than meaningful foreign policy objectives.

NOTE

1. Chaudhri Muhammad Ali, *The Emergence of Pakistan* (New York: Columbia University Press, 1967), p. 378.

9

Pakistan's Relations with the Islamic World

Apart from the perennial preoccupation with India, there have been some other important dimensions in Pakistan's foreign policy. In particular, Pakistan's strong attachment to its Islamic ideology has prompted it to espouse the causes of Muslims all over the world. Indeed, the 1973 Constitution imposes an obligation on the Pakistan government to develop closer relations with other Islamic countries.

Pakistan's founding party, the Muslim League, had supported the Palestinian cause even before Pakistan came into being. This was reflective of the strong sentiments of the Muslims of the subcontinent, even during the period of British colonial rule, in support of all Islamic causes, whether in Turkey in the First World War or Libya when Italy occupied it in 1911. The issue of retaining the Caliphate in Turkey, following the First World War, gave rise to a serious political campaign by Muslims in British India, known as the Khilafat Movement. Moreover, the poet-philosopher Iqbal has been a great influence on the Pakistani people in their Pan-Islamic yearnings.

After Pakistan became independent in 1947, it started to extend enthusiastic support to Muslim causes all over the world. Pakistan helped in the liberation struggle of several Muslim countries in Africa, namely, Tunisia, Morocco, Algeria, Libya, Sudan, Somalia, and Eritrea. Similarly, Pakistan strongly supported the liberation struggle of Indonesia in 1948.[1] In later years, Pakistan was sympathetic to the aspirations of Muslims in Southern Philippines. After the Soviet military incursion in Afghanistan in 1979, support for the Afghan resistance, of course, became the centrepiece of Pakistan's diplomacy. More recently, the cause of the Bosnian Muslims has received strong support from Pakistan. Sympathy for the cause of the Muslims in Chechnya and Kosovo has also been evident.

The Palestine issue gripped Pakistan's attention from the outset. Jerusalem's status as the third most holy city for Muslims has deeply influenced Pakistan's attitude. In the UN forum, Pakistan's first Foreign Minister, Sir Zafrulla Khan, became the leading proponent of the Palestinian cause after the Arab–Israel dispute erupted in 1948. He was to be elected as the president of the UN General Assembly in 1964, the only time that Pakistan has held such a high elective office, and later on as a judge of the International Court of Justice (aka World Court), mainly due to Arab gratitude for his role in the Palestinian cause.

Pakistan has remained unwavering in its support for the Palestinian and Arab cause. In the process, the Arabs have been gratified but Israel and the powerful Zionist lobby, particularly in the US, have been deeply antagonized. This has hurt Pakistan in both tangible as well as intangible ways. For instance, under the Zionist influence, the Western media, which dominates the world news coverage, has in general negatively projected Pakistan. This proved particularly damaging for Pakistan during the East Pakistan crisis of 1970–1971. Even in general terms it has denigrated Pakistan's image in the world.

Pakistan's friendship for the Arabs pre-dates the discovery of oil in most of the Arab countries, and certainly pre-dates the oil boom. The motive for this friendship was mainly ideological. Pakistan's friendship with the Arabs has also brought tangible benefits in the economic field and in terms of diplomatic and material support, consisting of economic aid, and manpower. Around two million Pakistanis are at present gainfully employed in the Arab countries whose home remittances are an important factor for the country's economy. On the diplomatic front, most of the Arab countries, with a few exceptions, have tended to support Pakistan in its problems with India, particularly on the Kashmir issue, in the two wars with India, and during the Soviet occupation of Afghanistan. In fact, Pakistan has all along drawn strong support from the Arab countries in a number of fields, including joint economic ventures and investment, which has helped the country significantly.

Apart from the Arab cause, Pakistan took the leading role in international forums to mobilize support for the Afghan cause after the Soviet military intervention in Afghanistan. Pakistan was in fact the main channel, despite its routine denials, in extending military support to the Afghan guerrillas—the Mujahideen. In international forums, Pakistan's efforts were successful and the Soviet Union was largely isolated on this issue. Pakistan also encouraged the UN to play a mediatory role in the Afghan crisis from the beginning. The pressure of international public opinion, including boycott of the Moscow Olympics, contributed along with other factors, to the Soviet decision to pull out of Afghanistan. The Geneva Accords on Afghanistan, negotiated under UN auspices over a period of seven years, were eventually signed by Pakistan and the Afghan regime in 1988, bringing about the withdrawal of Soviet forces from Afghanistan. This was considered as one of the more notable achievements of the UN and gave the world body a high profile in international diplomacy. The Geneva Accords were, moreover, a high moment for Pakistani diplomacy and allowed Pakistan to occupy the world's centre stage.

Turkey

Pakistan has always had a very warm and close relationship with Turkey. In the 1950s, both became members of the Baghdad Pact, later CENTO. They have had an active bilateral military collaboration from earlier years. Both also took active steps to foster economic and other kinds of collaboration on a regional basis under the aegis of the RCD, later re-named as the ECO.

The Turkish people have retained grateful memories of the support extended to them, in the beginning of the twentieth century, by the Muslims of British India. This contrasted with what the Turks regarded as betrayal by the Arabs during the First World War. Turkey was thus keen to establish a close relationship with another large non-Arab Muslim country like Pakistan following its independence in 1947. This fitted in well with Pakistan's search for friends and allies in the Islamic world. The two countries have tended to support each other on most issues of vital interest. In the more recent past, Pakistan was probably the only country in the world to support Turkey on its military intervention in northern Cyprus. Pakistan for its part has received steadfast Turkish support on the Kashmir issue and some degree of military assistance during the two wars with India. There is, of course, tremendous goodwill between the two peoples.

Pakistan–Turkey relations, nevertheless, suffer from some limitations. Turkey regards itself more as a European rather than an Islamic country. Defying the rest of the Islamic world, it has maintained friendly and even close relations with Israel, right from the beginning, and these relations have acquired a military dimension in the more recent past. Clearly, this has been something of an anathema for the other Muslim countries, including Pakistan. Turkey joined the OIC somewhat hesitantly, regarding its membership as a departure from its secular polity. However, the realization that absence from an important forum would be even more disadvantageous, made Turkey join this Islamic body. Besides, it could not ignore that in case of a security crisis for Turkey, the Islamic world would always be a natural supporter of Turkey.

For internal reasons Turkey plays down the role of Islam in its polity. In fact, it has sought to come down hard on all manifestations of Islamic orthodoxy. At times it appears that devotion to Islam is even considered as a security threat by the ruling elite in Turkey, particularly by the armed forces which have set themselves up as the custodians of the tradition of secularism of the founder of modern Turkey, Kemal Ataturk. The Europeanization of Turkish society has also put a distance between the two nations since most Pakistanis observe a more orthodox Islamic course. Similarly, in foreign policy, Turkey has been far more pro-West than Pakistan.

There is an odd dimension, therefore, to the bilateral relations between Pakistan and Turkey. In its expressions of friendship with Turkey, Pakistan is always vociferous in its emphasis on the Islamic bonds between them. On the other hand, Turkey tends to downplay this factor and instead emphasizes more the various bilateral linkages.

In the economic field, despite all the exhortations by the leadership in Pakistan and Turkey, the two countries have hardly ever been able to forge any significant cooperation. Evidently, the economies of the two countries are hardly complementary and they are even competitors producing the same kind of goods. Thus, there is more sentiment than solid substance in the bilateral relationship.

More recently in Central Asia, following the collapse of the Soviet Union, there seems to be some competition between Pakistan and Turkey for influence in the six independent Islamic states. Because of their common ethnic origins, the countries of Central Asia are regarded by Turkey as a kind of exclusive preserve. On the other hand, Pakistan hopes to spread its influence in these countries, which constitute Pakistan's hinterland.

In the last few years, Turkey has been alarmed by the rise of the Taliban to power in Afghanistan. Their revolutionary Islamic 'fundamentalism' is a cause of anxiety for the secular regime in Turkey, which faces a grave internal challenge from its own Islamic 'fundamentalists'. Turkey is thus impassive to such influences anywhere in the Islamic world. The Central Asian countries, with an ethnically Turkish background see the Taliban in next-door Afghanistan as a threat to the stability of their own regimes. Turkey has thus tended to make a common cause with the Central Asian countries against the Taliban regime in Afghanistan. This makes for a contrasting attitude with Pakistan, which is perceived as a supporter of the Taliban regime. Moreover, the increasing emphasis on Islamization in Pakistan and the adoption of the Shari'ah as the supreme law of the land does not strike a sympathetic chord in secular Turkey. Thus, the two countries are moving away from their earlier enthusiastic collaboration.

Saudi Arabia

Saudi Arabia has probably been the country closest to Pakistan's heart. As the birthplace of Islam and as the custodian of the two holiest cities of Islam, it has tremendous emotional and religious pull for the Pakistani Muslims who are second to none in their passionate attachment to Islam. In ideological terms also, there is great affinity between the two countries. Both have been generally moderate, even conservative in their foreign policy, with a great deal of emphasis on Islamic causes. Both have been wary of Arab radicals, particularly their emphasis on secularism and socialism, as also, in the case of Saudi Arabia, the radicals' calls for republicanism. By and large, Pakistan and Saudi Arabia have had a pro-West orientation, despite periodic differences with the US, particularly for its support for Israel. The Saudis were enthusiastic about the creation of Pakistan in 1947 as a new Islamic state. Muslim pilgrims from India had been coming to Arabia for centuries and were always welcomed for their piety and wealth, when the Arabian Peninsula was cash-starved. Thus, there had been a traditional enthusiasm for the Muslims of the Indian subcontinent. This background gave Pakistan a flying start with Saudi Arabia. In the late 1940s, oil wealth was beginning to flow into Saudi Arabia but the country was very backward. The first Pakistanis to arrive in Saudi Arabia were doctors and engineers. Thereafter, Pakistani collaboration started in practically every field. This expertise has been a key factor in Saudi Arabia's rapid growth.

There have been only two brief periods of estrangement between the two countries. In the mid-1950s, Pakistan's joining of the Baghdad Pact which also included Iraq, with which the Saudis had an old dynastic rivalry, led to a period of strain between Pakistan and Saudi Arabia. In this period, an exchange of visits between King Saud of Saudi Arabia and Indian Prime Minister Nehru also caused heart burning in Pakistan.[2] King Saud was also at times courting Arab radicals, many of whom had turned against Pakistan due to its membership of the Baghdad Pact as also its perceived pro-West role during the 1956 Suez crisis. However, with the exit of King Saud, relations with Pakistan became very friendly under King Faisal.

The second time when Pakistan–Saudi relations came under a cloud was when Z.A. Bhutto came to power in Pakistan in December 1971. The Saudis were apprehensive of the sympathy shown by Bhutto and his party men for the Palestinians and other Arab radicals who were, at that time, strongly critical of the conservative Arab regimes like that of Saudi Arabia. Even from an earlier date, King Faisal was unhappy with the movement led by Bhutto to topple President Ayub Khan, for whom the King had high regard. Bhutto's proposal to appoint an aide, who was believed to be from the heretical Ahmadi sect, as the Pakistan ambassador to Saudi Arabia, was rejected by the Saudis, creating a certain strain in bilateral relations. However, the strong support extended by Pakistan to the Arabs in the 1973 War against Israel and the oil boycott sponsored by King Faisal, followed thereafter by the successful holding of the Islamic Summit in Pakistan in 1974, restored the warmth in Pakistan–Saudi relations.

For the greater part in the history of their bilateral relations, Pakistan and Saudi Arabia have stood by each other on most political issues. Pakistan's unflinching support for the Palestinian and Arab cause against Israel has won it the lasting appreciation of Saudi Arabia and other Arab countries. Beginning from the 1960s, Pakistan provided security support to Saudi Arabia to strengthen its defence against Yemen and Israel. In the 1980s, following the incident of the seizure of the Holy Ka'aba by some Islamic militants, Pakistan's involvement in providing security support to Saudi Arabia developed on a scale unmatched by any other country. Thousands of Pakistani military personnel served in Saudi Arabia to strengthen the country's internal security. This military presence has remained an important area of collaboration between the two countries.

Saudi Arabia was very forthcoming in extending support to Pakistan during its wars against India. It has all along strongly supported Pakistan on the Kashmir dispute. During the Soviet occupation of Afghanistan, Saudi Arabia joined the US in extending strong military and other support to Pakistan. In the Saudi conception, the security of Pakistan was the motivating factor in determining their opposition to the Soviet military presence in Afghanistan.

Saudi Arabia has been a principal aid donor to Pakistan over the years. During the period of the oil boom (1974–84), Saudi assistance to Pakistan probably surpassed that of any other country. Since then, the Saudi aid has largely dried up, not only for Pakistan but also for other countries. This was primarily due to the heavy financial burden borne by Saudi Arabia during the Iran–Iraq War, followed by the Gulf War against Iraq, which strained the Saudi economy. Its immense foreign exchange reserves more or less dissipated. Also, over the years, the Saudis were besieged by so many countries looking for aid that a point of exhaustion had been reached by the early 1980s. Under these circumstances, it would be difficult for Pakistan to secure any significant aid from Saudi Arabia unless there is a new oil boom.

At the time of Pakistan's independence, Saudi Arabia was a very undeveloped country. Though oil exports from Saudi Arabia had started after the Second World War, affluence came only after the oil price went up in the early 1970s. In the early years, Pakistan even extended some aid to Saudi Arabia. Pakistan also came forward to provide expertise in diverse fields. This included military training of Saudis on a large scale. Saudi naval officers were nearly all trained in Pakistan until a few years ago. Pakistanis have, of course, worked in nearly all fields in Saudi Arabia right from the beginning. From the personal staff of the royal family to experts and workers in agriculture, banking, commerce, education, engineering, industry, and medicine, Pakistanis are to be found everywhere in Saudi Arabia. They are above all trusted by the Saudis and they get adjusted to Saudi cultural conditions more readily than many other nationalities. At present, over one million Pakistanis are working in Saudi Arabia whose home remittances are greater than that of Pakistani expatriates living all over the world.

Until Pakistan's defeat in the 1971 War and the oil boom which made Saudi Arabia one of the richest countries in the world, Pakistan was viewed as a kind of an elder brother by the Saudi government and people. That basic friendship remains but the relationship has since undergone a perceptible change in that Saudi Arabia has been, for many years, the senior partner. It is Pakistan, which is constantly wooing the Saudis for political or other support. The Saudi leaders hardly ever visit Pakistan whereas the Pakistani leaders keep flocking to Saudi Arabia most of the time. However, the Saudis realize Pakistan's continued importance in the region and the Islamic world. Pakistan's nuclear capability is an additional reason. More importantly, the Saudis regard Pakistan as a trustworthy friend who will come to Saudi Arabia's assistance whenever the occasion arises. This includes any requirement for strengthening the internal security of the Saudi regime.

The threat perception of the Saudis has changed in the last two decades. In the past, Israel was seen as the main threat. Pakistan could be counted upon to provide whatever assistance it could to defend Saudi Arabia against the Israeli threat, even though, in strategic terms, it was the US, due to its strong involvement with the production and export of oil from Saudi Arabia, which was expected to hold back Israel from committing any aggression against Saudi Arabia. During the 1950s and 1960s, the Saudis also felt threatened by radical Arab nations including Egypt, Syria, and even Yemen. Pakistan was a useful military partner of the Saudis in the event of any direct attack on Saudi Arabia.

However, with the coming of the Islamic Revolution in Iran, the Saudi threat perception became more preoccupied with Iran. It was this fear that propelled the Saudis to support Iraq against Iran in the eight-year war, which finally ended in 1988. This help was given to Iraq in spite of the fact that its own radicalism was feared by the Saudis and the other Gulf regimes alike.

The traditional rivalry between the Arabs and the Persians was clearly also a factor. Iraq was able to pressurize and extract massive support from its oil-rich conservative neighbours.

As it turned out, not content with the destruction wrought by the war against Iran, Saddam Hussein next turned against his benefactor, Kuwait, and occupied it in a sudden attack in August 1990. Iraq had an old territorial claim against Kuwait and the war with Iran had made it bankrupt. Saddam decided to attack the small and militarily hapless Kuwait. This led to the largest ever collection on Saudi soil of troops from several nations, led by the US, which defeated Iraq in a brief but deadly battle early in 1991. Pakistan also sent troops to join the alliance against Iraq, but Pakistani public opinion was clearly in favour of Saddam Hussein who was mistakenly considered another Sultan Salahuddin Ayubi fighting against the new Christian Crusaders. The comparison was, of course, ridiculous but was not uncharacteristic of the kind of illusions from which public opinion in Pakistan has suffered from time to time. Saddam Hussein had rarely shown any Islamic sentiments and, in fact, had ruthlessly crushed the Islamic opposition at home. As a committed Ba'athist, he was wedded to secularism and socialism. He had been close to the Soviet bloc and had adopted an unfriendly attitude towards Pakistan in the 1971 War against India. He had supported the Soviet-backed communist regime in Afghanistan. It was thus ludicrous to compare him with Salahuddin. The public sympathy for Saddam confused and irritated the Saudis and undid much of the goodwill generated by the sending of the Pakistani troops. Certain pronouncements that the Pakistani troops had been sent to defend the holy places in Saudi Arabia, rather than to fight Iraq to liberate Kuwait, also appeared like a dichotomy in the Pakistani stance. The Pakistani army chief, General Mirza Aslam Beg also caused annoyance in Saudi Arabia by his pro-Iraq comments.

The Gulf War revealed the declining military value of Pakistan for the Saudis. Their threat perception now involves possible wars against Iran or Iraq. Both are Muslim countries and Iran has been a close friend of Pakistan. In particular, Pakistani public opinion would simply not accept that Pakistani soldiers be involved in any large-scale fighting along with the Saudis against either Iran or Iraq. Fighting Iran would go against Pakistan's strategic interests since Iran has always been seen as providing strategic depth to Pakistan in the case of a war against India. The availability of Pakistan to come to Saudi Arabia's help in case of a war with Iran, in particular, is highly improbable. This obviously lessens Pakistan's importance for Saudi Arabia. As a consequence, since the end of the Gulf War, American influence has grown further in Saudi Arabia. It is obvious that it is the US alone that has the political will and the military muscle to assist Saudi Arabia in case of aggression from either Iraq or Iran. The US has long had an adversarial relationship with both of these countries.

Iran

Iran is another country in the Islamic world with which Pakistan has always had very strong ties. It is not only a neighbour but also a country with which Pakistan has had age-old relations based on cultural, ethnic, and spiritual links. Iranian influence is visible in Pakistan's languages and culture. In particular, Urdu, the national language of Pakistan, has been heavily influenced by the Persian language and its poetic traditions. There is also tremendous goodwill for Iran among the Pakistani people. A close relationship with Iran has been considered by defence experts as a strategic necessity for Pakistan, in particular because of Pakistan's perennial confrontation with India. Iran can provide Pakistan, which is a bit of a rectangular country in its shape, having a relatively small breadth, a certain degree of strategic depth. An unfriendly Iran could be quite damaging for Pakistan's security and the worst nightmare would be some kind of a pincer movement by India acting in consort with Iran. It is this background which has prompted Pakistan, ever since its independence, to establish very close cooperation with Iran in diverse fields, including common membership of military pacts.

Iran also sought to maintain a strong relationship with Pakistan. At the end of the Second World War, Iran was a vulnerable country. The Soviet Union, which had occupied northern Iran during the War, finally withdrew only after considerable pressure by the West. The Soviet expansionist designs in Iran were proved by the Soviet–German Pact of 1940. Iran had oil wealth of its own and was also the gateway to the Gulf. Left on its own, it was vulnerable to the Soviet Union as well as the threat from its local Soviet-inspired communists. Iran had, therefore, to look for an equalizer from the West. However, the oil interests of the West also made Iran vulnerable to manipulations by the Western countries in its internal and external policies. The West even intervened in Iran in the 1950s to overthrow the nationalistic government of Prime Minister Mohammad Mosaddegh.

Iran, therefore, welcomed in its vicinity the emergence of a friend like Pakistan as a counter-balance against these security threats. Till 1971, Pakistan was also viewed as militarily stronger than Iran and relatively more developed than Iran in the technical and industrial fields. Pakistan's geo-strategic importance was also understood by Iran. In view of the traditional rivalry between Iran and the Arab countries, Iran took satisfaction from the presence of Pakistan as another non-Arab Muslim country in the region. In consequence, the fifties and sixties saw a kind of special relationship between Iran and Pakistan, marked by close co-ordination between the two countries in the political, military, and other fields. In particular, Iran extended valuable military assistance to Pakistan in the two wars against India.

With the defeat of Pakistan in the 1971 War, the emergence of Bangladesh and the growth of centrifugal tendencies in Pakistan, the Iranian posture, under its increasingly imperious ruler, the Shah—now styled as the Shahenshah—underwent a change. The growing affluence of Iran in the seventies, as a result of the oil boom, added to his arrogance. In this period, Iran also extended some financial assistance to Pakistan. This, if anything, added to the Shah's condescending attitude towards Pakistan. He openly hinted that in the case of a 'further disintegration' of Pakistan, Iran might take over Pakistan's Balochistan province located on Iran's eastern border. The Shah started to act as the senior partner in the relationship. For instance, he declined to participate in the Islamic Summit held in Pakistan in 1974 because it was also being attended by the Libyan leader Colonel Muammar Gaddafi, whom he despised. The Shah was, in fact, furious when Gaddafi was given a big welcome in Pakistan. He commented contemptuously that 'supplicants' before Gaddafi (meaning Pakistan) did not rank high in his esteem. It took a great deal of effort from Pakistan before the Shah could be mollified.

As the Shah's relations with the Gulf Arab countries deteriorated in the early 1970s, following Iran's seizure of three islands belonging to the UAE, Pakistan's friendly ties with these countries came under Iranian suspicions. The Arab insistence on calling the Persian Gulf as the 'Arab' Gulf angered the Shah. It was somewhat characteristic of the bilateral relationship with Pakistan in this period that the Iranian ambassador in Islamabad, instead of working on the positive elements in the bilateral relationship, was spending his time looking at all kinds of official and unofficial documents in Pakistan to find out if any nomenclature other than the Persian Gulf had been used. Indeed, diplomatic protests were lodged with Pakistan whenever the correct name was not used, reflecting poorly on the state of bilateral relations in which even such a trivial 'offence' by Pakistan drew Iranian ire. Moreover, the absurdity of this exercise was clearly not understood by the Iranians, nor by the Arabs for that matter, either at that time or even now. The fact of the matter is that a geographical name confers no political rights, otherwise the Arabian Sea would belong to Saudi Arabia, the English Channel would belong to England, and the Indian Ocean would belong to India!

The fall of the Shah of Iran in January 1979 and the coming of the Islamic Revolution under Ayatollah Khomeini's leadership brought about a transformation in Iran's external as well as internal policies. In view of the new regime's ideological commitment to Islam, it would have been logical to expect a strengthening of relations with Pakistan which was so heavily committed to Islamic solidarity. Moreover, it was also the first country to recognize the revolutionary Iranian government which renamed the country as the Islamic Republic of Iran. Whereas the Shah was pro-West and highly Europeanized, the new Iranian regime, like Pakistan, swore by Islam. Moreover, the Islamic revolutionaries in Iran were influenced, among others, by the Pakistani poet-philosopher Iqbal who had written some of the most stirring poetry, in the early twentieth century, both in Urdu and in Persian, on Islamic renaissance and the concept of Islamic brotherhood. All of this pointed towards a common ideological affinity with Pakistan. Similarly, the communist takeover in neighbouring Afghanistan in 1978 was another area of common concern for Pakistan as well as Iran, as it represented both an ideological and a strategic threat to the two countries.

In spite of these common factors, the revolutionary regime in Tehran showed a considerably lukewarm attitude towards Pakistan. Probably the only point on which Pakistan could really take satisfaction was that revolutionary Iran did reaffirm, like the Shah's government, support for Pakistan on the Kashmir issue. In fact, the new regime's professed attachment to Islamic causes probably left no other option. By and large Iran did not fully reciprocate Pakistan's many gestures of friendship in as positive terms as was warranted. Its news media was often critical of Pakistan.

It seemed, at first, that Pakistan's old links with the Shah had aroused the suspicions of the new regime, which evidently did not differentiate that Pakistan's friendship was with Iran as a country and not with the Shah as an individual. The Iranian revolutionaries, who regarded the US as the 'great Satan,' were also inclined to view Pakistan as a pro-American country which, along with the ousted Shah's government, had been members of Western military pacts. In truth, Pakistan could not be equated with the Shah. The latter had remained strongly pro-West till the end but Pakistan's honeymoon with the US had ended more than a decade earlier. In holding Pakistan to be pro-US, the Islamic revolutionaries also seemed to have ignored the fact that around 1979 Pakistan was actually facing US sanctions, on account of the latter's suspicions that Pakistan was seeking to develop a nuclear capability.

To add to Pakistan's discomfiture under the new revolutionary regime, Iran, which is a Shia Muslim stronghold, showed a disposition to take an active interest on behalf of Pakistan's minority Shia population. This served to accentuate communal differences inside Pakistan between the majority Sunnis and the Shia community. Some observers believe that in order to counter the Iranian interest in the Pakistani Shias, Saudi Arabia and other Gulf countries started to extend support to Pakistani Sunni militants thereby playing a part in the rise of Pakistan's ominous sectarian problem and the resultant internal destabilisation, notably since the early 1980s. Moreover, this has given India the opportunity to fish in troubled waters in Pakistan, for strategic reasons of its own.

Pakistan, however, remained steadfast in its efforts to woo the Iranian regime. In order to remove the misgivings of the new Iranian government about any military association with the US, Pakistan agreed to disband the already moribund military pact CENTO in 1979. During the Iran–Iraq War, in the 1980s, Pakistan secretly tilted towards Iran, while maintaining an overtly neutral attitude. Not surprisingly, Pakistan's help to Iran could not remain unknown for a long period of time. This brought bitter complaints from the Gulf Arab states with which Pakistan had always maintained very close relations and where hundreds of thousands of Pakistanis were gainfully employed. Yet Pakistan took this risk in its keenness to secure greater Iranian friendship.

Pakistan also joined the OIC's mediation efforts to end the fratricide between Iran and Iraq. This helped Iran at the time when Iraq was pushing deep into Iranian territory. As the tide of the battle turned in Iran's favour around 1983, Pakistan tried its best to persuade Iran to accept a deal which would have vindicated its stance on the disputed Shatt-al-Arab and, in addition, would have secured massive reparations from Iraq and its Arab supporters. This was not agreed to by Iran, which held that there could be no peace with the 'devil' Saddam Hussein. Iran did not merely reject this deal but seemed to harbour suspicions that Pakistan was trying to rescue the Iraqi regime. Belatedly, after five years of further bloodshed in which thousands of Iranian youth sacrificed their lives unnecessarily, Iran finally agreed to a ceasefire with the same hated Iraqi leader, but on much less advantageous terms.

Throughout this period, Pakistan tried to help Iran break out of its regional and general isolation by using its good offices with Saudi Arabia, USA, and others to improve their relations with Iran. This created difficulties for Pakistan in its own friendly ties with these countries. The leadership in Tehran hardly seemed to worry about its international isolation. Pakistan's 'good Samaritan' motives carried the risk of being misunderstood on both sides.

Driven by its hatred for the US, the Iranian leadership seriously explored the possibility, around 1994, of establishing an anti-US bloc in Asia consisting of Iran, India, and China. The idea got nowhere, as neither India nor China was willing to join an anti-US grouping. Besides, the proposal made little sense since the three countries concerned are so very different in their outlook and systems. India clearly sees no security threat from the US. Neither China nor India has any intention, at least at the present time, to join in any anti-US alliance. However, from Pakistan's point of view, such a proposal coming from Iran was exceedingly disappointing. It showed a total disregard of Pakistan's strategic interests and its threat perception from India as also the sensitivities of Pakistan. Such a proposal also indicated that Islamic ideology is not a determinant in the formulation of Iranian foreign policy, at least in this particular instance.

Iran has often shown little regard for Pakistan's strong attachment to the Kashmir cause. In the OIC forum, Iran often kept aloof from the numerous resolutions and initiatives on the Kashmir issue, sponsored by Pakistan. For instance, despite urgings by the Pakistani delegates, the Iranian representatives in various OIC meetings held at Jeddah, between 1993 and 1997, made it a point not to speak on the Kashmir issue. This attitude was in strong contrast with the position taken by Saudi Arabia and others.

Pakistan's proposal in the OIC to hold a commemorative special Islamic summit in Pakistan in 1997, to mark fifty years of its independence, aroused strong suspicions in Tehran which feared that such a summit would deprive Iran from holding the regular OIC summit in Tehran, which was also scheduled to be held that year. Iran more or less accused Pakistan of trying to sabotage the summit in Tehran. For more than a year, this subject caused strains in Pakistan–Iran relations in spite of Pakistan's protestations that the special summit would be devoted to a single issue and would not be a substitute for the regular summit which had its own long agenda. However, Iran remained suspicious that the special summit was merely a Pakistani ploy, in collaboration with Saudi Arabia with American backing, to deny Iran the opportunity to host the Islamic Summit and thus become the OIC chairperson for three years.

Libya

Libya has also figured prominently in Pakistan's relations with the Islamic world. Pakistan had played an important role in Libya's independence, just as it had done in the case of the other North African countries—Tunisia, Algeria, and Morocco. As a result, Pakistan enjoyed considerable goodwill in Libya from the very beginning. Libya, with a small population of about four million people, only gained international prominence around 1970 when the oil boom made it one of the richest countries in the world. The seizure of power in Libya by young military officers led by Colonel Gaddafi also transformed the country. A firebrand revolutionary, deeply influenced by Egypt's Gamal Abdel Nasser, Gaddafi has remained one of the most vociferous enemies of Israel. Similarly, Arab unity has been his abiding passion and dream. Gaddafi has also been bitterly critical of the US for its support of Israel. Anti-imperialism and anti-Zionism have thus been the main planks of Libya's foreign policy under Gaddafi.

Gaddafi also espoused Islamic causes. For instance, he denounced India for the 1971 War and also extended some military assistance to Pakistan. This had an electrifying effect on Pakistani public opinion. As a result, when Gaddafi visited Pakistan to attend the Islamic Summit in Lahore in 1974, he received a rapturous welcome as a great Islamic hero. During this visit, Libya and Pakistan signed several very ambitious and wide-ranging agreements, including one on nuclear collaboration. However, Pakistan soon found out that Gaddafi's promises of big economic support hardly ever materialized. Contrary to popular perceptions which somehow continue to persist in Pakistan and elsewhere, very little money ever came from Libya to Pakistan, as compared to, say, what Pakistan received from Saudi Arabia or UAE or Iran. Similarly, contrary to impressions in some quarters, there was never any meaningful cooperation between Libya and Pakistan in the nuclear field.

A basic difficulty was that the Libyans were insistent, in general, on locating any joint projects in Libyan territory. This made little economic sense since it was obvious that the manpower and expertise was to be found in Pakistan while the capital was available in Libya. Hence, logically, the location of the projects should have been in Pakistan. Libya's growing notoriety and international isolation, as a state encouraging international terrorism, made Pakistan hesitant to establish close contacts with Libya in the nuclear field which would only have jeopardized Pakistan's more important relations with Iran, Saudi Arabia, and the US. Hence, the various agreements with Libya remained largely on paper only. This was not a unique case. Libya had signed similarly ambitious agreements with several other countries and nothing seems to have come out of them. Impractical schemes have been a trademark of Gaddafi.

In the mid-1970s, Gaddafi was coming increasingly under the influence of the Soviet bloc and was moving closer to socialistic ideas. Practically all business establishments in Libya were nationalized, leading to great shortages of consumer goods in the country. In opposition to both capitalism and communism, Gaddafi espoused his own 'third theory' of political and economic system, which was supposed to be neither like the West nor the East. He developed his own version of the socialist concept of the 'withering away of the state.' In Gaddafi's version, the state would be replaced by the *jamahiriya* or a kind of people's self-rule at the grassroots level. In such a state, in theory, there would be no government, no ministers, no army, no embassies etc. Instead, everything would be decided by the people themselves operating through people's committees. Libya was even declared to have become the first such *jamahiriya* in the world and other countries were expected to follow suit. But, of course, all the state institutions in Libya including the army continued to function, albeit under different names.

In the process of this ideological slant towards socialistic ideas, Gaddafi was in fact moving away from traditional Islam. His 'Green Book' is mainly a hotchpotch of socialism and anti-imperialist ideas and makes practically no mention of Islam. The slogan displayed in some places in Libya that 'the Quran is our Constitution' has been devoid of any meaning. The most determined internal opposition to Gaddafi has come from the Islamic circles who, in turn, have been suppressed by Gaddafi with an iron hand. Abroad, he has been at odds with nearly all Islamic countries, including Saudi Arabia. The impression that Gaddafi is an ardent Muslim spread from such early acts like prohibition, the ban on nightclubs and Gaddafi's publicized leading of Islamic prayers. However, as the saying goes, a man is known by the company he keeps. Until the collapse of the Soviet Communist bloc in 1991, Gaddafi's best friends were the communist countries and he had hardly any friends among governments in the Islamic world. When the Soviet Union sent troops into Afghanistan, Gaddafi felt no concern for the Afghan Muslims. In fact, Libya was one of the few Islamic countries to receive the representatives of the Afghan communist regime. Gaddafi was even bitterly critical of Pakistan's support for the Afghan Mujahideen in collaboration with the US. He once publicly said in 1980 that he did not believe in 'the Islam of Islamabad whose Ka'aba is Washington.'

Gaddafi's friendship with Prime Minister Zulfikar Ali Bhutto has received much publicity. The main reason for this warmth for Bhutto was the big popular reception that Gaddafi received during his visit to Pakistan in 1974. Actually, the Pakistani people had idealized Gaddafi as a great Muslim leader and friend of Pakistan for his role in the 1971 War. This spontaneous reception had even embarrassed Bhutto because the Shah of Iran had already kept away from the Lahore Summit due to Gaddafi's presence and was further peeved by the popularity of Gaddafi in Pakistan. For his part, Gaddafi assumed that it was Bhutto who had specially organized this great welcome. After having signed the various ambitious agreements for collaboration with Libya, Bhutto had second thoughts and he ordered a go-slow on these agreements. This was partially done for fear that too close a friendship with Libya would adversely affect Pakistan's important relations with Iran, Saudi Arabia, and the US. Moreover, Libya's reluctance to part with money for various projects also cooled down the enthusiasm in Pakistan for Gaddafi.

It is true that Bhutto's overthrow was seen as a setback by Gaddafi. However, General Ziaul Haq, who had ousted Bhutto, visited Libya in 1978 and there were also other high-ranking visits exchanged between the two countries. In fact, Gaddafi, who was having problems with several neighbours, was very keen in this period to secure Ziaul Haq's approval to allow Pakistanis to serve in the Libyan armed forces as mercenaries. It was Ziaul Haq's refusal to permit such use of Pakistani manpower that really irked Gaddafi. Moreover, his appeals for clemency for Bhutto were turned down. There is no doubt that Bhutto's execution greatly shocked Gaddafi. The Libyan ambassador in Islamabad was quietly recalled. The collaboration with Pakistan, however, continued and a large number of Pakistani military deputationists remained in Libya. But the bilateral climate had been vitiated by a number of factors mentioned above.

In this situation, Pakistan's abrupt decision, in early 1980, to recall all military deputationists from Libya, ostensibly because their services were needed back home due to the Soviet intervention in Afghanistan, triggered a grave crisis in the bilateral relations. Libya found out that military deputationists were not being withdrawn at that time from Syria and elsewhere. Angered, Gaddafi issued secret orders for the expulsion of some 80,000 Pakistani workers in Libya within a period of three months. Officially, the Libyans denied that any such orders had been issued. Only after considerable persuasion on both sides, the two governments revoked their respective orders. However, Gaddafi's main focus still remained on securing Pakistani mercenaries and his clandestine efforts to do so provoked a fresh crisis in relations with Pakistan in 1981. Having failed in this bid again, Gaddafi tried to make amends with Ziaul Haq. In 1982, he extended an invitation to General Ziaul Haq to visit Libya. Opinion was divided on the Pakistani side on this issue but, finally, this invitation was not accepted.

Islamabad concluded that it made little sense to adopt an unfriendly attitude towards Gaddafi. For one thing, his reputation for harbouring political opponents of various regimes in the world also dictated prudence for Ziaul Haq who had no shortage of opponents. This was illustrated by the case of hijacking of a PIA plane in 1981 by the Al-Zulfikar terrorists, headed by the late Bhutto's son Murtaza, which was heading for Libya but was finally not allowed to land there. With the consent of Ziaul Haq, the political activists released on the demand of the hijackers were given political asylum in Libya. Islamabad thus agreed with the recommendation that the prudent course for Pakistan was to have a balanced relationship with Libya, getting neither too close to it nor too distant from it. This policy has since been maintained and was not materially changed even when Bhutto's daughter Benazir twice became the Prime Minister of Pakistan (1988–90 and 1993–6).

Egypt

Even before Pakistan's independence the Muslim League had established a good equation with Wafd, the main Egyptian political party. Pakistan's strong espousal of the Palestinian and Arab cause endeared it to the Egyptians and other Arabs. However, the early efforts by Pakistan to set up an Islamic bloc were rebuffed by King Farouk who evidently saw this as a move by Pakistan to bid for leadership of the Islamic world.

The radicalization of Arab public opinion, following the Egyptian Revolution in 1953, adversely affected relations with Pakistan because of the latter's close identification at that time with the Western world. Even a traditional friend like Saudi Arabia was critical of Pakistan's joining the Baghdad Pact, which enrolled an Arab country, Iraq, in a Western-sponsored military pact. The strongest criticism of Pakistan came from Egypt, Syria and, later on, from Iraq after the overthrow of its monarchy in 1958. Arising out of their opposition to US support for Israel, these countries also drew closer to the Soviet bloc.

As a philosophy, Pan–Arabism in general excluded the non-Arabs and thus worked to Pakistan's disadvantage. The influence of Nasserism and Ba'athism in some of the Arab countries like Egypt, Syria, Iraq, and Yemen, apart from the Palestinians, also created strains with Pakistan. Their emphasis on Arabism, socialism, and secularism left Pakistan out in the cold. At the same time, their relations with India warmed up. Subsequently, Nasser and Nehru became the founders of the Non-Aligned Movement. In any case, India's large size has always been a strong attraction for at least some of the Arab countries.

Pakistan's diplomatic bungling during the 1956 Suez crisis angered the Egyptians and the radical Arabs. Thus, the gains made by Pakistan's staunch support of the Palestinian cause in the late 1940s were at least partially eroded. In fact, Pakistan–Egypt relations reached their all-time low during the Suez Canal crisis when Egypt accused Pakistan of going back on its promises of support. The irony was that Pakistan had been supportive of Egypt during this crisis. Prime Minister Huseyn Shaheed Suhrawardy even warned the British that Pakistan would withdraw from the Commonwealth if British aggression against Egypt were to continue.[3] Nevertheless, Pakistan showed inconsistencies in its policy towards Egypt during the crisis, arising out of its dilemma which was not to upset relations with the West whose military and economic assistance was needed by Pakistan to strengthen itself against India. On the whole, there had been a failure in communications between Pakistan and Egypt. The latter evidently saw Pakistan only as a Western lackey. An important Muslim country like Egypt's show of preference for India over Pakistan hurt the sensitivities of the Pakistani people. Nasser's reported remark that 'Suez is as dear to Egypt as Kashmir is to India'[4] was particularly resented by Pakistanis. Bitter charges were exchanged between the two countries.

Relations, however, started to improve somewhat after Iraq withdrew from the Baghdad Pact in 1958. When Ayub Khan came to power in Pakistan, Nasser paid a friendly visit to Pakistan in 1960 followed by a return visit to Egypt by the Pakistani President. However, Nasser remained close to Nehru whom he joined in setting up the Non-Aligned Movement in 1961. Thus, during the 1965 War, Egypt seemed relatively more sympathetic to India. A second reason for Nasser's coolness towards Pakistan was that he had a strained relationship with King Faisal of Saudi Arabia who was very friendly towards Pakistan.

Egypt's disastrous performance in the 1967 War with Israel brought a mellowing of Nasser's radicalism. His successor Sadat was basically pro-West and was also more sympathetic to Islamic causes. Moreover, Pakistan's strong support for the Arabs during the Ramadan War of 1973, in which Pakistani pilots on deputation with Syria even shot down Israeli jets, also resulted in a warming of relations with Egypt as well as with Syria. Later on, Sadat strongly supported Pakistan in the struggle against Soviet occupation of Afghanistan. Pakistan won the gratitude of Egypt in 1984 for its efforts to bring back Egypt in the OIC and the Arab League from which it had been expelled after signing the Camp David Accords.

Other Islamic States

The Gulf states have long been a priority area for Pakistan, mainly for economic reasons. They gained independence in 1971, after the British decision to withdraw from the east of Suez. These states were tiny in size and population and were generally quite backward. However, oil was found in the Gulf states and the oil boom, which started from around 1974, made them very rich. Pakistan was able to establish a relationship of trust and close mutual cooperation with the UAE, Kuwait, Qatar, Bahrain, and Oman. In particular, the President of the UAE, Sheikh Zayed bin Sultan Al Nahyan has been one of the best friends of Pakistan. He made Pakistan his winter home where he spent long periods on vacation for bird hunting, particularly the Houbara bustard. During his long stewardship of his country, Pakistan has received very substantial economic aid from the UAE, second only to that of Saudi Arabia. Pakistanis have been prominent as advisers and trainers in various fields of activities in the UAE. Its air force was at one time like an extension of the Pakistan Air Force. Thousands of Pakistanis have been employed in the UAE.

In varying degrees, the same has been the position of Pakistan in the other Gulf states. Qatar has had a large number of Pakistani workers who at one time, and possibly even now, exceeded the number of the indigenous Qatari population. In all of these countries, Pakistani workers enjoy a reputation of being hardworking and dependable. They pose no political threat to the security of these small states, unlike the suspicions of the local authorities regarding workers from Arab countries like Egypt or Sudan. In the case of Oman, Pakistani Baloch have for long served in its armed forces. The Omani coast is only about 180 miles from the Pakistani coast. In fact, it takes less time to fly from Karachi to Muscat than from Karachi to Islamabad.

Kuwait too has extended considerable financial aid to Pakistan in the past twenty-five years and a large number of expatriate Pakistanis work there. The armed forces of all the Gulf states have had an active training programme with Pakistan. For these reasons, it can be said that Pakistan enjoys a special relationship with the Gulf countries, particularly with the UAE. There is a clear strategic dimension to these relations. In reverse, if an unfriendly country acquires dominance in these countries it would be injurious to Pakistan's vital interests.

With the rest of the Islamic world, Pakistan's relations have been generally good without being very consequential. In general, Pakistan is admired as a large Islamic country with considerable expertise in diverse fields, including nuclear technology. Pakistan's sincere support for the Arab and Islamic causes has won it considerable goodwill among most of the Islamic countries. But there has been a varied pattern to these relations, which is not surprising when one considers the large number of Islamic countries.

The radicalization of Arab opinion following the Egyptian Revolution of 1953 hurt Pakistan's relations with several of these states, particularly during the 1950s and the 1960s. The Palestinians were angered by Pakistan's military support for King Hussein of Jordan in the early 1970s. The Ba'athists, who seized power in both Iraq and Syria during the 1960s, have followed a secular and socialist ideology and the Islamic factor has mattered little to them. Thus, Syria and Iraq have been generally cool towards Pakistan and have shown pro-Indian inclinations on the Kashmir issue. In fact, Iraq even sided with India during the 1971 War. Later, in 1973, Pakistan broke off diplomatic relations with Iraq after arms were found to have been smuggled by the Iraqi Embassy in Islamabad, meant for militants in Iranian Balochistan.

As Pakistan's relations with the US started to cool in the 1960s and, more so, as a result of Pakistan's strong moral and even material support for the Arabs in the 1967 and 1973 Wars with Israel, Pakistan's stature rose again in the Arab world. It is notable that during the India–Pakistan War of 1971, the Arab countries generally supported Pakistan. Even afterwards, on the issue of the recognition of Bangladesh, the Arabs showed solidarity with Pakistan.

From the early 1970s, Pakistan sought to adopt a policy of keeping out of inter-Arab disputes and by following a policy of bilateralism in relations with the various Arab countries. In the case of an Arab consensus, Pakistan usually went along with whatever the Arabs wanted to do in matters pertaining to the Arab world itself. This helped Pakistan to avoid the pitfalls involved in the case of inter-Arab disputes. The Arab world has never been a monolith and has had a wide variety of political ideologies and divergent pulls.

The signing of the Camp David Accords by Egypt and Israel in 1978 shook the Arab world to the core. It reacted angrily by expelling Egypt from the Arab League. Pakistan went along with the majority Arab view. The loss of Egypt greatly weakened the capacity of the Arab world to challenge Israel militarily. In time, the rest of the Arab world had to come to the grudging conclusion that some kind of accommodation with Israel was inevitable. At the 1984 Casablanca Islamic Summit, President Ziaul Haq took the lead in pleading that Egypt should be allowed re-entry into the OIC and the Arab League. This was found generally acceptable, ushering in an era of warm friendship between Pakistan and Egypt. Pakistan had been appreciative of the strong support given by President Anwar Sadat to Pakistan in the context of the Soviet occupation of Afghanistan. The Egyptian government, however, had been alarmed by the role played by Arab extremists trained in Afghanistan in opposing the pro-West Egyptian regime. Thus, Egypt applied strong pressure on Pakistan to expel all such Arab 'fundamentalists' from its soil.

The Arab Maghreb—Morocco, Algeria, and Tunisia—have generally been very friendly with Pakistan without having much concrete collaboration with it. They remember the key role played by Pakistan in their liberation struggle in the 1950s and this has been the source of great goodwill for Pakistan in these countries. However, Algeria has been relatively less enthusiastic about Pakistan. It has had a long rule of the socialist-minded National Liberation Front (French: Front de libération nationale [FLN]) which had close links with the Soviet bloc. In Algeria's dispute with Morocco on the Sahara issue, there have been misgivings in Algeria that Pakistan was leaning towards Morocco. More recently, the Algerian armed forces have cracked down on the growing Islamic movement in the country, which has unleashed counter-terrorism by the Islamists. The Algerian regime has been accusing Islamic 'fundamentalists', trained in Afghanistan, of involvement in terrorism and thus in some ways Pakistan has also been implicated in this controversy.

With most of the African Muslim countries, Pakistan has enjoyed not only goodwill but also a certain degree of admiration. Pakistan was active in the liberation struggle of many of these countries. On the issue of liberation from colonialism, as also in opposing racial discrimination, Pakistan has always been outspoken. Moreover, Pakistan has been extending technical assistance to many African countries since the early 1980s. In spite of these advantages, Pakistan has tended to neglect the countries of Africa and has instead concentrated much more on Western countries. The African countries are remembered by Pakistani policymakers only when Pakistan needs their votes at the UN or elsewhere. This has been a shortsighted approach.

With the South-East Asian Muslim countries, Pakistan's relations have been cordial without having much content. In the early 1960s, there was a period when Indonesia, under President Sukarno, showed a pronounced leaning towards Pakistan and extended some military support to Pakistan during the 1965 War. This was the period when Sukarno was very pro-China. China's problems with India and its friendship with Pakistan also had a beneficial effect for Pakistan in its relations with Indonesia.[5] However, after Sukarno's fall, Indonesia adopted an even-handed policy towards India and Pakistan. There have been instances when Indonesia has refused to support OIC resolutions in favour of Pakistan on the Kashmir question and has either abstained or reserved its position.

Brunei Darussalam too has at times followed Indonesia's example on Kashmir. Malaysia has been generally more forthcoming towards Pakistan.

But, ironically, in the 1965 War, Pakistan took the unprecedented step of breaking diplomatic relations with Malaysia on the ground that its representative at the UN (a Hindu of Indian origin) had made some unfavourable comments on the creation of Pakistan. Foreign Minister Z.A. Bhutto was evidently responsible for this extreme reaction and it was some time before Pakistan–Malaysia relations could be put back on the rails. In fact, most Malaysian Muslims have always had a soft corner for Pakistan. However, by and large, the south-east Asian countries have been more preoccupied with their own region and have maintained a relatively low profile in issues of the Muslim world.

Conclusion

All of these complexities have not always been appreciated by Pakistani public opinion and even by the policymakers. They have had difficulty in understanding as to how there could be anything but love for an Islamic country like Pakistan which has been such a strong supporter of the Palestinian cause and had done so much for the liberation struggle of many Arab countries. No doubt, these Pakistani policies have been appreciated by all Arab countries but there have also been other factors in operation like ideology and strategic interests. The Soviet bloc was a natural ally for the radical Arabs because of the strong American support for Israel. Substantial military assistance and strong diplomatic support was extended to the Arabs by the Soviet bloc which was crucial for their security against Israel. There had to be some quid pro quo for the Soviet support. It was thus unfortunate for Pakistan that in the two wars against India in 1965 and 1971, some of the Arab countries not only kept aloof from Pakistan but like South Yemen and Iraq were actively sympathetic towards India.

Even the Arab and other Muslim countries, which have been very friendly to Pakistan, have only been willing to give a limited amount of material support to Pakistan, in terms of military hardware and financial assistance. Their priority has obviously been closer to home. The oil-rich Arab countries have given much more assistance to fellow Arab countries than to Pakistan.

The conclusion from the foregoing account has to be that Pakistan has only received limited assistance in the past from the Arab and Islamic world in its confrontation with India. Indeed, some Islamic countries, for reasons of their own, have been sympathetic to or even helped India. There has also been a decline in the degree of support for Pakistan. For instance, the support received in the 1971 War was less than the support received in the 1965 War.

Moreover, the degree of diplomatic support for Pakistan from the Islamic countries on the Kashmir issue has also been declining.

Under the circumstances, it would be risky to make any strategic planning for the future on the premise of any kind of solid support from the Arab and Islamic world for Pakistan in its conflict with India. Some Pakistanis feel that the Islamic world is a solid entity and would come to Pakistan's rescue in meeting the challenge of India. In reality, this kind of thinking is little more than a romantic illusion. Among the Islamic countries, there are always diverse interests at play, which pull different countries apart. The Islamic world is not, and probably cannot be, a monolith. Islamic solidarity exists but it is not an overriding factor in determining national priorities. Some of these countries are secular in their outlook and have had a problem in matching their membership of the OIC, an organization based on religious affinity, with their secular ideology. Turkey and Syria have been members of the OIC more for political than for religious reasons. Basically, they did not want to be left out of this large grouping and also hoped to use it for their own political and economic objectives. There is no such thing as an Islamic bloc. For one thing, most Islamic countries do not have the kind of ideological commitment to Islam as a political philosophy which Pakistan has had. Pan-Islamism as a philosophy has had little appeal in Islamic countries in the twentieth century.

NOTES

1. Burke and Ziring, op. cit., p. 67.
2. *Dawn*, 27 September 1956, cited in Burke and Ziring, p. 205.
3. *Dawn*, 9 November 1956, cited in Burke and Ziring, p. 188.
4. *Round Table*, March 1957, cited in Burke and Ziring, p. 204.
5. Burke and Ziring, op. cit., pp. 307–10.

10

Pakistan's Relations with China

Pakistan has enjoyed a remarkably close relationship with China, almost from the very early years of its independence. Considering that the two countries have been ideologically far apart, and have at times even belonged to two opposite military blocs, China–Pakistan friendship has aroused considerable curiosity and various explanations have been offered for this seemingly odd couple. Indian observers have described this friendship as being based on opportunism, expediency and, even, collusion directed mainly against India since, in their view, apart from a common dislike for India, there was little else which was common between Pakistan and China.

An analysis of the history of the relationship reveals that the two countries had proceeded step-by-step towards establishing friendship on the basis of a mutuality of interests, which overcame ideological differences. India, no doubt, figured in an important way in the calculations of both sides. However, both Pakistan and China were moved by wider geo-strategic considerations as well.

When the communists seized power in China in 1949, Pakistan was quick to recognize the new regime. It was assumed by Pakistan and many others that China's seat at the UN would, henceforth, be occupied by the new Communist regime. Since the Kashmir dispute was before the UN Security Council, it would not have been in Pakistan's interest to alienate the new Chinese regime by delaying its recognition since China's veto could have adversely affected Pakistan's case there. Also, Pakistan was faced with a major economic problem in 1949 when India had suddenly stopped trading with Pakistan since it had not followed India's example in devaluing its currency. Pakistan was, therefore, desperate to find an alternative market for selling its raw jute and cotton as also to locate a supply source for coal. Trade with China thus fitted in very admirably with this situation. For these reasons, Pakistan was among the first nations to recognize Communist China and establish diplomatic relations with it.

Communist China had inherited old territorial claims on Tibet, and even in the Himalayas, which ran counter to India's position. Thus, when

China moved its troops into Tibet in 1950, India protested, although it later decided to acquiesce in the Chinese claim on Tibet. But the differences on the delineation of the India–China border, both in Kashmir as well as on the eastern side, were to acquire an increasingly bitter dimension. Even more importantly, from the beginning, China foresaw the potential of friction with India not only on the border question but also in the context of the leadership of Asia.

It was this background of actual or potential friction with India, which made Pakistan an attractive proposition for China. It was aware of Pakistan's anti-Indian stance and probably calculated that friendship with Pakistan could be handy when China ran into problems with India. Thus, during the 1950s, even in several instances when Pakistan took steps which were not to China's liking—such as joining SEATO or sympathizing with the US during the Korean War—China did not lose patience with Pakistan.

Moreover, as China developed differences with the Soviet Union in the mid-1950s and as the latter moved closer towards India, China found a commonality of interests with Pakistan. At the Bandung Conference of Afro–Asian countries in 1955, China was helpful to Pakistan in several ways. This led to the first-ever visit by a Pakistani prime minister to China in 1956, followed by a return visit to Pakistan by Premier Zhou Enlai when he said that, although Pakistan was a member of SEATO, there was no reason why China could not be friendly with her. He added that the two countries had 'no conflict of interests.'[1] On his part, Pakistani Prime Minister Huseyn Shaheed Suhrawardy predicted, early in 1957, that 'I feel perfectly certain that when the crucial time comes, China will come to our assistance.'[2]

With the seizure of power in Pakistan in 1958 by General Ayub Khan, China–Pakistan relations initially entered into difficulties. Ayub Khan was, in the beginning, strongly pro-American and anti-Communist. Thus in 1959 when India's relations with China soured, Ayub offered, in a surprise move, to have joint defence with India, evidently against Communist aggression from the north, involving either China or the Soviet Union or both. India immediately rebuffed the offer, mainly because it was conditional to resolving the Kashmir dispute.[3] China was clearly not pleased with Pakistan's move for joint defence with India. It even asked officially as to whom the Pakistanis were proposing joint defence against.[4] The Chinese news media was more openly critical and Pakistan was advised 'to pull up the horse before the precipice.'[5] It was, however, remarkable that, on the whole, China still maintained its sang-froid. It seemed to have made the correct calculation that India–Pakistan differences were too profound to be spanned by an unexpected, but conditional, offer of joint defence with India which the latter, in any case, rejected swiftly.

In the corresponding period, there had been a steady cooling of China's relations with India, particularly after the border clashes between the two countries in 1959. In the same period, there were growing differences between China and the Soviet Union. Not surprisingly, the Chinese took a very dim view of Moscow's strong support for India. In early 1961, it was announced that China and Pakistan had agreed to demarcate their border. Next, China proposed, and Pakistan agreed, that the border agreement would be a provisional one, pending the settlement of the Kashmir dispute.

By October 1962, China's relations with India had reached their lowest ebb when there was a brief but serious border war between the two countries. India suffered serious losses in this war. Pakistan was upset with the Western decision to rush military aid to India following its border war with China. Pakistan considered this to be a serious breach of its understandings with the US government that any US military aid would be given to India only after prior consultations with Pakistan. Moreover, Pakistan felt convinced (and was later proved right), that the military hardware supplied to India, ostensibly to fight China, would eventually be used against Pakistan.

The border talks between Pakistan and China were, therefore, taking place in the backdrop of growing tensions between China and India, as well as Pakistan's alienation with the West. The Pakistan–China border agreement was signed in March 1963, a few months after the border war between India and China. In the view of many observers, Pakistan was able to secure a favourable border settlement with China under which the latter had made important concessions when judged against its previous position.[6] India angrily denounced the agreement since it claimed the whole of Kashmir and regarded the Pakistani control of the relevant portion of Kashmir where the new border was agreed as illegal.

In January 1963, Pakistan and China signed a trade agreement followed a few months later by an agreement on air services. In fact, relations between Pakistan and China kept improving to such an extent that, in July 1963, Foreign Minister Z.A. Bhutto told Parliament that, in case of an India attack, Pakistan would not be alone as such an Indian attack would involve 'the territorial integrity and security of the largest state in Asia.'[7] In February 1964, Zhou Enlai paid an official visit to Pakistan and, for the first time, China declared open support for Pakistan on the Kashmir dispute.[8]

Pakistan became a vigorous supporter of China's membership of the UN and other international bodies. The years which followed saw Pakistan staunchly supporting China at the UN, often alone with Albania, at that time China's only friend in Europe. This evidently made a lasting impression in China. Pakistan came to be considered a special friend who had stood by China in good times and bad. In fact, Pakistan's strategic relationship with the US was put under severe strain in the early 1960s due to Pakistan's budding friendship with China. Pakistan's strategic calculation that in case of a war with India, the assistance of China would be more readily forthcoming than that of the USA ultimately proved correct. Despite the annoyance of the Americans, particularly that of President Lyndon B. Johnson, Pakistan stuck to its policy of befriending China. When President Ayub Khan visited China in March 1965, he was probably accorded the biggest-ever public welcome in China to any foreign visitor. This was a moment of triumph for Pakistani diplomacy. Pakistan had won over China almost completely while still maintaining a strong relationship with the US and, in the same period, had also improved relations with the Soviet Union. This had clearly been a successful case of following the policy of bilateralism to great advantage.

China's friendship with Pakistan reached its peak during the India–Pakistan War in September 1965. China not only denounced India for its aggression against Pakistan but also applied strong military pressure on India to stop the war. Immediately after the war began, China declared publicly that it was strengthening its alertness along its border with India. It accused India of serious violations of Chinese territory and warned it of serious consequences. On 16 September, China issued an ultimatum to India to dismantle all its military works on the Chinese side of the border and return all captive Chinese nationals and livestock, within three days, or else 'bear full responsibility for all the grave consequences arising therefrom.'[9] This ultimatum created global alarm and also led to decisive action by the Security Council which insisted on a ceasefire. Moreover, China sent a warning to India, through the American Embassy in Poland, not to attack East Pakistan.[10] This was believed by many to have deterred India from attacking the lightly defended eastern wing of Pakistan.

The strong Chinese support for Pakistan in the 1965 War won over the hearts of Pakistanis and this goodwill has survived the political changes in both countries in the past three decades. However, there was a realization in government circles in Pakistan that, despite this Chinese support, the country must maintain a good equation with the US, as well as the Soviet Union with whom relations had been on the mend in the 1960s. The Chinese understood Pakistan's geo-strategic compulsions and did not think ill of the efforts of Pakistan to improve relations with the other two major powers even though, at that time, China did not have amicable relations with either.

Pakistan was anxious to bring about an improvement in the bilateral relations between the US and China. Although the Americans had periodically shown interest in establishing a better relationship with China, there was no real progress. American involvement in Vietnam and the status of Taiwan were obviously very sore points for the Chinese. However, during a visit to Pakistan in 1969, when President Richard Nixon showed interest in using Pakistan as an intermediary for this purpose, the latter agreed to do so. During his visit to the US in October 1970, Yahya Khan was requested to set up a secret meeting between an emissary of Nixon and Premier Zhou Enlai. The latter welcomed the intermediary role of the president of Pakistan. Pakistan was to prove a good channel for communication and the US Secretary of State Henry Kissinger eventually flew secretly from Islamabad to Beijing in July 1971 on an historic mission which normalized relations between the US and China after years of hostility. Nixon profusely thanked Yahya Khan for the 'great service to peace and to mutual relations which he is rendering by acting as a true friend of two parties' (i.e. USA and China).[11] This role played by Pakistan was one of the reasons for Nixon's pro-Pakistan posture during the India–Pakistan War which broke out in December 1971.

China, too, was highly appreciative of Pakistan's role, which fitted in with the special ties existing between the two countries in the past decade. In fact, Kissinger told Yahya Khan on return from Beijing that the Chinese had said that they would 'intervene with men and arms' if India moved against Pakistan. However, the message from Zhou Enlai, conveyed by the Chinese Ambassador in Islamabad, was that it had been indicated to Henry Kissinger that 'in case India invaded Pakistan, China would not be an idle spectator but would support Pakistan.'[12] There was no mention of intervening with men and arms. According to Sultan M. Khan, Pakistan's Foreign Secretary at that time, during the talks held in the days prior to the war with India, 'China never…held out any possibility of coming to Pakistan's aid with her armed forces'[13] and that 'there was never any question of active Chinese military involvement and such an eventuality was never even discussed.'[14]

The impression in some quarters in Pakistan that Chinese troops were poised to apply pressure against India to rescue East Pakistan never had any basis. For one thing, China was too engrossed in its own internal situation during the ongoing Cultural Revolution to have been able to do so. Also, China could not risk a confrontation with Moscow, which was fully supporting India during the Bangladesh crisis. Moreover, China was no doubt aware that the majority of the people in East Pakistan had been irreversibly antagonized and little could be gained by its intervening under such circumstances.

Friendship between Pakistan and China has remained unaffected by the 1971 War. The Chinese have continued to extend significant moral and material support to Pakistan. In the meantime, China has liberalized its economic policies and achieved remarkable success in raising its exports and per capita income. Politically, China feels no longer menaced by the superpowers. The Soviet Union is no more there and its successor Russia is a very different country. The US has, despite some differences, established a harmonious relationship with China. Since the 1980s, China's relations with India have also improved, until the Bharatiya Janata Party (BJP) government in India unexpectedly soured the pitch in 1998. Under these circumstances, China no longer needs Pakistan in the manner it did in the 1960s and the 1970s, though it continues to show goodwill towards Pakistan and remains helpful to the latter in concrete ways. Nevertheless, it would be unwise for Pakistani policymakers to expect China to give the kind of assistance which it did in the past in any kind of confrontation with India.

NOTES

1. *Dawn*, 24 October 1956, cited in Burke and Ziring, p. 215.
2. National Assembly of Pakistan Debates, 25 February 1957, p. 1097, cited in Burke and Ziring, p. 215.
3. Burke and Ziring, p. 233.
4. *The New York Times*, 13 October 1959, citied in Burke and Ziring, p. 233.
5. *Peking Review*, 28 July 1959, cited in Burke and Ziring, p. 217.
6. *The Times*, London, 4 March 1963, cited in Burke and Ziring, p. 292.
7. *Dawn*, 18 June 1963, cited in Burke and Ziring, p. 293.
8. Burke and Ziring, p. 294.
9. Ibid., p. 339.
10. Disclosed by Foreign Minister Bhutto to the National Assembly, 15 March 1966, cited in Burke and Ziring, pp. 338, 348.
11. Sultan M. Khan, *Memories & Reflections of a Pakistani Diplomat*, pp. 261–2.
12. Ibid., p. 269.
13. Ibid., p. 308.
14. Ibid., p. 347.

11

A Reappraisal of India–Pakistan Relations

The Negative Elements

In retrospect, it can be said that Pakistan's foreign policy in the past fifty years seems to have been dominated by its security concerns against India. Almost everything else has been subordinated to or, at any rate, eclipsed by the India factor. The principal objective of Pakistan's strategic policy has been at least to prevent India from overrunning or subjugating Pakistan and, at the most, to pose as an equal of India. In Pakistan's threat perception, India has constantly figured as the number one danger. This mindset has been influenced by both ideology and geopolitics, hardened by public postures, all of which have converged to reduce the room for manoeuvrability. It can be said that Pakistan's foreign policy through most of its history has been India-obsessed.

In the political arena, Kashmir has occupied the centre stage in India–Pakistan relations. It was the scene of actual fighting between India and Pakistan in 1948 though this had remained confined to the disputed area only. However, in 1965, the two countries had a full-scale war, which was fought specifically over Kashmir. The 1971 War was no doubt caused by the Bangladesh crisis but the dispute on Kashmir had been mainly responsible for the acute hostility. In fact, early in 1971, an Indian Airlines passenger airline named Ganga had been hijacked to Lahore by Kashmiri separatists, suspected to be Indian agents provocateurs. The hijackers, who were greeted as heroes by some Pakistanis, later blew up the aircraft, reportedly at the instigation of Z.A. Bhutto, the PPP leader. This action had been seized by India as the justification for closure of its air space to flights between East and West Pakistan, thus creating serious logistic problems for Pakistan ahead of the 1971 War.

After its defeat in the 1971 War, Pakistan had to tone down its espousal of the Kashmir cause for some years, but as Pakistan regained its strength and confidence, particularly after acquiring nuclear capability around 1980, its line on Kashmir once again stiffened. An even more significant ossifying in Pakistan's attitude has taken place since 1990, when an unprecedented anti-India resistance movement erupted and soon gained momentum in the Indian-occupied Kashmir. Pakistan enthusiastically welcomed this anti-India uprising and announced its intention to extend to the Kashmiri people every possible moral and diplomatic support. In addition, some material support is allegedly going to the resistance in Kashmir, even if this charge is denied by Pakistan. India has been accusing Pakistan of conducting a 'proxy war' in Kashmir and insists that Pakistani infiltrators are behind most of the trouble.

Another reason for the hardening of Pakistan's attitude on Kashmir in the last decade has been its internal politics. With the restoration of parliamentary rule, the political parties in Pakistan have sought to gain popularity by whipping up anti-India feelings in the populace. Consequently, the two main parties, the Muslim League and the PPP, have vied with each other in sounding tough on Kashmir. The right wing religious parties like the Jamaat-i-Islami have always been ahead of everyone else in breathing fire on Kashmir and in fanning hatred against India. Any party which softens its stance towards India runs the risk of being accused of treason by its political rivals. In addition, the Pakistani army, which wields a strong influence in policy matters, has always maintained a hard line attitude towards India. In such a volatile atmosphere, any voices suggesting moderation or compromise are drowned out. In a sense, Pakistan has painted itself into a corner in which there seems to be little manoeuvrability.

In the context of bilateral negotiations with India, following the anti-India uprising in Kashmir since 1990, Pakistan has adopted an uncompromising position, namely that without progress on Kashmir, there can be no normalization of relations with India. Pakistan has been insistent that Kashmir is the 'core' problem and that everything else is peripheral. Pakistan has also accused India of serious violations of human rights in Kashmir by its deployment of 600,000 military personnel. As an inducement for talks with India, Pakistani leaders have from time to time stressed their desire to establish a durable peace with India, but have always linked this with prior progress on Kashmir.

On the other side of the border, the picture is not very different. There is a similar rigid stance on Kashmir. The Congress Party was in power for the first thirty years after independence and the Kashmir dispute started under Congress rule. The two wars with Pakistan were also fought when Congress regimes were in power. In particular, Prime Minister Indira Gandhi and her son Rajiv, who succeeded her, had made a habit of stepping up war fever against Pakistan whenever they needed to raise their popularity in India.

Pakistan-baiting was their trump card. The other parties have not been far behind. In recent years, the popularity of the Hindu fundamentalist party, the Bharatiya Janata Party (BJP), has been on the increase, which has had an even tougher stance against Pakistan than that of the relatively secular Nehru–Gandhi family that has provided three prime ministers to India. As soon as the BJP came to power, early in 1998, the relations with Pakistan came under an alarming strain, accentuated in particular by India's conducting of nuclear explosions.

The net result of the rigid and emotionally charged attitudes adopted by both India and Pakistan in the past fifty years has been that their bilateral relations have nearly always been under a serious strain, primarily because of the deadlock on the Kashmir issue. In the view of some observers, the centuries-old antagonisms between Hindus and Muslims are the real disease whereas the Kashmir dispute is a mere symptom. In any event, national egos and considerations of 'loss of face' on both sides have prevented any flexibility. Thus, the two countries seem be caught in a time warp in which they keep repeating their respective arguments, which merely fall on deaf ears of their opposite number.

On account of this mutual hostility, the two countries have had to pay a very dear price. Large portions of their scanty resources have been diverted to unproductive pursuits—their military budgets—at the expense of economic development and alleviation of the poverty of their masses.

There is also a sinister dimension in the bilateral relationship which has vitiated the atmosphere between India and Pakistan even further in the last decade. This has been the apparent involvement of their respective secret agencies in acts of terrorism on the other side of the border. There have been numerous bombings, assassinations, and various terrorist incidents in which the urban civilian population has been the target, resulting in a general sense of fear and insecurity. There have been selective killings carried out with a view to instigate sectarian vendettas, particularly among Muslim sects in Pakistan. This is widely believed in Pakistan to have been the handiwork of RAW, the Indian secret agency. The alleged support of Pakistan's secret agency, the ISI, for the Sikh insurgency in Indian Punjab in the 1980s and covert support for the Kashmiri resistance movement in the 1990s is cited by some quarters as justifying the response from India.

The difference is that the Kashmiris are involved in a genuine struggle for national liberation which has received international recognition, in the form of UN resolutions. Their resistance to Indian suppression cannot be equated with terrorism. The suspected Indian involvement in urban terrorism in Pakistan, however, has no such justification. A distinction is drawn all over the world between the struggles for national liberation and terrorism, especially if it is state-organized. Nor, for that matter, can there be any defence for the involvement, if true, of Pakistani agents in terrorist acts in Delhi or Bombay. State-sponsored terrorism is a highly odious phenomenon whatever its rationale or justification.

As for the economic and other consequences of the Indo-Pakistan hostility, there can be no doubt that both countries have been hurt badly. This is all the more unfortunate since India and Pakistan are amongst the poorest countries in the world in terms of per capita income. As costs of military hardware increase, the defence establishments in both Pakistan and India go on demanding more and more resources in their unending armaments race. The latest and the deadliest competition at present is in developing of nuclear weapons and missiles. The unexpected Indian nuclear explosions, carried out in May 1998, have raised frightful possibilities of devastation of apocalyptic proportions. Two weeks after the Indian tests, Pakistan retaliated by carrying out six nuclear explosions of its own. India had been clearly guilty of this dangerous escalation in the arms race. Pakistan would not have carried out any nuclear explosions if it had not been compelled by India. There was immense pressure of public opinion in Pakistan to counter the Indian nuclear explosions, even if this led to aggravated economic sufferings. Economic sanctions have followed, exacerbating Pakistan's economic woes. In India too, the loss of economic assistance has been quite substantial, even if the Indian economy is better geared to meet the situation. In the process, the loser, as usual, is the common person in both countries. Millions in both countries live below the poverty line and desperately need economic uplift, rather than having to bear the burdens arising out of the arms race.

Pakistan's adverse political relations with India have had their fall-out in other fields as well. Considering itself as the aggrieved party, Pakistan has sought to cut off links with India in diverse fields. Trade was one of the first casualties (although the first trade cut-off in 1949 had come from India).[1] Cultural links have also been discouraged. The rationale, in the first case, has been the old protectionist argument that India as the larger economy would not let Pakistan's infant or smaller industries grow. On the other hand, fearing dependence on India in respect of strategic items, import of iron ore and coal from India was discouraged for Pakistan's steel mills even though that would have made a lot of economic sense. Transit trade through Pakistan has been denied to India for fear that this would be detrimental to Pakistan's security. Politics have thus come in the way of trade in one way or the other, time and again. It seems that Pakistan has had to suffer greater economic losses and in several instances, the Pakistani consumer has been made to bear the burden of higher costs.

Pakistan's discouragement of cultural links has been due to reasons that are more complex. Though it was the clash of civilizations, no less than conflicting national aspirations, which had led to the demand for Pakistan, there also exist common strains in the cultures of the two countries. The subcontinent has always had diverse groups as well as cultural overlaps. This is inevitable in a population of over one billion people in a region whose history goes back several thousand years. Such cultural overlaps can also be found elsewhere in the world. For instance, many European countries have similarities in culture and overlapping strains. The same is true of the Arab world and Latin America. However, India has always sought to give a political interpretation to such cultural similarities with Pakistan. It has argued that the cultures of the two countries are the same, the peoples are the same and thus—and this is where the sting comes—there was no need for the political separation. In other words, the commonalties in culture have usually been given a political twist by India to deny the very rationale for the creation of Pakistan. This has understandably forced Pakistan to put up its shutters. The extremist elements—the super patriots—in Pakistan have reacted by going to ridiculous extents to deny altogether the common strains in cultures of the two countries, thus exposing Pakistan to the charge of being narrow-minded and paranoid.

It is also a fact that the peoples of the subcontinent speak many common languages and there are certain similarities in food, dresses, and customs. The music is more or less the same. However, this is true of many countries in Europe also but, on that basis, the separate national identities of such European countries have seldom been questioned. In the case of India and Pakistan, even where there are seeming commonalties in culture, there still exist sharp differences. For instance, the food seems to be similar, but Muslims eat beef whereas the Hindus are vegetarians.

Similarly, on the surface, it seems that both countries speak the same language, but a closer look shows sharp differences. India has followed a national policy of encouraging Hindi and downgrading Urdu on the spurious grounds that it is a 'Muslim' language. That by itself shows the deeply ingrained prejudices against the Muslims.

Urdu is the national language of Pakistan, even though relatively few Pakistanis speak Urdu as their mother tongue. This is because Urdu is the lingua franca, the link language between the four Pakistani provinces, and the most highly developed among the many languages spoken in Pakistan. Urdu has, moreover, one of the world's richest literatures. It is also the reservoir of most of the Islamic religious writings of the subcontinent.

Furthermore, Hindi and Urdu have two separate scripts; Urdu is written from right to left and Hindi from left to right. Hence, the superficial impression that the two countries speak the same language is quite faulty. The spoken language, in its bare essentials, is no doubt understood by both, but the moment more advanced vocabulary is used, the differences become evident. Urdu turns to Persian and Arabic sources for its more advanced vocabulary whereas Hindi looks to Sanskrit for this purpose. In fact, to use the words of George Bernard Shaw, who had England and USA in mind, the two countries of the subcontinent are also 'divided by a common language.'

The two countries could have shown more maturity by promoting mutual friendship on the basis of the several common elements in their cultures. A parallel could have been drawn from the examples of the US and Canada, or that of New Zealand and Australia. Indeed, many European countries, despite their linguistic variations, have drawn closer to each other because of the many common strains in their cultures and ethnic origins. The same is true of Latin America. Sadly, this has hardly ever been the case between India and Pakistan and the ingrained prejudices of the two countries have worked to the mutual detriment of both.

Another painful consequence of the adversarial relations between India and Pakistan has been the difficulties faced by millions of their citizens, belonging to divided families, in meeting their kith and kin. Even in less acrimonious times, travel between India and Pakistan has generally been difficult, but the situation becomes worse in times of political tension.

The Positive Exceptions: Indus Waters Treaty and the Rann of Kutch Arbitration

In an otherwise barren landscape, there have probably been only two important instances of mutual accommodation and rational resolution of difficulties—the Indus Waters Treaty and the Rann of Kutch arbitration. Both involved foreign intermediaries: in the former, the World Bank and, in the latter, an international tribunal in which the chairperson was appointed by the UN secretary general.

The question of the distribution of river waters flowing into Pakistan from the Indian side erupted into a crisis soon after independence. The Indus River and its five tributaries—Jhelum, Chenab, Ravi, Beas, and Sutlej—flow into Pakistan from Kashmir and India. Out of these, the three western rivers—

Indus, Jhelum, and Chenab—flow from Kashmir into Pakistan. The Indus River system is the source of Pakistan's agriculture and its basic livelihood. The partition of the Punjab in 1947 cut across the rivers and canals of the entire irrigation system, making India the upper riparian and Pakistan the lower riparian. At the time of independence, a committee of officials was set up consisting of representatives of the two sides which unanimously agreed on the maintenance of the pre-Partition division of water resources between East Punjab (India) and West Punjab (Pakistan). This principle was endorsed by higher level committees and was not referred to the Arbitral Tribunal because no dispute existed on this matter. The East Punjab ministers and officials also repeatedly assured their Pakistani counterparts that there was no question of any change in the pre-Partition formula. But no formal document was drawn up recording this agreement. The same declarations were made by the East Punjab officials before the Arbitral Tribunal.

It later transpired that the Indian side was secretly planning something very different. A few months after independence, on 1 April 1948, the day after the Arbitral Tribunal ceased to exist, India cut off the water supplies in every canal crossing into Pakistan. Pakistan was thus faced with the threat of famine and agricultural ruin. A Pakistani delegation was sent to India, which imposed its own unilateral terms on Pakistan before restoring the flow of water. India now insisted that the 'proprietary rights in the waters of the rivers in East Punjab rest wholly in the East Punjab Government.'

Pakistan's repeated proposals to refer this issue to the World Court were rejected by India. In September 1950, India did offer to submit the issue to adjudication, but this had to be a court consisting of two Indian and two Pakistani judges. Pakistan's proposal to have an impartial chairperson was not accepted by India. Finally, in September 1951, the President of the World Bank, Eugene Black, made an offer of good offices, which was accepted by India and Pakistan. Protracted efforts by the World Bank over several years eventually produced an agreement on water sharing. This included financing of construction works for water replacement which would have been otherwise clearly beyond the capacity of India and Pakistan. In fact, this financial aid might well have been an inducement for India to accept third party mediation.

The final agreement had been made possible by the steadfast perseverance of the World Bank and the financial assistance of the US, UK, Canada, Australia, New Zealand, and West Germany. The Indus Waters Treaty was signed on 19 September 1960. The World Bank rightly took credit for its successful 'economic diplomacy.' It is noteworthy that the Treaty has been respected by the two countries ever since, despite wars and all kinds of tensions and crises.

The second major instance in which a bitter India–Pakistan dispute was resolved amicably was the issue of the border in the desolate marshland of the Rann of Kutch. The two countries had their own historic claims to a largely marshy area involving 7,000 sq. mi. of territory. India, as the successor of the former princely state of Kutch, claimed title to the whole of the Rann of Kutch. Pakistan, as the successor of British rule in Sindh Province, adhered to the argument that the Rann was an inland sea in which the median line should be the border. It held, moreover, that Sindh had traditionally exercised control over the northern half of the Rann of Kutch.

After India and Pakistan gained independence, the issue was discussed between the two sides on several occasions but no solution was found. Border clashes were first reported in 1956. In April 1965, serious fighting erupted in the Chhad Bet region in the disputed territory. This was the first time since independence that the two countries had fought across their international border, using sizeable military forces (Kashmir's case being a different category). In the fierce but brief fighting, Pakistan fared better and took a number of Indians as prisoners. Incidentally, both sides made use of the American weapons received by them, to be used in the event of communist aggression.

Stung by the Indian losses, which were attributed to the difficult terrain where India was at a considerable disadvantage, Prime Minister Lal Bahadur Shastri warned on 29 April 1965 that if the fighting continued, 'the (Indian) Army will decide its own strategy and deploy its manpower and equipment in the way it deems best.'[2] This was seen as a threat to widen the scope of the fighting by attacking Pakistan in other sectors as well. This spurred an effort by British Prime Minister Harold Wilson to halt the fighting. The two countries agreed to a self-executing procedure. It was stipulated that an effort would first be made to settle the question by bilateral discussions at the ministerial level. If no agreement was reached within two months of the ceasefire, the two governments would have recourse to an international tribunal whose decision 'shall be binding.' Consequently, a three-member tribunal was set up at Geneva in which one judge each was nominated by India and Pakistan respectively. The Indian nominee was Ales Bebler from Yugoslavia whereas Pakistan nominated Nasrollah Entezam, an Iranian diplomat. The chairperson, nominated by the UN secretary-general, was Judge Gunnar Lagergren from Sweden. It was his decision, which became the tribunal's award.

Legal teams from the two countries, assisted by experts, argued their respective cases at great length before the tribunal in Geneva for several months, in a generally congenial atmosphere. Documents of the former British administration as well as the ex-princely state of Kutch, going back to nearly 200 years, had to be studied. For this purpose, the India Office Library in London was an important source. India also produced the old records of the state of Kutch, mostly in Gujarati language, which were examined by the Pakistani side.

In the main, the Indian case was that the British government in the colonial days had, in effect, accepted the claim of the princely state of Kutch to whole of the Rann. Several British Indian maps had shown the Rann as belonging to Kutch. Moreover, in 1914 a portion of the Sindh–Kutch boundary was even demarcated on this basis. As the successor state to the British in Sindh province, Pakistan was, therefore, bound to accept that border. On the other hand, Pakistan produced considerable evidence to show that, during the British period, Sindh's jurisdiction also extended to the northern half of the Rann. Criminal cases instituted in this region had always been handled by the police of Sindh on the premise that the northern half of the Rann belonged to Sindh province. There was also documented evidence that in 1885, the senior British officer in Nagarparkar, the Sindh district adjacent to the Rann of Kutch, had contended to higher officials that the northern half of the Rann had always been considered to belong to Sindh. No one had argued at that time that the whole of the Rann belonged to Kutch.

The Pakistani counsel, Manzur Qadir, painstakingly demonstrated that the physical limits of a geographical survey in the late 1880s came erroneously to be shown as the Sindh–Kutch border. No doubt, this gave rise to the belief even among some top British officials that the whole of the Rann of Kutch belonged to Kutch State. The Pakistani counsel argued persuasively that the maps printed subsequently had merely repeated this cartographic error, but that sovereign rights could not be acquired by Kutch simply through a misunderstanding. The British, as the paramount power, could not be deemed to have relinquished legal title to Kutch State simply by default and as a result of a mere cartographic error. There had never been a conscious political decision to surrender the northern half of the Rann to Kutch and in any case, the Sindh administration continued to exercise jurisdiction in the northern half in the belief that it belonged to Sindh.

The tribunal's award, announced in February 1968, was basically the verdict of the Swedish chairman, Judge Lagergren. As expected, the Yugoslav judge supported the Indian claim. The Iranian judge, who sided with the

Pakistani claim, said that he would support the chairperson in order to produce a majority judgement. The award was a compromise settlement in which Lagergren in effect drew out a new borderline. The Indian claim to the whole of the Rann of Kutch was rejected. Although Pakistan's claim to half of the Rann was also not accepted, Pakistan had the satisfaction of securing all of the tenable land areas adjacent to Sindh province, including Chhad Bet, whose possession had spurred the main border clashes. In strategic terms, this denied India the advantage of having a foothold on solid land across the largely marshy area. There was sharp disappointment in India when the award was announced and Prime Minister Indira Gandhi even said that this was the last time that India would go for international adjudication. However, she affirmed that India would accept and implement the boundary award.

The next stage was the actual demarcation of the border in accordance with the award of the tribunal. There were apprehensions in Pakistan that India would not live up to its public commitment and new obstacles would be raised to prevent or delay the implementation of the award. This did not happen as the officials in charge of demarcation maintained a good rapport to resolve any difficulties. The border was thus demarcated without a hitch, ahead of schedule, and border maps were formally signed in July 1969. In this manner, an old border dispute involving thousands of miles of territory was resolved in an honourable fashion.

It is, however, ironic that a small bit of the border in the Sir Creek lying just beyond the Rann of Kutch, which was not within the ambit of the Geneva Tribunal, has ever since remained unresolved.

Unfortunately, aside from the few important exceptions, mentioned above, the path of peaceful resolution of disputes has not generally been followed by India and Pakistan. The record bears out that, by and large, particularly in the last thirty years, it has been India which has opposed reference of bilateral disputes to third parties for mediation, arbitration, or adjudication. Pakistan has generally favoured this course even though the first such case of adjudication—the Radcliffe border award in 1947—had greatly disappointed Pakistan.

In a speech to the Indian Parliament on 12 September 1958, Prime Minister Jawaharlal Nehru had said that:

> We have thought, and we still think, that the best course to decide any outstanding matter, that cannot be decided by mutual talks, is to refer it to an independent party or tribunal. Either we come to an agreement ourselves or ask somebody else to advise us and accept whatever decision

is arrived at, whether it is in our favour or against us. *There is no other way.*[3] (My italics)

Following ministerial-level talks between India and Pakistan, the two sides issued a joint communiqué on 24 October 1959 in which they accepted the principle of referring all border disputes, if not settled by negotiation, to an impartial tribunal.[4] Subsequently, this very communiqué became the basis of British mediation in 1965 in the Rann of Kutch border dispute.

Similarly, when India suffered a serious military setback against China in 1962, Prime Minister Nehru again showed interest in referring the border dispute to adjudication. He told the Indian parliament on 10 December 1962 that he was prepared 'to refer the basic dispute of the claims on the frontier to a body like the International Court of Justice at the Hague' or to 'arbitration if it was agreed to.'[5]

But India has since, more or less, abandoned this course of action. Pakistan's repeated offers to refer the Kashmir issue and other disputes to mediation, arbitration, or adjudication have always been flatly turned down. In fact, after signing the Simla Agreement of July 1972, following Pakistan's defeat in the 1971 War, India has tended to rule out any kind of role by 'third parties' in India–Pakistan disputes.

This attitude clearly shows India's volte-face on its own previously expressed views for the pacific settlement of disputes between any two countries. Its first prime minister and founding father, Jawaharlal Nehru, went back on his solemn commitments with respect to Kashmir as well as Goa. The succeeding Indian governments have continued defiantly to disregard India's pledges on Kashmir. In fact, all Indian governments, ever since the announcement of the Rann of Kutch award in 1968, have abandoned Nehru's categorical belief in referring inter-state disputes to mediation, arbitration, and adjudication. Apart from going back on its own words, India's approach is also contrary to the provisions of the UN charter to which India, like other member states, is fully committed. Good offices, mediation, arbitration, and adjudication are specifically mentioned in the charter as the appropriate means for settling disputes between states. Besides, these are widely respected international practices.[6]

Nuclear Explosions by India and Pakistan

Looking back at the record of the past fifty years, it seems clear that acrimony and tension have been more typical of India–Pakistan relationship rather than accommodation or peaceful co-existence, in spite of periodic protestations by both sides to the contrary. It seems that the hangover of centuries of conflicts and recriminations has nurtured psychological attitudes which have, more often than not, led to irrational behaviour at various levels. In any event, the harsh truth is that, for the greater part in the past half century, neither the Indian nor the Pakistani rulers have really shown the ability to rise above narrow-minded and short-sighted considerations. In the absence of a genuine commitment to peace and the vision of a long-term cooperative relationship on the part of the leaders, small problems have been allowed to develop into major disputes and bigger problems have escalated into wars. This has been the melancholy history of the past fifty years.

A stage has clearly been reached when things can no longer be allowed to drift. The nuclear explosions by Pakistan and India, ushering in an arms race of weapons of mass destruction and long-range missiles, represents an exceedingly dangerous escalation of tensions. Paradoxically, at the same time, these developments also hold the possibility of promoting the long-elusive peace between them.

To recall the recent developments, in April 1998, the BJP, a Hindu fundamentalist party, came to power in India. Since then, temperatures in the subcontinent have risen to a very dangerous level. In particular, there has been an unprecedented escalation in the arms race. To counter the threat of India's long-range missiles, Pakistan test-fired the Ghauri missile with a range of 1,500 kilometres. There were celebrations in Pakistan that this missile (provocatively named after the Muslim conqueror of Delhi in the medieval ages) could hit the farthest Indian cities.

India's newly-formed BJP government then sent shock waves around the world by carrying out five nuclear explosions. Since India had already conducted a nuclear explosion as far back as 1974, there seemed to be no compelling technical or even strategic need to carry out fresh nuclear explosions, which could not but invite international condemnation. Several previous Indian governments had ruled out conducting nuclear tests even though Pakistan was widely believed to have acquired nuclear capability since the early 1980s. In their judgement, India stood to lose more than it could gain by carrying out nuclear tests. If the nuclear tests had been considered really advantageous for India, the previous Indian governments would surely have done so.

It was not altogether comprehensible as to what prompted this fateful decision, by the BJP government, to take the plunge. No doubt, becoming a nuclear power was part of the BJP's election manifesto. However, the BJP had been obliged to form a coalition government and had to modify some of its planks. Thus, the objectives announced in the common programme of the coalition government did not include any reference to becoming a nuclear power or carrying out immediate nuclear explosions.

In suddenly deciding to carry out the nuclear tests, Prime Minister Atal Bihari Vajpayee was apparently influenced by two factors. One-upmanship against Pakistan, particularly after the latter test-fired the Ghauri missile, could be one explanation. But domestic politics could have been a more compelling consideration. The BJP government had begun its term as a weak coalition and was straight away losing its hold on power because of internal bickering. Vajpayee was thus evidently tempted to turn the tide by conducting nuclear explosions which, no doubt, instantly won him popularity internally because of the jingoistic feelings unleashed by India's becoming a nuclear power.

Interestingly, the ostensible fear of China was advanced as the justification for the tests by the Indian Defence Minister, George Fernandes, even though Sino–Indian relations had been on the mend for several years. As far as the Indian public, specially the majority Hindu population, was concerned its jubilation had more to do with anti-Pakistan feelings. The nuclear explosions were seen as a slap on the face of Pakistan which had earlier boasted about its missiles reaching every major city of India. There was a lot of euphoria and bragging in India following the nuclear explosions. In this environment, the powerful Indian Home Minister L.K. Advani started to flex his muscles by using threatening language against Pakistan whom he accused of conducting a proxy war in the Indian-held Kashmir. Advani even threatened that India could seize by force the Pakistan-held portion of Kashmir.

Some observers believe that there could also be a third explanation for India's decision to conduct nuclear tests. The argument forwarded was that some circles in the BJP government did not actually believe that Pakistan already possessed nuclear capability. By carrying out nuclear explosions, India's design might have been to force Pakistan to show its hand. However, this reasoning runs counter to the frequently expressed belief in statements and writings of Indian military experts that Pakistan was in possession of the 'Islamic' bomb since the early 1980s. Further, it is the nuclear deterrent which has kept the peace between India and Pakistan in the past two decades.

Another possible explanation could be that India conducted the nuclear tests deliberately to step up an arms race with Pakistan so as to put back-breaking pressure on the latter's weaker economy. After India had carried out its nuclear tests, some prominent Indians including former Prime Minister I.K. Gujral, as also some officials in the BJP government, had encouraged

Pakistan to carry out nuclear explosions by openly saying that it would be understandable if Pakistan also carried out such explosions.

In any event, whether India had or had not anticipated it, the BJP government's action did in fact force Pakistan to retaliate, two weeks later, by carrying out six nuclear explosions of its own, despite intense international pressure on it not to do so. The public euphoria in India was, therefore, short-lived.

Not surprisingly, the Indian explosions attracted strong international condemnation, arising from the global consensus in favour of nuclear non-proliferation. There is genuine worldwide horror about the possibility of any nuclear war which, apart from the havoc caused in the actual area of impact, could spread radioactivity beyond the borders of the combatants. The Nuclear Non-Proliferation Treaty (NPT) enjoys the overwhelming support of the international community. The US led the way in imposing economic sanctions against India and many aid-giving countries followed suit. The UK and France were also critical of India but stated that, in principle, they were opposed to the application of sanctions.

The US, Japan, and many other countries began to apply strong pressure on Pakistan not to carry out nuclear explosions of its own, in retaliation against the Indian explosions. Pakistan was warned that if it went ahead with the explosions, it too would have to face economic sanctions. If Pakistan resisted the temptation, it would not only stand on a moral high ground against India but would also be able to secure substantial economic and other benefits. These could have included the waiving off or substantial reduction in the country's huge foreign debts which were crippling its economy. Such a trade-off has taken place in the recent past in Egypt and Israel.

After considerable debate, the final decision of Prime Minister Nawaz Sharif was in favour of carrying out nuclear explosions. The Pakistani public opinion had been inflamed by what was interpreted as a grave Indian challenge to Pakistan's security and its very existence. Some provocative statements by the Indian Home Minister L.K. Advani about forcibly taking away Azad Kashmir had alarmed many in Pakistan who thought that India, intoxicated by its nuclear might, was planning to attack the Pakistani part of Kashmir. National pride was also a factor in favour of conducting nuclear tests. Pakistani politicians, especially the rightist religious parties, threatened to launch campaigns to topple the government if it delayed conducting the nuclear tests. The Pakistani public opinion was thus increasingly in favour of matching India's nuclear explosions. The armed forces, who are always a decisive factor in Pakistan's power structure, evidently also applied strong pressure on the government.[7]

The general sentiment in Pakistan was that the West, which was urging Pakistan not to conduct nuclear tests, had not been forthcoming enough in extending credible security assurances to Pakistan in the event of an Indian nuclear threat. Pakistani public opinion was also highly sceptical about the reliability of any kind of security assurances coming from the West, particularly from the USA which, in the popular perception, had let down Pakistan twice in times of critical need, in the wars of 1965 and 1971 against India. In addition, there were some circles in Islamabad who did not take the Western threat of economic sanctions seriously and tended to regard it as a mere bluff. There were others who thought that the Pakistani people, in the flush of national pride, would be willing to put up the needed sacrifices and make a supreme effort to stand on their own feet. They argued that it was high time that the nation learnt to practise austerity and get rid of its bad habits of dependence on foreign loans. All in all, there seemed to be a nation-wide emotional frenzy to match or even outdo India.

In this general state of euphoria, some hard facts were overlooked. Out of these, the most important fact was that Pakistan already possessed nuclear capability since the early 1980s which had proved its value in the previous decade or more by effectively serving as the nuclear deterrent against India. Carrying out nuclear explosions—while an exhilarating experience for the masses—did not materially change the reality on the ground that Pakistan already possessed nuclear capability. This had been an open secret, known all over the world for several years.

The reality that Pakistan already possessed nuclear capability was demonstrated by the fact that, in a matter of ten days or so, after the Pakistani Prime Minister decided to carry out the nuclear explosions, the tests took place in the remote hills of Chaghi. Even the tunnels used had been dug many years ago. This showed beyond doubt that the Pakistani nuclear weapons were already available on the shelf for quite some time. By carrying out explosions, the fact was made public. This did score some points in a strategic and political context but did not add much to the knowledge of the military and official circles in the countries which mattered—India, the US, and others.

From the late 1970s onwards, Pakistan's progress towards the acquisition of nuclear technology had been followed closely by the Western countries, Israel, the Soviet bloc and, of course, by India. The US had even fallen out with Prime Minister Z.A. Bhutto, as early as 1976, on this very issue. Later on, President Jimmy Carter had cut off US economic assistance to Pakistan to express American disapproval of Pakistan's efforts to secure nuclear capability. The concern about the so-called 'Islamic Bomb' of Pakistan was also the subject of many books and articles in the world media. Since 1990, the US sanctions had actually come into force on the ground that Pakistan's nuclear programme was weapons-oriented.

In spite of international, particularly American, pressures on Pakistan since the 1970s, it had gone ahead resolutely with its nuclear programme. By the early 1980s, Pakistan was generally believed to have crossed the threshold and to have acquired the requisite knowledge for producing nuclear weapons. According to Dr A.Q. Khan, the 'father' of the Pakistani nuclear bomb, (interview published by the daily *Jang* dated 30 May 1998), the work on the technology used in making the bomb had commenced on 4 April 1978 and the technology had become operational in 1979. By 1982–3, high-enrichment level, required to produce weapons, had been reached. Pakistan conducted 'cold tests' in 1983 which have since been repeated. This achievement was publicly disclosed shortly thereafter by President Ziaul Haq and other sources. There was hardly any doubt, either in India or anywhere else in the world, that Pakistan had possessed nuclear capability for the past two decades. Thus, there seemed to be no compelling strategic necessity for Pakistan to give overt proof of something which was already known all over the world. In fact, if a nuclear explosion had been considered necessary from a strategic or technological point of view, Pakistan should have carried out such a test in the early 1980s, immediately after it had acquired the necessary know-how.

Israel's example had already shown that a country could be a nuclear power without actually carrying out any nuclear explosions. Probably, few serious observers have ever doubted that Israel has produced and is in possession of nuclear weapons, even though it is not known to have carried out any nuclear explosions. It is also believed that South Africa had acquired nuclear capability although it too did not carry out any nuclear test.

The argument that nuclear weapons need updating or that a country has to build bigger and better nuclear weapons is also not very tenable. A small nuclear weapon can do so much harm that it is unnecessary to raise its destructive capability ten times or more, which would only be a case of 'over-kill'. The six nuclear explosions carried out by Pakistan in May 1998 were not a compelling strategic necessity. Emotional considerations and the requirements of 'face saving' were perhaps the more compelling factors. National morale was raised by the ability to do one better than India and, psychologically, the explosions were important. But in terms of strategic necessity and national interests they were not. Hence, it seems that emotions rather than reason prevailed with the policymakers in Islamabad. The possible motivations of India have been outlined above.

One more argument has been advanced by some circles in Pakistan, namely that if Islamabad had not carried out nuclear explosions to prove that it also possessed the nuclear deterrent, India would have attacked and conquered Azad Kashmir. In this connection, they have cited some threats on Kashmir held out by the Indian Home Minister Advani, shortly after India's nuclear tests. A closer look shows that this argument could not stand scrutiny for several reasons. In the first place, there were no significant military movements on the ground suggesting that India was about to launch an armed attack against Azad Kashmir with a view to conquer it. Also, Azad Kashmir is a very mountainous territory which cannot be conquered in a quick military operation. Pakistan is well entrenched in Azad Kashmir to defend it against any Indian attack. In the case of a limited fight, confined to one theatre of war, Pakistan's smaller size has never been much of a disadvantage. Pakistan did well enough against India when there was fighting in the Rann of Kutch in 1965, and in Kashmir itself in the prelude to the 1965 War, as also during the more protracted fighting in Kashmir, way back in 1948. Pakistan's smaller size becomes a disadvantage only in the event of an all-out war with India, as in 1965 and in 1971. If Advani's threats were serious and India was indeed planning to attack only Azad Kashmir, Pakistan should have been able to defend its portion of Kashmir reasonably well.

India knew very well that it could not have attacked Azad Kashmir without risking an all-out war with Pakistan. In view of Pakistan's widely known progress in nuclear technology, India would, in effect, have been taking the risk of a nuclear war by trying to take over territory in Azad Kashmir. Thus, the logic of the situation was entirely against India actually carrying out Advani's threats of forcibly taking away Azad Kashmir from Pakistan's control. Furthermore, for such an all-out or limited war with Pakistan, the BJP regime would have prepared the ground by mobilizing Indian public opinion, but there were no indications that this was being done.

Under the circumstances, it may be said that Pakistan was not necessarily under any strategic compulsion to carry out its own nuclear explosions. However, there were other considerations, and among them was the political advantage to be gained by the Nawaz Sharif government from the emotional euphoria and boost to national morale that followed the nuclear explosions.

A sense of national pride swept the nation and there was even a semblance of national unity. But all of this was short-lived. Just a month later, the controversy over building the Kalabagh Dam was to shatter this illusion. Even worse, the country's economic woes were compounded by the sanctions that ensued.

Quite characteristically, it seems that transient emotional factors rather than cold calculations had prevailed with the policymakers in Islamabad in taking this fateful decision. The tragedy was that, in so doing, Pakistani policymakers ignored the country's real strategic interests which, at this time, were economic rather than military in nature. By not carrying out the nuclear tests, Pakistan could have extracted important financial and political concessions from the West and Japan. At the same time, it would have occupied a moral higher ground as against India in the eyes of the world. For a change, India would have been in the doghouse of world public opinion. In the words of President Clinton, 'Pakistan...missed a truly priceless opportunity.'

While the economic sanctions have been applied equally against both India and Pakistan, they have had a more deleterious effect on Pakistan's economy which, in its present precarious state, is ill-equipped to pay the price of economic sanctions. Pakistan's foreign exchange reserves are very low and it has a large imbalance in trade. Besides, it is encumbered by heavy foreign and domestic debts. Against this background, economic sanctions could become crippling for Pakistan. The country is likely to regret the Pyrrhic victory of having carried out its six nuclear explosions. India too would suffer but, relatively speaking, it might be able to withstand the international economic sanctions better than Pakistan because of its larger foreign exchange reserves, and a more self-reliant economy. The Vajpayee government may yet find that the odium of international disapproval and forcing Pakistan to react— thereby only achieving a dangerous nuclear stalemate with Pakistan—will, in the long run, prove more damaging than whatever domestic political mileage it had secured by carrying out the nuclear explosions.

The situation now is that both India and Pakistan have shown to each other and to the world that they are nuclear powers. They have thus joined the exclusive club of five (USA, Russia, Britain, France, and China) which possess nuclear capability. But the five original members of the club have exhibited by their conduct that, though they are in possession of this monstrous power, they also have a sense of responsibility and forbearance. In general, they have inspired confidence in the world that they would not act rashly or take the world to the brink of a nuclear holocaust. But the question is whether the two countries of the subcontinent can also act with a similar sense of responsibility.

For instance, a statement by the then Pakistani Foreign Minister Gohar Ayub Khan, that 'the next war between India and Pakistan would last one-and-a-half hours in which Pakistan will be victorious' is hardly reassuring. The point here is that the past fifty years of controversy, tensions, and warfare, resulting in wasteful expenditure and great hardships, have been bad enough, but are India and Pakistan headed for an even more perilous confrontation? The qualitative difference now is that both are in possession of nuclear capability and have missiles which can reach each other's main cities. The possibility of a nuclear holocaust, in which millions could be killed, can no longer be ruled out. The consequences, of course, would not be confined to the subcontinent alone. In a nuclear war, the radioactivity released would pose major health hazards not only to their own nationals but also to those living in the neighbouring countries and the world at large. In fact, in a nuclear war, there can be no winners: there are only losers.

It can also be argued that nuclear weapons can, by their very destructive nature, help to maintain peace between India and Pakistan. This in fact did happen in Europe from 1945 to 1991 between the two rival blocs and, at the global level, in the nuclear stalemate between the two superpowers, the US and the Soviet Union. Nuclear weapons are basically a deterrent and may also keep the peace in the subcontinent.

Considering the emotionalism rife in both India and Pakistan, it would unfortunately always be a precarious peace which could be jeopardized by a false move at any time. Neither country has genuine political stability nor are their leaders known for composure and sense of responsibility. Their peoples can be driven to emotional frenzies in given situations by demagoguery, chauvinism, and religious fervour. Some voices have already been heard saying that out of a population of 130 million, a loss of, say, a few million should be sustainable! One can only shudder at the prospect of such nervous fingers and heartless strategists holding the nuclear trigger.

In particular, the statement of Pakistan's foreign minister about winning the nuclear war against India within hours shows appalling ignorance and irresponsibility. It is sadly also characteristic of the self-delusion and bravado which has afflicted Pakistani policymakers from time to time. While making such an astonishing statement, the minister clearly forgot that victory means little in a nuclear war. To put it more graphically, if, for instance, in a hypothetical future nuclear war with India, the main Pakistani cities, e.g. Karachi and Lahore, are wiped out, and thus millions of Pakistanis are dead or wounded, and their future generations are horribly contaminated by deadly germs and diseases, the notional 'victory' for Pakistan over India, even if it could be achieved after 'one-and-a-half hour,' would in fact be worse than defeat in conventional warfare. The same, of course, will apply to any such wishful and macabre thinking emanating from India as well. It should in fact be self-evident to any sane person that a nuclear war is something that has got to be avoided at all costs.

Even if it is assumed that there will be no actual nuclear war between the two countries, the likelihood of nuclear brinkmanship between them will remain very real. Thus, the sword of Damocles would be hanging over their heads most of the time. In the process, the rest of the world too would be kept on tenterhooks, being always apprehensive of the fearsome consequences of an India–Pakistan nuclear confrontation, not only for the subcontinent itself but also for countries beyond. Hence, whether the path is leading towards nuclear destruction or, at the minimum, towards nuclear brinkmanship, the option for peace and compromise must surely be more appealing.

This prospect of a nuclear confrontation in South Asia could, perhaps, induce the world community and, in particular, the USA to make a more sustained effort to bring about an improvement in India–Pakistan relations. There could be renewed pressure on India to resolve the Kashmir dispute. Thus, Pakistan has been pressing the US to play the kind of role it had played in mediating between the Arabs and the Israelis as also in Bosnia between the Serbs and the Muslims. The US has pointed out that in those disputes, the two sides had been willing to accept US mediation. In the case of Kashmir as well, both India and Pakistan would have to agree to American mediation. So far India seems determined to shut out any kind of third party role in the context of Kashmir or, indeed, in any bilateral disputes with Pakistan. Hence, there do not seem to be good prospects for an American intervention while India sticks to its intransigence.

The Case for Fresh Thinking

Will Pakistan and India ever be able to live together in relative harmony as good neighbours, or will the next fifty years of their existence bring even more tension and strife, with a real possibility of a nuclear holocaust? Is there some kind of a law of nature that India and Pakistan must forever be enemies? These questions are increasingly being asked by many people on both sides of the border, by the common man as well as by the intellectuals and others.

The founding fathers certainly had spoken in favour of a relationship of peace and cooperation. Mohammad Ali Jinnah, who had led the Muslim struggle for the creation of Pakistan, had even favoured joint defence by the two countries, after independence, against any external aggression. India's first Prime Minister Jawaharlal Nehru had also come to the conclusion, several years after independence, that 'India and Pakistan cannot help playing an important role in Asia...If India and Pakistan follow a contrary policy

and are opposed to each other, they will obviously be neutralising each other and cannot play that role…This conflict and wasteful effort will wipe us out from the face of the earth.'[8]

Things went awry right from the beginning. Jinnah was far less optimistic about the course of bilateral relations, merely seven months after independence. Thus, on 11 March 1948, when asked whether there was any hope that the two countries would ever be able to settle their differences, he had replied: 'Yes, provided the Indian government will shed its superiority complex and will deal with Pakistan on an equal footing and fully appreciate the realities.'[9]

The truth is that the bilateral relationship would have been very different if the requisite vision and statesmanship had been shown by the leaders of the two countries. At the minimum, there could have been mutually beneficial trade, easier communications, and cultural links.

The onus lay mainly with India, the larger country, which could have shown magnanimity and adopted a policy of letting bygones be bygones. In reality, the situation turned out to be the opposite. In the early years after independence, it was India's menacing attitude towards Pakistan that created a deep sense of insecurity in the latter. This, more than anything else, pushed Pakistan into military pacts with the West which, in turn, hardened India's attitude on the Kashmir issue. Also, once Pakistan became militarily strong, its posture towards India became more defiant and this probably led to the 1965 War. During the subsequent years, the relationship has remained marred by deep suspicions, acrimony, and tensions.

The course of policies followed after Independence belied the early hopes. Contrary to the views of the founding fathers of the two countries, distrust and hate have been more characteristic of their relationship rather than peaceful co-existence and accommodation. The hangover of centuries of conflicts and recriminations has nurtured psychological attitudes which have subverted rational thinking. For the greater part in the past half-century, neither the Indian nor the Pakistani rulers have shown the ability to rise above conservative and myopic considerations. They have allowed small problems to turn into major disputes and bigger problems have escalated into wars. Their periodic negotiations have been a dialogue of the deaf, marked by posturing and playing to the galleries. Neither side has been willing to make any concession for fear that this would expose them to charges of betrayal and surrender.

The nuclear explosions carried out by the two countries have given a dramatic new turn to the situation and should jolt them out of their melancholia. Now, the stark choice before India and Pakistan is between

survival on the one side and a nuclear holocaust or, at the minimum, the constant threat of such destruction, on the other side. This is one aspect of the fateful choice confronting the two countries. The other aspect is that the continuation or acceleration of a nuclear and missiles race is bound to take a heavy toll of their severely stretched economic resources, imposing ever-greater hardships on their citizens. Even if a nuclear war between India and Pakistan can be avoided, the cost of developing nuclear weapons and missiles would become crippling for the economies of the two countries, which are already under severe pressure. To add to their woes, the nuclear explosions carried out by the two countries have attracted international economic sanctions on them, placing additional burdens on their struggling economies. The prospects of debt default, financial bankruptcy, run-away inflation, and even widespread famines and starvation cannot be ruled out. The choice for the two countries is thus between grinding poverty or even destruction on the one hand, and peace and prosperity, on the other.

It should be increasingly evident that the most compelling inducement in favour of peace between Pakistan and India is economic. The two countries are amongst the poorest in the world, based on per capita income, although Pakistan is comparatively a little better off on this count. In relative terms, both countries have come a long way since Independence in agricultural and industrial development. In technology in general, both have made significant progress. In the nuclear field, they are ahead of most countries in the world. There has always been an immense potential of mutually beneficial cooperation between them. Among other avenues, the forum of SAARC (South Asian Association for Regional Cooperation), set up in 1984 could have ushered in an era of institutional cooperation, possibly on the model of ASEAN or even the European community.

The bitter political divide between India and Pakistan has effectively stymied any kind of meaningful progress under the aegis of SAARC. Whatever progress has been made by either of them in the economic field has been largely devoured by the crushing defence burden on both, apart from their inability to keep their population growth in check. It is paradoxical and even absurd that both are willing to spend, for instance, $80 million just to buy a single combat aircraft for their air force, which might well perish in an air crash or soon become obsolete, but they cannot spare even a minuscule fraction of the price of such an aircraft to build schools and hospitals, to provide clean drinking water and basic sanitation for their long-suffering peoples. This is both cruel and absurd.

There is a case now, more than ever before, for fresh thinking in both India and Pakistan about their bilateral relationship. The case for re-evaluation

becomes irresistible when it is realized that a nuclear war and the present arms race, including the development of short- and long-range missiles, carries the serious risk of bringing mutual destruction. The politics of the status quo are leading towards nuclear destruction and economic ruin. On the other hand, peace and compromise, based on a drastic reduction in armaments, would be infinitely more advantageous for both. The common person in the two countries would, of course, be the greatest beneficiary. Hence, the establishment of good relations between the two countries need not any longer be motivated by considerations of high morality which, in any case, is always in short supply. A harmonious relationship in the subcontinent has now become an imperative of national self-interest which should carry weight with even the most myopic policymakers in their midst.

The matter need not be viewed in terms of negative imperatives only. It can also be analysed in a more positive framework. The peoples of India and Pakistan are the proud inheritors of some great civilizations going back to nearly nine thousand years in history. Until overwhelmed by the English colonialists in the nineteenth century, the Indian subcontinent had been generally ahead of most other countries of the world in culture, wealth, system of government, and other spheres of activity. It was the fame of the riches of India, particularly under the Mughal dynasty, which had originally brought the Europeans across 10,000 miles of ocean to South Asia. Even today, the countries of the subcontinent have the capability of doing very much better than many other countries of the world in technology, science, agriculture, industry, and diverse fields. Their peoples are talented and hard-working and can secure high living standards. But this will only be possible provided that Pakistan and India can live together in peace, cut down their expenditure on defence, and establish regional economic cooperation.

The conditions of peace will facilitate normal friendly contacts between Indians and Pakistanis who, like Europeans of diverse nationalities, share many things in common: music, literature, fashions, festivals, sports, and food. While abroad, even now, Indians and Pakistanis often gravitate towards each other. When their sports teams are not in contest with each other, Indian fans tend to support the Pakistani team against a third country and Pakistanis often support the Indian team. Their musicians, singers, actors, and sportsmen have numerous fans and admirers across the borders. This is something instinctive and is reflective of a degree of togetherness brought by co-habitation in the same region for centuries. As long as Pakistan's separate sovereign existence is respected, the common strains in the cultures of the two countries would always work to draw their peoples closer.

Time is a great healer. The bitterness, both ideological as well as personal, which had been accentuated by the Partition in 1947, has lost at least some of its intensity, particularly for the majority of their population consisting of the generations born after independence. Many among them do argue, that if India (or, conversely, Pakistan) can develop good relations with Thailand or Brazil, why can't they be friendly to their immediate neighbour with whom they also have many things in common?

Of course, the big question is as to how should the two countries proceed to improve their bilateral ties. It would seem that, in the first instance, the political elites and intellectuals in both India and Pakistan need to do some real soul-searching and honest self-appraisal as to why things have gone wrong for the past fifty years. There will have to be a genuine conviction that the policies pursued so far by them have hurt both countries; and that the politics of hate, misrepresentation, and inflexibility have been barren, wasteful, and destructive. Neither country has gained in the process. More so, after the acquisition of nuclear weapons capability and missile technology by both countries, the situation has taken a qualitative turn for the worse. The policies of the status quo will no longer work since they will lead inexorably towards nuclear brinkmanship and unthinkable destruction. Therefore, both sides have to make a conscious effort to move away from the barren old policies and stereotyped logic.

The new thinking will have to be based on hard realism and cold calculations, free of self-delusions and emotionalism. Perhaps, this might be less difficult now than before. India and Pakistan are now face-to-face with the horrendous possibility of nuclear brinkmanship or even holocaust and, at the minimum, an alarmingly expensive arms race. Therefore, the first conscious decision that the two countries must make is to avoid a nuclear war at all costs. This will have to be a policy decision based on genuine conviction and should not merely be a tactical manoeuvre or a pro forma verbal exercise. To give this conviction a formal shape, the two countries could sign a 'no war pact' and 'no first use of nuclear weapons' which should be formally ratified by their parliaments and endorsed by their peoples through national referenda. Such a commitment not to go to war will have to be the fundamental premise for establishing a new *modus vivendi*.

But beyond that, in the spirit of a new realism, India and Pakistan should seek to address the underlying causes of tension between them with a view to establishing a durable peace. It seems that there are three main problems: firstly, the Kashmir dispute which both agree is a fundamental stumbling block. There are two other major problems even though they

have received less public attention and about whose existence there could
be lesser unanimity, and that is, Pakistan's perception that India has never
been reconciled to its existence and seeks to reabsorb it into India and India's
perception that, despite its smaller size, Pakistan poses a serious security
threat to India as well as a permanent nagging challenge to it in all spheres
of activity.

To examine the Kashmir dispute, the existing position is that Pakistan has
been insisting that this is the 'core' issue which must be resolved on the basis
of the UN resolutions, passed between 1948 to 1957, asking for an impartial
plebiscite to determine whether the Kashmiri people wish to join India or
Pakistan. India too regards Kashmir as the main dispute with Pakistan though
its prescription for a solution is the opposite, that Pakistan should accept
Kashmir as an integral part of India. That is to say that Pakistan should
accept *de jure* India's *de facto* control over the larger portion of Kashmir and
also yield the Pakistan-controlled portion of Kashmir. The positions of the
two sides have remained frozen for a long time. The new thinking would
require some way to resolve or, at least, to defuse the Kashmir dispute.

There are fears in Pakistan that India seeks to turn Pakistan into a satellite
of some sort, say, into another Bhutan. In general, most Pakistanis view India
as a chauvinistic country with hegemonic designs. Thus, ways must be found
to overcome and remove these fears on a credible and durable basis. On the
other hand, India perceives Pakistan as a destabilizing factor, even apart from
the Kashmir problem, and also as a serious security threat. The ruling Hindu
majority in India cannot easily forget the history of the past one thousand
years during which the Muslims, despite their smaller numbers, were able
to rule most of India. True, times have changed and India has proven its
military superiority against Pakistan, more particularly in the 1971 War. But
Pakistan's persistent efforts to match India in every field are interpreted by
many Indians to mean that Pakistan refuses to recognize the physical reality
of its neighbour's larger size and resources which, in the Indian view, warrant
a wider and more important role for India in the region.

There are suspicions in India that Pakistan has had a hand in fomenting
sabotage and subversion in India. It is also resentful that Pakistan never seems
to miss any opportunity to oppose or embarrass India in every international
forum. Also, from the Indian point of view, Pakistan's strident emphasis on
its Islamic identity is viewed as a destabilizing factor for India's secular polity
and territorial integrity, keeping in mind that over 100 million Muslims, as
also other large non-Hindu minorities like the Sikhs, are living in India. The
new thinking would have to address these Indian concerns as well.

Indian Acceptance of the Irreversible Separation of Pakistan

Leaving the Kashmir dispute for later analysis, it might be more logical, first of all, to address Pakistan's apprehensions regarding the threat to its territorial integrity and sovereign existence posed by India. Obviously, no country can compromise on its sovereignty and territorial integrity. Hence, in order to establish a durable peace and mutual understanding between the two neighbouring countries, there needs to be a definitive realization and a credible affirmation, on the part of India, that the separation of Pakistan, which was brought about by the popular will of the Muslims of India in 1947, is an irreversible fact. There can be no going back to the concept of a united India. This controversy must end once for all, since more than enough energy has already been spent in this vain pursuit.

It may be correct that not everyone in India who thinks on the lines of a reunion is motivated by jingoistic feelings. But there must be a realization even by well-meaning people in India who believe that the Partition was a mistake, resulting from some kind of rectifiable misunderstanding between brothers,[10] that they must reconcile themselves to the ground realities. So much water has passed under the bridges in the past half century as to rule out any kind of reversal or going back in time; secondly, there is absolutely no acceptance in Pakistan of the idea of reintegration with India. The Hindu chauvinists in India, who would like to use force if necessary to secure Pakistan's break-up and reintegration with India, must understand that such an attempt can only cause the worst catastrophe because of the possession of nuclear weapons by the two protagonists.

An erroneous analogy must not be drawn in India from the secession of East Pakistan in 1971. In ideological terms, India can take little encouragement from the break-up of Pakistan at that time. The creation of Bangladesh was certainly a grave set-back for Pakistan's territorial integrity, but it did not mean any kind of acceptance of the 'one people' theory propounded by the Hindu leadership while opposing the demand for Pakistan, in contradistinction to the 'two-nations' theory propagated by the Muslim League leadership. No doubt, for political and economic reasons of their own, the people of East Pakistan broke away from united Pakistan. But the important point, in terms of ideology, was that they did not opt to rejoin India. Had they done so, it would have constituted the rejection of the philosophy which brought Pakistan into existence. What happened was that Bangladesh chose to maintain its sovereign identity, within borders whose demarcation was based solely on its Muslim identity. This was also what had been visualized in the original Pakistan Resolution of 1940, namely, the break-up of British India by the creation of sovereign Muslim autonomous areas in the north-west and north-east of the subcontinent. Pakistan did break into two parts in 1971 but the *raison d'être* of the Partition of India in 1947 continued to hold good, namely that the Muslim majority areas in the north-west (today's Pakistan) and the north-east (today's Bangladesh) should have sovereign status.

The original concept of a separate Muslim homeland, given by Iqbal in his famous Allahabad address in 1930, did not include Bengal in such a state. Iqbal had said, 'I would like to see the Punjab, North-West Frontier Province, Sindh and Baluchistan amalgamated into a single state. Self-government within the British Empire or without the British Empire, the formation of a consolidated North-West Indian Muslim State appears to me to be the final destiny of the Muslims, at least of North-West India.' The Lahore Resolution, which was the basis of the struggle for the creation of Pakistan, mentioned independent states (in plural) 'in the north-western and eastern zones of India.' It was on the later insistence, mainly of the Bengali Muslims, that the concept of a single Muslim homeland was put forward. Hence, the separation of Bangladesh did not go counter to the original concept of Pakistan.

Those in India who still have dreams of reintegration of Pakistan (and Bangladesh) with India must also understand that, with the passing of time, the situation on the ground in the present day Pakistan has changed completely. The sizeable Hindu and Sikh population living in Pakistan at the time of its creation in 1947 had left shortly thereafter. Today's Punjab and Sindh provinces are over 90 per cent Muslim majority areas. In pre-Partition Punjab, for instance, the non-Muslims were a powerful political force, even though they were overall in a minority. Similarly, Hindus in Sindh were quite well entrenched and had a significant political voice. Even in the NWFP, the non-Muslims, though small in number, had the ability to manoeuvre politically. The situation has since changed beyond recognition and the past simply cannot be resuscitated. After fifty years of existence, the territories constituting today's Pakistan are a solid Muslim block with a huge population of over 130 million people. They are intensely conscious of their Pakistani identity and would resist any attempt to make them a part of India.

What is probably even more important is the fact that such a large block of Muslim population simply cannot be absorbed by India or be reintegrated in it. Even if, for the sake of argument, it is assumed that Pakistan is somehow brought back into the Indian fold, this would be a recipe for constant secessionist activity and horrendous bloodshed. Hence, even from the point of view of India's own self-interest, the objective of re-absorption of Pakistan in India does not make political sense. It would destabilize India itself and throw that country into a vicious cycle of political crises, terrorism, and secessionist movements. International opinion today is solidly against any such forcible retention of territory. The two examples of the separation of Bangladesh in 1971 and the more recent disintegration of Yugoslavia (more specifically Bosnia and Kosovo) are pointers to which way the international opinion is moving.

There has to be a definitive realization by even the most rabid circles in India, including the extremist Shiv Sena and the RSS, that there is no option left but to accept Pakistan's permanent separate existence. The only scenario, very hypothetical and illusory, in which such an integration can take place would be if Pakistan itself were to make such a move, arising out of its own changed convictions or requirements. In fact, even in such a scenario, the hazards posed by Pakistan's hypothetical return to the Indian fold would be such that it would make more sense for the Indian leaders to refuse such a move because, in the event of reintegration, the demographic composition of India would change very drastically and the existing Hindu domination of the country would be seriously jeopardized.

India must come to accept that it is in its own interests to proceed on the basis that the Partition of 1947 has become an irreversible phenomenon. Perhaps, such a realization is already there. It had started to dawn in India after the first decade of independence when India's founding leader and first Prime Minister Jawaharlal Nehru himself had to admit that 'conflict and wasteful effort will wipe us (India and Pakistan) out from the face of the earth.' Paradoxically, the 1971 War, which India had won, only reinforced this realization. For instance, while talking to the author, a leading Indian journalist Girilal Jain, commented bitterly in 1976, 'What did India get out of the 1971 War? Instead of one Pakistan, now there are two Pakistans.' Strong anti-India feelings had surfaced in Bangladesh, despite India's crucial role in securing its independence. The fact that there was practically no sentiment amongst the people of Bangladesh—after it broke away from Pakistan, with India's military support—to rejoin their ethnic and linguistic brethren in West Bengal (India) proved that the two-nation theory, on the basis of which Pakistan was created in 1947, still held good in 1971 and afterwards.

India could draw a useful lesson from Pakistan's historical experience. The attempt to hold on to East Pakistan, after its people were alienated, proved to be utterly futile. A salutary conclusion could be drawn from Pakistan's subsequent reconciliation with Bangladesh. In spite of all the bitterness preceding the break-up of Pakistan in 1971, the two former wings re-established ties of friendship and a normal relationship just five years after the traumatic event. To its credit, Pakistan has shown no ulterior designs to reabsorb Bangladesh and is fully reconciled to its separation. There is a clear moral here for India as well. Whatever might have been the Hindu majority's reasons for opposing Partition in 1947, it did happen and nothing can be gained by crying over spilt milk or by trying to re-write history.

Finally, it can be said that the passing of time has made the reality of Pakistan a settled fact for most Indians. The younger generations in India have never lived in a united subcontinent. Not even a small percentage of Indians have ever visited Pakistan and the majority have probably never in their lives even met any Pakistanis face-to-face. Instead, they have been raised on an anti-Pakistan diet and tend to view Pakistanis as aliens and unfriendly creatures. Hence, the 'we' feeling which is the basis of a common nationhood simply does not exist in India, and certainly not in Pakistan. Many Indians say that for them Pakistan is as remote a country as Poland or Panama. Indeed, the consciousness of the nearness of Pakistan comes only for the negative reason that many people in India have a threat perception from this particular neighbour.

For the foregoing reasons, the new thinking must perforce be that India will have to expressly renounce any interest whatsoever in seeking the dismemberment of Pakistan or its reintegration in the Indian fold. Indeed, the dismemberment of Pakistan could be destabilizing for India itself. There has to be a realization in India that this very fear of dismemberment, whether real or perceived, has been a fundamental reason for Pakistan's distrust of India. It was this sense of insecurity felt by Pakistan which led to its joining the military pacts, and the tensions and the wars which followed. By alleviating these Pakistani fears, India would be acting in its own best interests. For these reasons, it is time that India went to all possible lengths to instil an abiding sense of confidence in Pakistan on this score. This could take the shape of formal statements, legal treaties and, above all, confidence building measures on the ground. The modalities of this process could be worked out through mutual consultations.

Pakistan's Acceptance of the Realities in the Subcontinent

Pakistan also needs to take a fresh look at its policy of keeping up a permanent confrontation with India in every field, whether it is defence or diplomacy, trade or technology. This would require that emotionalism, fanaticism, and simple one-upmanship should be set aside. Any kind of cool-headed reappraisal of the course of bilateral relations over the past fifty years must lead to the conclusion that this confrontation has hurt Pakistan more than India.

There is no getting away from the hard fact that Pakistan has the physical disadvantage of smaller size and lesser resources than India. Its bid to match India despite this fact has taken a heavy toll of its resources and energy. The early Muslims no doubt gained spectacular victories against much larger forces but they were imbued with a rare spirit of sacrifice and singular dedication. In addition, they used new war strategies, including short supply lines as against the traditional armour-heavy armies. The more recent parallel of little Israel prevailing over the larger Arab neighbours is also not accurate. It has been the vital support of a superpower, the US, which has really given Israel the edge in confronting the Arab countries which, in addition, have been weakened by internal divisions. Indian armed forces are not only larger in size and have training standards comparable to Pakistan, but they also have the backing of a bigger economy and a more elaborate infrastructure. Also, over the past forty years, India received massive military and diplomatic support from a superpower, the Soviet Union.

The dice has thus always been heavily loaded against Pakistan. In particular, this unending competition with India has placed a disproportionate burden on the common person in Pakistan who is constantly required to make ever greater financial and other sacrifices in the unequal bid to match India. To illustrate the point, if India spends merely 5 per cent of its budget on defence, Pakistan has to spend, say, 40 per cent of its budget to keep up with India. Had such sacrifices not been made necessary, the per capita income in Pakistan could have been significantly higher and, on a comparative basis, Pakistan could have made far greater progress in the economic, scientific, social, and other fields. The policymakers in Islamabad, living in secluded luxury, and the motley crowd of drawing room politicians and fire-breathing demagogues seem to have paid scant attention to the woes of the average person who, in the final resort, bears the cost of the ambitions of the rulers and politicians.

The example of the Soviet Union needs also to be kept in mind by policymakers in Pakistan. For decades, the Soviet Union had spent heavily on defence and, from the military point of view, it had made itself invincible. Eventually, it fell without a shot being fired because, in its bid to keep up with the West, the Soviet Union had bled itself white. Its economy simply could not sustain the enormous burdens of defence spending any further. The Soviet Union had collapsed in spite of the fact that it had the advantage of enormous natural resources of its own, supplemented by the resources of its empire, plus a huge regimented work force—all operating under a dictatorial command. As compared to the Soviet Union, Pakistan has comparatively fewer natural resources and it has been pitted against a country several times bigger than itself. Unlike the Soviet Union, Pakistan has rarely enjoyed political stability and its work force is relatively uneducated and undisciplined. With this background, it requires a far greater effort by Pakistan to match India than had been the case of the Soviet Union *vis-à-vis* the US and the West.

It has been argued that Pakistan cannot lower its guard against India, which would pounce on Pakistan the moment it got an opportunity. Is Pakistan's case unique and is there no way it can survive in relative peace and dignity while living next door to an unfriendly larger neighbour? After all, Pakistan is not the only small country in the world living alongside a much larger neighbour, with whom relations have been strained. There is Cuba, a small country, which has survived for the past forty years despite having antagonistic relations with the US, a superpower in its very neighbourhood. Vietnam has survived with dignity though its relations with its huge neighbour China have been strained and had once even erupted in bitter fighting. Little Taiwan has faced the might of mainland China for nearly fifty years and has not only survived but also done exceedingly well in the economic field. To start with, Taiwan did have the military backing of the US, but this has greatly diminished since 1971 when the latter improved its relations with mainland China. How about Afghanistan which has had tense relations with Pakistan, during the periods of King Zahir Shah and President Daoud, but survived well enough against its larger neighbour? Nepal and Sri Lanka have survived despite having many problems with their next-door neighbour, India.

History is full of many examples of small countries managing to preserve their independence and territorial integrity, in spite of the antagonism of larger neighbours. This success was achieved by these small countries without attempting to match their bigger neighbours in armed strength. With the help of diplomacy and alliances, shrewd policies and prudence, the smaller states have, all through history, learnt to survive against their larger neighbours. Some might have done so by becoming vassals of the neighbouring giants, but this cannot be said for others, such as the more recent examples of Cuba, Vietnam, or Taiwan. In other words, it is not indispensable for a small country, living next door to a larger and even unfriendly neighbour, to seek to match the latter in military strength. While maintaining a certain defensive capability, the smaller country should be able to survive by making use of shrewd diplomacy, exercising prudence and, where feasible, by building alliances.

On the contrary, from the beginning, Pakistan has sought to build up its military strength, rather than relying on other means as the basis for its survival and security against its larger neighbour. At times, Pakistan's military strategy has sought to go beyond the defensive, to achieve the level of a military balance or parity with India, with visions of even securing a military victory over it. This is where the real difficulty has come. Being one-eighth the size of India, Pakistan has obviously been at a great disadvantage in its bid to keep up with India. Pakistan has, therefore, been obliged to spend much more, on a per capita basis, to build its armed strength than would have been warranted by a purely defensive strategy.

Cuba, for instance, in the past forty years, has never planned in terms of a military balance with the US or defeating the latter in battle. Cuba's only interest has been in surviving against the US, without having to compromise on its national sovereignty and the freedom to pursue policies of its choice. Until 1991, Cuba could look to the Soviet bloc for support but this has since disappeared. Instead, President Fidel Castro has been building bridges with his neighbours and others, and relying on international public opinion to keep the US at bay. Similarly, Taiwan has never sought to build up its military strength to be able to achieve military parity with China. Such an ambition would have altogether broken the back of the Taiwanese economy and would even have increased the threat of a Chinese attack.

It would seem that historical memories of a thousand years of domination of India by the small Muslim minority, over the much larger Hindu majority, have something to do with this Pakistani attitude. However, what is forgotten in this historical comparison is that in the past, the Hindu kingdoms were divided in small entities whereas today's India is a solid giant. Moreover, the present is a very different age, in which modern technology has all but eliminated the relevance of the heroic swordsman cutting through a phalanx of adversaries and winning the battle for Islam. Unfortunately, romantic illusions of this kind persist in Pakistan, fed by the pure demagoguery of its politicians. It is this peculiar mentality which explains why Pakistan has remained over-stretched in the past fifty years.

The never-ending confrontation with India has resulted both in a siege mentality and placed a disproportionate burden on Pakistan's resources. Moreover, this confrontation has distorted nearly all of Pakistan's policies—internal as well as external.

It can be argued that Pakistan's political upheavals and internal destabilization in the first fifty years of its existence have been directly or indirectly affected by the conflict with India. The confrontation with India has forced Pakistan to spend far more than it could afford on its defence. Thus, the armed forces have always been given the lion's share in the country's meagre resources. As a consequence, the armed forces have also come to play a larger than life role in the country's internal politics. Four times in Pakistan's history, the armed forces have seized power, ruling directly for nearly twenty-four years out of fifty years of Pakistan's existence. The army first seized power in 1958, but the commander-in-chief had already become something of a kingmaker for some years prior to that date. From 1958 to 1971 and again from 1977 to 1988, the army chief actually ruled as the president. Similarly, even after parliamentary democracy was restored in 1988, the army chief has acted as one of the 'troika' in the power structure. Considerations of 'national security' have been cited as the reason for such a direct or indirect role for the armed forces in the running of the country. Of course, the personal ambitions of the army chief, and the top generals, have been no less important in determining such a political role by the army. As I write, the army has once again taken charge of the country. On that fateful day of 12 October 1999, General Pervez Musharraf had Prime Minister Nawaz Sharif ousted from power and placed under arrest. General Pervez Musharraf is now chief executive of Pakistan and the constitution is held in abeyance.

These repeated interventions of the armed forces in the running of the country have thwarted Pakistan's political democratic evolution. Human rights have also been a major casualty. The suppression of political activists, the news media, and intellectuals has been a black mark in Pakistan's history. Moreover, lack of democracy has fanned regional grievances and this is what had contributed *inter alia* to the secession of Pakistan's eastern wing. The imposition of military rule also lowers Pakistan's international image and gives impetus to Indian propaganda against Pakistan. India has thus been able to win international sympathy by parading its democratic credentials against Pakistan's military adventures.

There is another key area in which Pakistan has suffered internally due to its confrontation with India. Right from the time of independence, India has evidently sought to promote secessionist activities in Pakistan. To begin with, the NWFP, on Pakistan's border with Afghanistan, had a leftover of supporters of the Khudai Khidmatgar Party of the 'Frontier Gandhi' Abdul Ghaffar Khan, who was a close ally of the Congress and had believed in a united India. However, when the people of NWFP voted overwhelmingly in favour of Pakistan, Ghaffar Khan changed tactics and started a movement for a 'Pukhtunistan' state. In this endeavour, he received some covert support from India.[11] More open support came from the royal regime in Afghanistan, which had irredentist claims over some of the areas constituting Pakistan.[12] Later, Ghaffar Khan went into self-exile in Afghanistan where he died and was buried. The 'Pukhtunistan' problem remained a headache for Pakistan's foreign policy planners with respect to Afghanistan until the Soviet occupation of Afghanistan when Pakistan's support for the Afghans brought about a pro-Pakistan shift in public thinking in Afghanistan. However, in Pakistan itself, the survivors of Ghaffar Khan's party have continued to play up Pukhtun regionalism.

Over the years, secessionists and even political opponents of the government of the day in Pakistan have, in many cases, received encouragement, and even material support from India. In the case of East Pakistan, it is indisputable that India played an active role to encourage Bengali regional aspirations. The final separation of East Pakistan took place as a result of the Indian military invasion. Similarly, India has also been encouraging regional feelings in Sindh province. Official circles in Pakistan have been convinced of Indian involvement in the training of various dissident Pakistani groups, including Sindhi nationalists and the activists of the MQM, i.e., Muttahida Qaumi Movement/Muhajir Qaumi Movement, an ethnic party now split into two factions in urban Sindh. In fact, it seems that anyone seeking to weaken the federation of Pakistan has a receptive audience in India and can secure clandestine support from that country.

Pakistan too seems to have encouraged Sikh secessionist activities in the Indian Punjab. This movement had acquired a serious dimension in the mid-1980s but, since then, seems to have lost its momentum. India has been accusing Pakistan of complicity with the Sikh secessionists. Pakistani involvement in minor secessionist activities in the north-eastern part of India has also often been alleged by India. Of course, the principal Indian grievance has been the alleged Pakistani encouragement of Kashmiri separatists and, in particular, the uprising since 1990 in the Indian-occupied Kashmir. India has accused Pakistan of conducting a proxy war there, a charge denied by Pakistan which claims that its help to the Kashmiris is confined to diplomatic and moral support only.

In addition to the encouragement of secessionist and regional feelings in each other's territory, a more sinister dimension to the India–Pakistan confrontation has emerged in the past decade. Though both deny it categorically, the two countries have evidently been involved in a ruthless, though clandestine, campaign to destabilize each other internally through subversion, sabotage, and terrorism. India's military training of the Bengali secessionists has been mentioned already. There is also evidence to show

India's support for the Al-Zulfikar movement in the 1980s, which was involved in political assassinations, bombings, and plane hijackings.   .

In more recent years, there seems to be a pattern that whenever there is a serious incident of killing or sabotage in the Indian-held Kashmir, shortly thereafter, there is a terrorist act in Pakistan. Indian complicity is usually suspected even if it has been difficult to prove it beyond a shadow of doubt.

While this may look like a tit for tat situation, the balance sheet in this 'secret war' between India and Pakistan shows that the latter has suffered more in the process. Pakistan was in fact cut down in half, losing its eastern wing in 1971. On the other hand, India remains territorially intact. The most serious secessionist attempt, that of the Sikhs in India's Punjab province in the 1980s, which probably received some degree of support from Pakistan, was eventually crushed by India. However, on the pattern of Bangladesh, India's involvement with secessionist elements in Sindh province could pose a more serious challenge to Pakistan's integrity.

In addition to encouraging secessionists, India is widely suspected of training terrorists operating in parts of Pakistan. Some of them are mercenaries who commit acts of terrorism in return for financial rewards. Others are moved by sectarian feelings. These growing acts of terrorism in different places in Pakistan have become a destabilizing factor for the country. They have shaken the confidence of the Pakistani people in their governments and also impaired Pakistan's reputation abroad portraying it as an unstable country with poor law and order, torn by factional fighting.

The rise of sectarianism among Pakistani Muslims in the last twenty years is a particularly ominous development. To begin with, the incidents involving Shia–Sunni groups were linked to the 1979 Islamic Revolution in Iran, the main Shia stronghold. Pakistani Shias, who are outnumbered nearly ten to one by the Sunnis, had started to look increasingly towards Iran for support. As a reaction, some Sunni groups turned to Saudi Arabia and the Gulf countries for sustenance and now both Sunni and Shia groups are heavily armed, trained and continue to sporadically engage in vicious acts of violence against each other. However, the sectarian conflict in Pakistan has worsened in direct proportion to the increased intensity of the Kashmiri rebellion against Indian occupation, thus giving credence to the belief that mercenaries paid by India are actually behind these heinous acts of terrorism.

The foregoing analysis suggests that the path of confrontation has harmed Pakistan more than it has harmed India. This trend is likely to continue, or even get worse, if the confrontationist course is maintained in the years ahead. Even on the basis of cost-effectiveness, policymakers in Pakistan need to ask themselves as to what have been the net gains achieved by the unending confrontation with India followed for the past fifty years. The hard and unpleasant truth is that confrontation has not been beneficial for Pakistan. It is true that India has also suffered but, comparatively speaking, Pakistan has suffered much more. This is because, as compared to India, Pakistan is inherently more vulnerable to internal subversion and sabotage.

Feelings of provincialism emerged from the very beginning when the Bengalis in East Pakistan started to grumble about the domination of West Pakistan. The merging of the West Pakistani provinces in One Unit in 1955 led to resentment against the larger province, the Punjab, as the smaller provinces believed that they had lost their traditional identity. Under the strongman rule of President Ayub Khan (1958–69), the centrifugal tendencies, on the surface, remained in check. But, the secessionist movement in East Pakistan actually gained ground after the 1965 War, with the announcement of the Six Points of Sheikh Mujibur Rahman, followed by the Agartala Conspiracy Case in which he was tried for planning secession in collaboration with India. It seems that since the latter years of the rule of Ayub Khan, the genies of provincialism and sectarianism have been let loose in Pakistan, greatly harming Pakistan's ideological basis. In particular, the tendency of some elements in the political opposition to look abroad, even to known adversaries like India, for support in Pakistan's internal disputes has done grievous harm to the cause of national integration and the sense of patriotism. It is not surprising that India has profited from such divisions and weaknesses in Pakistan.

Rethinking on Kashmir

Kashmir has, of course, been the main dispute throughout between India and Pakistan and the biggest stumbling block in the improvement of relations between the two countries. It would perhaps not be an exaggeration to say that India–Pakistan relations in the past fifty years have been a hostage of the Kashmir dispute. In particular, Pakistan has made it the cardinal test and pre-condition for any meaningful improvement in bilateral relations and the establishment of a durable peace in the subcontinent. There have been endless tensions and wars between India and Pakistan on this issue which is no nearer a settlement today than it was thirty or fifty years ago.

THE MORAL DIMENSION

Morally, Pakistan is on much firmer ground than India on the Kashmir issue. The twentieth century has seen the global acceptance of the principle of national self-determination of peoples all over the world. Thus, Pakistan strikes a sympathetic chord when it insists on allowing the people of Kashmir this right. Pakistan's demand also has international legality. There are UN Security Council resolutions asking for an impartial plebiscite to ascertain the wishes of the people of Jammu and Kashmir as to whether they want to join Pakistan or India. The passing of time might have blurred their memory but has not destroyed their moral or legal content.

It is undeniable that India had, at the outset of the dispute, promised to allow the Kashmiri people the choice to freely decide whether they wanted to join India or Pakistan. In particular, India had promised to abide by the UN resolutions to this effect. Jawaharlal Nehru, India's first prime minister, had made repeated pledges to the world, and to Pakistan bilaterally, that India would allow the people of Kashmir to exercise their right of self-determination in a UN-supervised plebiscite. For instance, in a telegram to the Pakistani prime minister on 30 October 1947, Nehru had said, 'Our assurance that we shall withdraw our troops from Kashmir as soon as peace and order are restored and leave the decision about the future of the State to the people of the State is not merely a pledge to your Government but also to the people of Kashmir and to the world.'[13] Similarly, the Indian representative, Gopalaswami Ayyangar told the UN Security Council on 14 January 1948:

> The question of the future status of Kashmir vis-à-vis her neighbours and the world at large, and a further question, namely, whether she should withdraw from her accession to India, and either accede to Pakistan or remain independent, with a right to claim admission as a Member of the United Nations—all this we have recognized to be a matter for unfettered decision by the people of Kashmir, after normal life is restored to them.[14]

Similar pledges were repeated by Nehru till the mid-1950s.

Any impartial observer would have to say that India has, since then, reneged on these solemn commitments. Making short shrift of India's subsequent sophistry and quibbling justifying the volte-face on its commitments, Krishna Menon, a close aide of Nehru, had stated frankly in 1965 that the real reason why India would not permit a plebiscite in Kashmir was that 'we would lose it'.[15]

India's self-serving argument that the people of Kashmir have, through the decisions of the popularly elected Kashmir Assembly, exercised their right of self-determination has not been accepted by the international community. Such local elections could not be a substitute for a UN-supervised plebiscite. This was so declared in specific terms by the UN Security Council.[16] Furthermore, these local elections were never held in a free atmosphere and, as testified by most foreign observers, they were blatantly rigged. The people of the Pakistan-controlled portion of Kashmir obviously did not participate in this election process or in the 'decision' of the Kashmir Assembly endorsing Kashmir's accession to India.

Even less valid is the Indian argument that the Indian constitution has declared Kashmir to be an 'integral' part of India and that this is a settled matter. Such a unilateral declaration can have no legal validity or international acceptance. India argues that any discussion of Kashmir by another country is an interference in India's internal affairs since Kashmir is an 'integral' part of India just like any other Indian state, like Uttar Pradesh (UP) or Orissa. But the point is that there are no UN resolutions with respect to UP or Orissa, whereas there are a number of such resolutions regarding Kashmir which the UN and other international bodies have expressly described as a 'disputed' territory.

There is also little merit in another Indian argument that the separation of Kashmir from India would damage Indian secularism or imperil the safety of India's large Muslim minority. India has a moral and legal responsibility to protect its minorities and this cannot be contingent to keeping Kashmir as a part of India. Such a spurious argument is tantamount to blackmail, i.e. Kashmir must be kept with India, or else the Muslim population of India would be terrorized. Furthermore, there is no question of 'separation' of Kashmir from India since it has never been accepted as a part of India by the international community, as shown by the UN resolutions on the subject.

The people of Kashmir have all throughout resisted the Indian occupation. In particular, since 1990, they have been involved in an unprecedented popular uprising, marked by unending political agitation, strikes, and protests. In addition, there has been large-scale guerrilla activity. Thousands of Kashmiris, as well as many Indian soldiers, have been killed while the number of those wounded is still higher. The economic life in the Kashmir Valley has almost come to a standstill. India has tried to suppress this popular resistance with a heavy hand and has deployed almost 700,000 military and paramilitary forces in a massive show of force. Impartial foreign observers and international human rights groups have confirmed atrocities committed by the Indian forces at a large scale in which torture, rape, and burning of houses, and even entire villages and localities, have taken place. There have been very serious violations of human rights committed by the Indian occupation forces.

In addition to the past record of broken promises, the more recent Indian actions in Kashmir, i.e. the brutal suppression of the Kashmiris have knocked the bottom out of the Indian case, which is morally unsustainable. India has argued that Pakistan has been involved in training and giving other material aid to the Kashmiri militants, or even fighting a 'proxy war' in Kashmir. If the Kashmiris were not willing to fight the Indian occupation, no amount of Pakistani training or aid would have made any real difference. The truth of the matter is that the people of Kashmir simply do not wish to be a part of India.

Any impartial observer will probably have to admit that, in comparison with India, Pakistan's case on Kashmir stands on much firmer moral and legal grounds. This is primarily because of Pakistan's insistence on giving the Kashmiri people the right to choose, and also its adherence to the UN resolutions. For instance, unlike India, Pakistan has not declared Azad Kashmir to be a part of Pakistan but regards the whole of Kashmir as a disputed territory. It is also noteworthy that Pakistan has said time and again that it would accept the verdict of the Kashmiri people even if they opt to join India. Moreover, Pakistan has always shown its willingness to accept any third party mediation for resolving the Kashmir dispute and it has also been willing to refer the matter to international adjudication and arbitration. There can be little doubt as to who is morally right in the Kashmir dispute.

THE PRAGMATIC CONSIDERATIONS

All of the above-mentioned moral arguments are quite valid, but there has to be a realization in Pakistan that pragmatic considerations are even more compelling. There is no getting away from the fact that we live in an imperfect world. History is full of instances of injustice and moral wrongs which were never, or were only belatedly, corrected. The unpleasant truth is that in real life, good does not always prevail. In the final resort, therefore, nations and governments, like ordinary people, have to learn to live with the harsh facts of life and the strident ground realities.

The example of the Palestinian problem is a relevant parallel to such a consideration. After years of bitter and tragic warfare for a just cause, the Palestinians came around to the view that they would have to come to terms with Israel. The other option was that the Palestinians would be condemned to live indefinitely as refugees. The Oslo Accords were signed which have secured for the Palestinians a homeland which is on the way to becoming a sovereign entity. But the bitter pill of Israel's existence had to be accepted by the Palestinians. Earlier on, Egypt had signed the Camp David Agreement and established normal diplomatic relations with Israel. Having borne the brunt of the fighting against Israel for several decades, Egypt concluded that Israel could not be defeated, more so because of the support it enjoyed of a superpower—the US—and hence the wiser or pragmatic course was to establish peace and a *modus vivendi* with Israel.

History is full of such examples. Early in this century, Turkey lost its possessions in the Balkans and elsewhere, in many cases through force and perfidy. But Turkey has not become a prisoner of the past by an obsession to regain those territories. Instead, it has successfully rebuilt itself as a strong nation, which plays an important role in the international arena. Japan has never been able to regain the four islands annexed by Russia at the end of the Second World War, but has not maintained a posture of antagonism with Russia for this reason. At the end of the same war, several East European countries were taken over by the communists by conquest and deception. This was bitterly resented by the West, but it grew to live with this reality. The building of the Berlin Wall was considered as an outrage by West Germany and the West but they had to acquiesce in this bitter reality. Indeed, Pakistan itself lost East Pakistan in 1971 but has come to terms with the emergence of Bangladesh.

Apart from the loss of territory, there have been other kinds of instances of nations coming to terms with reality. In 1945, Germany and Japan were defeated and occupied by the Allies. But, instead of planning revenge, the two countries embarked on a policy of cooperation with their former enemies and have emerged as two of the biggest power centres of the world. France and Germany are the best of friends since the end of the Second World War, having successfully laid to rest the bitterness of past enmities.

Any number of such examples can be given from modern and ancient history. Territories have changed hands, kingdoms rose and fell, and great wrongs took place, which remained unrectified or were only belatedly set right. Compromise with the harsh realities sometimes becomes inevitable. This does not mean that every wrong should be cheerfully accepted. A nation like any individual has to raise its voice for its legitimate rights. But when this becomes an obsession, which distorts all other needs and puts a nation in some kind of a time warp, then this can become counter-productive. Where everything is relative, the lesser need often has to give way to the greater need.

Coming to the Kashmir dispute, the fact of the matter is that all the main political parties in India—as also the Indian public opinion by and large—are adamant in their determination to hold on to Kashmir, right or wrong. Big power chauvinism is one reason. Centuries-old prejudices against the Muslims is another factor. Of course, India's victory in the 1971 War hardened its attitude even further on the Kashmir issue. Since then, there has been even lesser inclination in India to show any kind of accommodation towards Pakistan. During this period, several prime ministers have come to power in India, but none of them—including Morarji Desai and I.K. Gujral who were more well disposed towards Pakistan—has shown any real flexibility on Kashmir. Words and gestures apart, the operative policy of all rulers in New Delhi on Kashmir remains the same. Moreover, India has the resources and the political will to take the physical and financial losses arising from any insurgency in Kashmir as well as the diplomatic costs of this dispute.

Pakistan has not been able to, and probably cannot, force India to change its stance. In military terms, this was never a feasible proposition for Pakistan but, with the acquisition of nuclear deterrence by both countries, a 'solution' through war has simply to be ruled out. Short of being defeated in a war, there are few prospects of India changing its policy on Kashmir, at least, in the foreseeable future.

The deadlock on Kashmir is brought out glaringly in the manner in which the two countries have been locked in a bloody confrontation in the remote Siachen Glacier since 1984. This has become 'the highest battleground in the world' where the physical environment is most inhospitable all the year around. Located at about 20,000 feet above sea level, Siachen has Arctic conditions. It requires specially imported clothing and other logistic arrangements, which reportedly cost both countries millions of rupees daily, to keep this confrontation going. Hundreds of lives have been lost, mostly due to freezing rather than in actual fighting, while the two antagonists remain determined to fight on for these barren rocks jutting out from the snow at this altitude. This has been the story of the past sixteen years, with no end in sight. India had surprised Pakistan in 1984 by making advances in Siachen, but since then India seems to have suffered relatively more than Pakistan in this standoff. The costly attrition continues; men keep dying needlessly, while neither side has the political will to come to any kind of a sensible compromise. Pakistani hopes that India would call it quits have been unrealistic.

Even more damaging from Pakistan's point of view could be the unreality of another expectation. Contrary to Pakistan's hopeful belief, the parallels of the success of guerrilla resistance in Afghanistan or Vietnam might not be applicable in the case of Kashmir. In those two cases, neither the Russians nor the Americans were willing to stomach the extent of the losses of life which the Indians, on their part, have shown that they are willing to accept. It can be seen that there has been practically no protest from the Indian public against the losses being suffered by the Indian forces in Kashmir, or the financial costs of the involvement in Kashmir. India is poor and overpopulated and life is considered cheap. Hence, the loss of lives of a few soldiers, particularly when this happens in the fighting against the old enemy—Pakistan—has not evidently aroused any great uproar in India. On the other hand, public opinion in the US had turned decisively against the continued military involvement in Vietnam. In the case of the Soviet Union also, the war in Afghanistan had become exceedingly unpopular. Moreover, the Soviet economy, which was already overburdened, could not sustain the expenditure of the Afghan war. The diplomatic costs of the war also became unpalatable for the Soviet Union. It was also a fact that the Afghan Mujahideen were receiving massive, though clandestine, assistance from many sources, including the US, Saudi Arabia, and Pakistan. This is not the case of the Kashmiri freedom fighters.

Thus, Kashmir does not appear to have a parallel with the situation that had existed in Vietnam and Afghanistan. Above all, it seems that the nationalistic sentiment in India is so strong *vis-à-vis* Pakistan that whatever has been the loss of lives and resources suffered by India, in occupying Kashmir, has been borne without much demur by the Indian public and government.

Moral pressure of the world public opinion has also not been much of a factor in the case of the Kashmir dispute. Deplorable as it might be, for most countries of the world Kashmir is at best a marginal issue. For diverse reasons, their priorities seem to be elsewhere. Of course, the Kashmir dispute is not unique in this context. Many other problems around the globe have also received much less attention than they deserved. In the contemporary world, it is the news media, which determines as to which issue gets attention, and the world media is largely in Western control.

The case of Afghanistan is a pointer. While the threat of Soviet communism remained, which was a principal Western preoccupation, Afghanistan was the focus of world attention. It received constant coverage in the news media and the Soviets were roundly criticized by all and sundry. In the Hollywood films of that epoch, the Afghan Mujahideen fighter was depicted as a heroic figure. However, soon after the Soviet forces were withdrawn from Afghanistan and, later on, when the Soviet Union itself disintegrated, the Western-dominated news media lost all interest in Afghanistan, even though there have been some significant developments in that country affecting peace and security in Central Asia. Currently, the same Afghan fighter is portrayed in the news media as a dangerous, fanatical, Islamic 'fundamentalist'.

The same kind of neglect or selective news media coverage has been given to Algeria which has been undergoing a bloody civil war for several years, including horrifying massacres, but it seems that most of the world is unconcerned. Massive human rights violations in that country seem to have been ignored. The civil war in Sri Lanka is another such instance. The Kurdish problem too has been there for decades but has been grossly neglected and has rarely figured either in the news media or in serious international diplomacy.

In the case of the Kashmir dispute, evidently, no real Western interests are involved and, hence, it has generated little attention in the Western-dominated news media. For the West, Kashmir is a remote and strategically unimportant territory in Central Asia, which has hardly any natural resources apart perhaps from its beautiful scenery. Whatever value it has had as a tourist attraction has been destroyed by the unending political tensions and lack of security for the tourists in Kashmir.

The West is caught in a dilemma. It is aware that on moral grounds, the Indian case is weak but condemning India would hurt Western interests in this key country which is the second most populous in the world and is also a big economic attraction. Apart from periodic gentle nudges from the West, which the Indians promptly ignore, little effective pressure has been brought to bear upon India.

It is also an unfortunate reality that the West has shown little sympathy for the causes of the Islamic world. Afghanistan was perhaps one of the few exceptions, but there, it was the desire to thwart the Soviet Union, rather than any real sympathy for the Muslim Afghan people, which motivated the West in supporting the Afghan resistance. The case of the Bosnian Muslims has received more attention, probably because it has been something happening in Europe itself. Moreover, the atrocities, verging on genocide, practised by the Serbs were of such a magnitude that they could not be ignored by the West without appearing to be a total hypocrite in its own eyes. It was the news media coverage of Bosnia, which finally jolted the Western public opinion and stirred the conscience of the Western governments. Even then, it was only belatedly, when a great deal of destruction had already taken place, that Europe, more so the US, woke up to the need to do something concrete to secure some sort of solution of the problem.

Since the disintegration of the Soviet Union and the apparent end of communist expansionism, Islamic 'fundamentalism' has emerged as the main bugbear not only for the Western world but also for some of Pakistan's traditional friends. The latter group includes China and some Muslim Central Asian countries, apart from several conservative, pro-West Arab regimes. These Central Asian countries, even after independence, still have the same old communist-era leaders who were raised on a diet of atheism and secularism. Internal opposition to their rule is coming from the more traditional Muslim circles, whom they brand as Islamic 'fundamentalists'. The Chinese government too is facing an insurgency in the western province of Sinkiang, bordering Kashmir, from the local population who are ethnic Turkish Muslims. Here again, Islamic 'fundamentalists' get the blame.

In the case of the West, it is becoming apparent that the resurgence of the Muslims is a cause of anxiety because after the decline of communism, Islam now seems to represent the only serious challenge to the Western way of life. The number of Muslims in Western countries (in France, UK, Germany, Canada, and the US) has increased quite remarkably in the recent past. The memories of the Crusades and the Turkish rule over East Europe have not altogether disappeared. There are over fifty Muslim states in the world with the potential to become a power bloc.

The relevance of this particular Western mind-set for the Kashmir problem is that it is seen by the West as basically a Muslim cause and one more manifestation of Muslim 'militancy'. It therefore leaves the Western governments and the news media unmoved. This attitude works to India's advantage.

It is also unfortunate that terrorism is being increasingly regarded by the West, as a phenomenon associated with the Muslims. This is a grossly inaccurate accusation as terrorism is found in many other parts of the world as well. The Irish Republican Army (IRA) and the Basque separatists have long practised terrorism right in the heart of Europe. The Jews used terrorism in the 1940s to secure Israel, and one of those terrorists—Yitzhak Shamir—later became the Israeli prime minister. Subsequently, Israel has used state terrorism against its Arab opponents. The Tamils have used terrorism on a large scale in Sri Lanka for their own national objectives. Terrorism has also been rampant in Colombia and other countries in South America. It is, therefore, unfair to single out the Muslims in this respect.

It cannot be denied that the Palestinians, in their desperation, have in some cases resorted to acts of terrorism and that Muslim countries like Libya, Syria, and Iran are alleged to have been associated with the training, financing, and harbouring of terrorists. The insurgency in Kashmir has been associated in some circles with terrorism. The kidnapping and disappearance of four Western tourists in Kashmir not long ago, one of whom was later found decapitated, did not help the Kashmiri cause. Similarly, incidents of stray massacres of Hindus in Kashmir, allegedly by Muslim militants, have also disparaged the freedom fighters.

The Kashmir issue has been around for a long time. For the foreign observers who have followed the Kashmir dispute, there is a sense of *déjà vu* associated to various developments. They have heard the respective arguments of Pakistan and India time and again. While Pakistan accuses India of violation of human rights and disregard of its old commitments to give the right of self-determination to the people of Kashmir, India for its part accuses Pakistan of interference in India's internal affairs, inciting terrorism in Indian-occupied Kashmir and carrying out a proxy war there. The foreign observers have heard these accusations and counter-accusations for the past fifty years and some of them have developed a kind of mental fatigue. In particular, the kind of stereotyped propaganda dished out by the official Pakistani news media has hardly ever won any converts. Many foreign experts tend to shrug off the whole matter as a part of antiquated religious quarrels and the endless squabbling between India and Pakistan. This kind of apathy to the Kashmir dispute by foreign governments and observers helps to maintain the status quo which favours India. It already possesses most of the Jammu and Kashmir state, including the heartland of Kashmir, the valley, in which the capital Srinagar is located.

Furthermore, India's size, as always, helps it. In the typical application of realpolitik, it appears that most states in the world usually give preference to their material interests over moral niceties. For them, India commands much more clout, in comparison with Pakistan, as a regional and even global power, possessing the world's fourth largest armed forces and the tenth largest industrial economy. India has a huge population of nearly one billion people which, obviously, offers greater attraction as a market. Many states are, therefore, inclined to look away from the moral dimension of the Kashmir dispute for the sake of their material interests, obviously to Pakistan's chagrin and disadvantage.

The long stints of military rule in Pakistan have also hurt Pakistan's case on Kashmir. While having dictatorship at home, Pakistan has been seeking to uphold the right of free vote in Kashmir. As against this, India has held elections regularly. This gave India moral superiority in the world, particularly with the growth of demands for the respect of human rights in the last few decades. No doubt, with the restoration of democratic institutions in Pakistan since 1988, the moral edge enjoyed by India on this score was no longer there until the latest seizure of power in Pakistan by the military. India's claims to be a pluralistic, secular society also get a better reception in the Western liberal democracies, as compared to Pakistan's claim over Kashmir, essentially on the basis of a common religion.

The moral and even political edge of Pakistan's case on Kashmir has been diminished by Pakistan's internal divisions which have seen one province pitted against another on linguistic and other factors. This has harmed the very ideological basis for the creation of Pakistan, which is the main Pakistani argument in seeking the incorporation of Kashmir into Pakistan. Sectarian killings in Pakistan, which have increased in frequency in recent years, have done even more harm to its oft-repeated concept of an Islamic brotherhood and the unity of the Ummah. The unending bloodshed in Pakistan's largest city, Karachi, and the bitter grievances of the Urdu-speaking *muhajirs*— migrants from India who were in the forefront in the struggle for the creation of Pakistan—has hardly enhanced Pakistan's moral case. The adversaries can and do argue that if Pakistan cannot keep its existing Muslim population in harmony, how does it expect the Kashmiris to join on the basis of Islamic brotherhood. They may still not want to join India, but some could opt for independence rather than joining either India or Pakistan.

To sum up, for the diverse reasons mentioned above, the moral pressure of world public opinion does not appear to be such that India would be compelled in the foreseeable future to change its stance on Kashmir. Further, it would be an oversimplification to conclude that this state of affairs has been due to the poor projection of the Kashmir cause and Pakistan's case, as has become the standard lament in Pakistan in the news media and elsewhere. In this spirit, there has been a constant temptation to make scapegoats of Pakistani diplomats and press attachés posted abroad for their alleged poor performance. However, doubling the time for propaganda on Kashmir in the official news media, or sending out parliamentarians and other luminaries to foreign countries to project Pakistan's case better, have also not produced the desired results. The reasons for the relative global apathy towards the Kashmir dispute have been outlined above. Poor projection has not been the principal reason for the comparative lack of interest in the Kashmir issue by the world public opinion. In fact, such an appreciation of the world situation has merely created one more illusion in Pakistan that, unfortunately, has prevented a realistic appraisal of the situation. It is obvious that no sound policy decisions can be taken when the basic analysis of the situation is defective.

Options before Pakistan

Under the circumstances, there appears to be a compelling need for policymakers in Pakistan to take stock of the situation realistically and consider what are the options available to them.

The first option, obviously, is to continue to adhere to the policy followed so far, namely, to treat Kashmir as the crux of bilateral relations with India and to continue to insist that without a resolution of this dispute, on the basis of the grant of the right of self-determination to the Kashmiri people, there can be no normalization of relations with India and no durable peace. The prospect of a nuclear war could perhaps induce the UN, the US, and other countries to wake up to the urgent need for resolving the Kashmir dispute. Pakistan's projection efforts to highlight the Kashmir dispute could be improved and expanded.

In favour of this approach, the following rationale can be advanced. Firstly, this insistence on giving the right of self-determination to the Kashmiri people is morally justifiable. Secondly, the freedom fighters in Kashmir, who have sacrificed so much, certainly expect Pakistan to adhere to its present stance. In the third place, it can still be hoped that India would sooner or later come round to accepting a solution of the Kashmir problem. The insurgency in Kashmir is said to be hurting India more than the cost borne by Pakistan. Last but not the least, the considerations of Pakistan's national prestige or 'face' require the continuation of the same course. There will be cries of betrayal and treachery from the opposition parties and many others if any government changes course on the Kashmir issue.

The pragmatic question arises as to whether Pakistan can afford to allow the Kashmir dispute to continue to poison bilateral relations with India, say, for another fifty years. Any realistic appraisal would suggest that, at least in the foreseeable future, India is not going to budge on its stance on Kashmir and that nothing short of India's military defeat by Pakistan could bring about a change in its attitude. Inflicting a military defeat on a much larger power like India is not, and perhaps never was, a realistic prospect for Pakistan. The statistics would simply not allow this to happen. Perhaps sometime around 1960, fortified by free-flowing American military aid, Pakistan could think in terms of repeating the story of the medieval wars when Muslim armies were able to defeat Hindu forces many times their size. However, the actual experiences of the India–Pakistan wars of 1965 and 1971 took care, or should have taken care, of all that.

The qualitative difference now in the power equation is that both countries possess nuclear capability as well as medium-range and long-range missiles which can reach each others' cities and wreak total havoc in both countries in the case of a nuclear war. The premise, therefore, has to be that everything must be done to avoid an Indo-Pakistan war. For the sake of Kashmir, going to war with India or defeating it militarily are simply not viable options for Pakistan.

Short of a nuclear war, Pakistan can continue with the present course of confronting India and conducting a cold war against it. Time, however, does not seem to be in Pakistan's favour and the policies of the status quo have been working to Pakistan's disadvantage, more particularly, in the recent past which has seen both a serious decline in Pakistan's economic fortunes and a sinister accentuation of the process of its internal destabilization. In order to be able to confront India meaningfully, Pakistan needs, above all, internal cohesion and national unity. This seems to be sadly missing. The more recent controversy on the Kalabagh Dam, coming on the heels of nuclear tests, revealed the alarming extent of divisive politics and centrifugal tendencies in the country. There was open talk of breaking the federation, with the three smaller provinces breathing defiance against the domination of the Punjab, the larger province. To take on India, Pakistan needs to have a vibrant economy. Due to financial mismanagement and a variety of reasons, the economy is in a terrible mess. As always, the burden of defence expenditure has taken a heavy toll of the country's meagre resources and the economic costs of conducting the recent nuclear explosions have made matters worse.

To put it bluntly, a stark choice is now before Pakistan as to whether Kashmir is more important than Pakistan's own survival and welfare. Any objective analysis would show that, over the years, Pakistan has suffered more than its rival through the pursuit of policies of confrontation. But now, there is a particular urgency in the situation in Pakistan that can no longer be ignored or wished away.

In the wake of conducting nuclear explosions in May 1998, Pakistan's long over-burdened economy is facing real prospects of a collapse. To show their disapproval of Pakistani nuclear tests, the US and some other aid donors imposed economic sanctions against Pakistan, similar to what had already been done against India. The main difference, however, is that India has foreign exchange reserves of nearly US$ 29 billion as against Pakistan's rapidly dwindling reserves of about half a billion dollars. Matters were further aggravated when the Pakistani financial authorities showed very poor judgement by freezing foreign currency accounts in Pakistani banks, in utter disregard of the oft-repeated solemn commitments of successive governments in Pakistan that such accounts were absolutely safe. This dealt a deadly blow to the confidence of foreign investors, in general, but more particularly that of nearly four million Pakistani expatriates living abroad, many of whom had been maintaining foreign currency accounts in Pakistan. As a result of the freezing of foreign currency accounts, the inflow of nearly US$ 1.5 billion per annum in new foreign currency deposits, and probably a similar amount in foreign exchange remittances sent home annually by Pakistanis abroad, seem to have largely dried up.

Moreover, the application of international economic sanctions could deprive Pakistan of nearly US$ 2 billion in annual aid. Pakistan's economy, which was already under pressure even before the nuclear tests, seems to have been deprived of nearly US$ 5 billion annually, from the funds it was receiving prior to May 1998. Pakistan has a huge foreign debt of over US$ 30 billion and its annual debt repayment amounts to nearly US$ 3 billion. With low foreign exchange reserves at its disposal, Pakistan is thus facing the real prospect of default in repayment or even having to declare a unilateral moratorium in the near future. This would unleash a fresh crisis for Pakistan's fragile economy. Foreign credit would become even more scarce as well as expensive. In the meanwhile, the arms race with India could possibly increase, forcing Pakistan's hand to keep up with India, thereby placing ever-greater burdens on Pakistan's sick economy.

Drawing a parallel with the experience of the Soviet Union thus becomes both relevant and unavoidable. The Soviet Union had thousands of nuclear weapons at its disposal, and yet it disintegrated without a shot being fired. The main reason was that the country had bled itself white because its defence expenditure had over-burdened the Soviet economy over a long period of time. The collapse of the Soviet Union was a chilling reminder to the world that possession of nuclear weapons by itself does not provide security to a country—even to a superpower. It is a country's economic health which can be much more crucial to its survival. If a country has the money, arms and equipment can always be secured.

This lesson does not seem to have been learnt as yet by Pakistani policymakers. They continue to hope against hope that somehow rescue would come from somewhere—hopefully from Muslim brother countries like Saudi Arabia and the UAE or some other oil-rich countries—or that perhaps the economic sanctions themselves would be lifted. This seems again to be a case of living under illusions. But even if these possibilities materialize, that would at best give Pakistan a temporary respite. The hard reality is that Pakistan's economy has been going downhill for several years, through gross mismanagement and rampant corruption, though the nuclear explosions triggered a sharp decline.

It is said that the Muslims of the subcontinent have always looked to help from outside: that some fabled hero such as Mohammed bin Qasim, Mahmud Ghaznavi, or Ahmad Shah Abdali would obtain their deliverance from their problems, more or less like the *deux ex machina* in romantic stories. But times have changed and at the end of the twentieth century, it is a very different world. For instance, during the 1971 War, many in Pakistan were hoping against hope that either the Chinese army or the American 7th Fleet or perhaps the brother Muslim countries would come to rescue the sinking ship. Of course, nothing of the kind happened. Such unrealistic hopes are doomed to fail in the future as well. It is high time, therefore, for all sections of opinion in Pakistan to realize that a country has to stand on its own feet and live within its means. It is unrealistic, if not absurd, to expect a foreign country—howsoever friendly—to come and fight Pakistan's battles, or to bail it out of its financial crises, especially when these are self-inflicted.

Without doubt, Pakistan's present economic crisis has been in the making for years. It has been in no small measure due to the culture of plunder and embezzlement which has become prevalent among the ruling elites in Pakistan, particularly in the last decade. Wrong economic priorities—like the perks and privileges of the elite classes, the construction of fancy official buildings in Islamabad, and the building of the motorway—have eaten away the country's meagre resources, while the more important social sector, namely, education and health, has been neglected, to the long-term detriment of the country.

Over and above this financial mismanagement, there has been the unending defence burden on Pakistan's economy. Pakistan has been trying for half a century to match a foe who is eight to ten times bigger than itself in size and resources. Thus, the inevitable pressures on Pakistan's economy have taken their toll. This is probably going to get worse if there is a new arms race between India and Pakistan, which seems likely, to build better missiles and more numerous weapons of mass destruction.

Foreign governments and financial circles are aware of these problems as well as the gross mismanagement of Pakistan's economy. They cannot really be expected to respond in a meaningful way to Pakistan's frantic appeals for help to tide over its self-inflicted financial crises. Pakistani policymakers have to realize that the country's economy cannot bear all of these burdens and that the nation has got to live within its means. Above all, they will have to learn that a country, no less than any individual, should enter the fray to fight only those battles which it can win or where at least it can hold its own. For the rest, discretion is the better part of valour.

Against the above-mentioned background, the second option before Pakistan becomes more compelling than ever before, which is to rethink its entire approach to India–Pakistan relations and seek to establish a new *modus vivendi* with India. In particular, Pakistan needs to reconsider its rigid stance that without a solution of the Kashmir dispute, there can be neither a normalization of relations with India nor a durable peace. Perhaps it would be best to start by asking a simple question as to what exactly has Pakistan achieved by maintaining this inflexible stance over the years? After all is said and done, the course of confrontation and war has not resolved the Kashmir dispute in the last fifty years. But, in the process, Pakistan has had to pay a very heavy price. It has lost half of the country in very humiliating circumstances. And what remains of the original Pakistan is in a declining curve: destabilization marked by all kinds of fissiparous tendencies—provincialism, sectarianism, and terrorism—as well as poor law and order, fractious politics, and a general loss of national purpose. Perhaps even this sorry state of affairs might have been tolerable except that the alarming condition of the country's economy really leaves no option but to carry out an agonizing reappraisal of the policies followed so far which have brought Pakistan to its present woes. There is the example of North Korea, the last of the 'Stalinist' communist states, which managed to build a mighty war machine but had to pay a very heavy economic price for the same, to the extent that its people are today faced with famine. Even worse, North Korea has been forced to negotiate under duress to come to terms with its perceived enemies—the US and South Korea. These recent examples serve to emphasize the crucial part played by the economy in a country's survival.

Pakistan may well have developed an adequate nuclear deterrent against India and even achieved a strategic parity (as did the Soviet Union against the US), and yet it may find that its economy could be its Achilles' heel and undo what has been achieved in the military field.

The example of Egypt is also a case in point. For years, Egypt had borne the brunt of the Arab warfare and confrontation against Israel. The feeling started to grow in Egypt that while the other Arab countries mostly talked, Egypt was required to shed blood against the Israeli enemy. Hence, it decided in 1978 that enough was enough and came to terms with Israel. It concluded that while Palestine was dear, Egypt was dearer. In the US-brokered agreement with Israel, Egypt secured for itself an era of peace and very substantial economic benefits. The other Arabs fiercely denounced Egypt for this 'betrayal' but a few years later, the Palestine Liberation Organization and Jordan followed suit, while the other Arab countries started to reconcile themselves to the reality of Israel. It needs to be remembered that the Arab antagonism against Israel has been no less vitriolic and deeply ingrained than the sentiments in Pakistan against India. But pragmatic considerations finally prevailed with the Egyptians and many other Arabs.

To draw a further historical parallel, as in the case of Pakistan, there were probably as many military hawks and 'super patriots' in the Soviet Union, North Korea, and Egypt who kept arguing with the decision-makers not to slacken in the arms race and to continue to maintain an inflexible diplomatic posture with their bitter adversaries, namely, the US, South Korea, and Israel respectively. Unfortunately, in the end, the economic realities caught up. The mighty Soviet Union not only collapsed without offering any resistance but its successor, the Russian Federation, has been obliged to live on American and Western largesse. The hawkish lobbies in Pakistan would, therefore, do well to learn from these very recent historical experiences.

It is said that facts have an unpleasant habit of always catching up with us. India's much larger size is one of those unpleasant facts, which cannot be wished away simply by brave-sounding words and vociferous slogans, especially when they are unmatched by hard work on the ground. For too long, Pakistan has tried to wear shoes bigger than its feet. A small country cannot forever go on pretending that it is a bigger power than it actually is. For one thing, this is playing with fire. For another, this is being unfair to one's own people. At the altar of national pride and outright xenophobia, they are always called upon to make increasingly more sacrifices in order to match a neighbour several times their size.

Therefore, the new thinking for dealing with the overall situation facing Pakistan would require, in particular, a careful and down-to-earth reappraisal of the relationship with India and its consequences. It is quite evident that the Pakistani policymakers have shown a glaring lack of balance in their judgement and their sense of priorities. For the sake of bravado and false prestige, it seems they have put Pakistan's very existence in jeopardy. They seem to have acted almost like the gambler who puts his wealth, wife, and household on stake for the sake of winning a bet. For the sake of Kashmir, they have in effect put Pakistan's overall interests at stake by adopting an all-or-nothing attitude. Kashmir is no doubt important and dear, but surely Pakistan is even more important and dearer. Getting Kashmir would make little sense if, in the process, Pakistan were to be lost. It is time, therefore, to put the country's priorities right.

Does this evaluation of realities mean that the only other option is that Pakistan must accept Indian hegemony and forget all about Kashmir? The answer is an emphatic 'no'. There is no compulsion at all to swing between two extremes. In seeking a new *modus vivendi* with India, the fundamental premise and the driving motive must always be the preservation of Pakistan's sovereignty and territorial integrity. Egypt's peace with Israel is a clear precedent. Can it be argued that following the signing of the Camp David Accords, Egypt has lost its sovereignty or has been forced to play second fiddle to Israel? Similarly, in seeking an accommodation with India, there need not be any undue anxieties about Pakistan's future prospects as a sovereign and proud nation.

It should not be forgotten that, unlike the case of Egypt, Pakistan also possesses the nuclear deterrent, which has already been able to keep the peace between India and Pakistan in the past two decades. More recently, following the nuclear explosions and test firing of the Ghauri medium-range missile, the Pakistani deterrent has become even more credible. Thus, there should be every reasonable confidence that Pakistan's basic security interests can be preserved, irrespective of any Indian designs. The nuclear deterrent did succeed in ensuring the peace in Europe for forty-six years after the Second World War, in spite of the deadly hostility between NATO and the Warsaw Pact powers. Pakistan need not, therefore, have any fears that following peace and normalization with India, the latter would somehow induce or coerce Pakistan to live under Indian hegemony or find a way to overrun Pakistan by deception.

Since Pakistan's basic security has thus been ensured by the nuclear deterrent, its main objective should be to defuse the tensions in the subcontinent and establish a normal, if not harmonious, relationship with India. This, above all, should give some respite to Pakistan's economy. Indeed, given half a chance, Pakistan's economy is capable of out-performing India in many ways.

The establishment of peace would require a joint resolve by both countries to open a new chapter in their relationship. Indeed, the leaders of both countries have been saying for years that a harmonious relationship is their cherished objective. Millions of their peoples would dearly like to see a tension-free relationship between the two neighbours. This would open the door to normal commercial, social, and cultural contacts. Particularly happy would be the millions belonging to divided families, mostly Muslims, half of whom are living on one side of the border and the remaining half on the other.

It is, therefore, time to give peace a chance. Experience shows that sometimes the conciliatory approach works better in life than the hard line approach. To come out of this long-lasting impasse, it might perhaps be best if both sides could agree to put aside the Kashmir dispute for a period of time while the two countries embark on a process of establishing a closer understanding and cooperation in other fields. The US could play a key role in the peace negotiations which could, initially, be held on the pattern of the US–China dialogue of the 1970s and the Arab–Israel negotiations of the more recent past. Such diplomatic efforts could take the form of a No War Pact or Treaty of Non-Aggression as also an agreement on 'no first use of nuclear weapons'. To strengthen these pacts, there could be international guarantees from the US and the UN. The two countries could sign the CTBT and commit themselves to the objectives of the NPT. There could be international involvement in the keeping of peace between India and Pakistan. Trade, easier travel, and cultural links should, in particular, be encouraged between the two countries to establish mutually advantageous linkages that would help create a more favourable climate.

It is more likely that in such an atmosphere, within a few years, the Kashmir dispute would become susceptible to a solution. Of course, there can be no guarantee that a satisfactory solution is sure to be found. But the truth is that such a solution has also not been found through confrontation either, despite all the immense sufferings and sacrifices which such confrontation has entailed.

It would be difficult to predict as to what could be the final solution of the Kashmir problem. Various alternatives have been suggested over the years. Freezing of the present Line of Control and converting it into the international border between India and Pakistan has evidently been favoured by some circles in India, though the Indian official position is that even Azad Kashmir, the Pakistan-controlled portion of Kashmir, should be handed over to India. Pakistan, of course, favours the holding of a UN-supervised impartial plebiscite to allow the people of Jammu and Kashmir the choice to join either Pakistan or India. Giving the valley of Kashmir a special status under UN trusteeship, for a period of ten or twenty years, is another possible solution. Independence for the whole of Jammu and Kashmir state, or at least the valley of Kashmir, is another alternative. In fact, anything which reduces or eliminates the present Indian control over large portions of Jammu and Kashmir ought to be welcome from Pakistan's angle.

There is a section of opinion in Pakistan which holds that without Kashmir, Pakistan cannot survive or that Kashmir is the 'jugular vein' of Pakistan. This argument is demonstrably self-contradictory. Logically speaking, if this hypothesis is correct, then the question arises as to how has Pakistan managed to survive for a full fifty years, even though Kashmir has been largely under Indian control? Clearly, Kashmir cannot be quite as vital for Pakistan as has been claimed. The linked argument that India could divert the waters of rivers flowing from Kashmir into Pakistan, thus causing starvation in Pakistan, also seems to have little validity. If this were actually something feasible, India would have done so long ago. At least, during the war days in 1965 and 1971, it would have tried to block the water of these rivers flowing into Pakistan. In fact, the Indus Waters Treaty, signed in 1960, has never been seriously violated. These international commitments cannot be disregarded by India and, in any event, it would be logistically difficult, if not impossible, for India to attempt to hold back the flow of these rivers into Pakistan. Now that the two countries possess the nuclear deterrent, such a course of action becomes even more impractical. Moreover, in the scenario in which India and Pakistan actually embark on a course of harmonious relations, it would be highly unlikely that India would throw everything overboard just to deny Pakistan the waters of these rivers flowing from Kashmir into Pakistan.

There is little weight in the argument that, from a strategic point of view, Pakistan cannot survive without Kashmir. The fact is that, for the past fifty years, Pakistan has survived without Kashmir, or more accurately, without the portion of Kashmir that is in Indian possession. Nor has India enjoyed any notable strategic advantage by its occupation of the larger portion of Kashmir.

This leaves the moral argument which is that Pakistan cannot, after all these years, in effect dilute or abandon the principle of self-determination for the Kashmiri people, by putting it on the back-burner while normalizing ties with India. The argument goes that the Kashmiris are fellow Muslims and the kith and kin of the Pakistani people. The hearts of the Kashmiris are with Pakistan and, given any chance, they would join Pakistan. With this objective, they have been fighting against Indian military occupation for so long and have made great sacrifices of life, honour, and property. Their right to make a free choice in a plebiscite has the sanction of UN resolutions behind it. India has been guilty of massive violations of the human rights of the brother Kashmiri people and Pakistan must stand up for them.

At the back of Pakistan's moral argument that the Kashmiris must be given the right of self-determination, the real motivation arises from the confident belief that, in case of an impartial vote, the people of Kashmir would opt to join Pakistan. Here again, realism demands that the question be asked as to whether Pakistan is justified in its optimism that such a free plebiscite would really deliver the Indian-occupied portion of Kashmir to Pakistan. At present, this seems like an academic question to discuss as to when the people of Jammu and Kashmir would be able to secure the right of self-determination and how they would vote in a plebiscite. India seems dead set against the holding of a plebiscite and whatever Pakistan and the people of the Indian-occupied territory have been able to do has not made India budge from its adamant position. Nevertheless, assuming that, at some point of time, an opportunity is given to the people of the state of Jammu and Kashmir to vote freely on the issue of their future, what will be the likely outcome?

A closer examination of the situation suggests that the picture is probably not all that rosy from Pakistan's point of view. It seems that, while insisting day in and day out on the right of self-determination, little attention has been paid in Pakistan to some ground realities. In the Indian-occupied area, there are three distinct regions, namely, the Kashmir Valley, Jammu, and Ladakh. If ever there is a plebiscite or free vote, it is likely that the parallel of the division of the provinces of the Punjab, Bengal, and Assam—at the time of Pakistan's creation in 1947—would be invoked to insist that the wishes of the people of each region of Jammu and Kashmir state be ascertained. The whole of the state might not be allowed to vote as a monolithic entity. The division of the Punjab, Bengal, and Assam provinces could not be denied by the Muslim League in 1947, as a corollary of its demand for Partition of India on the basis of religion. The authoritative chronicler of the events leading to the creation of Pakistan, Chaudhri Muhammad Ali, has put it as follows, 'The Congress demand for the partition of the Punjab and Bengal, however distasteful it might be to the Muslims of these provinces, had behind it the logic of the Pakistan Resolution.'[17] Thus, the same logic could not be denied in the case of Jammu and Kashmir either.

The question about the right of vote of those who left Kashmir after 1947 as refugees and settled in Pakistan or elsewhere might not be easy to resolve after the passing of so much time. Records have never been kept in an acceptable form and trying to retrace the antecedents of those claiming to have originally been from the state of Jammu and Kashmir might be an interminable exercise. The voting might have to be confined to those actually resident.

In a region-by-region vote, Ladakh, which is mainly non-Muslim (being Buddhist), will almost certainly vote for India. Jammu also now has a non-Muslim majority (Hindus and Sikhs) and will probably vote for India. This basically leaves the Kashmir Valley which, it needs to be remembered, accounts for only a small portion of the overall territory of Jammu and Kashmir, even though it is psychologically important and can be described as the heartland of the disputed territory. Here again, it has probably not been fully understood in Pakistan that, with the passing of time, the situation in the valley has not remained static. In particular, it seems that over the last ten years, the pro-independence sentiment has been gaining ground steadily in the valley and even beyond. When the wishes of the people of Jammu and Kashmir are ascertained, the choice in the voting might not be restricted only to joining either India or Pakistan. There will also be insistence on a third choice—independence. The spirit of the right of self-determination would make it difficult to deny this third option, in addition to voting according to regions, as stated above. Thus, if and when an impartial plebiscite is held, the pro-Pakistan vote, even in the Kashmir Valley, could face a serious competition from the pro-independence vote, while probably a small percentage will also opt for India.

From this prognosis, a conclusion emerges that the exercise of the right of self-determination of the people of Jammu and Kashmir, which has been the persistent demand Pakistan for so long, might not in the end produce the favourable results that Pakistan seems to have so confidently expected. Indeed, it seems that very little attention has been given to this aspect of the debate.

Pakistani policymakers as well as the Pakistani public opinion in general have based the Kashmir policy on unrealistic premises. In the first place, Kashmir does not appear to be strategically quite as vital for Pakistan as has been made out by the political and military experts. The country has survived well enough for the past fifty years without Kashmir and presumably would be able to do so for another fifty years. Secondly, the expectation that a free plebiscite would deliver Kashmir to Pakistan is probably also unrealistic. Large portions of the Indian-occupied Kashmir have a non-Muslim majority and are more likely join India rather than Pakistan in a free vote.

These being the realities, the question arises as to why Pakistan has been so insistent on keeping Kashmir as the make-or-break issue in India–Pakistan relations and the touchstone for any improvement of relations with India?

The answer is probably very complex. Realism and cool-headed thinking have generally been missing from Pakistan's approach in foreign and defence policies. Emotionalism and anti-India public hysteria have clouded the judgement of policymakers. Moreover, politicians and opportunists have cashed in on the anti-India public sentiments to secure popularity by sounding tough on Kashmir. In fact, populist policies have dominated the political scene in Pakistan, more so, since Bhutto exploited the anti-India and Kashmir card in the late 1960s to gain popularity with the masses.

Pakistan's ideological and security perceptions have also been undergoing changes over the years, each time with a direct bearing on its thinking on the Kashmir dispute. In the first decade after its independence, Pakistan's main fear was that India was unreconciled to Pakistan's separate existence and was conspiring to bring about Pakistan's disintegration. In this framework, Kashmir apparently became a test case about the acceptance or non-acceptance of the Partition formula itself, namely that the contiguous Muslim majority areas would constitute Pakistan. By this exercise, Kashmir should have become a part of Pakistan. Pakistan felt that to yield to India on the Kashmir issue would weaken the very *raison d'être* for the creation of Pakistan. In addition, Pakistan felt encouraged by the UN resolutions asking for a plebiscite in Kashmir. Pakistan was fairly confident that the UN would be able to secure a plebiscite in Kashmir, leading to its accession to Pakistan. It was, accordingly, determined to make this issue the central point in all negotiations with India.

However, in the second phase, starting in the late 1950s, having been fortified by US military assistance, Pakistan became strong enough to the extent that it felt that it was not only able to defend itself but could even take the battle inside India itself. In this scenario, Kashmir became a matter of national prestige and the test of strength between the two countries. Hardliners in the ruling group in Pakistan like Bhutto, Aziz Ahmed, and General Akhtar Malik evidently thought that Pakistan could even force India to give up Kashmir. In this frame of mind, the doomed Operation Gibraltar was launched to ignite a popular revolt in the Indian-occupied Kashmir in the confidence that India would not dare to cross the international border and the fighting would remain confined to Kashmir. This was an enormous miscalculation as India reacted by attacking across the international border, leading to the 1965 War. In Kashmir itself, despite pro-Pakistan feelings, there was no widespread popular revolt against India.

The popular, though erroneous, perception in Pakistan was that the armed forces were close to winning this particular war when it was prematurely stopped by the weak leadership. The general mood of euphoria at the perceived military success against India further raised the feelings of the Pakistani public on Kashmir to a high pitch. As a result, even the well-entrenched regime of Ayub Khan fell on the wayside in the widespread public disappointment that he had, allegedly, lost on the negotiating table at Tashkent what was perceived to have been secured by Pakistani arms in the battlefield. The popular mood in Pakistan in this era was depicted by the slogans of 'Crush India' displayed everywhere. Indeed, it was this psyche which, at least in part, led Pakistan head-along into a new war with India just six years later; and this psyche also accounted for the country's total lack of flexibility during the Bangladesh crisis. However, Pakistan's high hopes came to nought and its defeat in the 1971 War dampened the fervour for the Kashmir dispute in the decade of the 1970s.

As Pakistan regained strength in the 1980s, with the acquisition of nuclear capability and fresh injections of American aid during the Afghan crisis, there was once again a hardening of the position on Kashmir. With the exit of President Ziaul Haq in 1988, democratic rule was restored and the politicians started to compete with each other in sounding tough on Kashmir and in adopting a hard line posture against India. When the anti-India uprising started in Kashmir around 1990, which has continued ever since, Pakistan decided again to put Kashmir on top of the agenda in all negotiations with India. Thus, repeated rounds of talks with India, mostly at the level of foreign secretaries, have failed to make progress on the stumbling block of Kashmir. Periodic meetings of the prime ministers of the two countries have fared no better.

Pakistan's efforts to raise the Kashmir issue at the international level, in the last few years, have had only limited success. The UN has largely remained unresponsive. The last time the Security Council discussed the Kashmir issue was way back in 1964 when it could not even agree on a new resolution and the meeting ended inconclusively with an innocuous statement by its chairperson summarizing the views of the members. Since then a majority has not been found in the world body to reaffirm the UN's own resolutions on Kashmir, the last of which was passed in 1957. Pakistan's bids to raise the Kashmir issue in UN forums in 1994 and 1995 thus got nowhere.

The OIC has been more forthcoming in support of Pakistan on the Kashmir issue. In the OIC forum, favourable resolutions are not difficult to secure. The weakness of the OIC is that many amongst its member states do not regard themselves as being bound by its resolutions and adopt different positions at the UN and other forums, as Pakistan found out when it sought to raise the Kashmir issue at the UN in 1994 and 1995. This shows that the Islamic World is far from being united and that many member states treat their main political organization more as a discussion club rather than a serious forum like the UN whose resolutions carry much more credibility. Hence, the evident satisfaction felt in Pakistan over the passing of strong resolutions on Kashmir by the OIC is rather misplaced. If the OIC member states were genuinely committed to the resolutions on Kashmir, Pakistan could have easily lined up more than fifty votes in its favour at the UN, which has not actually been the case. The rulers in Islamabad keep playing up the importance of the OIC resolutions on Kashmir to give the Pakistani people the illusion of widespread international support for the Kashmir issue. Such illusions in turn harden the posture on Kashmir of both the government as well as the public opinion in Pakistan, thus reducing the possibility of any flexibility on the Kashmir issue. Over the years, Pakistani politicians have vied with each other in adopting a tough attitude on Kashmir in the expectation that this would bring popularity. Not surprisingly, Pakistani public opinion has become inflamed on this issue and hence there is little 'give' in Pakistan's negotiating position on Kashmir. In this sense, Pakistan has painted itself into a corner from where a climb down is exceedingly difficult.

To sum up, the hard fact on the ground is that India has all along been in possession of the larger portion of Kashmir and has been unwilling to give it up, short of suffering a military defeat. That, however, is something that has never been in Pakistan's grasp. Fifty years of confrontation have not produced the desired results for Pakistan. In the process, it did, however, lose half of the country. The disproportionate burden of defence expenditure over the years has hurt Pakistan more than it has hurt India. Pakistan's economy has reached a serious crisis, with the prospects of bankruptcy and financial collapse. Due to Pakistan's own weaknesses, duly exploited by India, the country has been seriously destabilized.

In 1998, India and Pakistan carried out nuclear explosions. Both have also developed long-range missiles that could hit each other's farthest cities. It is clear that a nuclear war between them can only lead to unacceptable mutual devastation for both. Logically speaking, the military option is no longer available to either country. The military stalemate, however, exposes Pakistan's weaker economy and more vulnerable political fibre to greater risks than those faced by India.

Against this background, more than ever before, there is need for some cool-headed thinking in Pakistan. The question must be asked as to whether securing Kashmir (which in any event seems only to be a remote possibility) is more important than saving Pakistan? Indeed, if Pakistan sinks, what use it would be to get Kashmir? The realistic answer to these questions is self evident.

The policymakers in Pakistan must, therefore, make some hard calculations and adopt a rational policy that should focus relentlessly on what is in the best interests of Pakistan. Playing politics with the Kashmir issue has got to end. There must be an open dialogue and sharing all the facts and arguments with the political parties and the nation at large. The effort should be to develop a broad new national consensus on the country's priorities, even though total unanimity would obviously not be possible. In fact, given a chance, the Pakistani public opinion has shown the ability to face up to the realities. The separation of East Pakistan was accepted by the people at large as an irreversible fact, once the political leadership decided to adopt a forthright policy on this issue.

Experience shows that sometimes it is better to retreat and regroup rather than take the foe head on. Islamic history itself provides a prime example of such an approach. The Holy Prophet of Islam (PBUH) himself signed the Peace of Hudaibiya, in which the harsh terms of the pagan enemy were largely accepted. But this tactical retreat turned out to be a famous victory. Sometimes a nation might never be able to secure one of its cherished goals, but for gaining this single objective, it does not place its entire future at stake.

In the present case, fortunately, a change of thinking does not mean that Pakistan has to give up its traditional support for the right of self-determination of the Kashmiri people. That position can yet be sustained. However, the state of cold war and confrontation would have to be replaced by a more business-like relationship and the present insistence on treating Kashmir as the make-or-break issue in India–Pakistan relations would have to be dropped. Instead, Kashmir could be put on the back burner, at least for a given period of time. But this, too, must be done in the framework of a broad-ranging understanding with India as the quid pro quo for a change in Pakistan's long-time stance.

There will have to be a new *modus vivendi* between the two countries wherein the principal objective should be to establish a more normal relationship between them. This should include confidence-building measures, particularly in the military field which, inter alia, should include agreements on non-aggression and non-first-use of nuclear weapons. Above all, there should be an agreement on a credible, verifiable, and phased reduction in defence expenditures of the two countries. There could be an Oslo-like (PLO–Israel) agreement or a specific peace treaty wherein India could be required to give express assurances to abide by the irreversibility of the Partition of 1947 and to respect the independence, sovereign equality, and territorial integrity of Pakistan. Moreover, the two countries should commit themselves not to interfere in each other's internal affairs and eschew all kind of hostile propaganda against each other. The process of normalization of relations should include specific measures to promote bilateral trade and travel as well as cultural exchanges. The peace treaty could include a monitoring mechanism, possibly involving the UN, or the backing of the US, to ensure that the grievances of either side regarding non-implementation of the provisions of the treaty could be looked into and redressed promptly.

The point is that the policy of confrontation has not secured Kashmir for Pakistan in the past fifty years. Nor is it like to do so in the near future. It seems, therefore, worthwhile to try some other remedies. Indeed, it is high time to give peace a chance. As the two countries proceed to establish a more harmonious relationship, involving a reduction of tensions and an increase in mutually beneficial cooperation in diverse fields, tempers on Kashmir are more likely to cool down. It might be more feasible then to look into various alternatives to find a solution of the Kashmir problem.

A number of possible solutions have been suggested over the years, including independence for Kashmir. In fact, the movement for independence has grown over the years. As usual, the official Pakistani media has maintained an ostrich-like attitude and Pakistani public opinion has had little awareness about the growth of pro-independence sentiments among Kashmiris, some of whom clearly feel that Kashmir has an identity of its own and should, therefore, be independent. Then, there are those Kashmiris who, while holding pro-Pakistan feelings, have come to believe that India would never allow Kashmir to become a part of Pakistan. For them, the second best alternative, which might not be as strongly resisted by India, is to secure Kashmir's independence—in other words, to be neither with India nor with Pakistan. In theory, this might be a face-saving formula for India and, for that matter, even for Pakistan. While, officially, Pakistan has never been willing to consider the 'third option,' on the ground that the UN resolutions only contemplate two choices viz. joining either India or Pakistan, the fact of the matter is that anything which removes the existing Indian occupation of Kashmir should be welcome from Pakistan's point of view. Moreover, an independent Kashmir would inevitably gravitate more towards Pakistan than to India for economic, social, and logistic reasons. Pakistan would also probably be the most natural transit route for a land-locked independent Kashmir.

It is time to give thought to the possibility of an independent Kashmir, which might be the second best alternative from Pakistan's point of view. It has also the merit of being a more attainable objective than the 'first option' which is Kashmir's accession to Pakistan. From the point of view of Pakistan, and indeed from the point of view of the Kashmiris, if the choice is between the status quo, which is the Indian occupation of Kashmir for the foreseeable future, or the independence of Kashmir, surely the second-mentioned alternative would be far better.

It is high time to launch a peace offensive between India and Pakistan. The whole world is in favour of such an initiative. The global atmosphere is conducive to the promotion of such a dialogue and the international community will be supportive with such diplomatic or financial assistance as might advance this objective. No doubt, India would like to do everything in a bilateral context. This need not be a barrier to the success of the talks. In the case of peace secured between Israel and Egypt in 1978, the US was forthcoming with substantial economic incentives. Presumably, similar incentives would not be altogether unwelcome to India. A third party role can be visualized at some stage of the talks. Secret diplomacy on the pattern of the Oslo Agreement between Israel and the Palestinians could be helpful.

In sum, it makes little sense for Pakistan to press for the continuation of the status quo, a situation which is damaging Pakistan more than India. It is, therefore, in Pakistan's own interest to try to come out of the present impasse and seek a change for the better.

NOTES

1. Burke and Ziring, p. 14.
2. *Hindu Weekly*, 3 May 1965, cited in Burke and Ziring, p. 324.
3. Burke and Ziring, p. 231.
4. *Asian Recorder*, 1959, p. 3000, cited in Burke and Ziring, p. 234
5. Jawaharlal Nehru, *Speeches*, IV, pp. 254, 260, 408, cited in Burke and Ziring, p. 52.
6. The Indian Constitution (Art. 51 d) lays down that 'the State shall endeavour to encourage settlement of international disputes by arbitration'. Burke and Ziring, p. 42.
7. Interview of Gen. Faiz Ali Chishti, published in *Jang* Sunday Magazine, 20–26 June 1999, p. 6.
8. Jawaharlal Nehru, *Speeches*, II, p. 446, cited in Burke and Ziring, p. 3.
9. *Selected Speeches of the Quaid-i-Azam Mohammed Ali Jinnah*, p. 459, cited in Burke and Ziring, p. 395.
10. Even as late as 1962, Nehru told Selig S. Harrison (*Washington Post*, 19 December 1962) that 'Confederation remains our ultimate goal though if we say it, they are alarmed and say we want to swallow them up.' Burke and Ziring, p. 282.
11. Burke and Ziring, p. 75.
12. Ibid., p. 68.
13. Burke and Ziring, p. 27.
14. Security Council, Official Records, S/1430, 9 December 1949, cited in Burke and Ziring, pp. 28–9.
15. A.B. Tourtellot, *Saturday Review*, 6 March 1965, cited in Burke and Ziring, p. 384.
16. Security Council Resolution, 24 January 1957, cited in Burke and Ziring, p. 228.
17. Chaudhri Muhammad Ali, *The Emergence of Pakistan*, p. 121.

12

Learning from Experience

Looking back at Pakistan's short history of half-a-century, the main impression which emerges is that of missed opportunities. As a country, it has always seemed to have promised more than what it has been actually able to achieve. Blessed with vast natural resources, a unique geo-strategic location, a large and basically talented population, which is the inheritor of one of the world's great civilizations, Pakistan has, since its independence, been an active player in the global arena and, more recently, has also become a nuclear power. But it could have gone much farther if it had enjoyed greater political stability and had managed its affairs better. For this state of affairs, a lack of balance in determining the country's national priorities seems to have been the main culprit.

Pakistan has been stymied by its obsession to confront or compete with its much larger neighbour, India, and has shown a persistent inability to judge matters in perspective. Its policymakers have allowed themselves to be swayed by emotionalism and extremism more often than by logic or even simple common sense. This has probably been the main reason as to why Pakistan has not been able to rise to its full potential.

It is difficult to escape the conclusion that Pakistan has, time and again in its history, suffered much from the advice of its many hardliners—whether in the political arena, the armed forces, in the news media and elsewhere in society—who have sought to pressurize the policymakers to shun all compromises and instead opt for the maximum demands, unmindful and even disdainful of the fact that this must lead to a collision course. In this peculiar frame of mind, patriotism seems to have been equated with loud slogans, tall claims, and outright bravado. These hardliners, who should perhaps be described as 'romantics,' have generally favoured a defiant attitude against the conceived foes, based essentially on simplistic logic and a general disregard of facts and figures. They have tended to give a paranoid interpretation of international events, in which the perceived enemies of Pakistan and Islam—specifically, India, Israel and, increasingly, the US and the IMF—have been blamed for every evil which has befallen not only

Pakistan but, indeed, the whole Islamic world. The latter's own glaring follies and weaknesses have been, in general, glossed over in the search for convenient scapegoats.

In what such hardliners have conceived to be heroic defiance, the country has been egged upon, as it were, to go hit its head against the wall, with an underlying, and almost mystical, belief that somehow divine help will come to the rescue. Any sober advice suggesting that one should look before one leaps has been generally dismissed as lack of faith or even lack of patriotism. Unfortunately, the main problem with this kind of approach has been that it usually flies in the face of the reality.

To illustrate this quixotic mindset, some specific instances could be recalled from Pakistan's history. For example, the military wisdom in Pakistan had long remained that the defence of East Pakistan lay in West Pakistan. There were even claims that the Pakistani army would have reached Delhi, the Indian capital, before India could penetrate deep into East Pakistan! Hence, East Pakistan had been generally left lightly guarded. The experience, of course, turned out to be the opposite.

A Pakistani foreign minister (Bhutto) had vowed, using Churchillian oratory, 'to fight India for a thousand years' when, actually, the two wars fought by Pakistan could be barely stretched to a fortnight.[1] Bhutto was later to proclaim that the nation would be ready to 'eat grass' in order to make the nuclear bomb. When it comes to rhetoric, the government and the people alike are always ready to swear to make all possible sacrifices for the country's sake. However, when the critical moment came, following the nuclear explosions in 1998, there was little evidence of willingness to make any kind of sacrifices, despite all the euphoria. Thus, the imposition of agricultural tax or general sales tax has been vigorously resisted, even though the country is facing dire financial difficulties. There is rampant tax evasion, which has almost become a way of life in Pakistan.

Pressure groups in Sindh have prevented the repatriation of about 300,000 'Bihari' Muslims from Bangladesh to Pakistan. These non-Bengalis have had to suffer so much for their loyalty to Pakistan in the 1971 War, but the parochial pressure groups in Sindh remain adamant, while the government in Islamabad seems unconcerned. This is in sharp contrast with the case of Germany, for instance, which accepted the repatriation of millions of ethnic Germans from Poland and elsewhere, when they were forced out of areas long inhabited by them. This placed a great burden on Germany but it was willingly accepted. Israel has accepted Jews from all parts of the world despite having a small territory. Over the years, Turkey has also accepted many ethnic Turks from neighbouring countries. But there has been little willingness in

Pakistan, due mainly to partisan politics in Sindh, to make the sacrifices involved in the repatriation of a relatively small number of Urdu-speaking Pakistanis to their own country. What is worse, such an attitude goes against the very ideological concept on which Pakistan was founded.

Another instance of the gap between promises and reality about sacrifices is even more revealing. There has always been brave talk in Pakistan, especially by the hardliners, about 'shedding the last drop of blood' in the country's defence. But 93,000 armed forces personnel laid down their arms in East Pakistan in the 1971 War after putting up a minimal resistance, lasting two weeks.[2] Indeed, during the entire crisis in East Pakistan, including the war with India, only about 3,000 Pakistani armed forces personnel reportedly lost their lives. As against this, for example, the Soviet Union lost 20 million people in the Second World War against Nazi Germany. In the recent Iran–Iraq War, nearly one million laid down their lives. Thus, the tall talk in Pakistan about 'shedding the last drop of blood' has clearly not been matched by actual performance.

It is unfortunate that Pakistan seems to have almost developed a political culture consisting of rhetoric, fantastic claims, and empty slogans. Perhaps, the popularity of patriotic songs, containing all kind of hyperbole, so characteristic of poetry, has helped to create a world of make-believe about soldiers of Islam fighting heroically against impossible odds and yet emerging victorious.

It is said that hard words break no bones. This is probably true of Pakistan's enemies who have not suffered much from Pakistan's hard-lining policies. But it has done Pakistan itself a great deal of harm. This could be illustrated from some instances from Pakistan's history. The 1965 War, which derailed Pakistan from the course of progress, should never have taken place, but for the hard line approach of certain policymakers in the Ayub regime, particularly Bhutto and Aziz Ahmed in the Foreign Office and some hawks in the military, notably General Akhtar Malik, the author of Operation Gibraltar. This was the ill-fated plan under which infiltrators were sent across into Indian-controlled Kashmir in the expectation that they would ignite a popular revolt. That hope did not materialize and, instead, Pakistan blundered into an unanticipated all-out war with India. As a result, Pakistan, which was doing notably well in the early 1960s and was even being cited as a model developing country in the Third World, could never regain that kind of momentum.

Six years later, Pakistan went on to lose half the country. Showing a similar mentality during the Bangladesh crisis, the hardliners ensured that the path of compromise was repeatedly turned down, till the very end.

First, they refused to accept the results of the 1970 elections and power was not handed over to the majority party. Despite its insistence on maximum provincial autonomy, the Awami League was still wedded to the concept of a united Pakistan. Overruling the advice given by the two top military officers incharge at that time of East Pakistan, namely, Governor Admiral S.M. Ahsan and the Martial Law Administrator Lt. Gen. Yaqub Khan, President General Yahya Khan instead unleashed a bloody suppression, directed by Lt. Gen. Tikka Khan, to crush the popular will.

The hawkish circles in West Pakistan, true to form, applauded. But this brutal operation, which evoked severe criticism of Pakistan from around the world, greatly weakened Pakistan's moral authority in handling the crisis. India was thus able to exploit the situation to its own advantage, so much so that its eventual intervention in East Pakistan was even viewed by some circles abroad as a humanitarian rescue operation! Moreover, during the fateful days prior to the outbreak of war with India, no effort was made by Islamabad to reach a deal with the Bengali separatists, although some amongst the latter (as Khondakar Mushtaq Ahmed, an associate of Mujib, was later to confirm)[3] had sent out some feelers. Of course, the super patriots would have howled in protest if any such deal with the separatists had been even contemplated by the Islamabad government.

After war broke out with India and the military situation in East Pakistan took a nosedive, the last-minute diplomatic efforts at the UN Security Council to find a face-saving formula for the withdrawal of West Pakistani troops and handing of power to the Awami League were spurned by Pakistan. Just two days before the fall of East Pakistan, a draft resolution was presented to the Security Council by Poland, obviously with the blessings of the Soviet Union, which provided for an orderly Pakistani pullout from East Pakistan. Its acceptance by Pakistan could probably have spared it the humiliation of surrender and of 93,000 being taken as prisoners. But, as confirmed by Sultan M. Khan, the then Pakistani Foreign Secretary, the head of Pakistan's delegation, Z.A. Bhutto, 'rejected the Polish resolution there and then. Whether or not he tore it up in the Security Council is irrelevant.'[4] Incidentally, the tearing up of this resolution had been widely reported at the time though, later on, this was to be denied by Bhutto. In a dramatic gesture of defiance, he also walked out of the Security Council, to the applause of many back home who, having lost all sense of reality, kept hoping against hope that somehow East Pakistan could yet be rescued, perhaps with Chinese help or the intervention of the American 7th Fleet.

The facts caught up just two days later when 93,000 Pakistani armed forces personnel surrendered to the Indian forces. It was the lowest point in

Pakistan's fortunes and perhaps the worst defeat suffered in Islamic history for a very long time. In West Pakistan, the people were being fed such a rosy account of the fighting that for days they could not believe that the surrender had taken place.

Throughout this tragic crisis, the hardliners in Pakistan had kept shooting down all compromises, while relentlessly pressing for the maximalist demands. In the light of what actually happened, it could be said that any compromise would have been better than the manner in which East Pakistan was lost. Even after defeat in December 1971, these hardliners remained totally opposed to the recognition of Bangladesh, when there appeared to be not a shred of evidence that Pakistan could recover its eastern wing. It was only as late as February 1974 that Pakistan was able to extend recognition to Bangladesh. Ironically, these same hardliners, who had set so much store on non-recognition, thereafter promptly forgot all about East Pakistan, showing how little they believed in their own arguments.

More recently, the same kind of hawkish pressures forced the hands of Prime Minister Nawaz Sharif to conduct nuclear tests, as a tit-for-tat against the Indian explosions. These tests plunged Pakistan's already precarious economy into a dire financial crisis with the potential even to rock the boat of the state. The fact of the matter was that Pakistan already possessed the nuclear deterrent for more than a decade and had no compelling need to conduct nuclear explosions. By not doing so, Pakistan could have reaped important financial and diplomatic benefits. But this was not to be, because of the hysteria generated by the hawkish lobby and the right wing religious parties, in particular. They all seemed driven by a kind of primeval need to do one better than India in a supreme act of machismo. It was clearly ignored that since Pakistan already possessed nuclear capability, it was not obligatory for it to openly flex its muscles, more so because restraint at this time would have produced concrete economic and diplomatic dividends for Pakistan's hard-pressed economy.

The same kind of pressures have subsequently been worked up to prevent Pakistan from signing the CTBT which merely puts restraints on future explosions and does not in any way curtail Pakistan's existing nuclear capabilities. What is evidently not understood by the pressure groups is that such a strait jacket severely restricts Pakistan's diplomatic manoeuvrability and its ability to secure important financial benefits for the country, especially at a time when Pakistan's economy is struggling. There is much defiant talk against the IMF, but the hard reality is that it is Pakistan which needs credits from the IMF and not the other way around. The strategic reality is that, at this time, Pakistan's greatest weakness is its sick economy.

The truth of the matter is that a great many people in Pakistan have long been living in a world of make-believe. There has always been a yawning gulf between what they profess and the realities, and between their words and actions. Talking tough can only make sense if one could match it by deeds. Otherwise, the old wisdom holds good that 'discretion is the better part of valour'. It is indeed astonishing as to how, with the kind of track record mentioned above, hardliners in Pakistan seem still determined to push the country into further disasters.

Failures are not unique to Pakistan, but the point is that, in similar conditions, many others were able to learn from their mistakes and at least did not repeat them. However, the problem in Pakistan has been that, for the hardliners, anyone suggesting a course of caution and compromise—the need to live within a country's physical means and the wisdom of looking before jumping—must either be a weakling or must be lacking in patriotism. There has been an unwillingness to realize that real patriotism lies, first and foremost, in working for the preservation of Pakistan's independence and integrity, and the welfare of its people. Anything which adversely affects these objectives cannot be in the best interests of Pakistan. Overburdening the country by setting for it impossible targets to achieve will, in the long run, be counter-productive.

A country, like any individual, needs to chart out its course, particularly in vital matters, with its eyes fully open to the objective realities on the ground. It is simply unwise to frame policies in disregard of facts in an emotional frame of mind or an atmosphere of jingoistic fervour. 'Not too much zeal' was the sound advice given by Talleyrand, a noted French statesman of the nineteenth century, to all those practising diplomacy. A cool-headed analysis of all the relevant facts and figures, and an examination of all the pros and cons, is essential for making the right foreign policy decisions.

In charting out foreign policy, the first priority always has to be the preservation of a country's independence and territorial integrity. Everything else should be treated as secondary. Secondly, a country has to stand on its own feet, as has been proved by Pakistan's own experience, namely that it cannot expect any foreign power to fight its battles. Thus, there should be no illusions whatsoever in Pakistan that, when the chips are down, there is going to be any rescue act, either by the brother Muslim countries, or by China, and certainly not by the USA.

Pakistan needs peace, if nothing else, in order to regroup and set its house in order. In the present circumstances, when there are increasingly grave fears that the country seems to be sinking, because of its desperate economic situation and fissiparous tendencies, those who advocate confrontation—whether in the name of patriotism or Islam—cannot be Pakistan's well-wishers. It makes no sense at all to ignore the realities about the country's past experiences as well as its present difficulties.

The reappraisal of the foreign policy followed by Pakistan, in the past fifty years, shows that it has been India-obsessed, directly as well as indirectly. In the first place, relations with India have always been the major preoccupation of its policymakers. But even the policies followed by Pakistan in respect of other countries have been largely or partly influenced by the India factor. This applies to its relations with the two superpowers, with China and even the relations with the Islamic world.

Indeed, it would not be incorrect to say that if one digs deep into almost any aspect of the foreign policy followed by Pakistan so far, one would find the Indian dimension. For instance, Pakistan would not have joined the Western-sponsored pacts and the military alliance with the US, if it had not been eager to find an equalizer against India. This spoiled Pakistan's relations with the other superpower which was to hurt Pakistan in many ways. The adverse relationship with the Soviet Union was a key factor in Pakistan's military defeat in 1971, which broke up the country into two.

In the internal context, the overriding priority given to Pakistan's defence against India did not merely place a crippling burden on the country's economy. It also allowed the Pakistani armed forces, in particular the army, to assume a larger-than-life profile in the country's politics, leading to long periods of military dictatorship and disruption of the democratic process. That, in turn, spurred fissiparous tendencies, particularly in the former East Pakistan, and provided India with the opportunity to fish in troubled waters. The whole thing has indeed been a vicious cycle.

Pakistan's relations with the US have throughout been affected by the India factor. In the 1950s and 1960s, the Pakistani expectations that the US would support Pakistan in its confrontation with India created serious difficulties in the bilateral Pakistan–American relations. In the past two decades, ties with the US have been adversely affected by the Pakistani efforts to develop a nuclear capability, leading even to the imposition of sanctions against Pakistan. But Pakistan's motivation in developing a nuclear capability has mainly been the desire to keep up with India.

It is time, therefore, to see matters in the correct perspective. There has been much debate, in particular in the more recent past, about the travails of Pakistan and what has gone wrong with the country, along with the search for scapegoats. No doubt, there has been a great deal of misrule and mismanagement. Corruption at the highest level has had a multiplier effect along cross-sections of the society. However, relations with India, which have been the root cause of the malaise, have rarely been appraised in a realistic or honest manner. In fact, there has been a kind of taboo on saying anything about the relations with India, apart from the repetition ad infinitum of the usual clichés.

In order to come out of the grave difficulties in which Pakistan has landed itself and, indeed, for the country's very survival, some hard thinking has become indispensable. The truth of the matter is that the confrontation with India has cost Pakistan a great deal.

Fortunately, Pakistan has many plus points and can do quite well in its region and in the world beyond if it can put its act together. It has vast natural resources including a significant agricultural base. It has plenty of water and a fertile soil and can basically support its large population. Above all, Pakistan has a talented and enterprising people who—when properly led—are capable of rising to great heights.

Despite all the mismanagement and misadventures of the past fifty years, the country has many proud achievements to show. Since independence, it has been able to raise the standard of living of its people and enjoys a higher per capita income than most of its neighbours. Starting as an exporter of primary products, Pakistan's exports today consist mostly of manufactured and semi-manufactured items. At the same time, the country's production of agricultural crops like wheat, rice, cotton, and sugarcane has multiplied four to five times since independence.

Pakistan's progress in science and technology is demonstrated by the acquisition of nuclear status, the first country in the Islamic world, and only the second in the whole of the Third World, to do so. The number of doctors and engineers graduating annually in Pakistan runs into thousands. A Pakistani scientist, Dr Abdus Salam, won the Nobel Prize for Physics and Dr A.Q. Khan has made Pakistan a nuclear power. The country has a significant defence production industry and it has also made progress in missile technology. Women have come a long way since independence and are an active participant in public and political activities, including the first woman prime minister in the Islamic world. Women are increasingly entering in various professions from which they were previously excluded. In sports, Pakistan has made a name for itself in cricket, hockey, and squash. Outstanding musicians like Nusrat Fateh Ali Khan have won global repute for Pakistan. The Pakistani news media has grown remarkably and the quality of journalism is comparable to that of many developed countries.

The geostrategic importance of Pakistan has always been its plus point. It is true that, in the changed world scenario after the disintegration of the Soviet Union in 1991, the US has emerged as the only superpower in the world and it no longer needs allies against the Soviet bloc; nor could it be blackmailed by countries threatening to go over to the rival camp. The previous importance of a country like Pakistan, or for that matter India, has diminished. But this is only relatively so. India is so big in population, resources, and as a military power that neither the US nor any other country can ignore it. Similarly, Pakistan has a key geostrategic location. It is also one of the largest countries in the world and perhaps the most important in the Islamic world.

As viewed by the US, Pakistan is located in a strategic but 'troubled' area. In this region, the US has had a strained relationship with the revolutionary Islamic regime in Iran since 1979 and considers it as a hotbed of radicalism and a supporter of terrorism. At times, the US has even been wanting to carry out some kind of punitive military action against Iran, but has so far avoided doing so. In the same region, Iraq has become a kind of *bête noire* for the West and the Gulf Arabs. The US has had no hesitation, of course, to strike against Iraq. Nevertheless, Saddam Hussein survived and posed a security threat in the region. Afghanistan remains embroiled in a civil war, which could degenerate into a larger conflagration and fuel the dreaded Islamic 'fundamentalism'. Already, there is a fierce struggle going on in neighbouring Tajikistan between the secularists and the orthodox Islamic circles. Against this troubled background, Pakistan appears to the US, and others, as a stabilizing factor.

Beyond the security concerns posed by these smaller countries in the Middle East and Central Asia, the US is probably even more anxious about the future course of relationship with the two giants who have both a presence as well as interests in this particular region. The future of Russia remains a question mark, even though the Soviet Union is gone. Communism could yet stage a return in this country and the global security situation might again be transformed. On the other hand, China remains communist and, by adopting capitalist ideas to improve its economy, it has become wealthier and much more powerful. What the future holds for China's relations with the West cannot be predicted with certainty at this time.

Thus, in the international arena, Pakistan should continue to enjoy an important advantage by virtue of its geostrategic location. It holds the access to the sea for its northern neighbours. It is a kind of linchpin between the Middle East, Central and South Asia. It has had a basically moderate posture and has strong linkages with the West in diverse fields. Thus, from the West's point of view, conditions of anarchy in Pakistan, or its disintegration, could be highly destabilizing for a sensitive and volatile region, where the Islamic fundamentalists in Afghanistan and Iran are already viewed as a serious security threat. A stable Pakistan with a moderate pro-West government has been, or at any rate could be, a balancing factor. Hence, it would probably remain a plank of the US and Western policy to give a degree of support to Pakistan and, at any rate, not to let it sink into chaos or revolutionary instability. Perhaps, the same reasoning would interest India as well. Indeed, Indian sources have even said as much from time to time. There can be no doubt that China certainly has a vital interest in the preservation of Pakistan. The security interests of the Gulf Arabs also converge here. Hence, geostrategic considerations would continue to help Pakistan.

In spite of all of these factors working to Pakistan's advantage, its basic problem, for the greater part, has been poor leadership and outright misgovernment. As a result, the country has suffered both in the management of its internal as well as foreign policies. An examination of the reasons for poor government in Pakistan falls outside the purview of this study. However, there is no getting away from the basic reality that political instability, misrule, and economic malaise have raised serious questions about Pakistan's very survival and have adversely effected the conduct of Pakistan's foreign relations as well.

Malaysian Prime Minister Mahathir Mohammed is reported to have said when he first took over government that Malaysia should concentrate on its internal stability and economic growth. As the country grew stronger at home, success in foreign policy would come on its own. This did actually happen, at any rate until the more recent economic and other troubles of that country. In essence, this is good advice for Pakistan or, for that matter, any country, particularly those in the developing world.

It would make far greater sense for a country like Pakistan to concentrate, at least for some time to come, on its domestic situation, with a view to organizing itself better in various fields. Political stability, sound economic policies, good governance, universal literacy, and population control should be the target areas for securing tangible progress. In a sense, the nation should become more inward looking. Until the house is first put in order, foreign affairs should be given a lower priority. This would obviously necessitate reducing the present level of differences with India and, certainly, an end to the kind of confrontation, which has for so long eclipsed all other factors. For this purpose, the Kashmir issue would need to be put on a lower pedestal and a new *modus vivendi* would have to be found for co-existing with India. A solution to the Kashmir problem would eventually have to be found, but this would be much more likely when the two countries are able to establish a better equation between themselves.

As relations improve with India, the prospects for regional cooperation would also brighten. So far, SAARC has remained relatively dormant because of the grave tensions between two of its largest components, namely, India and Pakistan. There has indeed been reluctance in Pakistan, so far, to promote trade, investment, and communications due to political constraints. In the improved political environment, however, mutuality of benefits would become the main criteria for commercial projects and businessmen would be given a free hand. South Asia may have a low per capita income but it has the advantage of being a large market with cheap labour and relatively good know-how. SAARC has, therefore, the potential to become as effective as ASEAN.

It should be Pakistan's endeavour to establish meaningful economic cooperation with its neighbours in Central Asia. This would, however, require the end of warfare in Afghanistan. Peace in that country would be essential for the development of transit trade. Afghanistan itself has important mineral resources, which can only be exploited, with Pakistan's participation, when conditions stabilize there. It will clearly be in Pakistan's interest to make every possible effort to promote peace and stability in Afghanistan. This will necessitate the adoption of a conciliatory attitude by the Taliban regime in that country and the adoption of policies, which inspire confidence amongst Afghanistan's neighbours, including Iran. Against this background, ECO could also be activated. This presently stretches up to Turkey and provides a good institutional framework for promotion of wide-ranging economic cooperation in a vast region which has important resources. Central Asia has the potential to become a key area of economic activity in the foreseeable future.

Pakistan enjoys a great deal of goodwill amongst nearly all African countries. It played a leading role in supporting the cause for the liberation of North African Muslim Arab countries in the 1950s and 1960s at the UN and elsewhere. Similarly, Pakistan's strong support to Black Africa over the years in the struggle against anti-colonialism and anti-apartheid also won it much goodwill. In the 1980s, Pakistan extended some military assistance to the guerrilla movement of Robert Mugabe during the struggle against the white regime in the then Rhodesia. The African Muslims, in general, admire Pakistan as a relatively more developed brother country that has even attained nuclear status.

In spite of this favourable climate, Pakistan has rarely made serious efforts to channelize the goodwill of African states by establishing deeper ties, with the exception of the 'Africa Programme', launched by President Ziaul Haq, in the 1980s, as a conscious effort to promote tangible cooperation with African countries. It was, however, not really pushed in a meaningful way since the ruling elite in Islamabad has shown little interest in Africa. Even a modest effort in this direction by Pakistan can produce very good results. Pakistan has the expertise that can help in the development of African countries. At minimal cost, considerable political and other benefits could be secured.

The ruling elite in Pakistan has always shown an obsession with Europe and North America. The greatest number of delegations, which have gone abroad from Pakistan, have chosen the Western countries for visits. The largest Pakistan embassies abroad are in London, Paris, Washington, and New York. Partially, this is a hangover from the colonial past. England remains a magnet in many ways although the US and Canada have increasingly attracted many Pakistanis for education, shopping, and holidays. The yearning for the West's approval has always been an underlying factor. Perhaps, the charm of the 'good life' in the Western world has been an even more important pull.

Unfortunately, on a cost-effective basis, Pakistan's untiring efforts to win over the sympathies—or to influence the thinking—of the West have been unsatisfactory. Similarly, the results achieved by the numerous visits to Western countries of Pakistani political leaders and government officials have been highly inadequate. In the context of India–Pakistan disputes, the West has leaned more towards India than Pakistan. The Democrats in the US and the British Labour Party have always shown a partiality for India. India's bigger size and economic potential has clearly weighed in its favour. Moreover, the Western world has had a greater affinity with India's political values, such as secularism, as against Pakistan's strident emphasis on its Islamic identity. India has adhered to the democratic path as against Pakistan's frequent lapses into military rule. Until the collapse of the Soviet bloc, the West had, as a policy, sought to promote democracy as the better alternative against communism. This was particularly the case before 1971, prior to the US–China rapprochement, when the Americans were determined to project India as the democratic model against the 'totalitarianism' of communist China. India's credentials as the world's 'largest' democracy obviously tilted the West in its favour as against Pakistan.

In addition, Islam has always remained a kind of bugbear for the West and these anxieties seem to have been aggravated since the demise of Soviet communism. The West is fully committed to Israel whereas Pakistan has been outspoken in its opposition to Israel. The Zionist influence over the Western news media, as also over politicians, particularly in the USA, has discouraged receptivity to Pakistan's point of view. It needs to be realized that whatever

Pakistan might do, it has little chance of securing the enthusiastic support of the West.

The ruling elite in Pakistan has obviously not understood this hard reality, namely that the West would always have a propensity to lean towards India in preference over Pakistan. And yet, an enormous amount of energy and resources has all along been wasted in this diplomatic wild goose chase. A realistic foreign policy would necessitate a toning down of the efforts to woo the West. The junkets to the Western world would need to be curtailed drastically. The size of Pakistan's diplomatic missions in these countries would also need to be cut down considerably. Incidentally, the cost of keeping a middle-ranking diplomat in a Western capital is generally equal to maintaining a full embassy in an African country.

Pakistan's prospects in the Western world are more likely to improve as and when the country is able to have internal stability and a more flourishing economy. This obviously would require internal consolidation. Pakistan's adherence to the democratic path and adoption of 'moderate' policies would also make a good impact in the West. The need to remove the distortions about the image of Islam is something that concerns not only Pakistan but also the Islamic world in general. However, as one of the largest Muslim countries, which has had traditionally greater access to the West because of its colonial past and in being Anglophone, Pakistan can perhaps play a more active role in this context.

The high priority given by Pakistan so far to multilateral diplomacy would also need to be toned down. The search for international support and approval has been a factor of the perennial confrontation with India. Once relations with India improve, the raison d'être for such diplomatic activity would probably be minimized. In any event, the results achieved over the years by Pakistan in such a competition with India have been, at best, patchy on a cost-effect basis. Similarly, the perennial search for international posts and election to the various international bodies would need to be reduced. The actual results here too have been quite unimpressive but the country has had to invest a great deal of its resources in this behalf. A more realistic foreign policy would seek to adopt a balanced course in this context.

The tendency to make too many high-level foreign visits in the hope that Pakistani leaders would somehow be able to charm or cajole their counterparts into supporting Pakistan must be curtailed, if not given up. It should be evident that countries make their policies on the basis of calculations of their national interests and are not likely to be influenced by personal factors. A foreign visit, particularly at the level of head of state or government, should only be undertaken when sufficient ground work has been done to ensure that the visit would be productive and that it would not merely be a 'photo opportunity' or bring out a repetition of previously heard clichés. The past few years have seen numerous visits by Pakistani prime ministers and other high-ranking visitors who return home declaring their visits to have been 'highly successful'. Had this been really the case, Pakistan should have been doing very well indeed in the international arena. Unfortunately, by and large, this has only been a case of self-praise and living in a world of illusions sustained by the dutiful sycophancy of aides of the Pakistani leaders, who only say what their leaders would like to hear.

In short, realism and a cold calculation of national interests should become the hallmarks of the foreign policy of Pakistan in the twenty-first century. For its very self-preservation, Pakistan would have to say goodbye to overambition and ad hocism, which have done so much harm already to the country in the first fifty years of its existence. While the preservation of Pakistan's sovereign independence and territorial integrity should be the overriding objectives, internal consolidation and high economic growth would need to become the main priorities. Peace with honour with India and the promotion of regional cooperation should be adopted as the immediate policy objectives.

NOTES

1. Chou En-lai, Chinese Premier, expressed astonishment to a Pakistani military mission, in August 1966, about the wisdom of going to war with India while having fourteen days reserve supplies. Sultan M. Khan, op. cit., p. 182.
2. On 7 December 1971, just four days after the war broke out, Gen. Niazi 'broke into tears' in a meeting with Governor Malik and agreed to a ceasefire. Siddiq Salik, *Witness to Surrender* (Karachi: Oxford University Press, 1978), p. 194.
3. Meeting with Khondakar Mushtaq, former President of Bangladesh, reported in an article by Tanvir Ahmad Khan, *Dawn*, 14 December 1999.
4. Sultan M. Khan, *Memories & Reflections*, pp. 382–4.

13

The Kargil Crisis: An Assessment

The subcontinent witnessed a particularly grave crisis in May 1999 when according to the Indians they first became aware that some 'Pakistani intruders' had penetrated across the Line of Control (LoC) in the Kargil sector and had firmly entrenched themselves over several hilltops. The Indians seemed to view it not only as the most serious penetration and violation of the LoC ever from the Pakistani side but also one that threatened their strategic highway to Ladakh and access to Siachen.

The short summer in the region also gave the issue a certain urgency because failure to get the strategic heights vacated by August could have probably delayed military operations till the next May and, in the meantime, access to Ladakh would have been imperilled. India evidently could not accept such a change in the status quo and decided to take decisive military action to reverse the situation.

Two months later, India had evidently secured this objective and there was much jubilation and backslapping in that country. On the other hand, many people in Pakistan were crestfallen and, here, the air was full of bitter recriminations, particularly from the opponents of the Nawaz Sharif government. The ruling party and its official machinery were making claims of a historic achievement. This seemed rather bewildering and even paradoxical. Where lies the truth and how would history judge the gains and losses made by the two protagonists? There is need for sober reflection and a cool analysis.

On the face of it, India had had the better of the bargain. Otherwise, there would be no warrant for the kind of euphoria one saw in India and the conspicuous lack of it in Pakistan, except among the official lobbyists in Islamabad. It cannot be denied that India regained control over the Kargil heights, as the Mujahideen or 'Pakistani intruders' were asked to withdraw. The Indian military and political objective would thus appear to have been secured. During this crisis, Pakistan found itself relatively isolated internationally which, too, was a triumph for Indian diplomacy. International pressure was mainly being exerted on Pakistan rather than on India. This was a key reason that obliged Pakistan to back away.

A closer examination of the apparent Indian successes suggests a less rosy picture for New Delhi. In the battlefield, India did poorly. According to India's own estimates, the number of the 'intruders' was in several hundreds. They did not possess the weaponry of a regular army since they were, by conception, only a guerrilla force. To throw out this small number of 'intruders', India threw in a force, at least, of over twenty thousand (some accounts suggest twice this number) regular troops including some elite commandos, backed up by heavy artillery and the latest aircraft of the Indian Air Force. During the fighting, the Indians made painfully slow progress. Two months later, India had only made limited military gains on the ground. The eviction of the Mujahideen was eventually secured through a political decision. In the process, the Indians bore heavy losses: the official count was nearly four hundred dead, which was high enough against the small number of the Mujahideen. The Indian casualties were believed to have been higher. Despite enjoying overwhelming military superiority, and making allowance for the fact that the Indians had to climb up the hills, the Indian military performance was poor, whereas the Mujahideen seem to have fought like tigers. This clearly raises questions about the quality of the Indian military and its morale, despite all the hype generated by the Indian media.

India paid a heavy financial price for its military campaign, probably running into billions rather than millions. It lost at least two aircraft and one helicopter. The reported cost of firing one shell of a Bofors gun, in use of the Indian army, is about Rs 40,000, whereas thousands of such shells were fired. It also seems likely that, henceforth, India would be obliged to keep a large force on the Kargil heights to defend them, even during the severe winters when temperatures come down to minus forty degrees. This would entail substantial financial expenditure as well, apart from the physical hardship including frostbite and frozen death for the soldiers guarding these desolate heights. The military 'gains' for India of the recent Kargil crisis might well turn out to be a Pyrrhic victory.

For political reasons, the Indian government chose to play up the funerals of dead soldiers in the Kargil fighting. This could turn out to be a grave mistake. So far, the Indian public, by and large, had little awareness of the body losses in the Kashmiri insurrection since 1990. The parallels of Afghanistan or Vietnam did not quite seem applicable to Kashmir. India was taking casualties but there were no known protests from the Indian public because there was no highlighting of the casualties. But, the situation has changed with the public effusive mourning of the returning dead. For a while, no doubt, the war fever kept the morale high. However, history bears witness that this euphoria rarely lasts. The growing awareness of physical and financial losses would, sooner or later, probably tell.

There has been considerable gloating in India over the seeming success of Indian diplomacy in isolating Pakistan. In fact, this had little to do with India's own efforts. It was more a function of the global apprehensions regarding the outbreak of any nuclear war. Since India and Pakistan are both nuclear powers, there has been a deep anxiety worldwide that a full-scale war between them must be avoided. This global concern—rather than any superior Indian diplomacy—was what prompted pressures on Pakistan to bring about the withdrawal of the Mujahideen whose crossing of the LoC was seen as the immediate reason for the fighting.

India's overreaction, war fever, and open threats to wage a larger war with Pakistan, while raising international pressures on Pakistan in the short run, might have done more harm to India in the long run for not being a 'responsible' nuclear power. Thus, over a period of time, there might be greater pressures on India to respond to the international concern for non-proliferation.

On the moral plane, India seems to be smug, and even boastful, about having upheld the sanctity of Agreements (Simla and Lahore) and the LoC. It has been accusing Pakistan of bad faith and violation of International Law. In the Western news media, an expensive advertising campaign was launched by India, highlighting the alleged violation of international norms and treaties by Pakistan. Charges of being a 'rogue' state or having a 'rogue' army continue to be levelled against Pakistan.

It has to be conceded that the violation of the LoC in the Kargil area did in a way put Pakistan in the dock in the present crisis. But a closer examination shows that India has had a far worse record of breaking its word. It has been violating solemn commitments on Kashmir and, in particular, has shown disregard for the long-standing UN Security Council resolutions on this issue. In contravention of the assurances given by Prime Minister Jawaharlal Nehru[1] and Gopalaswami Ayyangar,[2] the Indian delegate to the UN Security Council, in October 1947 and January 1948 respectively that the people of Kashmir would be allowed to decide whether they wanted to join India or Pakistan through an impartial plebiscite, India reneged on its promise.

Ever since, India has been persistently guilty of violation of its solemn commitments on Kashmir and defying the UN Security Council resolutions and the views of other international bodies. Its stance on Kashmir has not been supported by any international body or by the overwhelming majority of states. India has also shown total disregard for the Partition formula, according to which the subcontinent was divided in 1947, with the consent of its founding fathers including Gandhi and Nehru. This formula was that the contiguous Muslim majority areas should be separated from the contiguous non-Muslim majority areas in order to form the two Dominions. The rulers of the Princely States were bound by the same formula. Thus, when the Muslim ruler of Junagarh signed the Instrument of Accession in favour of Pakistan, despite the fact that Junagarh had a non-Muslim majority, India accused him of acting 'in utter violation of the principles on which partition was agreed upon and effected.' India attacked and occupied Junagarh on this premise. India has since taken a diametrically opposite position in the case of Kashmir.

Currently when the principle of self-determination and respect for democratic rights has become a part of the global political culture, India has consistently defied international opinion by trampling upon the rights of the Kashmiri people. It has been guilty of gross violations of human rights, as testified by international human rights organizations and independent journalists. It keeps an army of occupation in Kashmir of 700,000 to suppress a population of four million, a ratio that has no other parallel in the world.

India has no grounds for parading its respect for international norms and treaties and Pakistan's lack of such respect. Morally and legally, the Indian case on Kashmir has always been very weak and, indeed, indefensible. Its pious mantle of standing up for international morality and respect for treaties is at best a hollow claim, if not an outright farce. India's claim of having achieved a diplomatic victory over Pakistan in the Kargil crisis by isolating it cannot be stretched beyond a point. The grave tensions generated by the crisis, fuelled largely by India's own war hysteria and aggressive military posture, did shake up the chancelleries in key world capitals and forced them to take notice of the crisis in the subcontinent and its underlying cause, namely, the Kashmir issue. A relatively dormant and neglected issue thus secured at least some of the attention due to it. Above all, the world's only superpower, the USA decided to take interest in resolving this problem. The assurance of President Bill Clinton that he would 'take a personal interest' in promoting the India–Pakistan dialogue on all issues including Kashmir was the first of its kind in the past fifty years. In this connection, President Clinton's telephone calls to Indian Prime Minister A.B. Vajpayee did amount to a third party role, something that India has stoutly tried to resist for many years. This could hardly constitute the diplomatic 'triumph' of the Kargil crisis, which India is claiming. At the end of some reckless brinkmanship by the two sides, Pakistan did secure a significant advance on Kashmir in the diplomatic chessboard.

The foregoing cannot, however, conceal the many glaring deficiencies and flaws in Pakistan's policy in the Kargil crisis. Whoever engineered the Kargil venture did not, evidently, take all the relevant factors into account. It was clearly not anticipated by the Pakistani leadership as to how sharp would be the Indian reaction and how much Pakistan would be isolated internationally on this issue. It was not realized that the prospect of a nuclear war is terrifying for the world opinion, which expects nuclear powers to show the greatest sense of responsibility. Playing with fire is always dangerous, the more so if you are a nuclear power. But even if it had been calculated in Islamabad that the nuclear deterrent would prevent the worst scenario, the fact remained that even a conventional war at this juncture, against a foe several times bigger than itself, made little or no sense, particularly when Pakistan's economy is in a precarious condition and there is little or no prospect of material help coming from friends abroad—at least on the scale of the previous two wars with India.

What made matters worse was the total lack of realism shown by many in the government, as also by the opposition parties and the legion of retired military officers who kept up wild talk of fighting the 'last war' and using nuclear weapons and missiles in a do-or-die war. They even conjured up visions of the Mujahideen proceeding from Kargil to Srinagar and eventually deep inside India itself to hoist the flag of Islam! To imagine that India, with its much larger army and far stronger economy, possessing nuclear weapons and missiles, would have allowed a walkover to Pakistan seemed sheer lunacy. These brave souls also seemed completely oblivious of the fact that in a nuclear war, there are no winners, but only losers. The fact that the then Leader of the House in the Senate, Raja Zafarul Haq, and the then Chairman of the Foreign Affairs Committee in the National Assembly, Mian Abdul Waheed, were among those brandishing nuclear weapons raised chilling questions about the maturity of their regime. Against this background, it was a great relief that wisdom did dawn, if belatedly, and the Washington meeting between President Clinton and Prime Minister Nawaz Sharif secured the needed de-escalation, which seems to have defused the crisis.

In the course of the crisis, government spokesmen, including the Foreign Office, made themselves a target of ridicule by pretending that the world opinion was with Pakistan. It was even claimed that the US and the G-8 were supportive of Pakistan when they had clearly put the blame on Pakistan for triggering the crisis by 'sending infiltrators' across the LoC in the Kargil sector. This was an unmistakable indictment of Pakistan and no amount of hair splitting could conceal this reality. Similarly, all kinds of claims were made about China's 'full support' for Pakistan, whereas all the Chinese statements on the subject were circumspect and neutral sounding. The Islamic countries were equally guarded in their stance; and the only fig leaf left for Pakistan was the OIC resolutions at Ouagadougou. Experience, however, shows that in the OIC forum, almost any resolution can be secured. Unfortunately, these same OIC countries, when the issue comes up at the UN or other forums, hardly ever live up to their OIC stance. Hence, to claim that the Islamic world was solidly with us was close to self-deception.

The government decided to send its political 'heavy-weights', i.e. certain cabinet members and other luminaries to lobby foreign leaders for Pakistan's stance. They carried letters from the Pakistan prime minister addressed to the various heads of states. As usual, these special envoys made all kinds of claims of support secured for Pakistan and the 'success' of their missions. The fact, however, was that the special envoys were, in several instances, able only to meet lower level functionaries, as the heads of states did not agree to meet them. Their pretensions of having converted these countries to Pakistan's point of view sounded absurd. In the process, the unfortunate thing was that instead of getting a clear-headed view of the global situation, Pakistani public opinion was largely kept ignorant of the world's reaction. The pullback from Kargil, therefore, came as a far greater shock.

The question also needs to be asked as to what were the objectives of the Kargil venture? It could not have been the military conquest of Kashmir, since getting a few hilltops in Kargil could not bring about that result. Yet after the relative success of the Mujahideen in Kargil, there were those who actually thought that Srinagar would fall next. The reality was that short of a major war, this simply could not be done; but anyone with even a modicum of common sense would eschew a war between two nuclear states. On the other hand, if the Kargil venture was aimed at securing the activation of the Kashmir issue, then the de-escalation should have taken place much earlier than on 4 July at which stage it appeared like a climb-down and almost succumbing to US pressure. The US media has reported that Nawaz Sharif had 'begged' for a last minute meeting with Clinton. Whatever the truth, in the end, it did look like a national humiliation.

The Kargil venture had two inbuilt defects. It was taking place too close to the LoC, thus strengthening the suspicion that Pakistan was involved. It threatened Indian access to a vital area and, hence, India could not digest the loss of such territory. Had the Mujahideen struck deeper in the Indian-held territory, far from the LoC, the accusation of Pakistani complicity would have sounded much less credible. Furthermore, the timing was wrong. It was too close to the Indian elections. The ruling party there could not afford to reconcile to this territorial loss without suffering a severe setback in the elections.

Pakistani credibility was another casualty of the Kargil crisis. Islamabad kept saying that it had no control over the Mujahideen who were indigenous Kashmiri freedom fighters. In that case, how was it that at Washington, the prime minister accepted to take 'concrete steps for the restoration' of the LoC, which meant withdrawing the Mujahideen from the Kargil sector. But the ink was barely dry on the Washington agreement, when the Pakistani foreign minister was saying in London that Pakistan could only appeal to the Mujahideen for withdrawal and they would do so only if there was some progress on the Kashmir issue. If that was all that we could do, then what was the point of giving the US an assurance about 'concrete steps' to secure withdrawals. The foreign minister also sought to link withdrawal from Kargil with the Indian withdrawal from Siachen. This was clearly not so agreed at the Washington meeting and the Americans were quick to point out that the withdrawals were Kargil-specific. This quibbling did little more than further damaging Pakistan's credibility. Our spokespersons also claimed that the Washington agreement did not represent a change in Pakistan's position when the whole world could see that it was not only a change but also a climb down.

Actually, the problem with our government leaders and officials has long been an obsessive desire to prove that all is well and that everything is in control. They fear that any admission of failure or lack of progress would perhaps damage or destroy their careers. Hence, every visit is described as a success and everything is said to be going Pakistan's way. Unfortunately, this can hardly be so. Such an attitude does grave disservice to a country's vital interests. The big problem with Pakistan's foreign policy over the years has been a propensity, especially at critical times, to live under illusions. Before the fall of Dhaka in 1971, there were illusions about the 7th Fleet and Chinese soldiers coming to our rescue. In 1965, our strategists had thought that we could bottle up the Indians in Kashmir by capturing Akhnur and still India would not cross the international border. The attack on Lahore thus came as a big surprise to them. Later on, many were under the impression that Pakistan was winning the 1965 War, when the reality was that our armoured attack at Khem Karan had ended in a fiasco and, in general, we had run out of supplies. At the end of the fighting, India was in possession of important territory in Sialkot as against some desert area secured by us.

Yet, the long-lasting myth arose that at the conference table at Tashkent, we lost what had been gained in the battlefield.

It seems that no lessons have been learnt either from the 1965 or the 1971 wars. In some ways, Kargil seemed to be a repetition of the 1965 experience. The country came close to falling into a precipice, before wisdom belatedly dawned. Foreign policy is a very serious business and has to be based on realism and hard calculations, not on rosy projections. The consequences of any given policy must be worked out in meticulous detail under the worst scenario conditions. It is reckless to act first and think later. It is high time that the country became brutally realistic about its limitations and priorities. First and above all, Pakistan's survival must precede everything else, including our attachment to the Kashmir cause. Secondly, it has to be understood that our economy is our weakest point and has to be given priority over any other consideration. Thirdly, we need to set our house in order and require a long period of internal consolidation, based on drastic reforms.

Finally, there must be a total awareness in both India and Pakistan that war is no longer an option for either country. Being nuclear powers, they would surely destroy themselves if war broke out between them and millions would perish. Surely, no bilateral dispute is worth such a mutually assured devastation. Hence, there is no option for both countries except to exhibit the greatest sense of responsibility.

NOTES

1. Jawaharlal Nehru in a telegram dated 30 October 1947 to his Pakistani counterpart.
2. Gopalaswami Ayyangar in an address given by the Indian delegate at the UN Security Council on 14 January 1948.

14

Strengthening the OIC

The first Islamic Summit was convened in Rabat (Morocco) in 1969 following the worldwide Muslim outrage on the burning of the holy Al-Aqsa Mosque in Jerusalem by an Israeli extremist. The Rabat Summit had a symbolic as well as historical significance. It was the first time when the heads of state and government of Muslim countries from different parts of the world had met formally on a political platform. The Rabat Summit sent out a message that Jerusalem was an issue of concern not only for the Arabs but also for the entire Islamic world. This summit conference thus helped to raise the morale of the Arabs after their stunning defeat in the 1967 Arab–Israel War. The Palestine Liberation Organization (PLO) also received a boost at Rabat as the representative body of the Palestinians.

Perhaps the most important outcome of the Rabat Summit was the decision to institutionalize cooperation among the 1,000 million Muslims in the world by establishing a permanent body of the Islamic countries. It was agreed that Jeddah would be the headquarters until Al-Quds (Jerusalem) was liberated from Israeli occupation. In 1971, a charter was formally adopted and a secretariat was established. Tunku Abdul Rahman, Prime Minister of Malaysia, became the first secretary-general of the Organization of Islamic Conference (OIC).

The Rabat Summit is also remembered for the stance taken by Pakistan that India should be kept out of representative meetings of Islamic countries. At the time, King Faisal of Saudi Arabia and some other leaders were in favour of the participation of Indian Muslims in the Islamic Summit on the rationale that the Indian Muslims, who then numbered nearly 80 million, were many times larger in number than the total population of several Islamic states. Moreover, historically speaking, Indian Muslims had always been an active participant in all Islamic causes.

Pakistan was not opposed to this move in the beginning.[1] But the Indian government's decision to send its ambassador in Rabat, a Sikh, to represent India in the conference, pending the arrival of an official delegation headed by a Muslim cabinet minister, outraged the Pakistanis. This was clearly not the case of participation of 'Indian Muslims' in the conference but, under this cover, it would be India that would secure representation in the Islamic world. At this juncture, Pakistan quite validly took the position that India could not be described as an Islamic country since its government was controlled by non-Muslims and its Muslim minority had been subjected to serious religious persecution. Even if Indian Muslims were to represent India in the OIC, they would be handpicked by the Indian government and would only toe the official line. Moreover, if India were to be brought in, then by the same logic, the Soviet Union, Yugoslavia, and China should also have been included. Pakistan's stance was opposed by the friends of India, particularly Egypt, and it was only after Pakistan threatened to walk out of the Summit that it was agreed to keep India out of the meeting.

In the aftermath, there was severe criticism in India itself regarding such a move to participate in an Islamic meeting, which was inconsistent with India's secularism.[2] This rebuff to India, which had been mainly engineered by Pakistan, also hardened India's subsequent attitude towards the OIC. India had been successful in the preceding years in establishing close friendship with several Islamic countries, mainly on the premise of a common opposition to the Western-sponsored military alliances. In seeking friendship of the Islamic countries, the strategic objective of India was probably more to prevent Pakistan from building up a phalanx of Islamic countries behind it. Hence, its publicized ouster from the Rabat Summit was a bitter setback for India's policies. For this reason, India's close friends in the Arab world, like Egypt, even felt the necessity to send high-ranking delegations to India to apologize for this episode.[3]

Eventually, the OIC adopted a criterion for membership, namely that the applying country should have a Muslim majority or Islam should be its state religion. This criterion has not been rigorously followed in the case of membership of some African countries, e.g. Benin, Uganda, and Sierra Leone, where reliable statistics for population have not been available.

To begin with, secular Arab regimes like Syria and Iraq were cool towards the OIC and did not participate in some of its initial meetings. Egypt also had certain reservations. It had been unhappy with the decision to exclude India. The decision to make Jeddah the seat of the OIC rankled with the Egyptians who had an uneasy relationship with the Saudis. However, the death of Gamal Abdel Nasser in 1970 brought a more pro-Islamic leadership to power and Egypt henceforth became an enthusiastic member of the OIC. Other Arab secular regimes like Syria and Iraq also concluded that keeping out of a large body like the OIC would not be in their interest.

The next Islamic Summit was again convened on an emergency basis, following the October 1973 Arab–Israel War. The OIC Secretary-General Tunku Abdul Rahman suggested such a summit and the Pakistani Prime Minister Z.A. Bhutto offered to host it. The summit took place in February 1974 in Lahore. This summit had a larger number of participating states, particularly from Africa. The presence in the Islamic summit and the OIC of several oil-rich countries evidently enhanced its attraction for the poorer Muslim countries who expected that their participation in this forum would be economically advantageous. This explains why even some non-Muslim majority African countries rushed to join the OIC.

The Lahore Summit, unlike the previous summit, covered several subjects of concern to the Islamic world and thus acquired a wider interest. It also broke the deadlock on the issue of the recognition of Bangladesh and secured some degree of reconciliation between Pakistan and its breakaway eastern wing. The summit also generated a great deal of goodwill for the host Pakistan whose people extended such an enthusiastic reception to the visiting delegations. The OIC too gained in stature because of the success of the Lahore Summit which gave the organization the necessary credibility for its continued existence.

There was a gap of seven years before the Third Summit was held at Taif (Saudi Arabia) against the background of the Iran–Iraq War, the Soviet military occupation of Afghanistan and the Arab anger with Egypt for signing the Camp David peace accords unilaterally with Israel. An important achievement of this summit was the decision to hold Islamic summits every three years. Since then, Islamic summits have been held in Casablanca (1984), Kuwait (1987), Dakar (1991), Casablanca (1994), and Tehran (1997). Moreover, a special Islamic summit was also held in Islamabad in March 1997 to commemorate fifty years of Pakistan's independence, as a tribute to Pakistan's role in the Islamic world.

The Islamic foreign ministers meet annually in various capitals, as also at the beginning of the UN General Assembly session in New York. Their senior officials hold detailed preparatory meetings at Jeddah. The agenda of such meetings has grown bigger over the years and covers political, economic, social, scientific, and administrative subjects. The OIC commission for economic, cultural, and social affairs also meets annually. A number of subsidiary bodies hold their own meetings from time to time, giving the OIC a fairly high profile in the activities of the Islamic world.

From amongst the subsidiary organs of the OIC, the Islamic Development Bank (IDB), which was established in 1974, has probably become its most successful institution. Modelled on the pattern of the world's leading financial bodies, the IDB has expanded significantly over the years and has made a notable contribution in the financing of a large number of projects in the Islamic world. Saudi Arabia has always played a key role in the IDB and a Saudi national has headed the IDB right from the beginning.

There is no doubt that the OIC has become the most important collective body in the Islamic world. There are more than one billion Muslims in the world and their number is increasing, both because of the high ratio of population growth in the Muslim countries as well as the result of propagation of Islam in Africa and elsewhere. The OIC has at present a membership of fifty-five states and there are three states which have observer status. This accounts for more than one-fourth of the UN membership.

The Muslim countries possess enormous natural resources, particularly oil. Saudi Arabia, Kuwait, UAE, Qatar, and Brunei Darussalam are amongst the most affluent countries in the world. Iran, Iraq, Nigeria, and Indonesia are also among the world's major producers of oil. The Islamic countries occupy a key strategic location in the world and some of the world's most important waterways pass through them, viz. the Suez Canal, Bosphorus, Persian Gulf, and the Malacca Strait. They also possess considerable military capability and one of them—Pakistan—has become a nuclear power. The Muslim world accounts for one-fifth of the world's population and has a distinct cultural identity of its own.

In the event the Islamic countries can forge unity in their ranks, they can act as a powerful bloc and influence world events decisively. Unfortunately, this has rarely happened, much to the detriment of the Muslims themselves. Even though Islamic unity and brotherhood is an ingrained belief of every Muslim, the actual state of the Muslim World shows a very different situation. There have always been sharp rivalries and suspicions between Muslim countries. Two of the most destructive wars in recent history, the Iran–Iraq War (1980–8) and the Gulf War (1991), involved fighting between the Muslims. Morocco and Algeria have been feuding over the former Spanish Sahara. Libya has had problems with many Islamic countries. Sudan has been at odds with Egypt and other neighbours. Iraq continues to have serious differences with its neighbours. Turkey has had serious problems with Syria and Iraq over the Kurdish issue. The Kurds have been involved in an unsuccessful war for national independence against Muslim brothers in Turkey, Iran, Iraq, and Syria. Afghanistan recently came close to a full-scale war with Iran and has serious problems with its Muslim neighbours. Yemen and Saudi Arabia have had a difficult relationship. Qatar has had problems with its neighbours.

The OIC basically reflects the attitudes and relationships of its member states. It would be difficult for an organization to be effective when its members are pulling in different directions. Thus, the OIC has had an uneven growth and a chequered history. This continues to bewilder Muslims in many parts of the world who believe in the Quranic injunction that 'all Muslims are brothers'. They are unable to comprehend as to what has been impeding closer ties between the Islamic countries.

The governments and ruling classes in various Muslim countries hold widely divergent views about the role of Islam in their body politic, particularly in foreign policy matters. The secularists, who are in power in several Islamic countries, feel distinctly uncomfortable with policies motivated by religious considerations. Some of these states have evolved close relations with non-Muslim countries, even those in conflict with one or more Islamic countries, as also with some countries which have a poor record of treating their indigenous Muslim minorities. Nevertheless, these secular regimes too have found it inexpedient to stay away from the OIC. For instance, despite their mental reservations and initial reluctance to join this body, Turkey, Iraq, and Syria realized that the OIC was an important forum and could, in a given situation, provide them useful support. Besides, even secular regimes cannot altogether ignore the yearnings of their Muslim masses for Islamic solidarity. All Islamic countries without exception have, therefore, become OIC members. At the same time, the differences in their policies have often prevented the OIC from acting as a cohesive group.

There are other areas of divergence as well. The Islamic world stretches over a large part of the globe covering diverse cultural and ethnic backgrounds. There are regional groupings which have differing agendas from the OIC. It is not uncommon that the regional grouping gets preference over the more distant and looser body. For instance, the ASEAN and the Gulf Cooperation Council seem to take precedence for their constituent states over the OIC. This is a depressing commentary on the current state of affairs of the OIC and shows how far it has to go to secure credibility and meaningful acceptance.

There is another distortion in the OIC resulting from the yawning economic disparities between its member states. The more affluent states are wary of the tendency of the poorer cousins to place financial burdens on them in the name of Islamic solidarity. For instance, the majority of the OIC member states, particularly the African states, have not been paying their dues to the OIC. In fact, some of the African countries had joined the OIC in the expectation that its oil-rich members would be forthcoming with financial aid. The tacit assumption on their part is that the oil-rich states should foot the bill for expenses incurred by the OIC. Though the annual contribution for membership is not much, as international bodies go, and the oil-rich states should have hardly any problem footing it, yet the latter have not been willing to do so. Their reasoning probably is that if the same poorer nations can meet their financial obligations to the UN and other international bodies, why can't they do so in the case of the OIC?

At any rate, the OIC has been beset by financial crisis as a result of this impasse. A visit to the OIC secretariat in Jeddah shows its general state of neglect. There are always delays in payment of salaries and emoluments to the staff members; house rents are often overdue and medical bills do not get paid. Matters are not helped by the tendency of OIC Secretariat officials to travel too much, not missing any invitation that comes their way.

The financial woes of the OIC have also been compounded by a tendency towards proliferation of bodies set up under its umbrella. There has never been a shortage of ideas about what the Muslim Ummah should do to meet the challenges of the time. However, the authors of these ideas have, more often than not, failed to take into account the wherewithal and financial feasibility of such projects. But in OIC meetings, there is a reluctance to enter into controversies, particularly if the sensitivities of the host country would be injured. The path of least resistance has often been adopted, resulting in the creation of new bodies under the aegis of the OIC for which funds are not available and staff cannot be paid. Although the OIC has belatedly adopted the policy of not creating new bodies, even the existing bodies are far too many and are always starved of funds, even for their routine operations. This has obviously not enhanced the credibility of the organization and speaks poorly of its planning mechanism.

It can be argued that there is insufficient motivation on the part of many Islamic countries to enhance concrete cooperation amongst themselves, even in highly beneficial areas. Science and technology is one such area. An early Pakistani proposal (prompted by Dr Abdus Salam, who was later to win the Nobel Prize for Physics) to set up an Islamic Science Foundation got nowhere. In the same way, the COMSTECH (Committee for Science and Technology) headed by the President of Pakistan has not been able to make any significant headway. Similarly, the development of food security and an Islamic common market, or even its regional variations have also remained only on the conference agenda.

There is a general realization among the Islamic countries that the world news media gives very inadequate or even negative coverage to developments in the Muslim world. The reason seems to be that the media is basically controlled by the Western countries where the Jewish lobby is very active. It was decided many years ago to set up an Islamic news agency. However, the paucity of funds as well as incompetent management has prevented International Islamic News Agency (IINA) from developing into a credible body.

Joint defence production could have been of great benefit to many OIC member countries which are, in any event, making prohibitively expensive purchases from the West and elsewhere. However, the affluent OIC countries have tended to regard such joint projects as an exercise by the less affluent brothers to extract money from the richer members. The location of such projects has also held up progress. For instance, a country like Pakistan, which has relatively cheap labour and technical expertise, would like the project to be based in Pakistan, with the expectation that the capital investment would come from one of the oil-rich countries. But the latter would rather have the project based in their own countries. Besides, the oil-rich Muslim countries have tended to assume that the Third World countries cannot match the West in technology and hence the products of joint defence production would not be of a high standard. Incidentally, it is ironic that some of the oil-rich Islamic countries have been willing to fund projects outside the Islamic world on a far larger scale but they are not willing to do so for the good of their own brethren.

Of course, concrete cooperation in the defence field, in terms of defence pacts or collective regional security, has rarely been discussed in the OIC forum; and wherever it exists, it has been due to arrangements made outside the OIC.

The only exception to this trend has been the relative success secured by the Islamic Development Bank (IDB) based in Jeddah which has been functioning on the model of international financial institutions. The IDB is relatively autonomous and has generally worked on sound lines. It has made a notable contribution in the economic development of the Islamic countries.

There is no shortage of lip service among Muslims in Pakistan and elsewhere about the imperative of Islamic unity nor of sentimental claims about the progress made so far in the context of the OIC. A sober assessment, however, suggests that at present, the OIC is more froth than substance. This state of affairs is not deliberate nor in keeping with the aspirations of more than a billion-strong Muslim Ummah in the world. There are those who see sinister international conspiracies behind this lack of progress and see the hand of the US, Israel, India, and other non-Muslim powers and their 'agents' in the Islamic world.

The question is also asked as to what can be done to improve cooperation between the Islamic countries. This requires political will at the highest level in the Islamic countries to give credibility and substance to the widely cherished objective of Islamic unity under the aegis of the OIC. There has to be a genuine commitment to forging closer links between the Muslim countries, followed up by specific and concrete measures. There is need for the Muslim heads of state and government to consult each other frequently and work out common strategies. Where bilateral differences exist, constructive efforts ought to be made to resolve them, using the OIC itself as a mediatory body.

Member states must pay serious attention to deliberations in the OIC and not merely treat it as a discussion body. They must put an end to the tendency to regard decisions of the OIC as non-binding or at best merely recommendatory. In this framework, it follows that issues raised in the OIC forums should be seriously discussed and vigorously argued before any resolution is passed. The present practice of following the path of least resistance and shunning controversies has resulted in any number of resolutions getting passed by the organization which are simply not being implemented.

Some commentators in Islamic countries may have taken satisfaction from the fact that the last Islamic Summit held in Tehran passed 142 resolutions, but this is more reflective of the reality that almost any resolution could be passed in the OIC forum, provided that it is not against one of the OIC member states. However, after the resolution gets passed, it is promptly ignored by most of the member states. What is needed, therefore, is that fewer resolutions should be passed, but before passing, they should be seriously debated and argued. If some country has objections to a proposed resolution, it should state so categorically and either the objections are removed or the resolution is dropped. Little is gained by the expediency of avoiding floor controversy and letting a resolution pass, but subsequently ignoring it.

The financial crisis faced by the OIC secretariat needs to be effectively resolved by ensuring that each member state pays its dues or else it would be denied participation in OIC meetings. However, in the case of states facing acute financial difficulties e.g. Somalia and Afghanistan, the OIC could make a special exception. The rest must pay their dues or face exclusion from OIC meetings, on lines of the UN. To overcome the perennial financial crisis faced by the OIC secretariat, and various subsidiary bodies set up under the OIC umbrella, an endowment fund of, say, US$ 200 million may be set up which could raise sufficient annual revenues to meet the OIC's needs. This will effectively make the OIC self-reliant and end the sorry spectacle of the secretariat making desperate appeals to keep itself financially afloat.

There is also need for strict financial discipline in the OIC secretariat and the various subsidiary organs. There is too much travel, particularly for meetings held in the US and Europe, which is quite ironical also since these are non-Muslim regions. It is evident that many secretariat officials are only interested in going on foreign junkets and making money from travel allowances.

More importantly, some hard decisions are needed to fold up several programmes and some OIC organs which have proved to be inconsequential or redundant. In each case, the interested state or the affected staff will protest, but this will have to be over-ruled.

The OIC can really become effective if it is headed by a strong secretary-general with the right contacts in the highest quarters in key member states, particularly the oil-rich countries. Someone like Saudi Foreign Minister Prince Saud-al-Faisal would be an ideal choice. The experience so far has been that most of the OIC secretary-generals have generally been passive figures, more involved in ceremonial events than in concrete work. Moreover, there has been a tendency on the part of the successive OIC secretary-generals to show excessive deference to the wishes of the host, the Saudi government, on whose generosity the secretariat seems to survive, rather than act as international civil servants like their UN counterparts.

NOTES

1. Sultan M. Khan, op. cit., p. 235.
2. *Statesman*, editorial, 27 September 1969, cited in Burke and Ziring, p. 374.
3. Iqbal Akhund, *Memoirs of a Bystander*, p. 183.

15

The Role of the Islamic World in Global Politics

Islam emerged on the world scene in the seventh century AD as an irresistible force with a highly revolutionary message. It propagated equality and unity, irrespective of race or colour, in a commonwealth of the believers. It emphasized discipline and sacrifice for the collective good. Good character and piety were given preference over noble ancestry and other privileges. Its followers were devout and totally committed, willing to die gladly for the holy cause—the jihad. In a stunning display of military capability, the desert Bedouins swept aside the two major powers of that era, the Eastern Roman Empire and imperial Persia, within twenty years of the Islamization of Arabia. The lesser powers simply melted away before the rising sun of Islam.

The various peoples conquered by the Islamic forces readily embraced the new faith and they themselves took the flag of Islam to territories beyond. The Muslims reached the Atlantic in the West and the Pacific in the East. Spain came under Islamic rule in the beginning of the eighth century, at about the same time that the Muslims entered Sindh in western India. Most of India was in Muslim control by the twelfth century. The Mongol conquests of the thirteenth century were a grave setback for Islam but, fortunately, the Mongols readily embraced Islam themselves. Thus, the Mongols who had conquered Russia were converted to Islam and the Kazan Khanate ruled Moscow for nearly 200 years. Constantinople (now Istanbul) was conquered in 1453 and in the middle of the sixteenth century, the advancing Turks had laid siege to Vienna. The Muslims ruled much of East Europe for over four centuries.

For nearly a thousand years, Muslim power dominated much of global politics. The efforts of Christian Europe to recover Jerusalem, which led to a series of Crusades beginning in the eleventh century, were unsuccessful. The more serious challenge posed by the Mongols in the thirteenth century did destroy the central Muslim power in Baghdad and caused a severe setback to the Islamic world but soon the conquering Mongols themselves got converted to Islam and thus Muslim power remained intact. Tamerlane, a descendant of the great Genghis Khan, established a large Muslim Empire based in Samarkand.

While it lasted, the 'Pax Islamica' from the seventh to the seventeenth century was by and large a benign and progressive rule, marked by general prosperity. The contrary allegations which have been levelled so persistently by Western and other non-Muslim circles do not bear the test of objective scrutiny. They allege that Islam was spread at the point of the sword. If it were so, then how was it that at the end of centuries of Muslim rule over India, nearly three-fourth of the population remained non-Muslims; or, how, after over 700 years of Muslim supremacy, there could be enough Christians left in Spain to defeat the ruling Muslims? On the other hand, when the Christians seized power in Spain in 1492, they used the sword decisively to expel, kill, and forcibly convert the Spanish Muslims within a short span of time through their infamous Inquisition. Similarly, little remains of the Muslims who had ruled Crimea (now in Russia) for over a thousand years. This shows the degree of contrasting intolerance shown respectively by the Muslims and Christians in the same country.

No Muslim armies ever reached Indonesia or Malaysia, which accepted Islam on their own some centuries ago. The fearsome Mongol rulers of Central Asia and beyond were converted to Islam by preaching and not by the sword. Islam spread in India because of the missionary work of great Islamic saints such as Nizamuddin Aulia, Khwaja Moinuddin, Qutbuddin Bakhtiyar Kaki, and Fariduddin Ganjshakar and others. In the contemporary times, Islam has been spreading in Africa, faster than any other religion, entirely through preaching.

It is also worth recalling that the Jews had found a haven in the Islamic world in the centuries in which Christian Europe was persecuting them. In Muslim Spain, Egypt, and Turkey, in particular, the Jews flourished and had never to face pogroms and the kind of racial abuse which was their lot in the Christian European countries. When the Jews were expelled from Spain, along with the Muslims after the Christian re-conquest, the Jews moved to Muslim Turkey and Morocco to find a safe haven. More recently, the Nazi holocaust, which killed hundreds of thousands of Jews, was the work of Christian Europeans. As against this, the Jews were never butchered in the Muslim countries.

This illustrates well the historic tolerance of other faiths by the Muslims, in keeping with the Quranic teaching that 'there is no compulsion in religion'. Thus, in the seventh century, while accepting the surrender of Jerusalem, Hazrat Umar (RA), the second Islamic caliph, assured the Christians that 'you have complete security for your churches which shall not be occupied by the Muslims or destroyed.'[1] Similarly, when Syria was conquered, the legendary Muslim general, Khalid bin Walid, signed a treaty assuring the citizens of Damascus that they would have 'security for their lives, property and churches. Their city shall not be demolished, neither shall any Muslim be quartered in their houses.'[2] However, there were instances of intolerance as well but, by and large, these were few and far between.

As for the Western charge that the Muslims were obscurantists or even 'barbarians', history shows that while Europe was sunk deep in the Dark Ages and the rest of the world (apart from China) was far away from civilization, the torch of learning—that of culture, science, and technology—was kept burning and carried to new heights by the Islamic world. The finest scientists, doctors, geographers, poets, historians, and artists were to be found in the Muslim world. Avicenna, Averroes, Ibn Batutta, Razi (Rhazes), Ghazali, Omar Khayyam, Sa'adi, Al-Khwarazmi, Al-Biruni, Al-Kindi, Rumi, and Ibn Khaldun are some of the better known among the scholars and scientists who made immense contributions to human learning. The 'Arabic numerals' are the basis of modern mathematics. Chemistry or alchemy started with the Muslims. Muslim medicine was widely copied in the West and the writings of Avicenna and others were used as textbooks in the teaching of Western medicine. These scholars were also the bridge between the learning of ancient Greece and old India with the modern world. It can even be said that without the Muslims, probably there would have been no renaissance in West Europe and few of the technological advances which later gave the West its ascendancy.

From the beginning, Islam's teaching of equality and unity attracted converts from all races, colours, and cultures. While the ruling families were often Arabs or Turks, it was accepted that, in theory, any Muslim was equal to another Muslim. Pan-Islamism was the central philosophy and the concept of a nation state was not in vogue. The belief was that all Muslims constituted one community and one nation (Ummah) in a kind of commonwealth where merit and piety were held out as the true mark of distinction and not one's colour or ancestry. There were, no doubt, frequent instances where Muslims were fighting Muslims, but this was always considered an aberration and not a rejection of the concept of the unity of the Ummah.

With the non-Muslim world, except during periods of war, there were normal diplomatic and commercial ties. The legendary Caliph Haroon-al-Rashid established cordial ties with Charlemagne in Europe. The Ottoman Turks had friendly links with France and other Europeans. The Mughals in India had a cordial relationship with the British, and Tipu Sultan of Mysore in southern India had good relations with Napoleon's France. There was no insistence that friendship was possible only with fellow Muslims or that there could only be an adversarial relationship with non-Muslim states. Indeed, Sultan Salahuddin Ayubi treated his Christian enemies—the Crusaders—with exceptional cordiality, which inspired the traditions of gallantry and chivalry among the Christian knights of Europe of the Middle Ages.

However, from the sixteenth century onwards, Europe started to gain ground at the expense of the Muslim world primarily because, after the Renaissance, Europe placed much greater emphasis on education and technology. In the same period, the Muslim world was becoming regressive as decadence and luxury sapped and destroyed the vibrant qualities of early Islam, while religious dogmatism crippled all scientific learning. The Muslims began to lag behind the West in technology, learning, and methods of modern warfare, leading to disastrous consequences. The Muslim countries started losing their independence one by one and, in some cases, they were entirely obliterated. In general, the Muslim world lapsed into a state of decay in moral, political, military, and social spheres.

Coinciding with the rise of the Christian West, the Muslim world went into a state of general decline. In particular, the period of nearly 200 years, lasting till the middle of the twentieth century, was the nadir of Islamic history. Muslims were all but wiped out from Europe—from Spain to start with and, thereafter, from Yugoslavia, Romania, Bulgaria, and Greece as well as from what is now south-western Russia, particularly Crimea. Vast Muslim areas in Central Asia also went under Russian and Chinese control. Muslim rule over India, lasting nearly a thousand years, also ended in the nineteenth century, as British colonialism took control.

In this gloomy scenario, reformers and revivers came to the rescue in many parts of the Islamic world. Imam Abdul Wahab strove for religious purity in Arabia, Sir Syed Ahmed Khan sought uplift in Muslim India through modern education; and the poet-philosopher Iqbal through a synthesis of revolutionary message of early Islam with the scientific knowledge of the twentieth century. Jamaluddin Afghani preached Pan-Islamism. Ataturk led the fight for Turkish recovery through an appeal to Islam-based patriotism and, later, sought to impose modernism and Europeanization as the recipe for progress. King Abdul Aziz unified Arabia and set it on course to become a key Islamic country. Quaid-i-Azam Mohammad Ali Jinnah led the fight for the establishment of a new independent Muslim state—Pakistan—after a sustained struggle against British colonialism in the South Asian subcontinent.

The exit of the British from South Asia heralded the end of colonialism in most parts of the world. Nasser, who came to power after the Egyptian Revolution of 1953, stirred the Arab world with a fervent call for Arab nationalism. Khomeini took Iran by storm with his Islamic Revolution in 1979.

The Muslim world became a beneficiary, among other peoples, of the global trend in the twentieth century towards the acceptance of the right of national self-determination of peoples and the spread of democratic ideas. This helped in securing the liberation of many Islamic countries. The second half of the twentieth century has thus seen the emergence of over fifty independent Muslim states. Finally, the end of the Soviet Union in 1991 made it possible for Muslims in Central Asia to recover their independence after more than a century of Russian occupation. Six Muslim states rose from the ashes of the Soviet Union. At present, there are nearly fifty-five independent Muslim states in the world. Large pockets of Muslims in Russia, China, India and elsewhere, however, remain under non-Muslim domination. The rapid spread of Islam in Africa also holds the prospect of the emergence of some more Muslim states in the future.

In the political arena, the Islamic world has re-emerged as a notable political entity. Over one-fourth of the UN members are from the Islamic world. The Muslim countries possess vast natural resources, particularly oil, as well as strategic minerals and many of them are exceedingly wealthy. There are over one billion Muslims in the world inhabiting in a largely contiguous land mass stretching from the Atlantic to the Pacific. The Islamic world has great geostrategic importance. Militarily, the Islamic countries are getting stronger. Among them, Pakistan also possesses nuclear capability and medium-range missiles, and has good expertise in defence production. Turkey, Iran, Iraq, Syria, Egypt, and Indonesia are important military powers. In industry and technology also, significant progress has been made. There is a general rise in literacy and education though, in comparison with others, the Muslims still lag behind.

Despite the re-emergence of the Islamic bloc on the world stage as a key player, the Muslim countries have been embroiled in serious problems which have sapped their energies. Firstly, the problem of Palestine has, for more than half a century, retarded the growth of the Arab and Islamic world. There can be little doubt that, without the West's support, Israel could neither have been created nor survived. Israel has been more than a thorn in the body politic of the Arabs. It has emerged as the key military power in the Middle East. It has expanded its territory through military aggression. It has shown itself to be more or less invincible against the Arabs who have had to divert their resources to military spending and have suffered heavy losses in life and property during the confrontation with Israel. The reverses suffered by the Arabs have, moreover, caused political upheavals, revolutions, *coups d'état*, and public disturbances in the various Arab countries over the past fifty years. Political radicalization and bilateral political feuds between the Arab countries have also weakened the Arab world.

Israel's occupation of the holy places in Palestine, particularly its capture of Al-Aqsa Mosque in 1967, had deeply hurt the sensitivities not only of the Arabs but also of Muslims all over the world. Pakistan played an important part in the adoption of resolutions at the UN demanding Israeli withdrawal from Jerusalem and from all occupied Arab territories.

Thirty years after Israel's creation, the Arab countries, starting with Egypt, have been forced to concede Israel's right to exist. In 1991, the Palestinians also decided to make peace with Israel, on more or less the latter's terms. Even then, the Israelis, particularly during the term of Netanyahu as the prime minister, have been creating hurdles in the way of implementation of the Oslo Accords. The non-Arab Muslim countries are likely to follow the lead of the Arab countries in accepting the status quo and the inescapable reality of Israel's existence. The argument would have to prevail that if the Palestinians are willing to acquiesce in Israel's existence, then the rest of the Islamic world will have to follow suit.

There can be no doubt that the West, and in particular the US, has played a key role in Israel's creation and its continued existence. It is true that the yearnings of the Jews to return to Jerusalem were always there. But it was the British control over Palestine, following Turkey's defeat in the First World War which facilitated large-scale Jewish emigration to this area. Hitler's atrocities against the Jews during the Second World War created a sympathetic climate in the Western countries towards the Jewish aspirations in Palestine. What was, however, clearly ignored by the West was that it made little moral sense to secure happiness for one set of people at the expense of the happiness of another people. There could be no legal or moral basis for dispossessing the Palestinians of their homeland. The evident reason for the West's partiality has been that most Israelis have come from the West itself and belong to the common 'Judaeo–Christian civilization.' Thus, the 'we feeling' in the West has always favoured the Jews over the Arabs.

The hold of the Zionists in the USA, in both the financial and political circles, has ensured strong American support to Israel. There are more Jews living in New York than in the state of Israel. It is said that no American politician can win an important election in the teeth of opposition from the Zionists. This largely explains the open-ended and, at times, almost blind support extended to Israel by successive US administrations. This has consisted of the supply of the latest US weapons as well as massive financial and diplomatic support to Israel, without which Israel would not probably have been able to exist.

The reason given by Egypt for coming to terms with Israel in 1978 was that while Egypt could fight Israel, it could not fight the US and Israel together. The West has found Israel a useful handle to keep the Arabs in check. It needs the oil of the Gulf and the sea routes through the Suez and the Persian Gulf. Israel has, of course, been more than willing to act as the West's sentinel and watchdog in the region. Until the collapse of the Soviet Union in 1991, the US also regarded Israel as an important strategic ally. The combinations of these diverse factors have enabled Israel to get Americans' support in repeated aggressions against its Arab neighbours. There have been few limits to America's bounty and military support for Israel.

Israeli ambitions have in general destabilized the Middle East. The past fifty years have seen big and small wars in the region, resulting primarily from Israel's hegemonic ambitions. The Arab failure to dislodge Israel has led to political upheavals in the Arab world and divisions between the radicals and the conservatives. Frustration has given rise to random terrorism and earned a bad name for the Arabs, and the Muslims in general. In short, Israel's presence has been a cause of wars and grave tensions in the Middle East in which the Arabs have, by and large, come out on the losing side.

This has generally worked to the advantage of the West, particularly the US, which has been both the contributor to the Arabs' torment as well as their protector from Israel's degradations. The West has powerful commercial interests in the Gulf region. The Israeli menace obliges the oil-rich Arab countries, in particular, to remain dependent on the US to keep Israel in check. Thus, the Arab countries are caught in a vicious cycle.

The Western military presence is most apparent in the Persian Gulf. According to the Carter Doctrine, the US will, if necessary, intervene militarily to keep the oil lanes of the Gulf open. In the Gulf War of 1991, the West did actually use military power decisively to overwhelm Iraq. The US has since also shown that it is prepared to attack Iraq once again if it attempts to assert itself in any way. The Gulf War, fought under UN auspices, had acquired a multi-national character but the real muscle was clearly provided by the Americans who used the latest military technology against Iraq. The latter proved no match in this contest. The oil-rich Gulf countries were made to pay the exorbitant bill for the war effort. The US not only protected its vital oil interests in the Gulf but also made handsome profits by a military venture against a hapless foe.

Iraq under Saddam Hussein has been, for its part, a disruptive force in the region for nearly three decades. History will probably hold Saddam Hussein personally responsible for the two destructive wars in which the Islamic world has suffered major physical and financial losses. The Iran–Iraq War of 1980–8 was a fratricide in which hundreds of thousands of young Muslim Arabs and Iranians lost their lives. Financial losses were staggering and possibly US\$ 1,000 billion went down the drain. This large sum of money, if wisely used, could have transformed the Islamic world. It needs to be recalled that for all its diverse projects for mutually beneficial cooperation between the Islamic countries, the OIC has not been able to raise even one billion dollars. The oil-rich Muslim countries have simply not been forthcoming enough, pleading their financial constraints. Yet, to fight this utterly wasteful war, these Gulf countries could, and did, find a thousand times more money. For the Muslim masses all over the world and the propagators of Islamic solidarity, this was the saddest part of the story, reflecting the wrong priorities of the Islamic world.

Not satisfied with the havoc caused by the eight-year long Iran–Iraq War, Saddam Hussein next embarked on the conquest and military occupation of a fellow Arab country, Kuwait. This led to the Gulf War of 1991 which not only devastated Iraq but also once again bled the oil-rich Arab countries white. Saddam Hussein's action was morally indefensible. He had attacked, without notice or provocation, a country, which was the benefactor of Iraq and a fellow Arab and Muslim state. His aggression created a deep chasm in the Islamic world. Many Islamic countries supported the US-led alliance which next attacked Iraq. Many Muslims felt that they had to sympathize with Saddam since he appeared to be defying the traditionally anti-Muslim forces.

In terms of the loss of lives and property, it can be argued that probably no one, ever since the havoc caused in the thirteenth century by the Mongols under Genghis Khan and Hulagu Khan, has done as much harm to the Muslim world as has been done by Saddam Hussein. As a result of these wars, which should have never been fought, two of the most powerful Muslim countries, namely, Iraq and Iran, stood greatly weakened; and the enormous wealth of their Muslim neighbours had been largely drained out. The net beneficiary in this exercise would appear to have been the West, particularly the US, which literally made billions out of arms sale. Moreover, the US has since clearly emerged as the protector of the Gulf and acquired greater influence than ever before among the oil-rich but vulnerable Muslim countries of this region.

The two other main military powers in the Arab world, Egypt and Syria, had been earlier checkmated and weakened by the long confrontation with Israel. At the end of thirty years of this conflict, Egypt decided to call it quits. Syria remains in the arena but, with the end of support from the former Soviet bloc, it is hardly in a position to take on Israel. With the exit of Egypt from the Arab camp, the military option is simply no longer available to the Arabs.

Another key Muslim country, Pakistan, has been weakened by its unending disputes with India, particularly on Kashmir. India has stubbornly flouted the UN resolutions on Kashmir calling for an impartial plebiscite to enable the Muslim-majority population to join either India or Pakistan. Several times larger than Pakistan in size and resources, and also enjoying strong backing, for the greater part, of a superpower, the former Soviet Union, in its confrontation with Pakistan, India has had the upper hand in the fifty-year-old conflict. Moreover, the confrontation with India has destabilized Pakistan internally. Its economy has been under severe strain. The country seems to have stumbled from crisis to crisis. Its eastern half was lost in 1971. Thus, a key Muslim country with great potential which, moreover, has probably been the greatest proponent of Islamic unity, has been kept at bay and has never been able to rise to its true potential.

Malaysia seems to be the latest among the leading Islamic countries to run into serious internal difficulties, which have impeded its spectacular economic growth and good international standing. In recent years, Malaysia had become a kind of a success story in the Muslim world and indeed in the Third World. All of a sudden, the country's currency came under speculative pressures for which its prime minister put the blame on some Western businessmen. Its economic growth has been adversely affected. This has been followed by a serious political crisis. Malaysia's future, thus, seems to be under a cloud.

Algeria, the largest Muslim power in North Africa, has been embroiled for several years in a savage internal crisis, arising out of the efforts of the Western-backed military regime to curb the popularity of Islamic fundamentalists. The West is never tired of preaching human rights but the gross violation of human rights in Algeria, which is Europe's next-door neighbour, has hardly drawn a word of protest from the West. France, otherwise a great champion of human rights, has even applauded the policies of the Algerian regime to suppress the popular Islamic movement. If an Islamic fundamentalist regime in Algeria had been crushing popular secular forces, the hue and cry raised by the West would have been loud and clear.

In Africa, two of the bigger Muslim countries, Nigeria and Sudan have also had their share of troubles. Nigeria's economy has been sliding downhill after a period of prosperity during the oil boom, which ended around 1984. Its internal political situation has since led to international pressures, especially from the West. Its prestige is at a low point and its influence in its region has been cut down. Sudan too has been under a lot of pressures from the West for its handling of the Christian south where a civil war has been raging for several years. Sudan has been ruled by the Islamic fundamentalists for several years which, by itself, is a sufficient reason for the West to put Sudan in the dog house. The US has been accusing Sudan of harbouring terrorists and this led to a US missiles attack on targets in Khartoum in 1998 where allegedly chemical weapons were being produced. This was apparently not so, but the US has not expressed any regrets for its action and the international community has been subdued in its reaction. The US has clearly arrogated for itself the role of the international police officer. However, it seems that Muslim areas are being singled out for punitive action even though they do not have a monopoly of mischief.

Can it be a pure coincidence that some of the key Muslim countries have thus been weakened militarily, politically, and financially and that, in the process, the net gainers seem to have been the West, Israel, and India? There are some observers who see a pattern of collusion between non-Islamic countries to keep the Islamic world in check, just when it looked that the latter was re-emerging as a significant force on the world scene. No doubt, many Muslim countries appear to have been guilty of a lack of foresight and sound judgement, thus contributing to their own deep discomfiture. The divisions of the Muslim countries on ideological and ethnic bases, as well as due to petty rivalries, have clearly weakened the Islamic world. However, there seems to be more to it than meets the eye. The machinations of unfriendly forces have probably been a key factor in this pattern of disunity in the Islamic world.

In the case of the Iran–Iraq War, the words of Henry Kissinger, the former US secretary of state, are perhaps illustrative of this reality. He had said that 'this is a war which neither side should win.' Thus, the West, as also the Soviet bloc, kept stoking the fire by supplying arms to both sides, at high prices, until they were both drained out. In the Gulf War that followed next, the West, of course, played the decisive role. There is a version that Saddam Hussein had gained the impression from the American ambassador in Baghdad that the US would keep aloof in the event that Iraq went to war with Kuwait. He had thus walked, as it were, into an American trap. But once he got drawn into his military adventure, the US engineered the alliance against Iraq.

Subsequent to Iraq's defeat, every effort has been made by the West to frustrate Iraqi efforts to regain military capability. Iraq has been accused of harbouring intentions to develop weapons of mass destruction. Nearly nine years after the war ended, Iraq remains subject to sanctions, as a result of which the Iraqi people have been the main sufferers. The odd thing is that Saddam Hussein, despite all his setbacks, remains in power. While he is in the saddle, smaller Arab neighbours in the Gulf must continue to look to the US for protection. All of this works admirably to the advantage of the US. It has even been said that if there were no Saddam, one would have to be created.

The Western stance on Islamic 'fundamentalism' is quite revealing. While the Soviet bloc lasted, and was perceived as the main threat to the West, little or nothing was heard about Islamic fundamentalism. The reason clearly was that Islam was considered as a useful ally in the fight against and the containment of communism, which the Muslims have generally opposed as an atheistic force. In the case of Afghanistan, the Soviets were pushed out—for the first time in history from a country which had been occupied by them—by Afghan guerrillas fighting under the Islamic banner, fully supported by the West. The setback in Afghanistan hastened the collapse of the Soviet Union. This was a most far-reaching development that brought to an end the global confrontation of the previous fifty years. Islam had thus played a key role in changing the global political equation in favour of the West.

As a moral obligation, the West should have been deeply grateful to and appreciative of this strategic contribution of the Afghan Muslim fundamentalists, backed mainly by Pakistan, in removing the global threat posed by Soviet-led communism. Instead, the moment the Soviet threat ended, it seems that the bogey of Islamic fundamentalism has been raised as the main threat to the West. Afghanistan has since been in turmoil, in a foreign-aided civil war. It has been branded as a country fostering terrorism and was recently the target of a US missiles attack.

The seeming logic behind this Western attitude perhaps is that the same determined resistance which had forced the Soviets out of Afghanistan could turn its hostility towards the West as well. The underlying hard reality is that Islam has been seen as a rival and threat by the West and other non-Islamic forces, notably Hindu India, for nearly 1,300 years. In the post-Soviet world, the US has emerged as the only remaining superpower, while the West dominates the world in most fields. Apart perhaps from China and possibly

Japan, which might at some stage become serious rivals, apparently the only challenge to the West's preponderant presence is posed by the Islamic way of life and the potential of the unity of the Islamic world in the political, military, and economic spheres. Pakistan's acquisition of nuclear technology adds to the West's concerns. The reported efforts of Iran, Iraq, and Libya to acquire missiles and weapons of mass destruction are viewed with great alarm by the West. Incidentally, the West has remained silent about Israel's nuclear capability, as it was about the nuclear explosion by India conducted earlier in 1974. But when any Muslim country takes a step in this direction, the West seems to regard it as an alarming development.

Leaving aside the issue of Muslim fundamentalism, it is interesting to note that the efforts of some Muslim countries to ape the West or to survive on its sweet will, have hardly fared better. Turkey's example is an obvious pointer. It has tried its best for over seventy years to adopt European ways, only to find that Europe would still not allow it to enter the European Economic Community. Turkey's Islamic background is probably enough reason for the refusal. On the Cyprus issue, of course, Turkey has received no support from Europe.

Taking the foregoing factors into account, the Islamic world would do well to make a realistic appraisal of the global situation and take such steps as might be necessary for its self-preservation. The Muslims are the inheritors of a great civilization and a glorious history and have every right to a place of respect in the contemporary world. Their numbers and resources justify such an expectation. However, in order to survive and prosper in the days ahead, it is essential for the Muslim countries, in the first place, to forge unity in their ranks and establish effective mutually beneficial cooperation. The acquisition of the latest technology and education will also need to be given high priority.

At the same time, there need not be a 'clash of civilizations' or any sort of political or military confrontation with anyone. In the twenty-first century, wars and tensions should no longer be considered as a viable option. The world is big enough to accommodate all kinds of people with diverse philosophies. With all the progress made by humanity, it should be possible to establish good lines of communications so that all countries of the world, with their differing religions and cultures, could live together in reasonable harmony and peace. However, this will require a conscious effort by everyone to eschew all kinds of extremism, vicious propaganda, and outright misrepresentation of each other's point of view.

On the part of the Muslim countries, it would be necessary to curb the negativism of religious zealots in Muslim societies who oppose moderation and compromises and thrive, for example, on a 'hate America' mentality. This has, in some instances, given rise to terrorism against American targets leading, in turn, to hostile responses from the US, including unilateral punitive military missions, unauthorized by the UN. Two wrongs, of course, do not make one right. Terrorism must be rejected as a political option. It is brutal and insane and can hardly ever secure the objectives for which it is launched.

At the same time, it would be unfair to single out Muslims alone for condemnation for acts of terrorism. Israeli state terrorism, such as punitive raids against targets in Lebanon, Palestine, and elsewhere, has taken a far heavier toll of innocent lives, over the years, but this has hardly ever drawn any condemnation by the US or the West. Israeli secret agencies have been involved in assassinations of Palestinians and others, even in third countries but, on each occasion, it seems that Israel gets away with its crime, with little disapproval by the West. But individual acts of terrorism by Palestinians or Muslims anywhere receive all kinds of publicity and are severely condemned. This is clearly indicative of the West's double standards that, in fact, breeds extremist feelings in Muslim societies.

Terrorism of various kinds is taking place all over the world. The Kansas bombing of the recent past was the handiwork of a white American extremist. The earlier massacre of a cult in Texas was also not the work of Muslims. The Irish Republican Army has long been involved in terrorism in UK and the Basques separatists in Spain. Sri Lankan separatists have carried out any number of acts of terrorism. Japan has not been immune from terrorism. And yet, in the Western news media, somehow the Muslims alone seem to get singled out for involvement with terrorism.

It also needs to be appreciated that to stamp out terrorism, a conscious effort has to be made to remove the causes of frustration which breed terrorism. There has to be a sense of justice and fair play and a willingness to understand each other's point of view. Furthermore, effective measures need to be taken in the West to end the distortions and misrepresentations of Islamic societies in its news media.

The Muslim world has to be more conscious that there is a growing 'image' problem for the Muslims. The Muslims need to do some introspection and make an objective evaluation of the realities. Militancy in words can be as alarming as extremist actions. The self-righteousness of Islamic societies and the frequent paranoia about the non-Islamic world has to be contained, if not eliminated. Moderate policies need to be adopted, in words as well as in deeds. In fact, moderation has always been a distinctive part of Islam's teachings, which lays down that the Muslims are the people of the 'middle way.' While protecting the rights of the Muslim world, therefore, the effort should be to act rationally and in moderation. There should be a genuine effort to promote greater understanding of the Muslim world's point of view. In particular, the distortions about the 'image' of Islam need to be corrected by taking positive steps to secure a favourable impression about Islamic societies and the Islamic way of life.

In a growingly materialistic world, where traditional values seem to be breaking down, Islam has a role to play. Its message remains vibrant but its presentation needs improvement.

NOTES

1. Ismail I. Nawwab, Peter C. Speers, Paul F. Hoye (eds.), *Aramco and its World: Arabia and the Middle East* (Aramco, 1981), p. 53.
2. Ibid.

16

The Fall of the Soviet Union: Implications for Pakistan

The most important political development of the past fifty years, has been the fall of the mighty Soviet Union in 1991. A superpower simply melted away while the rest of world looked on in disbelief. At the same time, the Soviet bloc also disappeared, putting an end to the fearsome confrontation with the US-led Western alliance which had dominated global politics for nearly half a century. The Soviet Union itself broke up into several new states.

The post-Soviet world is a very different scene. Most importantly, the human race does not live any longer under the horrendous threat of a global nuclear holocaust. Whatever crises remain in the world are local or regional in nature. The world is now unipolar with the United States emerging as the only superpower. That poses problems of its own, which warrant separate consideration. However, this analysis is confined to taking a look-back at the reasons for the fall of the Soviet Union, as to how and where it went wrong; and the conclusions and implications therefrom which could be drawn by the rest of the world, including a country like Pakistan. An objective analysis is, perhaps, still not easy as there has been so much propaganda for and against the Soviet state ever since its founding in 1917 and the ideological controversy continues. Nevertheless, an attempt to make a dispassionate evaluation seems worthwhile.

The Marxist philosophy, which inspired Lenin and the October Revolution, was an odd mixture of idealism and historical half-truths. It was based on a highly dogmatic and selective interpretation of human history and the behaviour of humans. Its evaluation of the historic role and the relative importance of the working class was unbalanced, if not lopsided. Its claim about the 'dictatorship of the proletariat' seemed absurd when judged against the actual situation in the Soviet Union and other communist states where the Communist Party—or more accurately the top leadership of the party—held all the strings of power and the proletariat was no more than pawns in their hands. Similarly, its prognosis about the future of humanity was largely unrealistic, notably its belief that, after the establishment of the socialist society, the state would simply 'wither away'. As it turned out, more than seventy years after the Soviet Union was established, the state was showing no sign of withering away and had, on the contrary, become even more powerful and all pervasive than ever before. Ironically, though, by a quirk of fortune, it turned out to be the Soviet state which suddenly went out of existence. But the state as an institution survived even here, with the re-emergence of the Russian state.

There were other communist promises and predictions, which remained unfulfilled or turned out to be false. The workers and peasants were supposed to rule the socialist state but the Soviet peasant was all but liquidated in bloody purges conducted by Stalin in the 1930s. During the collectivization campaign, 6.5 million people lost their lives, one-third of them in Central Asia.[1] The lot of the Soviet worker was paradoxical. While all praise was showered on him as a kind of a ritual, he was virtually denied even his fundamental right to go on strike. In fact, power was never in the hands of the workers. From the beginning, it was the Communist Party that was in control. The party itself was, for the greater part, dancing to the tune of the top boss, particularly under Stalin.

The Soviet propaganda made all kinds of claims about fundamental human rights, people's democracy and freedom, but much of this was denied to the people living in the Soviet bloc. The periodic elections held in this 'democracy' were a ritual farce in which 99 per cent amongst the voters duly voted in favour of whatever those in power wanted them to do. The press printed only the official line and read like a drab recital of government and party engagements. Nothing critical or different could be published. The whole country was supposed to have the same opinion on a given issue and, indeed, the thinking was done for the citizens by the party and the government itself! At the whim of the party leader, an erstwhile hero could overnight become a traitor and an enemy of the people. History was rewritten from time to time to accommodate the twists in the thinking of the current party leader. This was the truth about Soviet-style freedom and democracy. Anyone showing dissent was considered a counter-revolutionary or traitor and a threat to the state and society. The ever-present secret police was watching everyone. Any kind of dissent could result in arrest, interrogation, torture, jail, and execution or exile to Siberia or elsewhere, depending upon the gravity of the offence in the eyes of the authorities. Millions of people were killed in bloody purges and millions were forced to leave their homes and live in exile.

The Leninist–Marxist theory apart, in reality, the Soviet state became all-powerful and the average citizen was no more than a pawn in the hands of the authorities. Everything was done in the name of the people, but the people had very little say in the running of their own affairs. As a result of years of brutal repression and propaganda, the average Soviet citizen was turned into a docile and unquestioning camp follower, if not a robot. In every way, there seemed to be a great discrepancy between theory and practice. Democracy meant dictatorship; freedom meant enslavement; and people's rule meant the party's rule. Religious freedom was proclaimed but everything was done to curb religion.

Self-determination was the official policy but this was never practised at home. The constituent fifteen republics of the USSR were supposed to have the right to secede and each had its own president and foreign minister, giving the appearance of being autonomous or sovereign. On the contrary, the republics slavishly followed Moscow's wishes in every respect. It was often arranged that an ethnic Russian was holding the number two position in the republic and most key posts in the hierarchy were held by Russians. Of course, the KGB was always watching and it was ensured that the 'independent' Republic toed Moscow's every wish and command. Russification was enforced in the Muslim Central Asian republics and even names were changed. The Arabic script was abolished and the Cyrillic script was adopted. This cut off the new generations of Muslims from their cultural and religious roots. Suppression of Islam was rigorously followed. There were about 26,000 mosques in Central Asia in 1917 but only about 400 were functioning by 1985. The Quran was not available anywhere and even if a Muslim was able to get a copy somehow, it was more than likely that he could not read the Arabic script, since teaching of religion was banned.

The Communist Party ran the show most of the time but, under Stalin, one-man rule of the most despotic nature almost entirely eclipsed the party itself. Stalin unleashed the worst kind of terror. Indeed, succeeding Soviet rulers themselves had to admit that millions were liquidated by him and even more sent into exile: Ironically, all of this was done in the name of the people, democracy, and freedom. Though the worst oppression ended with the death of Stalin in 1953, the coercive apparatus for enforcing thought control, the secret police, surveillance, torture, and intimidation continued under the later rulers as well. 'Big brother' was always watching. Indeed, the Soviet Union resembled a vast prison where it seemed everyone was under watch, with no escape routes. A citizen needed permission to travel from one city to another. Telephones were tapped and letters were censored.

Photocopying was punishable. Yet the Soviet propaganda claimed that the people had every freedom.

Another Soviet claim was that there was complete freedom of religion but, in reality, the situation was the opposite. The State machinery was fully mobilized to suppress religion. Atheism was taught as a compulsory subject in educational institutions, even to foreign students. There was relentless propaganda against religion. The preaching of religion or any kind of missionary activity was banned. Old churches and mosques were mostly shut down and converted into museums or restaurants and even bars. Bukhara had more than 300 mosques before the communist takeover in 1920 but only three were left in the mid-1980s where only a handful of old men could be seen attending prayers. Young people were conspicuous by their absence, the theory being that they were enlightened and no longer believed in old superstitions. The authorities evidently did not mind some old people attending mosques or churches, as this gave some credibility to the claim that there was freedom of religion. The young, of course, could face varying degrees of persecution for going to mosques. At the minimum, their educational career and job prospects could be jeopardized if their religious inclinations came to notice. But it could get far nastier than that, as many found out to their regret.

A group of Moscow-based ambassadors, who visited Kazan, an ancient Islamic city east of Moscow, in the Tatar Autonomous Republic, in 1987 found only one functioning mosque there. During a meeting with the president of the republic, his attention was drawn to the promise of Lenin in 1918 to the Muslims of Kazan and all Russia that they would have full religious freedom and that the Czarist policy of demolition of their mosques etc. would be abandoned. The president was asked as to why there was only one mosque left in Kazan. Visibly embarrassed, the president asked his deputy to shed some light. The latter replied blandly that there could be any number of mosques if the people wanted them. The local rule was that a mosque could be opened if ten citizens were to make an application to the authorities. Evidently, however, in a city of one million, not even ten such Muslims could be found! The Tatar Republic had a Muslim majority. The president bore the classical Muslim name Umar—Russified as Umarov—but he made it clear that he was only a 'cultural' Muslim. This meant that he was not a believer although, culturally, he had a Muslim background.

Incidentally, with the fall of the Soviet Union, hundreds of mosques have been reopened in such Muslim areas and new ones have been built, proving that communist suppression could not destroy Islam despite the outward appearances in the Soviet era. The same, of course, has been the case with the Christian and Jewish places of worship. In fact, most people during the communist period had remained believers, though publicly they would say otherwise. It was revealing that even Communist Party bosses in the Central Asian republics and other Muslim areas, who were professed atheists, were known to have been given a religious burial in the Islamic tradition. After their death, evidently, they no longer needed to prove their pretensions of atheism. When asked as to how such a contradiction could exist, the reply would be that the Islamic burial was being given to please the old relatives who believed in those sort of things; otherwise, the dead leader was an enlightened person!

Similarly, most Muslim couples secured an Islamic *Nikah* (marriage vows) after their civil marriage, thus taking no chances about the legitimacy of their wedding and their progeny. On some visits to Central Asia in the mid-1980s, while serving as Pakistan's ambassador in Moscow, I found that local officials would toe the official line in formal meetings, but when they would get a chance to be alone with me, some recited the *Kalima* (Islamic affirmation of the oneness of God) to show their Islamic adherence. A local official named Abdulkarimov, when alone with me clarified angrily that his actual name was Abdul Karim, a typical Arabic–Islamic name. Under the Soviet system, all names including those of Muslims had to have a Russian-style ending. Indeed, some local officials in Soviet Central Asia privately expressed their support and admiration for the Afghan Mujahideen fighting Soviet troops in Afghanistan in those days and reviled in the Soviet media as bandits and cutthroats.

The Soviet system did have a number of positive features. There was a basic commitment to egalitarianism and social justice. Public good was given priority over individual benefits. Also, there was little evidence among the dominant Russians of any racial superiority of the kind shown by Europeans and Americans towards other races. Though the real power apparatus was undoubtedly in the hands of the Russians in the Central Asian republics, menial jobs, like sweeping the streets were being done by Russian women. Joseph Stalin and Nikita Khrushchev, the two most powerful Soviet dictators, were not ethnic Russians.

Illiteracy was largely eradicated in the Soviet Union and the number of scientists and PhDs produced by the country was quite remarkable. Women were, in general, given equality and were fully involved in the work force. (However, top political assignments were rarely given to women.) There was promotion of culture, including regional cultures: some famous old Islamic monuments in Samarkand were beautifully renovated. There was a great deal of emphasis on learning foreign languages. Law and order was generally good; the crime rate was low and life was disciplined and orderly. Prices were stable and the basic necessities were inexpensive. Education and health facilities were free. There was very little unemployment (though this was done by the expedient of creating new jobs even where there was no need). Most notably, of course, the country managed to come a long way since 1917 in technological progress. Indeed the Soviet Union had succeeded in becoming a superpower and being the first to reach the space.

In spite of these Soviet successes, the fact was that progress had been achieved at the cost of immense human suffering. 'Between 1920 and 1945 it is estimated that more than a quarter of the population of Central Asia died a violent death.'[2] While there have been monstrous cruelties in world history by individual conquerors, the world has hardly ever seen a system which was so brutal and coercive. There was no individual freedom and life was regimented. Despite the tall claims about the 'Soviet man', in reality, the ordinary citizen was treated as a faceless robot rather than as a human being. Conformity was enforced. Propaganda was continuous: usually false, dull, and contrived. The Soviet Union was portrayed as a paradise on earth whereas the rest of the world was supposed to be groaning under the worst oppression.

Life in the Soviet Union was monotonous and predictable, with hardly any variety or excitement. Consumer goods were in short supply and were shoddy in quality. There was little prospect of out-of-turn promotion, except for those with links to the Communist Party. The talented had little incentive to work since their salaries were no better than those of their mediocre co-workers. Since a job was more or less ensured for everyone—in keeping with the claim that there was full employment—the inefficient and the incompetent had little to worry about. This disheartened even the competent and the talented workers. In a kind of perverse logic, the salaries of doctors, professors, and engineers were abysmally low. Doctors were paid less than chauffeurs.

There was no doubt some degree of idealism present in the early years after the 1917 Revolution. But the revolutionary fervour of Vladimir Lenin's days was soon to vanish, as Stalin went on his bloody rampages for the next thirty years, when the brightest and the most idealistic among the communists were liquidated, leaving behind only the most servile and loyal. In later years, idealism seemed to be altogether missing in the party which, with the passing of time, became almost a bureaucratic set-up. The apparatchiks in the Communist Party were a motley crowd of opportunists and career seekers who, while mouthing the usual shibboleths and clichés, were involved more in petty intrigues for power. It was this set-up which allowed a mediocre figure like Konstantin Chernenko to rise to the top position of general secretary of the Soviet Communist Party in 1984. He was a party faithful incarnate, but little else. Leonid Brezhnev had not been much brighter either and was, moreover, known for his hedonistic ways and corruption.

In the field of foreign affairs, the Soviet Union strongly espoused the cause of anti-colonialism and anti-racism. However, this was mainly done to weaken the influence of the Western colonial powers, as also to secure popularity and influence in the Third World, as a part of the relentless effort, through propaganda, intrigue, or outright conquest, to spread communism all over the world. While never tired of espousing the cause of democracy, self-determination, and human rights abroad, the Soviet Union itself followed a policy of ruthless subjugation of a number of nations, firstly, in the Soviet Union itself and, beyond that, in East Europe and in Mongolia. The sporadic efforts made by the satellite nations to assert their independence were ruthlessly crushed, e.g. in East Germany (1953), Hungary (1956), Czechoslovakia (1968), and Poland (1980). In fact, wherever the Soviet forces had reached by the end of the Second World War, communism was imposed under a Soviet stranglehold. Once a country somehow came under Soviet sway, it stayed that way. The only exception turned out to be Afghanistan.

The Soviet system was an unnatural growth based on coercion and fraud. Its theory, the diagnosis of history, as well as its prescription were simply wrong. Its actual implementation under Stalin took it towards directions which were never even dreamt of by Karl Marx, and would probably have horrified Lenin. In retrospect, it seems astonishing as to how it could last seventy-four years. Eventually, the greatest failure of the Soviet Communist system, leading to its collapse, was probably the stagnation of its economy in the 1970s and its actual decline in the 1980s. The situation was aggravated and finally made impossible by the burden of the unending arms race with the far richer West. In the early phase of communist rule, there had no doubt been notable economic progress. But it had been achieved through centralized political stability, regimentation of the work force, slave labour, and the exploitation of the vast natural resources of the Soviet Union, and those of the Soviet Empire. By the 1960s, however, Soviet economic development had reached a plateau. Thereafter, it was a downward curve.

Lack of incentives, absence of competition, and centralized bureaucratic control in the Soviet system had led to this economic stagnation. There was great wastage in the 'command' economy in which projects were launched without proper feasibility. The economic deterioration was hastened by Brezhnev's foreign military adventures, notably the occupation of Afghanistan, the ever-growing burden of military expenditure, apart from the rampant corruption of his regime. Consequently, the Soviet Union in the 1980s had become a giant with the feet of clay. Its economic development was so lopsided that it could excel in producing space ships but could not make decent battery cells for torches, ordinary bulbs, or safety matches. The reason for this paradox was that where the authorities were determined to make progress, all the resources would be mobilized to produce excellent results but, where the state did not put high priority, the average product would be substandard. Thus, it was said that the Soviet Union was a superpower with an economy of the Third World.

It was against this background of economic stalemate, and indeed downward slide, that the reformist group of Yuri Andropov and Mikhail Gorbachev came to power around 1982, hoping to bring about a new dynamism in the economy. But the arms race against the West could not be halted. Increasingly, it emerged that while the West could sustain the mounting weight of defence expenditure, the Soviet economy kept sinking under the strain. Moreover, the policies of glasnost and perestroika ushered in by Gorbachev involved unleashing the freedom of thought. Thus, the genie was let loose and the repression of seventy years of communist rule produced the popular backlash under which the Soviet communist system and, ironically, Gorbachev himself were swept away into the dustbin of history.

The Soviet-style communist system turned out to be a great failure, even though its original authors were motivated by idealistic egalitarian considerations. Its denial of the economic laws and market forces could not be sustained over a period of time. It ran out of steam mainly because the military ambitions of its rulers imposed an unbearable burden on its resources. What successes were achieved by the Soviets were secured at the cost of immense human suffering imposed on the people living in the Soviet bloc. The 'brave new world' of the Soviet Union was a cruel system based on enforced conformity producing a regulated and dull existence. The oppression unleashed by Stalin had few parallels in world history.

In this context, the astonishing thing has been the attitude towards the situation in the Soviet Union adopted by the intellectual left and the socialists. Right from the beginning, the oppression of the Bolshevik regime was well documented and could not escape the notice of any careful observer. No doubt, there was also a great deal of propaganda against the Soviet Union by the capitalist world, which sought every opportunity to denigrate the communist rule. Nevertheless, it seems that many leftist intellectuals simply refused to look at the grim realities and kept portraying the Soviet Union in rosy colours. While shedding tears over the loss of democratic rights in dictatorial regimes around the world, the same intellectuals simply turned a blind eye to the monstrous cruelties of Stalin lasting over a period of three decades. But Stalin was not unique: the scale of oppression might have declined after him but the cruel state apparatus survived. The left, however, refused to see that practically all communist regimes relied on the use of brute force to survive and were guilty of massive violation of human rights.

The Soviet Union's ambitions to spread communism beyond its borders so as to bring the whole world under its sway created widespread apprehensions. Opposition to the spread of communism was thus morally sustainable, since the success of Soviet designs would have enslaved the whole world and taken human progress behind by some centuries. Even if the West had its own selfish motives in opposing Soviet communism, the larger interests of humanity were served by the counter-response from the Western world, led by the USA, to 'contain' the outward flow of communism through a chain of military alliances built on the periphery of the Soviet bloc. However, the eyeball-to-eyeball confrontation lasting over half-a-century created a highly dangerous environment in the world and distorted human development. Indeed, the Cold War was a traumatic experience for the whole world and smaller countries were, invariably, sucked into the vortex of the rivalries of the two power blocs.

While it lasted, the Soviet Union posed a serious security threat to Pakistan by supporting India in its hegemonic ambitions against Pakistan. Soviet military support for India was a decisive factor in the dismemberment of Pakistan in 1971. The Soviet Union also did significant harm to Pakistan by using its veto in the UN Security Council to block any resolution on Kashmir. Thus, the UN was more or less rendered a neutral player on the Kashmir issue.

The disquieting fact of the matter is that, like the Soviet Union, Pakistan too has been forced, all through the past fifty years of its existence, to bear a disproportionate defence burden in its confrontation with India. It is undeniable that Pakistan has a much smaller economy than that of its rival. In relative terms, therefore, the price of keeping up with India has put severe strains on the Pakistani economy. This, in turn, has taken a heavy toll of Pakistan's energies and its priorities have all along been distorted. Thus, for example, the social sector has received minimal funds and literacy has remained very low. This has prevented all-round development. It has really been a kind of a vicious circle. An alarming consequence of this confrontation with India has been that Pakistan has also been destabilized internally.

The development of nuclear capability has, no doubt, given Pakistan's defence a big boost. But, the example of the Soviet Union shows that nuclear capability itself is not enough. It does not necessarily guarantee a country's survival. After all, the Soviet Union did possess thousands of nuclear warheads, intercontinental ballistic missiles, and the latest weaponry, but it collapsed without a shot being fired, notwithstanding its nuclear might. The Soviet economy proved to be its Achilles heel and the ground simply gave in under its feet. It would be unwise to ignore this historical lesson since Pakistan's precarious economy can be its undoing as well. The truth is that living beyond means can be dangerous for nations, no less than it is for individuals.

NOTES

1. Robert Conquest, *Harvest of Sorrow: Soviet Collectivization and the Terror–Famine* (New York: Oxford University Press, 1986), cited in Ahmed Rashid, *The Resurgence of Central Asia: Islam or Nationalism?* (London: Zed/Karachi: Oxford University Press, 1994), p. 33.
2. Richard Pipes, *The Russian Revolution* (New York: Alfred A. Knopf, 1990), cited in Ahmed Rashid, ibid., p. 34.

17

Post 9/11 Developments in Pakistan's Foreign Policy

'War against Terror': US–Pakistan Relations

The deadly terrorist attacks in New York and Washington on 9/11 (11 September 2001) by Al-Qaeda, an Islamist extremist group, brought about a fundamental change in the global political scenario. American foreign and defence policy took a new shape. President George W. Bush, backed by the US Congress, launched a global 'war against terror' that was directed against Al-Qaeda specifically, but included Islamic extremism in general. An elusive and highly secretive group, Al-Qaeda, led by Osama bin Laden, an ex-Saudi national of Yemeni origin, had secured a sanctuary in Afghanistan where the fundamentalist Taliban regime had come to power in 1994. After the attacks of 9/11, the US demanded Osama bin Laden's extradition but this was turned down by the Taliban regime. A month later, the US and allied forces launched a military invasion of Afghanistan and removed the Taliban regime.

Until 9/11, Pakistan had maintained friendly relations with the Taliban regime and, left on its own, it would have stayed out of this war. However, President Bush put a blunt question to Pakistan: 'Are you with us or against us?' Pakistan's military leader General Pervez Musharraf came under intense US pressure to extend support to its military campaign against the Taliban regime. In making a choice, Musharraf had to keep in view three ground realities. Firstly, Pakistan was the only feasible route for the US forces to attack Afghanistan. Secondly, there was little that Pakistan could do to dissuade the US from invading Afghanistan. Thirdly, opposing the US could have resulted in dire consequences for Pakistan's own security and economic welfare. Realpolitik clearly demanded that Pakistan abandon its erstwhile support for the Taliban regime and join the US-led coalition in the war against terror.

The war against the Taliban must also be seen in the background of Pakistan's relations with Afghanistan. Pakistan has always had a history of troubled relations with Afghanistan with which it shares a long, mountainous, and largely unpoliced borders.

At the very outset, on Pakistan's independence in 1947, the Kabul regime raised an irredentist claim against Pakistan that would bedevil relations between the two neighbours in the years to come. In April 1978, the situation took a new turn when communists seized power in Afghanistan. An uprising against the communist regime started soon thereafter with some degree of support from Pakistan. To help the communist regime remain in power in Afghanistan, the Soviet Union made a military intervention there in December 1979. The Soviet military presence across the Khyber Pass was seen by Pakistan as a direct threat to its own security and it started to extend vital support to the resistance launched by the Afghan Mujahideen rebels. The US and the West, as well as China, were also opposed to the Soviet military presence in Afghanistan due to their global rivalry with the Soviet Union. Even such diverse countries as Iran, Egypt, Saudi Arabia, and Japan were against the Soviet military presence in Afghanistan. In a classic illustration of the maxim that politics makes strange bedfellows, an active alliance developed between Pakistan, the US and the Islamic fundamentalist Afghan Mujahideen who were carrying out an armed resistance or jihad against the Soviet military occupation. Osama bin Laden was one of the Arab jihadists who fought alongside the Mujahideen against the Soviet occupation.

After the Soviet withdrawal from Afghanistan was achieved in 1989, there was a war of succession amongst the various Mujahideen groups. The resultant bloodshed and anarchy helped bring to power a new group, the Taliban, who emerged on the scene in 1994 with the promise of peace and Islamic justice. By 1996, they had seized control over 90 per cent of the country. The Taliban were mainly Pukhtuns, the traditionally dominant ethnic group in Afghan society, who live in the south-eastern parts of Afghanistan adjacent to Pakistan. Pukhtuns also live on the Pakistani side of the border and share many things in common with the tribes on the Afghan side. This common ethnic factor and the fact that some of the *Taliban* (meaning students) had received religious education in Pakistani *madrassahs* (Islamic schools) gave rise to an impression in some quarters that the Taliban were a Pakistani creation. The reality was that the Taliban had seized power due to their popularity among some sections of the population in Afghanistan. However, there was some degree of covert military support for the Taliban by Pakistan when, during the period 1994–6, power was held by Prime Minister Benazir Bhutto.

The Taliban regime adopted an obscurantist version of Islam and became highly isolated in the world. Pakistan, too, had little ideological sympathy for the Taliban regime. As a moderate and generally pro-US country with a Westernized ruling elite, Pakistan had little in common with the fundamentalist Taliban. However, from 1994 to 2001, it sought to maintain a good relationship with the Taliban regime for three reasons. Firstly, Pakistan shared a long, common border with Afghanistan, with close commercial and people-to-people contacts, and needed to have a working relationship with that country. Secondly, the Pakistani military doctrine had always been that a friendly Afghanistan provided 'strategic depth' to Pakistan *vis-à-vis* India, its traditional rival. Thirdly, the Taliban regime adopted a friendlier attitude towards Pakistan, as compared to the previous Burhanuddin Rabbani regime. It is notable that this policy of befriending the Taliban regime was followed by Prime Minister Benazir Bhutto (1994–6), Prime Minister Nawaz Sharif (1997–9), and continued by General Pervez Musharraf (1999–2001). In 1996, Pakistan persuaded its close allies, Saudi Arabia and the UAE, to extend recognition to the Taliban regime.

Pakistan's friendship with the Taliban regime was based on geostrategic rather than ideological considerations. Islamabad tried to persuade its sceptical friends (e.g. the US, China, Turkey, and, Central Asian neighbours of Afghanistan) that by befriending the Taliban regime, Pakistan would be able to influence it to adopt more moderate policies. That turned out to be no more than an empty hope as the Taliban were highly rigid in their obscurantist views about Islam. They had a paranoid worldview in which they saw themselves pitted in a holy struggle against anti-Islamic forces, led mainly by the USA. The Taliban were also antagonistic towards Russia, India, and Israel.

Osama bin Laden, who had founded Al-Qaeda around 1990, resurfaced in Afghanistan soon after the Taliban took over and made that country his base to launch terrorist attacks against US facilities in East Africa and Yemen. This caused a severe strain on Washington's relations with the Taliban regime, leading to a US missile attack on Al-Qaeda bases in Afghanistan in 1998. The US demanded that the Taliban regime should stop giving sanctuary to Al-Qaeda. During this period, Pakistan tried to play a mediatory role and, for the next three years, the US held its hand. However, 9/11 was the last straw and led to the full-scale US invasion of Afghanistan in October 2001.

Under intense US pressure, when a top American official threatened to 'bomb Pakistan back to the Stone Age'[1] that President Musharraf made the fateful decision to switch Pakistan's policy towards the Taliban regime. This led to far-reaching consequences for the country, both externally as well as internally. The decision to join the US-led war against terror, moreover, generated an unending debate in Pakistan whether Musharraf should or should not have made a U-turn in Pakistan's policy towards the Taliban regime.

Pakistani public opinion has always opposed any attack on a Muslim country, as sentiments of Islamic solidarity and Pan-Islamism are ingrained in the Pakistani psyche. Moreover, the north-western border areas of Pakistan have common ethnic links with the Afghan Pukhtuns. Consequently, the US attack on Afghanistan, and the invasion of Iraq two years later, led to a significant increase in anti-American sentiments, notably in the Pukhtun tribal areas of Pakistan, and an upsurge in jihadist activities. In other parts of Pakistan as well, and among Muslims worldwide, anti-Americanism has been on the rise. Hence, the political opponents of Musharraf of various hues saw an opportunity to oust him because of the widespread public disaffection at the policy shift. Pakistani politicians joined hands in criticizing Musharraf's U-turn in policy towards the Taliban and accused him of betrayal and weakness and for acting, in their view, as an American pawn. The religious political parties were the most vociferous in such criticism. The exception in this exercise was Benazir Bhutto, leader of the PPP, who supported the switch in foreign policy but tried to convince the US that if she were in power, she would be more effective than General Musharraf in the war against terror.

In this politicking and emotionalism, many critics seemed oblivious of the fact that after 9/11, Pakistan had been left with little choice. The deadly terrorist attacks in the heart of America had made the US absolutely determined to punish Al-Qaeda and its head Osama bin Laden. When the Taliban regime refused to hand over Osama, a US attack on Afghanistan became inevitable. Since the only feasible access route for the invasion lay across Pakistan, its geophysical location made continued support for the Taliban, or even neutrality, impossible. Pakistan was also perceived as the only real friend of the Taliban regime. Had Pakistan refused to abandon its support for the Taliban regime, it, too, would have been seen by the US and the West—and by many others in the world—as a supporter of terrorism. Pakistan would have been branded as a terrorist state, with the following resultant consequences. Its aid would have been cut off and trade restricted. In the worst scenario, its nuclear assets could have been attacked by the US or Israel, and India given a free hand to deal with Pakistan. In such an isolated state, Pakistan could not expect to get any meaningful support even from its traditional friends like China, Saudi Arabia, or Turkey, since they were also supporting the US attack against the Taliban regime. In fact, by and large, the US-led invasion of Afghanistan in 2001 had the endorsement of the international community including the UN, Europe and Russia.

On the other hand, by making a switch in its policy, Pakistan was able to derive some significant advantages. It came in the mainstream of international diplomacy and instantly occupied a key position on the world stage. This was shown by the stream of Western leaders who started to arrive in Islamabad to express their appreciation of Pakistan's stance. Significant economic and military assistance was extended by the US to Pakistan amounting to US$ 10 billion over a period of five years.[2] Military hardware including F-16s was also secured from the US after a gap of several years. A part of Pakistan's foreign debt was written off and a part rescheduled. Pakistan's exports rose by nearly 50 per cent in this period, with the US emerging as its largest market.

Pakistan's close links with the US after 9/11 proved helpful when the news broke in the second half of 2003 that Pakistan's leading nuclear scientist Dr A.Q. Khan had been involved in passing nuclear technology to foreign countries, notably, Iran and North Korea that had been branded by the US as part of the 'axis of evil.' Under intense pressure from the US and the International Atomic Energy Agency, President Musharraf carried out a detailed enquiry into Dr Khan's activities which revealed that he had been involved in proliferation from as far back as 1987. However, Musharraf was able 'to assure the world that the proliferation was a one-man act and that neither the government of Pakistan nor the army was involved.'[3] This hardly seemed possible as Pakistan's nuclear facilities were in a high security area where unusual activities stretching over a period of fifteen years could not have remained unknown to the authorities. More likely, the US chose to turn a blind eye to the involvement of Pakistani official agencies in the proliferation because any punitive action against Pakistan would have jeopardized its indispensable assistance in the war against terror. Had Pakistan not made a switch of policy after 9/11, such a disclosure of nuclear proliferation would have blown up in its face.

As far as foreign policy calculations were concerned, Pakistan's switch of policy after 9/11 made eminent sense. However, the internal consequences of the policy shift were quite the contrary. The U-turn away from the Taliban regime and joining the US in the 'war against terror' was not supported by large sections of Pakistani public opinion. Its initial reaction was one of confusion and uncertainty but, later on, the public mood became more and more critical. Thus, a big gap developed between official policy and public opinion. The Pakistani 'street' became increasingly critical of what it saw as a betrayal of Muslims by Musharraf in order to please the West.

The Pakistani religious parties led the way in the hate-America propaganda by portraying the US as the enemy of Islam, mainly for its support for Israel that has been a perennial grievance of Muslims all over the world. In the recent context, the growing anti-American lobby accused the US of killing fellow Muslims in Afghanistan and Iraq. In many mosques all over the country, *mullahs* severely criticised the government and urged the faithful to join the jihad being waged by the Taliban and Al-Qaeda against the infidels. Citing early Muslim history, some religious zealots asserted that despite the obvious disadvantages in size and resources, Muslims could 'defeat' the US, like the Soviets had been defeated in Afghanistan a few years earlier. The Pakistani news media, particularly the numerous TV channels that came on the air during Musharraf's tenure, also played a part in fanning anti-US feelings through a one-sided projection of events.

Emotionalism and living under illusions has often been a bane in the Pakistani political scene. The anti-American propaganda deliberately ignored the fact that since its independence in 1947, Pakistan had received more economic and military aid from the US than from any other country. Pakistan was able to hold back Indian aggression in the 1965 war because it possessed superior weapons that had been supplied by the US for fighting communist aggression. It is also a matter of record that the US had played a key role in preventing India from invading Pakistan on at least three occasions. After the 1971 military debacle in East Pakistan, the US had prevented an Indian invasion of Kashmir and West Pakistan.[4] The US had dissuaded India from attacking Pakistan during the Kargil crisis in 1999, and during the grave confrontation between Pakistan and India in 2002–2003.

Elsewhere in the Muslim world, the US has helped Muslims in several instances. In 1956, it was the US that had forced the Israeli, British, and French withdrawal from Egypt. In 1978, it secured the Israeli withdrawal from the Sinai. In the 1980s, the US played a vital role in support of the Afghan Mujahideen in the jihad against Soviet military occupation. In the 1990s, the US had helped liberate the Muslims of Bosnia and Kosovo.

Although the foregoing facts could have been cited to rebut the one-sided propaganda against the US, the Musharraf regime was unable to effectively counter the emotionally charged, demonization campaign launched after 9/11. One possible reason could be that some elements in the government and the army itself were said to be sympathetic to the Taliban cause. There have been persistent accusations by the Hamid Karzai regime in Kabul and by US and NATO circles that 'rogue' elements in the ISI, the Pakistani military intelligence, acting either on their own or with the tacit support of the Pakistan government, have in some instances colluded with the Taliban.

Clearly, the anti-US sentiments helped the Taliban. Since 2004, there has been a notable resurgence in their activities in the Pukhtun areas bordering Pakistan where Al-Qaeda and foreign militants also became more active. As a result, the US and NATO forces in Afghanistan have come under greater pressure. They have in turn been making accusations that the Taliban, Al-Qaeda and other Islamic militants have been operating from safe sanctuaries in the tribal areas of Pakistan.

The Federally Administered Tribal Areas (FATA) of Pakistan have traditionally enjoyed a fair amount of autonomy. The tribes have a warlike tradition and most adults carry guns. During the anti-Soviet jihad in Afghanistan in the 1980s, this area had become awash with guns and ammunition, supplied liberally by the US and others to fight the Soviets. Many foreign jihadists, mainly Arabs, Uzbeks and Chechens, sought sanctuary in FATA and some of them have remained entrenched in this area. There is little doubt that these militants have been launching operations in Afghanistan against the US and NATO forces as well as the Karzai regime. Their supporters/sympathizers in other parts of Pakistan, and even outside Pakistan, have been extending financial and other support to these militants in the tribal areas. The Taliban have also been able to get an increasing number of recruits to their ranks from FATA and other areas in Pakistan.

Such cross-border activities have caused serious misgivings between Pakistan and the US and NATO forces as well as the Karzai regime. US 'Drone' aircraft have been involved in surveillance and periodic missile attacks on suspected targets in FATA in which there has been serious loss of innocent civilians. The US forces in Afghanistan have also made a few landings across the border to attack Al-Qaeda and Taliban targets in Pakistan. These operations were undertaken either unilaterally or with tacit Pakistani approval. During the US presidential election campaign in 2008, Barack Obama declared that he would authorize unilateral military strikes against Al-Qaeda elements in Pakistan if the Pakistan government was unable or unwilling to take them out. On the other hand, such US military strikes have enraged Pakistani public opinion and led to tensions in US–Pakistan relations. Pakistan has repeatedly asked the US to respect its sovereignty and stop Drone attacks. Islamabad says any such action against the militants should be undertaken by Pakistani security forces.

There has been growing pressure on Pakistan by the US and NATO to 'do more' to curb the jihadists supporting the Taliban and Al-Qaeda. While Pakistan has a large army contingent deployed in FATA to prevent cross-border operations since 2003, it has not been able to put an end to the activities of the militants. The dilemma that the Pakistan government has been facing is that if it comes down with too heavy a hand against the militants, there are bound to be many casualties, including collateral damage of non-combatants, leading to public protest that the government is killing its own fellow countrymen in order to please the US and foreign powers. On the other hand, lack of effective action against the militants puts a strains on relations with the US, NATO and the Kabul regime.

Pakistan's involvement in the war against terror has also had a serious fallout on the country's internal situation. In the last few years, Talibanization has started to grow in Pakistan itself, particularly in the Pukhtun tribal belt. Anti-American and pro-Taliban feelings are being whipped up in mosques and *madrassahs*. A kind of brainwashing is going on in these places using the war cry that 'Islam is in danger' and that it is the duty of every Pakistani Muslim to join the jihad. What is more ominous is that the religious extremists have resorted to terror tactics to intimidate not only their opponents but also the government and society in Pakistan. Public beheading of alleged collaborators and American spies, sabotage, bombing of various targets, kidnappings and, increasingly, suicide bombings has become the trademark of these Islamic militants. They espouse a very narrow-minded version of Islam. One of their main targets has been girls' schools which have been destroyed by the hundreds. They also attack video shops and barber saloons whom they accuse of un-Islamic activities.

Actually, religious extremism in Pakistan, notably in southern Punjab, predates the rise of the Taliban. Pakistan has had fanatical religious groups like the Lashkar-e-Jhangvi, Sipah-e-Sahaba and Lashkar-e-Tayyaba for more than three decades. They have been involved in sectarian killings in Pakistan and in covert operations in Indian-occupied Kashmir.

Thus, an internal crisis has been growing in Pakistan's body politic, pitting the religious extremists against the mainstream moderates. This has assumed a more acute shape with the rise in Taliban activities since 2004. There are fears that if the fanatics make headway in the settled areas, outside FATA, and start establishing their control over cities, they would impose a rigid conformity to their brand of Islam and would fight modernism in all forms. The biggest sufferers would be Pakistani women who would be deprived of education, confined to their homes and obliged to wear the shuttlecock *burqas* when going outside their homes. Men would be required to keep beards of a certain size, Western-style dress would be prohibited, and attendance of prayers in mosques would be made compulsory. If the religious extremists manage to come to power in Pakistan, they would probably impose the kind of oppressive dictatorship as seen in Afghanistan during the Taliban rule from 1994 to 2001. They would change Pakistan beyond recognition.

There would be no television, films, videos, radio, music, photographs, and sports. Freedom of expression, assembly, and the press would be severely curtailed. There would be no free elections or representative institutions and everyone would be required to conform to the mullahs' version of Islam. In effect, Pakistan would be taken back from the twenty-first century to medieval times.

Even if the religious extremists do not manage to come in power, the immediate problem that Pakistan faces is the rise in terrorism, particularly the gruesome attacks on military and civilian targets by suicide bombers. This has created a grave law and order problem affecting civil life and damaging the economy and infrastructure. The image of Pakistan in the world has suffered badly and it is seen by many as a lawless country full of dangerous fanatics and terrorists. Foreigners are reluctant to travel to Pakistan and foreign investment is pulling out of the country, adding to its multiple economic woes.

Important political changes took place in Pakistan in 2008. After its success in the general elections, the PPP government came to power in March 2008 and Pervez Musharraf had to quit as president in August. But there was no fundamental change in the foreign policy. The PPP government led by President Asif Ali Zardari and Prime Minister Yousuf Raza Gilani faced a serious dilemma. A modernist party with a pro-West leaning, the PPP government declared its commitment to the war against terror to curb Al-Qaeda and the Taliban. But it had to find a way to carry public opinion with it in this war. In the final resort, ideas had to be fought by ideas. Force should normally be used only as a weapon of the last resort. The obscurantist ideas of the religious extremists could best be countered by raising public consciousness and by securing the active support of the moderate and more educated *ulema*. Moreover, the government would need to intensify efforts to win over—by negotiations and political means—the various religious extremists and the pro-Taliban, jihadist groups.

After a year in power of the PPP government, during which efforts were made to find some political compromise with the Taliban in Swat and in FATA, talks broke down in May 2009. The government had even accepted the demand for the enforcement of the *Sharia* in Malakand but the Taliban continued to up the ante. In Swat, the writ of the government was challenged to a point that it seemed that the Taliban had seized control of that area. Consequently, a big military operation was launched in Swat. To avoid being caught in the crossfire, nearly three million people in the affected area had to seek shelter outside Swat. However, the difference between the Musharraf regime and the PPP government has been that the use of military force since May 2009 has been supported by larger sections of public opinion. The government also intends to extend the military operation to Taliban-dominated South Waziristan and other tribal areas.

President Barack Obama, who came to power in January 2009, has remained focused on Afghanistan and the war against Al-Qaeda. The pressure on Pakistan to 'do more' has increased. In some ways, Pakistan is being made a scapegoat for the failure of the Afghan regime and the US and NATO forces to suppress the resurgent Taliban. The truth is that the situation in the Pakistani tribal area is a fallout of the developments in Afghanistan: it is not the cause of the Taliban insurgency there. A durable solution of the problem would have to be found in Afghanistan rather than in FATA. The US has so far relied much more on military means. There are signs of some rethinking in the US about the two-pronged strategy advocated by Pakistan viz. emphasis on development and negotiations with the militants as well as the use of force.

The Obama Administration accepts that the US had made a mistake in abandoning Afghanistan and Pakistan after the Soviet withdrawal in 1989. It has repeatedly assured Pakistan of durable and long-term ties rather than an off-and-on, one-issue relationship. In spite of such assurances, it seems that US–Pakistan relations for some time to come would remain a hostage of the war in Afghanistan. The likely strengthening of US relations with India would also continue to create misgivings in Pakistan, unless a way can be found to improve Pakistan–India relations.

Pakistan–India Relations after 9/11

9/11 had direct consequences for Pakistan not only on its western border with Afghanistan but also in the context of its traditional rivalry with India. On the one hand, there was a revival of US–Pakistan military and economic ties, as Washington needed Pakistan's support for its military campaign in Afghanistan. On the other hand, India saw an opportunity to strengthen its already growing links with Washington by emphasizing the common fight against (Islamic) terrorism that had a focal point in Afghanistan and the neighbouring tribal areas of Pakistan.

Pakistan–India relations had come under additional strains since 1989 when there was an upsurge in the Kashmiri resistance. In India's view, some Pakistani and other militants who had been fighting the Soviet forces in Afghanistan had shifted to Indian-occupied Kashmir in the wake of the Soviet withdrawal from Afghanistan. India accused Pakistan of training militants and sending them across the Line of Control. Moreover, after the Taliban seized power in Afghanistan in 1994, India became critical of Pakistan for having friendly ties with the extremist Taliban regime.

After the Bharatiya Janata Party (BJP) came to power in 1998, Indian External Affairs Minister Jaswant Singh often contended that Pakistan had become the 'epicentre of terrorism'. India saw an opportunity after 9/11 to draw a parallel between the US action to crush Islamic extremism in Afghanistan and India's own fight against Kashmiri Muslim militants. It warned that, like the US action in Afghanistan, India could launch a punitive attack against Pakistan whom it accused of sponsoring cross-border operations.

In October 2001, some Kashmiri militants attacked the State Assembly building of Indian-occupied Kashmir, killing thirty-eight people. Chief Minister Farooq Abdullah called on the Indian government to strike at alleged militant training camps in Pakistani-held Kashmir and in Pakistan itself. On 13 December 2001, the Indian Parliament building in New Delhi was attacked by some militants. India asserted that they were Pakistani infiltrators. Parliament was in session at the time and several members of parliament and senior politicians narrowly escaped injury. Making this an excuse, the Indian government, led by Prime Minister A.B. Vajpayee, announced a mobilization of troops. It suspended flights to Pakistan, including overflights, and reduced the size of its embassy in Islamabad. It made a demand to Pakistan to hand over twenty individuals accused of terrorism who, it alleged, were hiding in Pakistan. A war fever was whipped up in India, on a much greater scale than seen during the Kargil crisis of 1999.

Hawkish circles in India came out in full cry against Pakistan. According to Stephen Philip Cohen, a US expert on South Asia, hawks in India continue to believe that 'Pakistan is an accident of history, and must be forced to its knees or destroyed'.[5] Cohen says that the hawks fall into three categories:

- those who would lure Pakistan into a military confrontation leading to a final triumph over the Pakistan army (the aborted 1987 Brasstacks model);
- those who believe that Pakistan only needs a push in the form of increased support for separatist forces in Sindh, NWFP and Balochistan leading to civil war and the break-up of Pakistan (the 1971 model); and
- those who believe that India's greater economic potential will enable it to dominate Pakistan making it a failed state (the Soviet model).

On the other side, Pakistan, too, is not without hawks in its military establishment. There is one school of thought in the military that believes that nuclear weapons possessed by both India and Pakistan deter an all out war in South Asia but provide the opportunity for a 'limited' war at a sub-nuclear level. However, the soundness of this doctrine was evidently disproved by the 2002 war crisis. The reaction of India to the attack on its parliament was so strident that it raised fears that the two countries were at the brink of a nuclear war. President Musharraf and some Pakistani spokespersons in public interviews found it necessary to hint at the possibility of the first use of the atom bomb if the pressure from India became too great.[6]

The US reaction in this context was also noteworthy. Washington was worried by the possibility that its own war on terror would be disrupted by a Pakistan–India war. Secondly, the prospects of a nuclear war in South Asia had unacceptable worldwide implications. Alarmed by the nuclear brinkmanship in South Asia, the US issued a warning to its citizens to leave India. It also airlifted non-essential US Embassy personnel and families from India. This US warning hit the Indian economy. Foreign investment declined resulting in an outcry from Indian businessmen.

In mid-2002, US diplomatic pressure grew on both India and Pakistan to pull back from the brink. The US extracted a commitment from President Musharraf in July 2002 to 'permanently' stop cross-border infiltration. Musharraf secured a commitment from the US to play a more positive role in resolving the Kashmir dispute. The US also put pressure on India. Secretary of State Colin Powell stated on 28 July 2002 in New Delhi that progress on Kashmir was 'on the international agenda' and America would 'lend a helping hand to all sides'.[7]

By the end of 2002, the worst seemed to be over. In April 2003, Indian Prime Minister Vajpayee launched his 'last' effort for peace between India and Pakistan and stretched a hand of friendship to Pakistan. In November 2003, Pakistani Prime Minister Zafarullah Khan Jamali announced a unilateral ceasefire along the Line of Control in Kashmir.

A historic turning point was reached in January 2004 when India and Pakistan decided to embark upon a journey towards peace. President Musharraf and Prime Minister Vajpayee signed the Islamabad Declaration. It contained two main points. Firstly, India and Pakistan agreed to resume their composite dialogue which, they were confident, would lead to a peaceful settlement of all bilateral issued including Jammu and Kashmir. Secondly, the president of Pakistan reassured that he would not permit any territory under Pakistan's control (evidently meaning Azad Kashmir) to be used to support terrorism in any manner.

The Islamabad Declaration was signed against the backdrop of nearly two years of eyeball-to-eyeball confrontation between the armed forces of the two countries and veiled threats of use of nuclear weapons against each other. The two states seemed to be on the brink of a catastrophe in which millions would have died and the whole region could have been contaminated for decades. Perhaps a belated realization of this doomsday scenario eventually compelled policy-makers in the two countries to pull back from the brink and opt for the path of negotiations and compromise. In this context, international pressure, particularly from the USA, clearly induced the two countries to move away from confrontation.

Though Vajpayee was ousted from power in the general elections of 2005, the succeeding Congress government under Prime Minister Manmohan Singh reaffirmed India's commitment to the peace process that was described as 'irreversible' in a joint statement issued in 2005. Since then, the peace process has been jolted and even temporarily halted by periodic terrorist incidents in India, for which India has always shown a knee-jerk reaction putting the blame on Pakistan. But the two countries have not so far abandoned the peace process. There have been detailed and indeed painstaking negotiations between the two countries on the various agenda items of the composite dialogue. After each meeting, the two sides have stressed the positive atmosphere in the talks and reaffirmed their resolve to continue the dialogue. However, the scorecard on the negotiations shows mixed results.

The two sides have made progress in confidence building measures (CBMs) that have facilitated better communication links, easier travel, greater trade, unprecedented cultural exchanges and a decrease in hostile propaganda. High-level meetings including summits have taken place from time to time.

But the dispute on Jammu and Kashmir, which has been the main source of tensions between the two countries ever since their independence, remains unresolved. It can be argued that emotionally charged issues like Kashmir cannot be resolved in a hurry, but there has been little concrete progress even on the less intractable issues viz. Siachen, Sir Creek, cross-border terrorism and a reduction in defence forces. As a result of the continuing impasse between the two big South Asian countries, regional cooperation under SAARC, including the important free trade area project, is making only lethargic progress.

Pakistan has urged that the two sides should move from dispute management to conflict resolution. Some Pakistani analysts believe that India is interested only in the CBMs, particularly in the cultural field. They fear that India would take advantage of the apparent bonhomie by sweeping the Kashmir dispute under the rug and getting de facto acceptance from Pakistan of its illegal occupation of the state. These analysts point out that India's main focus seems to be that the insurgency in Kashmir since 1989—which it contends has been due to cross-border terrorism from Pakistan—should somehow be brought to an end. Thereafter, these analysts fear, there would be no pressure left on India to resolve the Kashmir dispute.

In November 2008, Pakistan–India relations had a major setback when there was a spectacular terrorist attack in Mumbai. India immediately put the blame on Pakistan. One of the terrorists was captured alive and turned out to be a Pakistani national. It was said that several terrorists had come by the sea route from Karachi and carried out a highly sophisticated attack. India claimed that the Mumbai attack was organized by the Lashkar-e-Tayyaba, a Pakistani militant group involved in the anti-India resistance in Kashmir. India adopted a bellicose stance towards Pakistan with veiled suggestions of war. It suspended the ongoing peace process and insisted that it would not be resumed until Pakistan took effective action to destroy the terrorist network on its soil. Once again, the US played an important role to mediate between India and Pakistan and the situation gradually eased. Pakistan promised to punish any of its nationals involved in the Mumbai incident. Eventually, the two prime ministers issued a joint statement on 16 July 2009, on the sidelines of the NAM Summit in Sharm El Sheikh (Egypt), agreeing to resume dialogue. This episode, however, showed the fragility of the peace process that could be easily disrupted by terrorist groups whenever they chose to do so. Those responsible for the Mumbai attack probably wanted to disrupt any improvement in Pakistan–India relations. Unfortunately, such anti-peace elements exist in both countries.

Prospects for Peace in South Asia

Clearly, there is a bitter legacy of distrust between India and Pakistan that makes any objective evaluation a difficult exercise since partisanship and emotionalism seem often to cloud any rational judgement. Nevertheless, four elements that are working for peace and accommodation can be identified in the scenario that has emerged since the peace process was launched in January 2004, viz.

(i)   the growing peace lobby in both countries generated by the CBMs;

(ii) the geostrategic scenario after 9/11 that has produced a common stance against Islamist extremists;

(iii) the emergence of vested economic interests that want peace and stability in Pakistan–India relations to ensure economic collaboration; and

(iv) the pressure of the US and West as also many other countries in the world on both India and Pakistan to shun a nuclear war and opt for dialogue and peace.

Firstly, there can be no doubt that the various CBMs have helped improve the bilateral environment. Before 2004, war always seemed a possibility, whereas after 2004, both sides have generally avoided any kind of war talk. Moreover, there has been a remarkable increase in bilateral exchanges including visits by leaders known for their hawkish attitudes. For the first time since 1947, Kashmiri leaders from the two sides have exchanged visits. Limited travel and trade has also started across the Line of Control.

There is little substance in the allegation made by some quarters in Pakistan that the CBMs benefit India alone. To give an example, easier travel between the two countries has come as a great relief to millions of people belonging to divided families, who are by and large Pakistani and Indian Muslims. Better communication links have made supplies of commercial items much easier. Thus, whenever Pakistan has had a shortage of food items like onions, garlic, pulses, or meat, it has been able to import them from India within a few hours, rather than waiting for weeks to import them from elsewhere. The same benefits are being enjoyed by India. The opening of direct trade reduces smuggling, increases government revenues, and makes things cheaper for the average citizen.

The increase in cultural exchanges and reduction of hostile propaganda has resulted in an upsurge in public opinion in support of peace and friendship. There are now strong peace lobbies in both countries that want to bury the hatchet and are keen to open a new chapter of friendship in the subcontinent. Public opinion has influenced political parties in both countries to extend support to the peace process. It is significant that the right wing parties are also supporting the peace process. In India, the BJP that had traditionally taken a hawkish attitude towards Pakistan now wants good relations with Pakistan. The BJP cannot do otherwise since it is itself the author of the Islamabad Declaration, which was signed when it was last in power. The victory of the Congress in the general elections of May 2009 suggests that moderates enjoy greater support in India. Prime Minister Manmohan Singh has adopted a relatively more conciliatory attitude towards Pakistan and his re-election would give him a freer hand in dealings with Pakistan.

In Pakistan, the traditionally anti-India religious parties like the JUI and Jamaat-i-Islami support the peace process with India, more so because since 9/11, they have focused on the USA as the main enemy. The mainstream parties, the PPP and the two Muslim Leagues, (Q) and (N), are all for better ties with India and indeed claim to be the original sponsors of the peace process.

This apparent change of heart on both sides is diminishing the traditional pattern of tensions between the two countries and thus lessens the possibility of war. Defence expenditure might still be rising on both sides, but it would have risen much more had there been the previous pattern of tension in relations.

Secondly, Pakistan–India relations are being influenced by certain events in the international arena that have affected the current geostrategic scenario. It is clear that the world has changed since 9/11 in particular and, even earlier, since the demise of the Soviet bloc in 1991. The great international issue seems to be the war against terrorism, mainly against Muslim militants, in which the US is the driving force. But this war also has the support of many countries in the international com-munity, including Russia and China. The focus of this war has been against Al-Qaeda and the resurgent Taliban in Afghanistan and neighbouring tribal areas of Pakistan. However, Islamist fundamentalist groups have also emerged elsewhere who are alleged to be involved in militant or terrorist activities of one kind or the other, in a wide region stretching from Indonesia in the east to Morocco, Europe and USA in the west.

Islamist extremism is becoming a worldwide phenomenon primarily because anti-Americanism has grown in many Muslim circles since the US invasions of Afghanistan in 2001 and Iraq in 2003. Muslims in general feel aggrieved by what they see as the grave injustice done to their brethren in Palestine, Kashmir, Bosnia, Kosovo, Chechnya, and other places. This sentiment has mainly contributed to the rise of Islamic extremism and has turned moderates into extremists and some zealots into terrorists.

India itself has some 150 million Muslims. In case these Muslims are radicalized and some turn to extremism, they could pose a grave threat to India's internal security. Some Indian Muslims were recently accused of terrorism in Britain. There have been terrorist incidents in India itself involving Muslim extremists. While India has tended to put the blame on Pakistan's secret military service, the ISI, for such terrorist incidents, India's own courts have found in many such cases that those involved were either

Kashmiri or Indian or Bangladeshi Muslims. There is increasing evidence of emergence of Muslim militant groups in India.

India clearly has an interest in opposing Islamist extremism. There seems to be a greater realization in India that the Pakistan government—headed by Musharraf till 2008 and by PPP's Asif Zardari since then—is a key player in the fight against extremists. Pakistani politicians themselves, notably the PPP's top leader Benazir Bhutto who was assassinated in December 2007, have become the target of Islamist extremists. In fact, all moderate forces in Pakistan are facing a grave challenge from Islamist extremism. Therefore, it would be in India's own interest to strengthen rather than weaken the hands of the moderates in Pakistan. Prime Minister Manmohan Singh has said on several occasions that a strong and stable Pakistan is in India's own interest. There is realization in India that Pakistan's weakening or disintegration could unleash Islamic extremism on a massive scale and its nuclear assets could fall into the hands of such extremists. Such a realization could become the rationale for bringing about an enduring improvement in bilateral Pakistan–India relations.

The US, which launched the global war against terrorism in 2001, also has a vital interest to support moderate and pro-West forces in Islamic countries. It highly values the role of Pakistan as a key Islamic country with a unique geostrategic location, being located next to the epicentre of militancy and terrorism, i.e. the Al-Qaeda and Taliban. While Washington saw Musharraf personally as a bulwark against Islamic extremists, the US is more comfortable with the return of democracy in Pakistan under PPP rule. From the US point of view, confrontation or even tensions between India and Pakistan would distract attention from its focus on the war against terrorism. Moreover, the US and the entire world community would be adversely affected by a nuclear war in South Asia or elsewhere. For these two reasons, the US has been using its influence both in India and Pakistan in favour of peace, accommodation and dialogue. Europe too has a similar approach and the European Union has also been involved in a conciliatory role in South Asia. In fact, at present, Russia, China, and all other countries favour peace between India and Pakistan.

Thirdly, improvement in relations between India and Pakistan makes it possible to establish long-term economic linkages between the two countries. Trade has already been growing and the two commerce secretaries have fixed a target of US$ 10 billion by 2010. Undoubtedly, proximity is a key incentive for expansion of commercial links between India and Pakistan. Economic cooperation will have political fallout as well. Over a period of time, pressure groups are likely to emerge having vested economic interests in favour of peace and cooperation, since they will stand to lose in the case of war and tension. Of particular importance, in this connection, will be the bilateral trade with Pakistan, transit trade through Pakistan and the proposed Iran–Pakistan–India gas pipeline, as also the Turkmenistan–Afghanistan–Pakistan–India gas pipeline. Both India and Pakistan desperately need more energy to maintain their economic growth. Hence, these gas pipelines could become guarantors of peace and cooperation between the two countries.

Both sides are moving towards mutually advantageous cooperation by exploring opportunities in diverse fields, despite political reservations. The advantage of proximity, faster and less costly communication lines as well as awareness of each other's tastes, will continue to foster greater collaboration. This in turn will establish greater confidence in each other and will create vested interests in favour of peace and cooperation. Big business houses that stand to lose heavily if their commercial linkages in the other country are disrupted would use their influence on the two governments in favour of peace and harmony. Similarly, if better relations between India and Pakistan enable SAARC to take off, on the ASEAN model, that too would reinforce the peace process and even make it irreversible.

In sum, the above-mentioned factors are helpful in reducing the traditional distrust and antagonism between India and Pakistan. Against this background, the progress since 2004 on the main political disputes, including the key issue of Jammu and Kashmir, can be examined.

There are some indications that the Kashmir issue is moving towards a Northern Ireland type solution. There has been intensive back channel diplomacy whose details have not been announced but whose contours seem to be the following. Firstly, a solution would not involve a change of border, but a kind of condominium might emerge. There would be maximum autonomy given to the two parts of Kashmir, with easier travel and trade between the two parts.

It is notable that Musharraf's four-point solution had drawn support from All Parties Hurriyat Conference (APHC), the main anti-India political body in Indian-occupied Kashmir, as well as from the top Kashmiri leaders on the Pakistani side such as Sardar Abdul Qayyum Khan. In Pakistan, better ties with India are supported by the mainstream political parties, the PPP and the Muslim League as also by the religious alliance Muttahida Majlis-e-Amal (MMA). Only the hard line jihadist groups oppose it. The militancy in Indian-occupied Kashmir might gradually decline, leading to the withdrawal of the greater part of Indian troops.

Indian Prime Minister Manmohan Singh told an audience in Jammu on 15 July 2007 that the time was ripe for a pact with Pakistan and between the culturally and politically diverse peoples of Jammu and Kashmir. He announced his quest for a historic reconciliation with Pakistan for peace and cooperation in Kashmir, including a joint sharing of its water and land resources for the region's benefit on both sides of the Line of Control. He called for a 'historic reconciliation of hearts and minds in our region.' Singh said:

> I hope and believe that Jammu and Kashmir can, one day, become a symbol of India-Pakistan cooperation rather than of conflict. As I have stated earlier, borders cannot be changed, but they can be made irrelevant. There can be no question of divisions or partitions, but the Line of Control can become a line of peace with a freer flow of ideas, goods, services and people.

He said:

> I believe it is possible to pursue the development of a United State of Jammu and Kashmir even while respecting and addressing the legitimate aspirations of the peoples of each of the three regions—Kashmir, Jammu and Ladakh.[8]

No doubt, apart from the Kashmir dispute, there are also some other unresolved problems between India and Pakistan. On Sir Creek, there is still no agreement despite detailed talks. However, the international deadline for demarcation of the sea limits should induce India and Pakistan to find a compromise.

On the Siachen Glacier, the sticking point is Indian insistence to make an official note of the existing line of control. Pakistan contests the validity of the existing line, representing Indian de facto control, as being the result of Indian aggression in 1984. There are periodic hints from both sides that a solution is close. The two countries can possibly overcome this deadlock by using the Simla-like formula that had referred to the Kashmir issue 'without prejudice to the known position of either side'. An additional compulsion for the two countries could be the concern that due to military activities in Siachen for over twenty-five years, snow has started to melt that could lead to an environ-mental catastrophe due to loss of the glacier itself and resultant flooding. The two countries have a vested interest in managing water resources that is a key to their survival. Bilateral trade has been on the rise but could grow significantly if political understanding grows. This would also enable SAARC to become more effective.

Fourthly, prospects of peace in the subcontinent are strengthened by the pressure brought on both India and Pakistan by the international community to shun a nuclear war and opt for dialogue and peace. A nuclear war would destroy both countries and kill millions in the subcontinent. Atomic radiation would spread beyond South Asia and adversely affect others. This is unacceptable to the international community. The West and especially the US, in addition, oppose any diversion from their focus on the war on terror. For these reasons, the international community would continue to remain engaged with India and Pakistan in order to prevent war and continue the peace process.

* * * *

While the above-mentioned developments since 2004 have worked towards a long-term betterment of Pakistan–India relations, some elements in the current geostrategic scenario could complicate the situation in South Asia in the future. One of them is internal to Pakistan and the other is global in nature.

Progress in the peace process could be halted in the event that an Islamic fundamentalist government comes to power in Pakistan. In such an eventuality, the US would drop all pretensions of an even-handed attitude in South Asia. It would draw even closer to India and could probably also adopt a common strategy with New Delhi to contain and even weaken Pakistan. A primary concern of these two countries plus Israel in that scenario would be to bring about the denuclearization of Pakistan, for which purpose there could even be use of force. Secondly, the growing relationship between India and the US could have an adverse impact not only on Pakistan but also on China, its long-standing ally.

Until the fall of the Soviet Union in 1991, India had enjoyed a special relationship with Moscow, which provided 70 per cent of India's military hardware. In this period, India was also the leading spirit behind the Non-Aligned Movement. India's opposition to the military alliance between Pakistan and the US since 1954 had influenced India to adopt these policies. The US took a dim view of the India–Soviet axis.

After the demise of the Soviet Union in 1991, India continued to maintain a close relationship with Russia. But with the coming to power of the BJP government in 1998, India made a paradigm shift in policy to move closer to the USA. Washington responded enthusiastically for several reasons. India is the second most populous country in the world and it is an important military, political, and economic power. It is a democracy and shares Western values in political and economic spheres. Both the US and India are opposed to Islamist extremism and consider it a serious security threat. This adds to the mutuality of interests at this time that is bringing the US and India closer to each other. More importantly, the US sees India as a counterweight against China, which not only continues to adhere to a totalitarian philosophy but is also fast emerging as a potential superpower. China's spectacular economic progress since 1980 and its growing military strength pose a long-term challenge for the US.

For its part, India has hardly ever concealed its leadership ambitions and sees China as its main Asian rival. China's close friendship with Pakistan since the 1960s had caused serious concern in India. In 1962, India and China fought a border war. Since 1980, Sino–Indian relations have improved a lot but China continues to maintain a territorial claim on the Indian state of Arunachal Pradesh. India and China have been in competition for influence in Nepal and Burma as also in Southeast Asia.

China is aware that in the last decade, US–India relations have taken a quantum leap. India and the US have developed a 'strategic partnership' which has, notably, led to the signing of a nuclear deal. In March 2005, the US Secretary of State Condoleezza Rice publicly offered US help to make India 'a major world power in the twenty-first century'. Shortly thereafter, Indian Foreign Minister Pranab Mukherjee went to Washington and signed a ten-year framework defence agreement. India is planning to purchase top-of-the-range US weaponry worth several billion dollars and has conducted joint military exercises with the US. In an important initiative, the US, India, Japan and Australia met in May 2007 on the sidelines of the Asian Regional Forum in Manila to set up a new 'quadrilateral' grouping. This led to protests from Beijing. Prime Minister Manmohan Singh later said that India was not 'ganging up' against China and that the 'quadrilateral group was not a military alliance'. This has not satisfied China which fears that the US is fashioning a 'China containment' strategy involving India, Japan, and Australia.[9]

The Chinese policy for the past three decades has been one of building bridges with the US, India and others. China wants to concentrate on economic development, where its progress has been phenomenal. At the present rate of growth, China could emerge as a superpower by 2030 or so. It would like to see a stable international environment that does not distract it from pursuing its rapid economic growth. But if the strategic relationship between the US and India keeps growing, China might toughen its policy towards India. This could bring China even closer towards Pakistan.

The India–US strategic partnership could, in the long run, also result in Pakistan getting estranged from the US. Moreover, the growing anti-Americanism in Pakistan could at some stage force the government to review its relations with the US. The subcontinent faces an uncertain future in the days ahead.

NOTES

1. Pervez Musharraf, *In the Line of Fire: A Memoir* (New York: Free Press, 2006), p. 201.
2. Richard Boucher, the US Assistant Secretary of State for South Asia, quoted in, 'US pours cold water on hopes for immediate remedy', *Dawn*, 21 October 2008.
3. Musharraf, op. cit., p. 292.
4. Burke and Ziring, op. cit., p. 406.
5. Stephen Philip Cohen, 'Asian Aftershocks: Strategic Asia 2002–03', p. 20. https://www.brookings.edu/wp-content/uploads/2016/06/20021201-1.pdf.
6. Cohen, ibid., pp. 28–34.
7. Shahid M. Amin, *Realism in Politics* (Karachi: Royal Book Company, 2005), p. 271.
8. Jawed Naqvi, 'LoC can become symbol of peace, says Singh', *Dawn*, 16 July 2007. https://www.dawn.com/news/256637.
9. Praful Bidwai, 'India's growing relations with US annoy China', *Dawn*, 7 July 2007. https://www.dawn.com/news/255115/india-s-growing-relations-with-us-annoy-china.

18

Pakistan's Foreign Policy (2010–2020)

There were some important developments in Pakistan's foreign policy in the decade beginning from 2010. The traditionally strong relationship with USA showed a downward curve until it reached an all-time low in 2018 when the newly-elected US President Donald Trump more or less denounced Pakistan. Matters improved to some extent thereafter, as the US realized that it had little option but to turn to Pakistan in order to secure a negotiated settlement in Afghanistan, allowing a face-saving withdrawal from its unsuccessful war in that country. Painstaking negotiations eventually produced an agreement on 29 February 2020, which laid out a fourteen-month period for US military withdrawal from Afghanistan. US–Pakistan relations also improved as Trump evidently developed a personal rapport with Prime Minister Imran Khan, but the US aid flow to Pakistan was still not resumed.

Pakistan's relations with India had been deteriorating since the Mumbai terrorist attack of 2008, and became worse after three more terrorist incidents at Pathankot (2016), Uri (2016), and Pulwama (2019), for which India blamed Pakistan, raising serious war fears on all these occasions. India adopted a strategy to isolate Pakistan internationally, accusing it of being a 'sponsor' of state terrorism. India also rejected all attempts to hold talks to ease tensions between the two countries, insisting that first Pakistan would have to end its alleged support for terrorist groups such as Jaish-e-Mohammad and Lashkar-e-Tayyaba. In February 2019, there were air clashes between the two sides, in which Pakistan downed two Indian aircraft and captured an Indian pilot. International actors, thereafter, made hectic efforts to defuse tensions to avoid a nuclear war between the two neighbours. But in August 2019, India stoked up the tensions by ending the 'special status' of India-occupied Kashmir and putting some eight million Kashmiris under house detention in order to prevent public protests. Pakistan denounced these steps as violation of UN resolutions and a blatant disregard for human rights. Anti-Muslim legislation passed in India in December 2019 led to big demonstrations in that country, mainly by Muslims, and further heightened tensions with Pakistan. Pakistan denounced the anti-Muslim policies of the BJP government in India.

During this decade, Pakistan drew even closer to its traditional friend China, as the latter launched the highly ambitious China–Pakistan Economic Corridor (CPEC). This would give China a short, safe access route to the Persian Gulf through the Pakistani port of Gwadar, thereby reducing the travel time for oil shipments to one-fifth as compared to the existing Indian Ocean route. CPEC is expected to transform Pakistan's economy in many areas, viz. communication, energy, commerce, tourism, and agriculture. In strategic terms, CPEC would make both the countries even more dependent on each other, thus ensuring a long-term alliance.

Pakistan's relations with Afghanistan remained troubled throughout the decade. The main reason was the Afghan government's perception that the ascendant Taliban were using sanctuaries in Pakistan, with the tacit or active approval of the Government Pakistan and ISI (its main intelligence agency), in order to launch deadly attacks against NATO/Kabul forces. Pakistan's repeated denials of any complicity were given little or no credence by Kabul, which seemed convinced that the Taliban, who are mainly ethnic Pakhtun, had the support of Pakistan, which also has a large Pakhtun population. The reality was that Kabul was unable to break the growing power of Taliban and chose to make Pakistan a scapegoat for its own failures in the military and other fields. India kept stirring these misgivings through propaganda, while it also sought to build goodwill in Afghanistan by making big investments in hospitals, dams, etc.

Pakistan made efforts during this decade to improve its relations with Russia in order to secure a better balance of power. Moscow was more responsive towards these overtures than in the past, in spite of its traditionally close relations with India. But the prospects of building any Moscow–Islamabad–Beijing axis seemed remote.

Pakistan continued to maintain its special relationship with Saudi Arabia during this decade, though the latter made a paradigm shift towards a better relationship with India, mainly for economic reasons. Pakistan's economy was in a poor condition, mainly due to corruption and mismanagement during the previous two governments led by PPP and PML (N), which obliged Prime Minister Imran Khan to turn towards Saudi Arabia and UAE for a bailout. Both countries responded generously. While Pakistan also wished to maintain good relations with Iran, but found it increasingly difficult to do so, because of the cold war between Iran and Saudi Arabia.

Downward Slope in US–Pakistan Relations

In 2001, the US/NATO invading forces had little difficulty in ousting the Taliban regime, but in the long run it turned out to be a pyrrhic victory. Instead, the US found itself trapped in the longest war in its history. From around 2004, the Afghan Taliban re-emerged as a formidable guerrilla force and kept gaining ground and inflicting more and more casualties on the occupying US/NATO forces, as well as those of the Kabul regime. This fitted in with the pattern of successful fighting by Afghan guerrillas against foreign occupation forces that had earlier led to military failures of British imperialist forces in the nineteenth century and Soviet forces in the twentieth century. However, instead of accepting their military failure, the US-led occupation forces sought to make a scapegoat of Pakistan by accusing it of providing sanctuaries to and, even, aiding the Taliban fighters. Pakistan angrily denied this charge. The loss of trust generated by the Afghan war, therefore, became the main reason for the decline in US–Pakistan relations. Since launching the 'War on Terror' in 2001, the US has considered Islamist extremism as the main threat to its security and has often accused Pakistan of not doing enough to terminate this threat.

There was some truth in the accusations about Taliban sanctuaries in Pakistan but that is because the Durand Line (the border between Afghanistan and Pakistan) is porous and cannot be guarded all along its 2,400-km length. Pakistan also held that while it was being accused of not doing enough to prevent terrorists from going across the border into Afghanistan, why could not the US coalition do more to prevent terrorists from entering Afghanistan. It had to be a two-way exercise in order to secure success. Nevertheless, Pakistan has made efforts to better guard this border by building security fences on its side. It launched a major military operation against the Islamist terrorists and has sought to curb their activities inside Pakistan.

As for the US/NATO/Kabul accusations of duplicity by Pakistan, viz. aiding the Taliban militants, Pakistan argued that it was itself the biggest victim of pro-Taliban terrorists. Its military was constantly engaged in fighting and clearing militants' sanctuaries in remote tribal areas. While the US/NATO officials did periodically praise Pakistan's efforts against the terrorists, their constant refrain to Pakistan was to 'do more'. This angered public opinion in Pakistan and led to a growth in anti-Americanism. A common view developed in Pakistan that it had suffered so much from terrorism because it had become entangled in a war that was not its own. The war was actually between the US, NATO, and Kabul regime, on the one hand, and the Afghan Taliban, Al-Qaeda and Islamist militants on the other.

Pakistan had been more or less forced to support America's war by providing it the invaluable access route across Pakistan. That was the only reason why Islamist militants had turned against Pakistan and unleashed terrorism that took over 70,000 lives and inflicted economic losses of US$100 billion plus. The US military and economic assistance given to Pakistan was never enough to compensate Pakistan's losses and, yet, Pakistan was being asked to 'do more'.

The US–Pakistan relations were severely tested after 2011 by certain specific incidents.

THE RAYMOND DAVIS CASE

In January 2011, a CIA contractor, Raymond Davis, was involved in a traffic incident in Lahore when he opened fire and killed two Pakistanis who, he claimed, were planning to rob him. Davis was caught by the crowd and handed over to the police which put him on trial for murder. The US claimed diplomatic immunity for Davis but this was not accepted by the Pakistan Foreign Office. Pakistani public opinion was inflamed amidst reports that private US contractors like Blackwater had been acting with impunity in order to spy in Pakistan and committing other acts prejudicial to Pakistan's sovereignty. After a long standoff, a settlement was reached with the payment of compensation to the relatives of the two murdered men, and Davis was deported. Some reports suggested that Saudi Arabia played a role in securing this settlement.

THE DEATH OF OSAMA BIN LADEN

The circumstances in which the Al-Qaeda chief Osama bin Laden was killed in May 2011 put US–Pakistan relations under further strain. The US had obtained evidence of Osama bin Laden's presence in Abbottabad, Pakistan. President Barack Obama ordered a secret military operation that killed Osama on 2 May 2011. The operation, involving the flight of several US helicopters from Afghanistan to Abbottabad, about a hundred kilometres inside Pakistani territory, was conducted without the knowledge or approval of the Pakistan government. While Pakistan did officially welcome the killing of Osama, it protested against the violation of its territory by the US forces. On the other hand, in the US, there was strong criticism of Pakistan, with suggestions that Osama could not have been living in Abbottabad, near Pakistan's top military training academy, without the connivance of Pakistani authorities or some 'rogue' elements within the military. The then Prime Minister Yousuf Raza Gilani called for a review of the foreign policy. An Enquiry Commission was set up by the Pakistan government to examine the whole incident, including possible negligence or connivance of official personnel. After a long-drawn out investigation, a detailed report was submitted by the enquiry commission, though its findings have not been made public. No one was reported to have been punished for negligence of duties or connivance with the US.

According to Peter Bergen of CNN, 'there is no evidence that anyone in the Pakistani government, military or intelligence agencies knowingly sheltered bin Laden.' Bergen reported that he had spoken to nearly all top officials in the US government concerned with security 'but all of them told me in one form or another that Pakistani officials had no clue that bin Laden was living in Abbottabad.'[1] This was, no doubt, a huge intelligence failure, but there are other precedents in history of such intelligence failures, e.g. the US never knew that 9/11 was about to happen. Similarly, in 2003, nearly all Western intelligence agencies had the wrong information that there were weapons of mass destruction in Saddam Hussein's Iraq. In 1941, the US didn't know that Japan was about to attack Pearl Harbour.

A key geostrategic outcome of the killing of Osama was that it provided the US with a face-saving basis for extricating itself from Afghanistan by arguing that it had achieved the objectives for the invasion of Afghanistan in 2001, viz. it had taken revenge by killing Osama and had largely destroyed Al-Qaeda.

MEMOGATE SCANDAL

On 10 October 2011, a US-based businessman Mansoor Ijaz wrote an article in *The Financial Times* claiming that he had acted as an intermediary between the Pakistan government and the US administration when the former requested the help of the latter to avert a military coup in Pakistan, following the secret US raid that killed Osama bin Laden. He said that Hussain Haqqani, the then Pakistan ambassador to the US, had telephoned him with an urgent request on 9 May, a week after the raid against Osama. Haqqani asked Ijaz to deliver a confidential memo asking for US assistance against a possible Pakistani military coup. The memo was alleged to have been drafted by Haqqani at the behest of President Asif Zardari. Mansoor Ijaz delivered it to Admiral Mike Mullen and then to National Security Advisor James L. Jones.

Though the PPP government rejected Mansoor Ijaz's claims, it triggered a storm in the country's political circles, especially between the government and the military. A judicial commission was appointed to investigate the matter at the request of the Chairman Joint Chiefs of Staff, General Khalid Shameem Wynne, to the Supreme Court for an independent probe. The court rejected the government's contention that the issue should be investigated by a parliamentary panel. Tension between the government and the military reached a peak after Prime Minister Gilani said that the armed forces and intelligence chiefs had acted in an 'unconstitutional and illegal' manner by filing affidavits on the memo issue in the Supreme Court, without getting the government's approval. Prime Minister Gilani also maintained that he was only answerable to the Parliament. On 19 April 2012, a petition was submitted in the Supreme Court to arrest former ambassador Hussain Haqqani, through Interpol, following his refusal to return to Pakistan. On 12 June, the Supreme Court commission released its findings declaring that, after testimony by all parties and verifying the forensic results of Ijaz's BlackBerry conversations with Haqqani, it was 'incontrovertibly established' that Haqqani had written the memo and he should be called back to Pakistan to face likely charges of treason. This episode embittered the uneasy civil–military relations and raised apprehensions about US intervention in Pakistan's internal affairs.

Salala Incident

Pakistan blocked the supply lines for the US/NATO forces in Afghanistan in 2011 after an attack by NATO forces on two Pakistani military check posts at Salala in Mohmand agency. The incident occurred when, on 26 November 2011, two NATO Apache helicopters, an AC-130 gunship, and two F-15E Eagle fighter jets entered into the Pakistani border area of Salala and opened fire at two border patrol check posts, killing up to twenty-four Pakistani soldiers, including two officers, and wounding thirteen others. The army check posts were codenamed 'Boulder' and 'Volcano' respectively. This attack resulted in a sharp deterioration of relations between Pakistan and the US. Both sides put forward conflicting versions of what had transpired.

General Ashfaq Parvez Kayani, the Pakistan army chief, condemned the attack as an 'unprovoked act of aggression' and 'indiscriminate' violence. He said 'it was a blatant and unacceptable act, resulting in the loss of precious lives of Pakistani soldiers'. The Pakistani side saw Salala as the fourth such attack by the US/NATO forces in Afghanistan since 2006. Almost a similar attack in June 2008 had left eleven personnel of the Frontier Corps dead, prompting the Pakistan government to suspend NATO supplies for a few days. In another such incident, on 30 September 2010, two Pakistani soldiers had been killed; it again led to the closure of the NATO supplies route for ten days. In a hardening of its position, Pakistan demanded an official apology from the US. Other steps taken by Pakistan were closure of the NATO supplies route, boycotting of the Bonn Conference, demanding vacating of the Shamsi airbase in Balochistan and stopping of Drone attacks in Pakistani territory. As the crisis grew, NATO expressed regrets over the incident and admitted its mistake. The US government also offered its 'deepest condolences' but was reluctant to offer an unconditional apology. The Pentagon felt that its condolence and regret over the incident was enough to move on. President Obama called the attack a 'tragedy' but did not offer an apology. The Salala incident led to a hardening of Pakistani opinion towards the US. Many demanded a review of Pakistan's ties with the US and Pakistan's participation in the 'War on Terror'. The Parliament in Pakistan took up the matter and anti-US sentiments were shared across the political spectrum.

The closure of the two NATO supplies route across Pakistan created serious difficulties for the US/NATO military operations inside Afghanistan. The alternative transit routes were much more expensive and impractical. Lifting of goods by air from the Persian Gulf was ten times more expensive. Using the northern route across Russia was uneconomical, long, and undependable.

For Pakistan also, the deadlock with the US was seen as unproductive, jeopardizing the aid relationship, amounting to billions of dollars annually. Moreover, Pakistan's tensions with the US/NATO would have worked to India's advantage. Consequently, after long negotiations, on 3 July 2012, when the US Secretary of State Hillary Clinton officially apologized for the incident, Pakistan restored the NATO supply routes. However, the US facilities at Shamsi air base were never restored.

DRONE ATTACKS

From around 2004, the US authorities, mainly the CIA, started to use drones to attack and destroy militants involved in fighting the US/NATO forces in Afghanistan. Many of these militants were based in remote tribal areas of Pakistan adjacent to the Afghan border and were able to evade military operations. Based on intelligence, drones would be used to attack such militants. Several notable militant leaders were killed by drones. However, these attacks also caused collateral damage in which innocent civilians, including children, were killed and wounded. This stirred indignation amongst the local people and, over a period of time, many Pakistanis came to see drone attacks as barbaric, apart from being a violation of Pakistan's sovereignty. There was some evidence that at least some drone attacks were launched with the approval of Pakistani authorities, notably President Pervez Musharraf and, later on, the Army Chief General Ashfaq Parvez Kayani. Those killed were terrorists operating against Pakistan, and drones were the only practical method to trace and kill them in their hideouts in tribal areas. This connivance was never publicly admitted by Pakistani authorities and in most cases official protests were lodged against drone attacks as violation of Pakistan's sovereignty. Public opinion was definitely against such attacks and this issue stoked anti-Americanism in Pakistan.

The US authorities kept claiming that the collateral damage, both in Pakistan and elsewhere, arising from drone attacks was minimal. The statistics given by the US sources were between 158 to 965 civilians killed, as against 2,000 to 3,500 militants killed. On the other hand, the prestigious Brookings Institution, in 2009, said that on average, drone attacks killed about ten civilians for every militant that they killed.[2]

In December 2013, Pakistan's National Assembly passed a resolution against drone attacks, calling them a violation of the UN Charter, international laws, and humanitarian norms. Prime Minister Nawaz Sharif stated that the use of drones 'is not only a continued violation of our territorial integrity, but also detrimental to our resolve and efforts at eliminating terrorism from our country.' However, the fact was that among those killed in drone attacks were notable enemies of the Pakistani state such as Baitullah Mehsud, Mullah Fazlullah, and Hakimullah Mehsud. In any event, the US has practically ceased drone attacks in Pakistani territory since around 2014.

OPERATION ZARB-I-AZB

Pakistan has suffered more from terrorism than any other country. Nearly 70,000 people lost their lives and economic losses were over US$100 billion. However, there was a lack of political will to take effective steps to curb terrorism. The PPP government ruled over Pakistan from 2008 to 2013 but never launched a major military operation. Prime Minister Nawaz Sharif, who came to power in 2013, was suspected of having a soft corner for Islamist militants. He opposed a military solution to end terrorism, but eventually the policy had to be abandoned. General Raheel Sharif, the army chief appointed by Nawaz Sharif, pressed for a military operation in Waziristan, the main centre of the extremist groups. Though Nawaz Sharif held talks with the Taliban, nothing concrete emerged from several rounds of talks. A military operation codenamed Operation Zarb-i-Azb was launched in June 2014. Military spokespersons have since reported notable success in the operation. One important achievement was making Karachi safe. For years, the largest city in Pakistan had suffered from terrorism, mostly ethnic in nature. As a result of the anti-terrorism measures taken in Karachi since 2014, target-killing and other acts of terrorism have been largely eliminated, greatly improving the image of the city. However, terrorist incidents have not yet been fully eliminated from the country and are still taking place from time to time.

The international reaction has been very favourable. Additional measures taken in 2020 against banned outfits like Jaish-e-Mohammad and Lashkar-e-Tayyaba should remove a long-standing grievance of India and also improve Pakistan's international image. Pakistan is also building a fence along the Afghan border to put a stop to cross-border activities by militants. However, Pakistan has also been demanding that terrorists based in Afghanistan like the TTP should not be allowed to use Afghanistan as a sanctuary to attack targets in Pakistan.

TRUMP ACCUSES PAKISTAN OF DUPLICITY

The US President Donald Trump shocked Pakistan by issuing a Tweet on 1 January 2018:

> The United States has foolishly given Pakistan more than 33 billion dollars in aid over the last 15 years, and they have given us nothing but lies & deceit, thinking of our leaders as fools. They give safe haven to the terrorists we hunt in Afghanistan, with little help. No more!
> 5:12 PM Jan 1, 2018

This statement shook the foundations of US–Pakistan relations. An alliance of about seventy years seemed to be in jeopardy. At the heart of this accusation was the US frustration over lack of progress against the Taliban in Afghanistan. For years, the US official circles and analysts attributed this failure to the alleged use of Pakistan as sanctuaries by the Afghan Taliban. Pakistan has clearly been made a scapegoat for the US military failure in Afghanistan. The success of the Taliban has been due to their ideological and ethnic appeal, whereas the peculiar conditions of Afghanistan have helped guerrilla resistance against the US, just as it did against the British and the Russians. Trump's statement totally ignored the role played by Pakistan in the War on Terror. Since 2001, Pakistan had given vital support to the

US/NATO and Afghan forces by providing the logistic access route through Pakistan. Pakistan helped capture some key leaders of Al-Qaeda. The biggest military operation against Islamist terrorists was launched by Pakistan and large areas on the tribal border were cleared of terrorists. Due to this support for the War on Terror, the Islamist militants turned against Pakistan and their terrorism resulted in the death of over 70,000 Pakistanis and economic losses of over US$100 billion. It was manifestly unfair and untrue to accuse Pakistan of duplicity. Some sanctuaries did exist on Pakistani soil but that was due to the unpoliced border and hilly terrain.

Shortly after his unprovoked outburst against Pakistan, Trump sought to backtrack as the Pentagon, CIA, and the State Department stressed the need for Pakistan's cooperation. Matters were also helped by a successful visit to Washington by Prime Minister Imran Khan, in July 2019, when a personal rapport was established between the two leaders. Trump realized that Pakistan's help was necessary in order to persuade the Taliban to reach a negotiated settlement with the US in Afghanistan. An agreement was finally signed in Doha in February 2020, and withdrawal of US troops was scheduled to be completed in fourteen months.

CONCLUSION

The above narrative brings out the downward trend in US–Pakistan relations for the past many years. Anti-Americanism has grown significantly in Pakistan and the US is widely distrusted by Pakistani public. The same seems to be the case in the US where, too, Pakistan is seen as an untrustworthy ally. No doubt, some of the steps taken by the US in the decade of 2010 justifiably angered Pakistan. But a state has to base its foreign policy decisions on hard calculations rather than emotions. It cannot be overlooked that Pakistan has been a major recipient of US aid—both military and civil—since around 1954 when it joined the US-sponsored military pacts. Statistics show that overall Pakistan has received nearly US$75 billion in US aid, making the US as the single largest source of aid to Pakistan. The drying up of US aid since 2016 is one reason for the economic crisis that Pakistan has been facing since then.

The two countries have had a very close relationship for nearly seventy years. Apart from receiving aid from the US, Pakistan has also benefitted in some other important ways. It was able to hold back India in the 1965 war to a large extent because it had acquired the latest US arms, after joining the military pacts. Though Pakistan lost its eastern wing during the 1971 war against India, the US played a role, along with the Soviet Union, in preventing India from invading West Pakistan. Pakistan's Green Revolution in the 1960s that doubled its agricultural production and made Pakistan self-sufficient in food was the work of a US scientist, sent by the Rockefeller Foundation. At the present time, the US is the sole superpower and can harm Pakistan in multiple ways. It remains in Pakistan's national interest to maintain a mutually advantageous relationship with it and, at least, not allow any serious deterioration in relations, since that would only work to India's advantage.

Pakistan–India Tensions

The decade of 2010 saw a further deterioration in Pakistan's relations with India. In the background was the 2008 terrorist incident in Mumbai, for which India blamed Lashkar-e-Tayyaba (LeT), a banned Pakistani militant outfit. The Indian narrative was that LeT and similar groups were the creation of ISI, the Pakistani intelligence agency. Pakistan had offered to cooperate in investigations relating to the Mumbai incident but no real headway was made. The coming to power of Nawaz Sharif in 2013 was seen as a positive development since he was known to favour a better relationship with India. India's newly elected Prime Minister Narendra Modi invited Nawaz Sharif to attend his inauguration in May 2014. The two leaders also met at Urfa, Russia in July 2015, and later Modi made an unscheduled stopover in Lahore to attend a wedding in Nawaz Sharif's family in December 2015.

But the apparent bonhomie quickly disappeared when there was a terrorist incident in Pathankot soon thereafter, for which India blamed Pakistan-based terrorists. Next, there was a terrorist attack in Uri on 18 September 2016, in which nineteen Indian soldiers were killed, which raised war fever in India. India put the blame on Jaish-e-Mohammad, a Pakistan-based group. Next, India raised the stakes when it claimed that on 29 September 2016, it had carried out 'surgical strikes' across the Line of Control against militant bases in Azad Kashmir, inflicting thirty-five to seventy casualties. Pakistan rejected this claim and took foreign news media to the site in Azad Kashmir to prove that the Indian claim was baseless. Nevertheless, this claim marked an escalation in the nature of military response from India.

While Nawaz Sharif kept his stance of seeking better relations with India, there was a hardening in the Indian stance and it turned down any possibility of bilateral talks until Pakistan satisfied India that it was taking effective steps to eradicate terrorists, allegedly operating from its soil against India. In July 2017, Nawaz Sharif lost power after his disqualification by the court. In July

2018, the new general elections in Pakistan brought Imran Khan, leader of the Pakistan Tehreek-e-Insaf (PTI), to power. He started by reaching out to India with an offer of talks but drew a blank. It became apparent that Modi was seeking to win Hindu nationalist voters by keeping up a tough stance towards Pakistan.

PULWAMA AND 'SURGICAL STRIKES'

A sharp deterioration in India–Pakistan relations took place when a Kashmiri suicide bomber struck an Indian military convoy at Pulwama, killing forty Indian soldiers. The bomber was a local Kashmiri but India alleged that he was aligned to the Pakistan-based Jaish-e-Mohammad. Based on this assertion, even before investigations were made, a war fever was raised in India, whipped up by the government itself, with threats of retaliatory military action against Pakistan. This time, there was an escalation in Indian response when it claimed to have carried out a 'surgical strike' inside Pakistani territory. On 26 February 2019, twelve Indian Air Force planes entered Pakistani territory in Khyber Pakhtunkhwa (KP) province at night and dropped bombs at Balakot on an alleged training camp of Jaish-e-Mohammad. Pakistan took foreign journalists to the site bombed by Indian planes to show that no material damage had been done and only a few trees were destroyed. Still, Pakistan decided to retaliate and also raised the stakes. On 27 February 2019, PAF planes entered India-occupied Kashmir in broad daylight, dropped bombs around Indian military camps, avoiding to cause any material damage, in a show of their capability. While returning, the PAF planes were engaged in an air combat in which Pakistani planes shot down an Indian aircraft and captured its pilot. Pakistan also claimed to have shot down a second Indian plane, while India claimed that it had shot down a Pakistani F-16. Neither side produced conclusive evidence to back their claims. However, the capture of Indian pilot Abhinandan Varthaman gave credence to the Pakistani version, though Prime Minister Imran Khan released him a few days later. Probably, this effective Pakistani retaliation dampened the aggressive mood in India and prevented any further military escalation.

There were several other steps taken by India in retaliation for the Pulwama incident. India ended the MFN (Most Favoured Nation) status of Pakistan in trade, and ended all cultural contacts with Pakistan. It stepped up efforts to get Pakistan declared a terrorist state, but was unsuccessful. Kashmiri students in India were also maltreated and many were forced to end their studies and go back home. For its part, Pakistan retaliated by reducing diplomatic representation at chargé d'affaires level and cutting off trade links with India. The Pulwama incident thus represented a dangerous new low in India–Pakistan relations. The surgical strikes represented a 'new normal' in the military confrontation. The evidence of increasing security collaboration between India and Israel added to Pakistan's security concerns. Israeli weapons were used in the Balakot attack and there were reports that Israeli pilots were also involved in these incidents.

Indian Repression in Kashmir

The 1990s saw a decade of Kashmiri militancy when serious confrontations took place between Indian forces, numbering more than half a million, and freedom fighters. The militancy was probably aided by Islamic militants who had fought against the Soviet occupation of Afghanistan in 1980s but, after the Soviet withdrawal from that country, shifted their activities to India-occupied Kashmir. This gave rise to Indian propaganda about a 'proxy war' and 'cross-border terrorism' allegedly launched by Pakistan. The fighting in Kashmir caused the death of some 70,000 Kashmiris. It was followed by a relative lull in the first decade of the twenty-first century, and some Kashmiri political circles were willing to join the electoral process, suggesting a weakening of the opposition to India.

A new phase in the Kashmiri resistance against Indian occupation began in July 2016 when the Indian military killed Burhan Wani, who had become a legendary Kashmiri freedom fighter. He was a 22-year-old educated youth from a good family who gave up an easy life to carry out a fearless struggle against Indian occupation. He used YouTube to win a huge following. Wani was quite different from the image of the bearded jihadist and set in new trends in the resistance struggle. A large number of people attended his funeral and his death sparked unprecedented protests, which continued for a long time. Hundreds of thousands of Kashmiris—young and old, men, and women—came out in daily protests to show their opposition to Indian rule. There was a virtual shutdown for months. India resorted to use brutal force to put down the protests. This included firing by pellet guns that caused blindness among the injured, condemned by many as a war crime. One outcome of these protests was that the pro-India leaders like Chief Minister Mehbooba Mufti lost all credibility.

A new development in 2019 was the interest shown by US President Trump to mediate in the Kashmir dispute. This was against the long-held Indian stance that there was no scope for third party mediation. Trump's stance might have forced India and so it decided to stage a *fait accompli* in the context of Kashmir. On 5 August 2019, India revoked India-occupied Kashmir's special status or limited autonomy, given in the Indian constitution ever since 1954. India also ended its status as a province and bifurcated it into two Union Territories, administered by lieutenant governors, directly under control of the Indian government. It also removed Article 35A of the constitution that prevented Indian nationals from other states to purchase land or property in Jammu & Kashmir.

To prevent mass protests by Kashmiris against these drastic changes in their constitutional status, India simultaneously imposed draconian restrictions on the movement of some eight million Kashmiris inhabiting the Kashmir valley. All top political leaders, including those considered to be pro-India, were put under house arrest. Ever since August 2019, the Kashmir valley has become the world's largest prison. The Indian steps were a clear violation of UN resolutions on Kashmir as well as provisions of the Indian constitution itself. The Kashmiri people, even though denied public expression, showed total opposition to the Indian steps.

Pakistan was outraged and raised the issue at all possible forums. Addressing the UN General Assembly on 27 September 2019, Imran Khan strongly denounced the Indian measures. He also attacked the Hindutva ideology of the ruling party in India, which he compared to Nazi philosophy. He warned that tensions between the two South Asian neighbours could lead to a nuclear conflagration. The UN Security Council held a closed-door session on the Kashmir issue, the first time since 1964, but no formal resolution was adopted. However, UN human rights bodies condemned the Indian measures and asked for respect of the human rights of the Kashmiri people. Turkey, Malaysia, Iran, and the OIC also condemned India for its blatant disregard of UN resolutions and its violation of human rights. However, Saudi Arabia did not make any public criticism of India.

Ever since, Pakistan has kept accusing the Modi government of deliberately whipping up anti-Pakistan feelings in order to secure support from Hindu nationalist voters. It insinuated that the Pulwama incident might have been staged by India itself as an election ploy. At any rate, these tactics clearly helped the BJP in securing a landslide victory in the general elections in May 2019.

ANTI-MUSLIM LAWS IN INDIA

In December 2019, India promulgated some anti-Muslim laws that led to huge protests by Indian Muslims who, though a minority of less than 20 per cent, number some 200 million. The Citizenship Amendment Act (CAA) aims to give citizenship to minorities (excluding Muslims) who have been allegedly persecuted in Muslim majority neighbouring countries, viz. Pakistan, Bangladesh, and Afghanistan. The Indian government had a law for registering citizens which required documentary evidence such as birth certificates, which are not often available in India. CAA makes faith a basis for granting citizenship and is seen as contrary to India's declared status as a secular state. On that basis, Muslim residents could be declared non-Indians and could be deported from the country. The passing of these laws seemed a part of the agenda of the BJP government, whose ideological parent is the Rashtriya Swayamsevak Sangh (RSS), a Hindu paramilitary supremacist organization set up in the 1920s, which was inspired by European fascists and Nazis. RSS wants India to be declared a Hindu Rashtra, or a nation of Hindus.

Since December 2019, India has seen protests on an unprecedented scale. Spearheaded by Muslims, the protestors have included Hindus and other communities as well who were shocked by the anti-secular nature of these laws. Shaheen Bagh, a locality in Delhi, gained fame as a focal point of protest, where Muslim women of all ages have been sitting in the open 24-hours a day for months. In February 2020, there were attacks on Muslims by Hindu mobs who committed a veritable genocide, while the Delhi police either watched unconcerned or even joined the Hindu rioters in their killing and looting spree. The main opposition parties joined in strongly condemning the BJP government for this carnage. There were fears that India was heading towards some kind of a civil war that could fragment the country. In spite of these protests, the BJP government has remained unmoved and seems determined not to bring any changes in these draconian laws.

Against this background, there has been severe criticism of India in many countries by the media and by protestors who gathered outside Indian consulates. Turkey, Malaysia, and Iran have condemned India. Pakistan, of course, has been vociferous in condemning these laws and the Delhi genocide. Severe personal criticism of Modi by Imran Khan would also seem to have shut the door to any dialogue with him. India–Pakistan relations have been further embittered by these anti-Muslim laws. It is unlikely that there can be any improvement in bilateral relations unless there is a basic change of policy in India or the Modi government is ousted.

Despite claims of secularism, the Muslim minority in India has been systematically discriminated against since the independence of India in 1947. The Urdu language was the most widely used in government and academic circles during the eighteenth, nineteenth, and early twentieth century during the British rule. But with the rise of Hindu nationalism, Urdu was dubbed as a 'Muslim language', and a virtual cultural genocide has been taking place. Its teaching has been restricted to the extent that even those whose mother tongue is Urdu cannot read the Urdu script. The treatment of Muslims has become far worse under BJP rule. There are lynchings of Muslims on the charge of eating beef. Muslim representation in the political arena is far less than their percentage in population. Muslims are denied jobs and housing; traditional names of cities and localities with Muslim connotations are being changed; the police and the judiciary fail to protect the Muslims, instilling a sense of insecurity. Ironically, the ill-treatment of Muslims under BJP government provides a fresh proof of the prediction made during the Pakistan struggle, viz. Muslims would be treated as second class citizens in a Hindu-dominated, independent India. Therefore, Partition of India was the only way through which the Muslim way of life could be preserved and protected, i.e. by ensuring Muslim rule in the north-western and eastern zones of India where Muslims were in majority.

KULBHUSHAN JADHAV CASE

India–Pakistan relations were also strained by the strange case of espionage by Commander Kulbhushan Jadhav. On 10 April 2017, a Pakistani military court awarded him the death sentence on the charge of espionage and subversion in Pakistan. Jadhav was the highest-ranking Indian spy arrested in Pakistan. He was a serving officer of Indian Navy (serial 41558Z), whose services were acquired by RAW, the Indian intelligence agency. He possessed an Indian passport with a fake Muslim name, Hussein Mubarak Patel, and was based in Chabahar in Iran since 2003, from where he carried out espionage activities in Pakistan. Jadhav was arrested on 3 March 2016 by Pakistani authorities in Mashkel in Balochistan. He made a full confession of his espionage activities before a magistrate and gave names of his Pakistani accomplices. A video of his confession was played on television, where he is seen relaxed and smiling, with no sign of any coercion. His trial was conducted by Field General Court Martial under Section 59 of Pakistan Army Act of 1952 and Section 3 of the Official Secrets Act of 1923.

The announcement of death sentence by the court brought a severe reaction from India. Some of its ministers threatened that India would go to any extent to save Jadhav's life. India claimed that Jadhav had been 'kidnapped' from Iran and brought to Pakistan. However, it produced no evidence to prove this claim. There was no explanation as to why Jadhav was carrying an Indian passport with a false Muslim name.

On 8 May 2017, India raised the issue at the International Court of Justice (ICJ), The Hague, under the cover of the Vienna Convention on Consular Relations 1963, contending that Pakistan had violated its provisions for consular access to India to the accused prisoner. In its Order of 18 May 2017, the ICJ directed Pakistan to ensure that Jadhav was not executed pending a final decision in the case. On 25 December 2017, Pakistan allowed Jadhav's wife and mother to meet him in Islamabad. Jadhav assured them that he was being well treated. This did not generate much goodwill in India, which objected to the conditions under which this meeting was held. Public hearings in the ICJ on the merits of the case were held from 18 to 21 February 2019. In its judgment of 17 July 2019, the ICJ found that Pakistan had violated several provisions under the 1963 Convention and should allow India consular access to the accused Indian national. But the ICJ rejected the more important Indian request to the court to annul the decision of the Pakistani military court and restrain Pakistan from giving effect to the sentence or conviction and release Jadhav. However, the court found that 'Pakistan was under an obligation to provide, by means of its own choosing, effective review and reconsideration of the conviction and sentence of Mr Jadhav, so as to ensure that full weight was given to the effect of the violation of the rights set forth in Article 36 of the Vienna Convention.' Pakistan gave India consular access when it allowed a senior Indian diplomat in Islamabad to meet Jadhav for two hours on 2 September 2019.

KARTARPUR CORRIDOR

Second only to the Golden Temple in Amritsar, one of the holiest Sikh shrine is the gurdwara at Kartarpur in Shakargarh tehsil in Pakistan. It was set up by the founder of Sikhism, Baba Nanak, in 1504, who established the first Sikh commune here. Nanak lived in Kartarpur for years until his death in 1538 and his remains are buried in this gurdwara. It is so close to the India–Pakistan border that pilgrims can see it through telescope from Dera Baba Nanak on the Indian side. For years, Sikhs sought access to this gurdwara and, in 1998, the possibility of a corridor was discussed by prime ministers Vajpayee and Nawaz Sharif but nothing came out of it.

Tensions in India–Pakistan relations prevented real progress until August 2018 when Navjot Singh Sidhu, a provincial minister from Indian Punjab, attended the swearing-in ceremony of Prime Minister Imran Khan—the 22nd Prime Minister of Pakistan. Pakistan Army Chief General Qamar Javed Bajwa told him about Pakistan's willingness to open the corridor to facilitate participation of Sikhs in the 550th birth anniversary of Guru Nanak in

November 2019. The plan was approved by the Indian cabinet in November 2018 and construction work was started by both sides, though the main work was to be done by Pakistan. An agreement was signed by the two countries on 24 October 2019, paving the way for 5,000 Indian pilgrims to visit the holy site on a daily basis. Each visitor would have to pay US$20 as service charge. India imposed passport restrictions for each traveller but Pakistan waived off most requirements and made it a visa-free travel. The inauguration of the Kartarpur Corridor by Imran Khan took place on 12 November 2019. Since then, it has enabled thousands of pilgrims from India and elsewhere, not only Sikhs but others as well, to visit the magnificent gurdwara which has a huge white marble courtyard and excellent facilities.

Great goodwill for Pakistan among Indian and non-Indian Sikhs and other pilgrims has been generated by the access given to this Sikh holy site. It shows that non-Muslim minorities in Pakistan are being treated well. This has helped erase the negative image of Pakistan resulting from years of hostile propaganda, and has promoted the peace lobby on both sides. Indian visitors have been full of praise for Pakistan's generous hospitality and excellent arrangements. The opening of the Kartarpur Corridor has turned out to be a very positive diplomatic move by Pakistan, with far-reaching consequences. For some 400 years, the Sikhs had been very anti-Muslim, due to their centuries-long struggle against Muslim Mughal rule. The Kartarpur Corridor is bringing a historic reconciliation between the two groups. The Sikhs are traditionally fierce warriors and today constitute 20 per cent of the Indian military. They are concentrated in the province of Punjab, which borders Pakistan.

Pakistan–China Relations

The traditionally strong ties between Pakistan and China kept deepening during the decade beginning 2010. There were many high-level visits and reaffirmations of friendship, which was described as 'deeper than the seas and higher than the mountains'. The most important single initiative in promoting bilateral ties was the launching of CPEC, which is the most important project under what was first dubbed as One Belt One Road (OBOR) and later as Belt and Road Initiative (BRI). Its aim is to boost China's domestic growth and it is also a part of the country's economic diplomacy. By connecting the less-developed regions like Xinjiang with neighbouring nations, China hopes to raise their economic activity. The BRI is expected to open up and create new markets for Chinese goods. It would also enable the manufacturing powerhouse to gain control of cost-effective routes to export materials easily. An excess capacity in terms of production can be channelized effectively to regions along the BRI routes. China has announced investments of one trillion dollars in various infrastructure projects and is funding them by low-cost loans to the participating countries. Some analysts see BRI as a strategic move by China to attain control at a regional level and to play a larger role at the global level by controlling a China-focused trading network. While the US is posing challenges for Asian nations through tariffs and other measures, China sees this as an opportunity to emerge as a regional leader.[3]

CPEC is an extension of China's twenty-first century Silk Road initiative. Although under discussion for several years, Pakistan and China signed agreements in 2015 to launch the CPEC. Chinese President Xi Jinping has named this project the most important achievement of his tenure and has pushed it with remarkable vigour. In his vision, the CPEC will not only cover Pakistan but will also extend to other countries in Central Asia, and beyond to Europe. There is also a sea link part of the Silk Route, coming via Malaysia to Bangladesh, Sri Lanka, the Persian Gulf and the Red Sea to Europe.

Most analysts believe that CPEC will transform Pakistan's economy and will be a game-changer. It has already gone a long way to overhaul Pakistan's transportation infrastructure. Spanning the length and breadth of Pakistan with a network of highways, it will link the south-western Pakistani port of Gwadar to China's north-western region of Xinjiang. It includes overhauling and expansion of the existing Karakoram Highway from Islamabad to the Chinese border at Khunjerab Pass. The Karachi–Peshawar main railway line will also be completely overhauled to allow trains to travel up to 160 km per hour. The railway network will be improved and the northern-most Pakistani railway terminus at Havelian will be connected to Kashgar.

The CPEC consists of a number of projects presently under construction at a cost of about US$62 billion. Though its main thrust is on the development of communications infrastructure, it has more projects relating to energy production, which is much needed by Pakistan. Gwadar has a pivotal role in CPEC as the sea outlet from where oil and gas of the Persian Gulf will flow to China. Chinese access to the Persian Gulf via Gwadar will reduce the distance by one-fifth, as compared to the existing sea route to China. At present, oil supplies meant for use in western China require, first, a long sea journey from the Persian Gulf to Shanghai in eastern China and, then, a long haul over land from Shanghai to western China, some thousands of kilometres away. This shorter and safest access to the Persian Gulf oil is probably China's main motivation in launching the CPEC. The strategic link will bind Pakistan and China in a long-term alliance, as neither would be willing to lose the advantages ensuing from the CPEC.

Despite its obvious advantages, there has been criticism of the CPEC both in Pakistan and abroad. Some Pakistani politicians have been bickering on CPEC due to parochial, short-sighted considerations. Some of them might have become the unwitting accomplices of covert intrigue by external powers. It seems that there are some powers which do not want to see Pakistan making a quantum leap towards economic prosperity. Some of them fear that their current economic importance could be eroded by the success of CPEC. In addition, there are powers that are uncomfortable with China's steady advance towards superpower status and are worried that CPEC will give an important strategic gain to China. The US has remained critical of the CPEC. It has been suggested that Pakistan is falling into a debt trap and might compromise its sovereignty. Comparisons are made with the rise of East India Company in India, which began as a trading company but went on to establish British imperial rule over India.

The BRI is the brainchild of Chinese President Xi Jinping who believes that China has adapted socialism to modern conditions and in doing so created a unique Chinese answer to 'the problems facing mankind'. Xi believes that the time has come for 'Chinese wisdom and Chinese approach' to benefit those outside China by developing the world's poorer regions. However, Chinese experts have articulated more down-to-earth goals for the initiative. For them, BRI promises to integrate China's internal markets with those of its neighbours, thus bringing them closer to China politically and bring stability to the region. By increasing economic activity in China's regions such as Xinjiang and Tibet, BRI will lessen the appeal of separatists.

Apart from the CPEC, Pakistan's relations with China kept growing in diverse fields during 2010–20. China consistently defended Pakistan against the charge of terrorism and used its veto at the UN in support of Pakistan. In the defence field, China helped Pakistan develop the JF-17 Thunder aircraft, which has become a key component of Pakistan Air Force. The aircraft is also being sold by Pakistan to some other countries. At the same time, a key pillar of China's foreign policy is avoiding war or conflict in the region and beyond, since it wants to concentrate on its economic growth that is bringing it closer to superpower status. It, therefore, counsels both Pakistan and India to resolve their issues peacefully. China has been only mildly critical of India on the latter's repression in Kashmir. China's own relations with India have grown over the past three decades, notably in the commercial field. There are periodic high-level visits as well. However, border issues with India continue to cast a big shadow over the bilateral relationship and at times have led to tensions between the two Asian giants. China's friendly relations with India have not been at Pakistan's expense and China continues to stand solidly behind Pakistan on nearly all issues.

In strategic terms, the traditional US influence in Pakistan has been waning since around 2007 and has been mainly replaced by China, which has become its main partner in both military and economic fields. Unlike the US, China has never been accused of interfering in Pakistan's internal matters, or imposing its views on foreign policy issues. China has helped Pakistan to develop its arms industry and has transferred vital knowhow to Pakistan. Under the CPEC, it is helping Pakistan to develop its economy. Most Pakistanis view China as an indispensable ally, whereas the US is perceived as an unreliable and overbearing ally, with a latent anti-Muslim agenda.

Pakistan–Afghanistan Relations

The US/NATO war in Afghanistan, dubbed in 2001 as the War on Terror, continued during the decade of 2010–20, with increasing indications that the Afghan Taliban were gaining ground and the US was fighting a losing battle. By 2009, the Taliban appeared to be in control of several regions in Afghanistan. The US military commander General David Petraeus insisted on a troop 'surge'. In 2010, President Barack Obama deployed an additional 30,000 soldiers over a period of six months but proposed that troop withdrawal would begin by 2012. The 'surge' strategy had failed by 2013. Obama next set a deadline of end of 2014 for the withdrawal of troops.

The inauguration of Donald Trump as President in 2017 saw new developments in Afghanistan. He made it clear that he favoured an end to the war in Afghanistan and withdrawal of US troops from that country. He wrote to Prime Minister Imran Khan on 3 December 2018 requesting his help in bringing the Taliban to the negotiating table. Pakistan responded favourably and talks between the US and Taliban took place in Abu Dhabi, in which Pakistani, Saudi and UAE officials were also present. On 21 December 2018, Trump announced that he had decided to pull out 7,000 US troops from Afghanistan, nearly half of the total US forces there. Prolonged negotiations were conducted between the US and the Taliban, with the help of Pakistan, and led to the signing of a peace agreement in Doha on 29 February 2020, providing that the US troop withdrawal from Afghanistan would be completed in a period of fourteen months.

Incidentally, some senior Pakistani military analysts had long been saying that they did not expect that the US would withdraw from Afghanistan in the foreseeable future. Their argument was that Afghanistan was viewed by the US as a key base against both China and Russia. Moreover, it had immense mineral resources that the US wanted to control. However, this line of reasoning ignored Trump's repeated view that this war was the longest in US history and was futile and had eaten away immense US resources.

Throughout the 2010–20 decade, Pakistan–Afghanistan relations were poisoned by Kabul's accusations that Pakistan was supporting the Afghan Taliban by providing them with safe sanctuaries and other help. The Kabul regime attributed the successes of the Taliban, including their destructive terrorist attacks, to the planning or aid of Pakistan. However, no proof was put forward to substantiate such allegations. Pakistan's hot denials evidently carried no weight for Kabul. The reasons could be that the Kabul regime, though headed by Pakhtuns like Hamid Karzai and Ashraf Ghani, has mostly consisted of the former Northern Alliance (NA) of Tajiks, Uzbeks and Hazaras, or the non-Pakhtuns. During the Afghan Civil War of 1992–4, a perception grew that Pakistan was supporting Gulbuddin Hekmatyar, a Pakhtun, who was pitted against the Tajiks led by Ahmad Shah Massoud. Later, from 1994 to 2001, Pakistan supported the Taliban, who are mainly Pakhtuns.

The abovementioned is the basis of the impression in Afghanistan that Pakistan supports the Pakhtuns—who live both in Afghanistan and Pakistan—and has given rise to the accusation that Pakistan has been interfering in Afghanistan's internal affairs and seeks to foist a pro-Pakistan Pakhtun regime there. India has played on these fears and misapprehensions to win support among the non-Pakhtuns in Afghanistan (the former Northern Alliance). It has extended nearly US$3 billion in aid to Afghanistan to build hospitals, the parliament building, dams and other facilities, which has generated goodwill. Another factor for Kabul's tilt towards India could be the maxim: 'my enemy's enemy is my friend'. It is ironic that Pakistan did so much for the Afghans during the jihad against Soviet occupation and has ever since hosted some three million Afghan refugees, whereas India supported the pro-Soviet Kabul regime in the 1980s. Even since 2001, Pakistan has provided the vital access route to the US/NATO/Afghan forces fighting against the Taliban. Most of Afghan foreign trade has used Pakistan for transit. Pakistan is the main market for export of Afghan fruit. Moreover, both Pakistan and Afghanistan are Muslim countries, whereas India is non-Muslim. In spite of these facts, Afghan public opinion today seems to be pro-India and is often hostile to Pakistan. The explanation for this paradox seems to be that the Afghan people are told day in and day out that the unending war in their country, and the bloodshed caused in periodic terrorist acts, are all due to Pakistan's support for Taliban, who are dubbed as a proxy for Pakistan's ambitions in Afghanistan. The truth, of course, is that the Taliban have grown in strength due to their own ethnic and ideological appeal. They take their own decisions and do not take orders from Pakistan. They were in power in 1990s and never heeded Pakistan's requests to accept the legality of the Durand Line, or expel Osama, or not to destroy the Buddha statues in Bamiyan, etc. Where Pakistan can take satisfaction is that the Taliban are not anti-Pakistan, unlike the Northern Alliance in Afghanistan.

Afghan President Hamid Karzai (2004–14), who had spent years in Pakistan as a refugee, used to blow hot and cold towards Pakistan. In October 2011, Afghanistan signed a strategic pact with India. The military assistance included training of Afghan security personnel in India. Karzai told the media: 'This strategic partnership is not directed against any country.' He added: 'Pakistan is our twin brother, India is a great friend. The agreement we signed with our friend will not affect our brother. However, our engagement with Islamabad has unfortunately not yet yielded the result that we want.' In fact, Karzai routinely accused Pakistan of fuelling the Taliban insurgency to destabilise his country, as a hedge against Indian influence. Pakistan saw Karzai as 'a deeply mercurial man whose attitude towards Pakistan veered wildly between occasional spasms of warmth and long periods of outright hostility.'[4]

After Ashraf Ghani took over as president, he said he wanted to improve relations with Pakistan which, in turn, could pave the way for peace with the Taliban. His first visit to Pakistan took place on 14 November 2014. He went straight to the military headquarters and had talks with the army chief. He declared himself satisfied with these talks which, he said, had solved long-standing issues in a matter of hours. Afghan officials welcomed the statement of Army Chief General Raheel Sharif (given in Kabul in February 2015) that 'the enemies of Afghanistan are enemies of Pakistan.' However, the continuation of attacks by the Taliban against the Kabul regime made Ghani openly critical of Pakistan and in 2017 he declared that Pakistan was carrying on 'an undeclared war of aggression' against Afghanistan.[5] Similarly, after two deadly attacks by the Taliban in Kabul in January 2018 Ghani called Pakistan the 'centre of the Taliban'. No proof was provided to sustain such allegations, which was clearly a case of making Pakistan a scapegoat for the military failures of the Kabul regime.

In June 2019, Ghani visited Pakistan for the third time to meet Prime Minister Imran Khan. The latter reaffirmed Pakistan's position that an

Afghan-led and Afghan-owned peace process was the only viable option to end the conflict in Afghanistan. Ghani seemed appreciative of Pakistan's efforts for a peace settlement in Afghanistan. But in early 2020, Ghani accused Pakistan of meddling in internal politics of Afghanistan. He said that the keys to the war were in Islamabad/Rawalpindi (base of Pakistan's civil–military leadership), and in Quetta, the alleged hideout of Taliban leaders. On 24 January 2020, Ghani accused Pakistan of 'giving sanctuary to an insurgent group [Haqqani] that helps the Taliban in its war against US/Kabul forces'.[6]

The signing of the US–Taliban Agreement in February 2020 has been acclaimed widely in the expectation that this would bring an end to the US war in Afghanistan. Pakistan's help in reaching this agreement is acknowledged. However, it remains to be seen as to how far this agreement is actually followed by the two sides. The agreement does not mean an end to fighting between the Taliban and Kabul regime, for which separate talks would be held. There is a big question mark whether such talks will succeed. If not, even after the US withdrawal, fighting would continue in Afghanistan in the form of a new civil war. The long-desired peace would still not come to the region and Pakistan would continue to have serious difficulties in relations with Afghanistan.

Prime Minister Imran Khan feels vindicated by the success of the talks between the US and Taliban. He says he had always advocated such talks, since 'wars never solve any problems'. He recalls that since around 2005, he was dubbed as 'Mr Taliban Khan' for advocating talks with the Taliban. Unfortunately, his historical recall is less than accurate. Imran was opposing military action against the Tehrik-i-Taliban Pakistan (TTP), the Pakistani Taliban, who were mainly responsible for the rampant terrorism in Pakistan. Every time the use of military force against TTP was contemplated, Imran and religious parties would oppose it and instead proposed negotiations. Such talks with TTP did take place, without any result. It was not until 2014 that the decisive military operation Zarb-i-Azb was launched, which helped eradicate terrorism in Pakistan. In retrospect, it must be said that the delay in launching of this operation, due to opposition from various quarters, caused thousands of deaths. It is also ironic that while still arguing in favour of negotiations as against war, Imran Khan now praises Zarb-i-Azb, the military action against the TTP and other militants that began in 2014 and has continued ever since.

Of course, the case of Afghan Taliban is quite different. They have waged a long guerrilla war against the occupying US/NATO forces, which has produced a bloody stalemate. In such a stalemate, political talks are seen as the way out, as happened in Korea in 1953 and in Vietnam in 1974. But the assertion that wars never solve issues is not borne out by historical record. In fact, wars have had the most decisive impact in history. For example, centuries of Muslim rule over India was the outcome of successes by Muslim military figures such as Mohammad bin Qasim, Muhammad Ghori, and Zahiruddin Babur. British rule over India was established through military conquest. Napoleon was defeated through war. The horrors of Nazi rule ended by military defeat of Hitler. Pakistan lost its eastern wing in 1971 due to military defeat. The most decisive changes in world history have come through wars.

CHABAHAR AS TRANSIT ROUTE

Afghanistan, Iran and India agreed in 2016 to develop a transit route to Afghanistan via Chabahar in Iran. Since Pakistan has all along denied a land transit route (via Lahore) to India to trade with Afghanistan, this alternate transit route was developed. India extended over US$100 million to develop facilities at Chabahar. India also helped build a railway link from Chabahar to Zahedan, as well as a road linking Zahedan with Zaranj, a border town in Afghanistan. The first shipment through this route was made in February 2019. Many observers see the Chabahar transit route as a rival of the Gwadar route and the traditional route through Karachi. But the Chabahar route passes through uninhabited desert areas and might not be a practical alternative to the Pakistan routes.

Pakistan–Russia Relations

There was some improvement in Pakistan's ties with Russia during the past decade (2010–2020). The decline in US–Pakistan relations has motivated Pakistan to turn to Russia for balance of power. There has always been an argument that Russia is a great power (previously a superpower) in Pakistan's neighbourhood and antagonizing it, while depending on a distant (and unreliable) ally, did not make sense. What this argument ignores is that in 1950s, Pakistan was desperately short of military weapons and was deeply threatened by a far larger India, and joining the US-sponsored military pacts was the only feasible way to strengthen itself. However, this is old history. After the end of the Cold War and the collapse of the Soviet Union in 1991, geopolitics has changed. By 2000, India and USA had decided to form a strategic alliance. The old New Delhi–Moscow axis diminished significantly. However, in the defence field, India has continued to rely on Russia to a large extent. Russia, too, has remained keen to keep its influence in India. One way to do so is to warn India that Russia could come closer to Pakistan. As a part of this diplomatic manoeuvring there has been an increase in exchange of high-level visits between Russia and Pakistan, but President Vladimir Putin has not yet visited Pakistan. Even his occasional meetings with Pakistani leaders on the sidelines of international summits have been of an informal nature. In contrast, there are regular summit level meetings between Russian and Indian leaders.

Russia does see Pakistan as an important player in the region, particularly in the context of Afghanistan, where the likely US withdrawal has revived Russian interest. Moscow is worried that Afghanistan might not become a source of Islamist extremism, which could have security implications for Russia since it has a significant Muslim population. Russia also continues to have considerable influence in Central Asia and fears the rise of fundamentalist Islam, particularly the Islamic State (Da'esh). Pakistan is seen as a key to a political settlement in Afghanistan. Pakistan is a strong military power with nuclear capability and cannot be ignored by Russia or any other country. Pakistan's inclusion as a full member in the Shanghai Cooperation Organization (SCO) in 2017 brings it closer to Russia and China. Pakistan and Russia have been conducting annual joint military exercises since 2016. After the visit of Russian Defence Minister Sergei Shoigu to Pakistan in 2014, Russia decided to lift its embargo on Pakistan and agreed to supply four MI-35 helicopters, besides agreeing to build a US$1.7 billion gas pipeline from Karachi to Lahore. Pakistan's alliance with China and the growing impact of CPEC is also enhancing its importance. Russia itself has drawn closer to China.

However, the talk of a Russia–China–Pakistan axis is premature. Russia has no intention of giving up on India, while Pakistan still hopes to retain an equation with USA, its long-term ally. In this context, a comparison of Russia–India ties, as compared to Russia–Pakistan ties, is quite revealing. Russia's annual trade with India is over US$10 billion, whereas trade with Pakistan is around US$800 million. In 2018, India decided to secure from Russia the S400 missile defence system worth US$5.2 billion, and four frigates worth US$950 million, followed by a US$3 billion deal for a nuclear submarine the next year, the purchase of 464 T-90 tanks for $2 billion and the joint manufacture of AK-203/103 rifles.[7]

Pakistan–Saudi Arabia Relations

An important pillar of Pakistan's foreign policy since long has been to maintain a special relationship with Saudi Arabia. The two countries have supported each other in war and peace. They consult each other on most issues and seek to adopt a common position. Pakistan is committed to protect Saudi Arabia against any foreign aggression and even for its internal security. Saudi Arabia, in turn, has been the main aid giver to Pakistan, apart from USA and China. It has nearly three million Pakistani workers whose remittances are the largest from any single country. Saudi Arabia is the second largest trading partner of Pakistan in the Middle East. The overall trade volume ranges between U$3 and US$4 billion annually. (The trade volume with UAE is US$8 billion.) Pakistanis have a deep attachment to Saudi Arabia as the holy land, which has the two most important Islamic sanctuaries.

While all regimes in Pakistan have enjoyed good relations with Saudi Arabia, record shows that the Saudi rulers have been more comfortable with military regimes in Pakistan. Among civilian governments, they have been less keen towards the PPP rulers, viz. Zulfikar Ali Bhutto, Benazir Bhutto, and Asif Zardari. King Faisal greatly admired President Ayub Khan and was disturbed by his fall in 1969 due to a countrywide political agitation in which Bhutto played a key role. The PPP used revolutionary rhetoric during its rise to power and was critical of the pro-West regimes in the Middle East. After coming to power, Bhutto developed close links with Libya's Colonel Muammar Gaddafi, Syria's Hafez al-Assad and PLO's Yasser Arafat, who were all distrusted by the Saudi rulers. However, the latter were realistic enough to know that relations were essentially between states and tried to maintain working relationships with successive PPP regimes in Pakistan.

King Abdullah was the effective Saudi ruler from 1995 to 2015. He had a close relationship with President Pervez Musharraf and tried till the end to keep the latter in power. But when Musharraf made a deal with Benazir Bhutto in 2007 to share power, King Abdullah insisted that Nawaz Sharif be allowed to return to Pakistan from the Saudi-brokered exile. Though Sharif had broken his promise to the Saudis, he was still seen as Saudi Arabia's own man in Pakistan. The assassination of Benazir Bhutto generated a sympathy wave that brought the PPP into power in 2008. Her husband Asif Zardari remained the President till 2013. True to the pattern, Pakistan's relations with Saudi Arabia lost their warmth. King Abdullah made no secret of his dislike for Zardari.[8] His Shia affiliation and pro-Iran stance sealed the matter, as far as the Saudis were concerned. There was no high-level visit from Saudi Arabia to Pakistan during Zardari's tenure. Saudi economic assistance also stopped.

Against this background, the Saudis warmly welcomed the return of Nawaz Sharif to power in 2013. High-level visits from Saudi Arabia increased notably, including that of Crown Prince of Saudi Arabia, Prince Salman bin Abdulaziz Al Saud, in 2014. Saudi economic aid of US$1.5 billion was also announced. However, the bilateral relations received a jolt in 2015 when Pakistan did not join Saudi Arabia in its military intervention against the Houthi Shia rebels in Yemen. Public opinion in Pakistan was against any such involvement, and neither the powerful Pakistani army nor the political parties wanted Pakistan to get involved. Nawaz Sharif himself seem inclined to respond positively to the Saudi request but finally decided to pass the buck to the parliament. After a protracted debate, a consensus resolution was adopted in favour of neutrality in Yemen fighting. Some members of the parliament made critical references to Saudi Arabia. The Saudis had somehow assumed that Pakistan would support them on this issue and were clearly disappointed when it did not do so. Actually, the long-time Pakistani commitment to Saudi Arabia has been of Pakistani military support in case of any invasion of Saudi Arabia itself, and not of joining the latter when it got into a war with some other country. (For the same reason, Pakistan declined to take sides when Saudi Arabia developed a quarrel with Qatar in 2015.) However, it was notable that the UAE, a close ally of Saudi Arabia, reacted strongly against Pakistan when it adopted neutrality in the Yemen war. UAE's Minister of State for Foreign Affairs Dr Anwar Mohammed Gargash issued a warning of adverse consequences.

No doubt, the warm reception given to Indian Prime Minister Narendra Modi during an official visit to Saudi Arabia in April 2016 was a kind of retaliation against Pakistan. He was conferred the highest Saudi civilian award by King Salman bin Abdulaziz Al Saud. To show India's old links with Islam, Modi presented a model of the first mosque built in India (Kerala) in the seventh century by Arab traders. In a joint statement, both strongly condemned terrorism and rejected any attempts 'to link this universal phenomenon to any particular race, religion or culture.'[9] The two sides signed five agreements including intelligence-sharing, defence cooperation, provision of Indian labour and promotion of bilateral investments in the private sector. Bilateral trade stood at US$39 billion in 2014. Saudi Arabia is the largest supplier of crude oil to India. It has adopted a policy of looking towards the East in its trade partnerships and wants to increase its oil exports to India.

Earlier in August 2015, UAE had received Modi with much fanfare during the first visit of an Indian prime minister to that country since 1981. UAE's trade with India is US$60 billion annually. Annual remittances from about three million Indian workers in UAE are US$14 billion. They constitute the largest foreign nationality group in the UAE.

While Saudi Arabia is now more willing to draw closer to India, mainly for economic reasons, it continues to see Pakistan as its most important ally. In case of any external or internal threat to Saudi security, it is Pakistan alone that has shown by its proven record in the past and its firm resolve for the future to stand shoulder-to-shoulder with Riyadh. India simply cannot fill this role. The warm reception given to Modi was a tit-for-tat for Pakistan's unwillingness to support Saudi Arabia in the Yemen war. In diplomacy, such manoeuvring often takes place. While Pakistan must not ignore the significance of a Saudi shift towards India, the fundamentals of Saudi–Pakistan relations remain intact and there is no strategic shift in Saudi priorities. Saudi Arabia will continue to need Pakistan in the days ahead, and vice versa. The fact that Saudi Arabia appointed the former Pakistani army chief, General Raheel Sharif, as the first commander-in-chief of the 41-member security alliance Islamic Military Counter Terrorism Coalition (IMCTC) shows the Saudi trust in Pakistan. This coalition was announced on 15 December 2015. Its main aim is military intervention against the Islamic State (aka Da'esh) terrorist group and other counter-terrorist activities. IMCTC was seen by some analysts as anti-Shia because of its omission of Iran and Iraq from this coalition. But General Sharif has stressed that its objective was to take joint action against terrorist groups like the Islamic State.

The coming to power of Imran Khan in July 2018 has seen a notable warming in relations with Saudi Arabia. He has reaffirmed Pakistan's commitment to Saudi security. He has visited Saudi Arabia several times and has established a personal rapport with Crown Prince Mohammad bin Salman whose visit to Islamabad in February 2019 was a high point in the bilateral relationship. He won the heart of Pakistanis by saying that he should be regarded as Pakistan's own ambassador in Saudi Arabia. He made commitments of generous Saudi support for Pakistan including an investment package of US$20 billion. Another success of Imran Khan's 'economic diplomacy' is establishing of a warm relationship with Abu Dhabi's Crown Prince Sheikh Mohammed bin Zayed Al Nahyan, who too has extended important financial aid to Pakistan. The likely explanation for this warming of relations with Imran Khan is that he is seen as the honest and strong leader that the Saudis and others were hoping to see in Pakistan, unlike its former leaders who were tainted by corruption.

Pakistan–Iran Relations

Iran is a neighbour of Pakistan with which the Pakistani people have age-old historical and cultural ties. After Pakistan's independence in 1947, close strategic and military ties were also developed between the two countries, including membership of US-sponsored military pacts. Military strategists in Pakistan saw friendship with Iran as providing 'strategic depth' to Pakistan in its confrontation with India. No doubt, Iran extended important military and diplomatic support to Pakistan in the wars with India in 1965 and 1971. Iran, under the Shah, was not worried about Pakistan's close ties with Saudi Arabia because the latter, like Iran, was a pro-West monarchy. But much would change after the Islamic Revolution in Iran in 1979. The new regime was stridently anti-US and had reservations towards pro-West regimes in the Gulf States, both for ideological and sectarian reasons. Though Pakistan was quick to recognize the Islamic regime in Iran, it continued to have reservations towards Pakistan as well, due to its old friendship with the last Shah of Iran, Mohammad Reza Shah Pahlavi, and continuing close ties with the US.

From around 1994, Iran adopted a 'look East' policy that brought it closer to India. It planned an anti-US alliance with India and China, though the latter showed little interest in joining this alliance. Such an initiative by Iran could hardly please Pakistan. Another complication was the civil war in Afghanistan, after the withdrawal of the Soviet forces, in which Pakistan was supporting the Pakhtuns—first under Hekmatyar and then under the Taliban—whereas Iran was supporting the other ethnic groups—Tajiks, Uzbeks and Hazaras—constituting the Northern Alliance (NA).

In 2003, at a time when there was a tense confrontation between India and Pakistan, Iranian President Mohammad Khatami was the chief guest at the Indian national day celebrations. He signed the 'New Delhi Declaration' with Prime Minister Vajpayee for a 'strategic partnership' between the two countries. This was followed by joint naval exercises and training of Iranian military personnel in India. Along with Russia, the two countries agreed to create a Russo–Iranian–Indian transport corridor. India also started work on the Chabahar port in Iran, providing an alternate transit route to Afghanistan and Central Asia, in competition with Pakistan. Another disturbing thing for

Pakistan was the periodic anti-Pakistan demonstrations by Iranian crowds besieging Pakistani consulates in Iran.

Little progress has been made on an important project that could bring Pakistan and Iran closer, viz. the gas pipeline that could provide Pakistan with badly-needed gas. A preliminary agreement was signed in 1995. India also joined the scheme in 1999 but withdrew in 2009 over price and security issues. Presidents Asif Zardari and Mahmoud Ahmadinejad inaugurated the construction works on laying the pipeline in 2013. But the project remains incomplete, mainly, because of political considerations, such as US sanctions on Iran. Iran has accused Pakistan of a breach of contract.

Iranian President Hassan Rouhani paid a two-day visit to Islamabad (25–26 March 2016). He assured that Iran is a strategic partner for the Pakistani nation for provision of Pakistan's energy security. Iran had already constructed its part of the joint gas line project and expected Pakistan to complete the work on its side. President Rouhani gave an assurance that Pakistan's security is our security and Iran's security is Pakistan's security. However, he kept silent on the Kashmir issue, as Iran has done since the 1990s. Another area of concern for Pakistan was the arrest of Indian spy Kulbhushan Jadhav, who had been based for years in Chabahar in Iran under a false Muslim passport.

Pakistan–Iran relations have also been adversely affected by the activities of Baloch secessionists, viz. a group called Jundallah. Iran has been complaining that this group has carried out terrorist attacks in Iran by using sanctuaries in Pakistan. There have been periodic threats by top Iranian officials of sending Iranian troops inside Pakistan to exterminate these terrorists. General Qasem Soleimani,[10] the top commander of Iran's elite force, warned Pakistan on 21 February 2019 that Saudi Arabia was pumping money into Pakistan to break up Pakistan by pitting it against its neighbours. He claimed that 'Saudi-sponsored terrorists on Pakistani soil are causing trouble for all of the country's neighbours'. He said that Pakistan must not turn into a place for activities that disturb regional states such as Iran, India and Afghanistan. General Soleimani's comments were made at the height of India–Pakistan tensions, following the Pulwama incident. Pakistan was concerned that he was clearly supporting Indian allegations against Pakistan of sponsoring terrorism in India and elsewhere.

On 20 April 2019, Pakistan protested to Iran when Iran-based militants ambushed a bus in Balochistan and killed fourteen passengers, mostly armed forces personnel. The attack took place shortly before Prime Minister Imran Khan was to visit Iran. A similar attack took place on 20 March 2020 when a Pakistan army convoy was ambushed in which six soldiers were killed.

The cold war between Iran and Saudi Arabia is probably responsible for some of the tensions that have arisen between Pakistan and Iran. No doubt, since the Islamic Revolution in Iran, sectarian tensions have grown in Pakistan. There have been accusations that the Saudis are supporting Pakistani Sunni militants and Iran has been backing Shia groups.

NOTES

1. Peter Bergen, 'Pakistan sheltered Bin Laden? Prove it,' 21 March 2014, https://edition. cnn.com/2014/03/21/opinion/bergen-bin-laden-new-york-times/index.html. Peter Bergen is CNN National Security Analyst.
2. Daniel L. Byman, 'Do Targeted Killings Work?' Brookings, 14 July 2009, https://www. brookings.edu/opinions/do-targeted-killings-work-2/.
3. *Investopedia*, 28 January 2020.
4. Jon Boone, 'Ashraf Ghani visit may mark new chapter in Afghan-Pakistan relations', *The Guardian*, 14 November 2014, https://www.theguardian.com/world/2014/nov/14/ ashraf-ghani-visit-pakistan-afghanistan.
5. *Investopedia*, 28 January 2020.
6. Stephen J. Adler and Simon Robinson, 'Afghanistan President: Pakistan still Shelters Insurgents', 23 January 2020, https://www.reuters.com/article/us-davos-meeting-ghani/ afghanistan-president-pakistan-still-shelters-insurgents-idUSKBN1ZM276.
7. Nivedita Kapoor, 'Russia-Pakistan relations and its impact on India', Observer Research Foundation (ORF), 3 July 2019.
8. https://www.dawn.com/news/586856/250000-secret-us-cables-released-king-abdullah-criticised-zardari-arab-leaders-urged-air-attack-on-iran-us-trying-to-remove-enriched-pak-uranium-wikileaks.
9. https://www.ndtv.com/india-news/india-saudi-arabia-sign-several-pacts-as-pm-modi-meets-with-crown-prince-2124298.
10. BBC News, 'Qasem Soleimani: US kills top Iranian general in Baghdad air strike', https://www.bbc.com/news/world-middle-east-50979463.

Index